THE CONCEPTS OF VALUE:
FOUNDATIONS OF VALUE THEORY

FOUNDATIONS OF LANGUAGE

SUPPLEMENTARY SERIES

VOLUME 12

HUMANITIES PRESS / NEW YORK

KARL ASCHENBRENNER

THE CONCEPTS OF VALUE

FOUNDATIONS OF VALUE THEORY

D. REIDEL PUBLISHING COMPANY / DORDRECHT-HOLLAND

SOLE DISTRIBUTORS FOR U.S.A. AND CANADA
HUMANITIES PRESS / NEW YORK

Library of Congress Catalog Card Number 70–159651

U.S.A. SBN 391 00126 4

That people who invented the word *charity*, and used it in a good sense, inculcated more clearly and much more efficaciously the precept *be charitable*, than any pretended legislator or prophet who should insert such a maxim in his writings.

— HUME

Im Ganzen – haltet euch an Worte!
Dann geht ihr durch die sichre Pforte
Zum Tempel der Gewissheit ein...
Doch ein Begriff muss bei dem Worte sein.

— GOETHE, *Faust*

PREFACE

The task of presenting for explicit view the store of appraisive terms our language affords has been undertaken in the conviction that it will be of interest not only to ethics and other philosophical studies but also to various areas of social science and linguistics. I have principally sought to do justice to the complexities of this vocabulary, the uses to which it is put, and the capacities its use reflects. I have given little thought to whether the inquiry was philosophical and whether it was being conducted in a philosophical manner. Foremost in my thoughts were the tasks that appeared to need doing, among them these: explicit attention was to be given to the vocabulary by means of which we say we commend, judge, appraise, or evaluate subjects and subject matters in our experience; it was to be segregated from other language at least for the purpose of study; the types of appraisive resources that are at hand in a language such as English were to be classified in some convincing and not too artificial manner; and an empirical standpoint was to be developed for a better view of appraisal, evaluation, and judging within the framework of other ways we have of responding to our surroundings such as appetition and emotion on one side and factual registering and theorizing about states of affairs on the other. Such an inquiry has never been undertaken in quite this manner before.

It soon became apparent that it was worth doing at all only if it were carried out in considerable detail. But if one merely wanted to present as large a corpus of appraisive terms as possible, many thousands more could be added to this stock. The reason is that appraisal is precisely the area of man's greatest linguistic creativity: we are never satisfied with the "standard" vocabulary to which this study is by choice confined, but we are all of us expanding it with devices of one or another degree of novelty through metaphor, slang, the adaptation of what is ordinarily nonappraisive language to appraisive purposes, foreign borrowings, poetic turns of thought and speech, and the inevitable mutations that words undergo by the wear and tear upon them of millions of speakers. If one wishes to take the trouble one may expand the present store through the magpie method of Roget and the other compilers of "synonyms." To confuse our effort with theirs is to misunderstand its purpose altogether.

Philosophers may expect more palpable results for their work in value theory, ethics, and similar studies than have here been arrived at. I have, however, pointed repeatedly at implications in these directions and have reserved for further study a good many of the consequences for philosophy. If many problems and possibilities have been suggested here that others wish to follow out, even to the revising and redoing of the whole task, I will have accomplished much of my purpose. I am convinced that one cannot carry value studies much further without a detailed study of this material. I shall agree with the possible objection that the investigation of the mere vocabulary of value for the purposes envisaged may not be sufficient. Beyond this vocabulary, itself an inevitable abstraction and extraction, there stretches the limitless expanse of possible contexts for its use in the form of sentences and more extended discourse. Unfortunately, if one of these is too little, the other is too much. But a beginning must be made.

As an ulterior purpose, I wish to show that philosophers, too, have some empirical tasks to perform. And even more than this, I wish to depart as far as I can from the inherent dogmatism of those philosophers who can never see themselves as doing a part of a larger work but must always write as if every article and book were the final, whole, and irrevocable truth on its subject.

Touching on this matter, I may quickly draw attention to some of the principal orientations of this study. I have affirmed the centrality or priority of what I call characterization to appraisal, evaluation, and judgment; the essential meaningfulness in a familiar sense of the vocabulary of value against those who regard it as an elaborate way of writing exclamation marks or as simply venting our emotions; the essential formalism, in a manner explained, of the notions *right*, *just*, and *good* for which the vocabulary of characterization must provide the matter; the useful role that may be played by the ancient notions of virtue and vice, and their explanation in terms of function, at least in reference to man; the distinctness of the several acts and procedures of appraisal and of the other acts akin to them or somewhere bordering them.

As to the tasks that might yet be done if life were long enough, or if others were to join their efforts, one might mention the following: first of all, the study of the appraisive resources in hundreds of other languages, particularly those that lie far from English; thereafter the investigation of subjects such as these: the actual genesis of characterisms, in which direction man shows a genuine (but to me still puzzling) creativity; the allied problem of the translatability or nontranslatability of appraisives and the effect of this on the nature and difference of human appraisive communities; the determinism of our appraisals by the shape and content of our linguistic instruments for appraisal; the nature of the manner in which formal commendatives such as *good* are referrable to material characterizations for explication or evidence; the human appraisive ideal that is apparently implied in a language by what it records as virtue and vice; the factual basis of characterization or the relation of characterization to the facts characterized; and finally the relation of all of this to the concerns of ethics in a narrower sense. Beyond this one might hope for a study of the writing of history to ascertain the degree to which it employs evaluative language and an inquiry into the relation of this to the aspirations of history to record the facts objectively, and for a study of law in the area in which its concerns intersect with those that have been taken up here. Some parts of this must be done by philosophers, but there is also much to enlist the aid also of those who are not philosophers.

I wish to express my thanks to Miss Ruth Anderson for kind and unfailing assistance at many of the tasks in the writing of the book, and to my colleagues who encouraged me in this effort. I would also like to thank those who taught me about the virtues I have discussed if I could do so without leading anyone to believe that I possessed any of them. But even our vices are a school for virtue provided we have a command of the concepts of value and we call things by their right names.

TABLE OF CONTENTS

INTRODUCTION

1 THE PURPOSE OF THIS STUDY

The approach of this investigation is quite different from that of most other investigations of value. The good is literally the last thing we are concerned about: we shall not encounter it in explicit form until we are nearly at the end of our study. We can hope for a clearer notion of the good only after exploring the ground from which it arises. The sequent order of this study is, therefore, one of its most important features.

Virtually nothing will be said that touches on the controversies about naturalism or utilitarianism or intuitionism and on the question of choice among these. Yet it is difficult to think what is said will have no bearing on them if such standpoints are seriously concerned with the process of evaluation. What may be claimed for the present study is its effort to survey in detail the verbal means employed to carry on this process. While this approach does not exclude others, neither has it been tried before.

The distinction of fact and value, of descriptions and value judgments is encountered everywhere. If we cannot truly say that everyone understands this distinction, we may say that the learning of it is a fairly sure mark of an educated mind or at least of one that has begun its education. The distinction is not hard to make or to apply, but saying exactly what it consists in is not so easy. Can it be recognized by a certain vocubulary, a mode or manner of expression, a tone of voice, or all of these? The appraisive capacity of language may derive from all of them.

We have chosen to concentrate attention on a distinct body of concepts or terms embodied in the more or less standard vocabulary that is presented in dictionaries. These concepts seem to have been created for the very purpose of appraisal; but 'creation' and 'purpose' are used for want of better terms since, of course, only a small part of any language comes into being in such a manner. The choice of terms of this appraisive vocabulary may at first appear somewhat arbitrary. For the time being we avoid offering any precise criteria for this choice since these will fully emerge as we proceed.

Assuming that we can identify a kind of standard appraisive vocabulary we should immediately recognize that it does not and cannot exhaust even the elements of appraisive language. We must also recognize the resources to be found in other areas such as metaphor and slang whose purpose is more often than not inherently appraisive. We cannot explore this vast field as well as the one we have chosen. The reader may, however, agree that, apart from such terms, the appraisive terms already found in our language enjoy a definite authority and priority. We would not resort to what amonts to the creation of new appraisive terms in slang and metaphor unless we already possessed a body of such terms and understood their purpose, use, and application. We resort to this either because we find the existing stock of appraisives inadequate for our purposes or because we have certain creative, or even poetical inclinations, or perhaps for both of these reasons.

The appraisive concepts named by this core appraisive vocabulary are to be found particularly under the more material parts of speech: nouns, verbs, adjectives. But here more general classifications will prove to be appropriate: *substantives*, such as **upstart, bully, sycophant, boor,** and **oaf,** which try to get to the innermost character of their targets; *processives*, such as **besmirch, execrate,** and **flay,** which characterize acts or actions; *attributives*, such as **happy, lonely,** and **wretched,** which characterize states or properties of subjects. We shall also speak of *elicitives*, such as **delightful, boresome,** and **repulsive,** that seem to attribute to objects characters which are really the responses that may be had or are expected to be had toward subjects; *conformatives*, such as **authentic, normal,** or **sound,** that point toward a norm for subjects; and various other classes.*

The facts of appraisive language, not attitudes, not emotions, not institutions, not actions are here considered to be the *explicandum* of the foundations of value theory. A theory must, of course, be determined by the facts it seeks to explain. Perhaps a few very specific things may be said at the outset about the choice of facts to be explained.

(1) Since, of course, what is essentially the same word can readily appear in various forms, as noun, verb, adjective, adverb, and also in negative form, certain restrictions are in order. The form we quote is the parent form, which is nearly always clearly recognizable. For example, **profound** appears instead of **profundity,** and **profoundly; guilt** instead of **guilty, guiltiness, guiltless;** and

---

* With the first appearance at this point in the text of appraisive terms such as will be constantly under discussion, a brief explanation of the typographical conventions employed is in order. We make little distinction between 'term' and 'concept': what we are in general discussing is concepts, but it is often easier to refer to them as terms. Whenever concepts are listed or in any way under discussion, they will appear in bold type, thus: **happy.** The concepts of Part One, though generally not themselves appraisive, also appear in this type. The concepts, however, will not appear in bold type if the usual grammatical conventions do not require it, thus: "The good and the bad, in effect, have been under study here," (p. 374). Or: "When we hear someone characterized as dignified, vulgar, reserved," etc. (p. 16). But: "We may proceed with some confidence toward the examination of ultimate appraisives such as **good** and **bad**" (p. 371). Where in rare cases we need to speak about a word, about its spelling, let us say, we generally use single quotation marks. Double quotation marks are used in the conventional manner.

so on. What is said of the first can generally be applied with fairly obvious qualifications to the others. Our aim is not to present a glossary of appraisive terms, but to arrive at a theory of appraisal and appraisive language by scrupulous attention to the language itself. (2) In general, we have tried to follow a *rule of one* so that each term appears once. Although dictionaries readily offer expositions of the several uses of terms, it is for the most part unnecessary for us to pursue all of these. The fact that, for example, **sensuous, fool, melancholy, rash**, or **tender** may have several uses is, of course, obvious, but not always particularly instructive for our purposes. It should be observed that pluralizations of meaning through processes of metaphor are often particularly significant for appraisal even when they are not formally recorded. (3) We assert that the uses of the terms quoted *are* appraisive in the contexts explored here, but we do not deny that many of them have non-appraisive uses elsewhere, nor even, for that matter, appraisive uses elsewhere. In other words we are not necessarily denying what it did not seem necessary to assert. (4) Evaluation is also conducted with other than specifically appraisive terms. This is explained below. Poets sometimes tell us that they hear virtually all terms as appraisive. I leave it to them to explain this. (5) The power of appraisive terms to credit or discredit, which we occasionally refer to as 'valence,' is sometimes affected by the context in which terms appear, shifting even from credit to discredit, as will be explained. (6) It may be said the author could have reduced the number of terms quoted by eliminating the numerous synonyms. We agree that the mere multiplication of synonyms may be left to Roget, who incidentally was rarely of any use here. But sheer numbers also have an importance. It is instructive that we have virtually only one way to say "make sense," namely **make sense**; but we have some three dozen alternatives of one sort or another to **nonsense**. Our ways of registering complaints of invasive contention (11.111) against ourselves are to be numbered in many more dozens, as compared with the few creditable modes of contention.

In all of this we are interested not just in a mountain of words. We are the first to concede that when these are wrenched from their contexts they are nearly as mutilated and grotesque as a heap of animal organs of many species. But even granting this, a great deal can be learned about appraisive terms so long as we have contextual examples of them constantly in mind. We seek the thought that accompanies them, their interrelations and differences, the purposes they serve, and above all the way in which they constitute the devices or instruments by which responses, appraisals, and judgments are made. They are referred to by the term 'concepts' in order to indicate that they are not "mere words," whatever they may mean, and that they are instruments of *thought*.

We undertake the survey of what is a fairly vast array of such concepts (some two or three thousand) partly in order to show that ethics and value theory are but stunted growths if they try to confine their attention merely to the vocabulary of general or ultimate appraisives: **good, bad, right, wrong**. This would be like trying to carry on a sociological investigation of a country only by reading its constitution, or observing the etiquette of the queen's court. It is obvious that the court and the constitution will look and sound differently if one has first acquainted himself with the *realia* of the nation, its wealth and poverty, slums and homesteads, work and leisure pursuits, loves and hatreds. This is why we shall come explicitly to the question of the good only as we approach the end of our study. I believe it will look considerably changed under this light.

2   OVERVIEW OF THE INQUIRY

Our study falls into three main parts. In Part One we take up the acts or processes of mind that are involved in our responding, appraising, and judging, and in the creation or enactment of values. In Part Two we present numerous concepts that we make use of in these acts or processes of evaluation. We have restricted attention in this part to the characterization of human life and action. Part Three culminates in the presentation of completely general and ultimate appraisive concepts such as **good**.

The restriction of Part Two to the appraising of man by man is a necessity in this exposition, yet there are also other areas that involve values which are not considered here. We say that propositions are true, that consequences follow from premises and that arguments are valid, that some things are real, others illusory or imaginary. Truth, validity, and reality have all been called values, but we shall not pause to look for what all things called values have in common. Brief consideration of these other values is given in the Appendices.

There is another large area of value that has the strongest kind of claim to our attention but must be excluded here, except for brief treatment in an appendix, namely aesthetic value. Moreover, one must admit that the consensus about this value, more than any of those preceding it, except economic value which in some ways it closely resembles, is that it is value solely *for us*. We exclude it largely because it is such a wide and difficult field that it deserves extended, separate treatment. What would particularly find a place here is taste or sensitivity or the capacity for aesthetic discrimination since this enters into the appraisal and characterization of man, to which all of Part Two is devoted. Even this can be accorded only the briefest consideration.

3 MODES OF ATTENDING

In this and the following two sections we offer a brief sketch of what enters into each of the three main parts of this study. In Part One we shall be considering concepts whose normal or usual form is that of verbs. These are not themselves appraisive concepts. We begin with notions such as *enjoying, desiring, admiring, detesting, fearing,* and *spurning* where we appear to be responding with our feelings. We consider next the appraising and assessing of things, processes, persons, or aspects of these in our environment. Having appraised them we avoid, applaud, or disparage them and we may evidently err in our appraisals since we speak of overrating and underrating them.

But appraisal is not the end of the matter. We also dedicate ourselves to certain values, purposes, or destinies, and we ordain the observance of them. Here we note the progressively more serious tone of these processes. If we are skilled at self-observation, we can discern the shape of our body of values, or our ideology; this may be part of a religious system of thought and practice. But matters do not stop there, for ideologies and religions may not be deliberately constructed, nor if they simply grow, do they grow merely in order to entertain or edify us. Decisions are taken on the basis of them, and as a result we are in the thick of accusation, correction, condemnation, and even vengeance. Beyond these involvements or directly connected with them, is the necessity to justify the actions we are involved in or the decisions we have taken. In this we hope to bring this process to a decisive end. We wish to say of these outcomes that justice has been done. What this means will eventually be considered in some detail.

In broad outline then we begin, in Part One, with the capacities of the mind to respond or react appetitively or emotionally to the environment, that is to say, to nature as it concerns man, and proceed towards the capacities to establish values and to appraise and judge in the light of them, proceeding through five topics: *enjoyment, response, appraisal, enactment,* and *moral involvement.* One should avoid thinking of these as marking stages of man's history or of the individual person's development. They may occur in conjunction with one another, but they are clearly distinguishable. We shall offer reasons for refusing to accept the absolute primacy of response and the reduction of appraisal to this, as is so often proposed by naturalist philosophers.

4 THE INSTRUMENTS OF APPRAISAL

Part Two comprises the entire area of the means of appraisal of man by man. The concepts that are here the object of study can be looked upon as the devices or instruments by means of which appraisals are made, specifically the instruments or the results of the acts of evaluation, appraisal, or discovery which have been set forth in Part One. This then is the heart of the subject because the appraisal of man and the appraisal of the universe as it affects man or as he affects it, are the principal although not the only subject matter of axiology, the theory of value.

We may observe that the concepts of Part One are used to name, report, or describe certain acts: but they are not themselves part of the appraisal of these acts. There is, however, one departure from this, made for certain purposes of exposition, namely the Responsional Characterizations in 2.4. For the most part, all of the concepts of Part One are simply those for reporting or describing our acts of appraising, responding, and judging, whereas actual appraisives make their first most significant appearance in Part Two.

We should notice in this connection the use of the terms 'appraisal' and 'appraisive.' Appraisals are themselves acts and the statements that issue from them. The linguistic or conceptual instruments or devices by means of which appraisals are made are called appraisives. Many terms in '-ive' are used in this manner, and not only in the present study.

When we consider now how man appraises man, we can, of course, offer a great variety of systems of classification. What *are* the main areas or dimensions of man's being? Obviously no one scheme is likely to be authoritative or final. We are familiar with the classical ternary distinction of thought, feeling and action. This might have served here but no real need was found for it. Precisely in order to avoid leaning on this classical framework, unless it seemed entirely necessary, a different tactic of discovery, as it may perhaps be called, was necessary. For this one may proceed in an inductive manner in what seems at first sight a rather primitive sense of the term 'inductive'. Having collected a vast array of appraisives, we sort them out by such resemblances as they appear to have to one another. Of course, any body of particular items whether they be matches, or pebbles, or concepts can be sorted in innumerable ways. What is worse, they may show no clear or interesting principles of division whatever. In fact, however, the concepts of valuation fairly readily fall into place in reference to various general features of man's life. While others may come to strikingly different results pursuing this method, they may nevertheless, working toward the same end, agree that this is one way to do justice to the similarities. These are what must stand uppermost in attention. The fact that language has the unique built-in characteristic of certain "natural similarities," so to speak, namely synonymity, of course tends to abbreviate the process. (But synonymity can be utterly misleading here, as we shall explain later on.)

Perhaps a single example will show the procedure. Eventually the terms **resolute, makeshift, pertinacious, pitfall,** and **maladroit** seemed to fall into the general area of man's engagement in actions, undertakings, enterprises – I have called this area the Tendentive. But further distinctions are possible within this. Eventually, **resolute** seems to fall "naturally" (the inverted commas indicate a certain intellectual apology) within the class called Address to Enterprise, **makeshift** to Means and Management of Means, **pertinacious** to quality or degree of Engagement, **pitfall** to Situational Aids and Impediments, and **maladroit** to Exercise of Powers. But, of course, the invention of these classes is possible only after a great deal of trial and error.

This will suffice for the moment as a sketch of the method pursued. What is more important are the classifications arrived at. These will emerge as this introduction proceeds.

5 HUMAN APPRAISIVES AND GENERAL APPRAISIVES

We must now draw attention to the fundamental distinction between the appraisives of Part Two and those of Part Three. Part Two concerns man more or less exclusively. Part Three is broader in scope, and its appraisives are general and ultimate. Here ultimacy includes generality, but the converse does not hold. The classes of ultimate commendatives (e.g. **good**) and discommendatives are general as well as ultimate. They invite questions of specific meaning, application, and interpretation: so far as these are applied to man this is to be found only by further reference to those appraisives in Part Two which may be deemed appropriate. For example, **catastrophe** is a general characterization. In use it must be given a reference to appraisives of Part Two, if the subject matter is human, and it also points toward an ultimate discommendation (**bad**). When we declare some event a catastrophe, we see it as characterized by deprivation, want, frustration, and defeat, and accord it unreserved discommendation. Characterizations thus point toward commendation and discommendation, because they credit or discredit, and commendations gain significant content only by reference back to characterization. We shall examine these relations or movements in detail as we proceed.

There is a considerable variety of terms comprised under Part Three. All of them have in common the fact that they are apparently not devised for the appraisal *of man* in any narrow sense but are general in scope. So we have classes of appraisives variously titled elicitives, deservatives, normatives, etc. And under them we have such concepts as **benign, catastrophe,** and **momentous.** Now, of course we tend to think of that which is benign as benign to us, to all or some of us human beings. But the subjects we characterize as benign need not be man or any work of man. The disappearance of *Bronto-saurus* was, for his race at least, a catastrophe, although it is hard to see how humanity could have arisen and flourished if the Mesozoic age had continued indefinitely. Again, *what* is characterized as momentous may have only a remote connection with man. The emergence of amphibians was, in natural history, momentous. But though it was a necessary condition, biologically speaking, for the emergence of man, it is nevertheless for man, as he has lived the last hundred centuries, a remote and unmomentous event.

The subjects appraised may thus be extra-human and even remote from man. Their appraisal *usually* indicates what significance they have for us but we may also adopt, and often we try to adopt, standpoints other than our own. We need, then, a vocabulary to express appraisals of things other than man, and of things which inhabit or seem to inhabit a world of their own apart from ourselves.

The matter may, therefore, be put so. The appraisives of Part Two concern particularly the powers of man. If we wish to characterize traits, bodies, objects, qualities, relations, and other extra-human things as such, we employ first the special appraisive vocabulary appropriate to them (e.g., the cognitive, religious, aesthetic vocabularies sketched in the Appendices), and then also the general and ultimate appraisives in Part Three. If we use the appraisives of Part Two in speaking of things or animals, we generally do so by humanizing, or animizing them. Our use of Part Three appraisives generally does indicate the importance of the extra-human *for us*, but as applied to such things they can also suggest evaluation from a more timeless and eternal standpoint. It was perfectly meaningful for the medieval philosophers, or others, to ask whether the world or matter was evil or good, and they were not thinking of its *use* to man, whatever else they may have had in mind.

The appraisives of Part Three can thus be applied to subjects other than human, and we have also other vocabularies at our disposal for this purpose. In general, and this is an essential part of what is urged in the whole of this study, the appraisives of Part Three are significant only when they are taken in conjunction with those of Part Two for man and with comparable appraisives for other things. By themselves they are largely void. To decide whether something is felicitous, deleterious, moderate, potent, prosperous, salient, flagrant, trivial, invaluable, natural, good, or bad we must have some more specific appraisive clue, some means of interpreting and specifying the application of the terms. We ask, "What do you mean?" "Why do you say so?" Either there is a way of specifying or interpreting the appraisives in Part Three in terms of those in Part Two, or comparable characterizations, or 'A is good' is a mere void that gets whatever meaning it has by coasting downhill on the strength of its resemblance to other contexts where speci-fication *has* been made.

In the case of extra-human subject matters, with substances, for example, such as animals, we can often support a commendation by appeal to ideal generic characteristics of the class in question. Part Three includes the class of normative and quasi-normative terms. These we can and regularly do apply to both animals and machines to indicate how nearly these things accord with norms seemingly found in nature (a typical and healthy polar bear, *ursus maritimus*, found wild, let us say, in northern Alaska or Canada), or in human manufacture (a perfect Hispano-Suiza of 1923 of a certain type). But of course, we also have a host of terms appropriate to each of the classes of this sort, for example, a manufacturer's specifications, or the appropriate characterization of a horse in Shakespeare's *Venus and Adonis*, or terms used in the appraisal of a certain type of animal for certain purposes, e.g., the production of milk, and so on. The use of normative terms in these cases is meaningful only when reference can be made to generic characteristics. Whether there is anything comparable to this for man will be discussed at length in connection with the virtues and vices in 14.0.

6   DEFINITION AND THE VOCABULARY OF APPRAISAL

One of the principal purposes behind our investigation of the language of evaluation is to show its vast subtlety and complexity, but not only that. It is also that investigations of value have shown unpardonable neglect of this vocabulary of concepts in their zeal to come to a decisive analysis of good and to settle victoriously for one side or another the conflicts over ethical naturalism and its alternatives. One will seek in vain, in most volumes on ethics, for explicit study of the rich treasury of appraisive terms such as is assembled here. They manifest themselves there at most when examples are alluded to. This is not because such investigations are backward or oriented toward the past. The fact is, they have lost touch with kinds of investiga-tions that the great historical figures undertook. One can readily mention some five or six at least of these who were immediately concerned with a body of appraisive terms.

The first is Plato. He devotes himself directly and explicitly to the study of the Good in several dialogues, but the bulk of his effort in the study of value lies in dialogues on very specific values and virtues: *piety, courage, temperance, justice, wisdom*. The second is Aristotle, who shows the keenest concern for the whole range of ethical terms and their relationships, notably in the *Nicomachean Ethics*, Book Two. Setting aside the medieval philosophers as too varied to consider, the next name should be that of Descartes, whose

Passions de l'Âme is concerned not only with the psychological questions that surround ethics on all sides but also with study of a host of ethical concepts taken for themselves. A fourth great name is that of Spinoza. In Book III of the *Ethics* nearly fifty terms which are either responsives or appraisives, to use our terminology, are considered and given the most painstaking definitions in characteristic consecutive and cumulative order. Further, one should mention the second book of Hume's *Treatise*. One does not often find due appreciation of the fact that Hume treats morals and ethics only *after* the passions, and moreover that the passions with the understanding form one of the three pillars of *human nature*. Hume's analysis is one of his most ingenious efforts and is also undoubtedly the least read portion of the *Treatise*.

Finally, Kant devoted considerable space to what one may call the philosophy of virtue (*Tugendlehre*), but this part of his writings has lain in neglect for generations. Yet he himself regarded it as the culmination of his moral theory. Since his time the naturalists and their opponents, the intuitionists, have occupied what they suppose is the center of the field of ethics and value. But in the process, everything which could interest a larger public has disappeared from view whilst interminable debate rages over matters of definition and analysis of a small range of concepts.

It is time to turn aside from these diversions and from concentration on a mere handful of terms, as if the value vocabulary consisted only of them. It is hard to see what further analytical microscopy can accomplish with them, and it is by no means obvious that everything hangs on their analysis or definition.

In the realm of value, hatred, jealousy, love, and war are stirred. Here men bless, curse, and blaspheme. Here they utter every known oath, obscenity, and endearment and invent new ones to suit their moods. *This* is what the theory of value must reflect.

7   THE SOURCE AND HABITAT OF APPRAISIVE TERMS

We must now survey our body of concepts from a broader point of view. Are these the entire body of appraisive terms and are there no others? The answer is that they are by no means all of the appraisives that there are or are possible even in the English language. Let us first survey the sources from which appraisive language grows, and second, show why we have confined our attention to the present selection.

Some four sources of appraisives can be identified. Besides the core vocabulary explored here, there are vocabularies originating in slang, metaphor, and non-appraisive language. Since we are able to appraise only because we possess appraisive language, the question arises how appraisive terms are introduced into and become part of the language. They seem to have extremely varied histories. Only empirical study can hope to throw light on this matter.

The first source of appraisives is ordinary or plain language, language not explicitly appraisive which has been pressed into service for the purpose of appraising. We readily recognize the appraisive force of the following sentences, but scarcely a single word would, by itself, seem to have any appraisive force. I shall have occasion to refer to this kind of appraising again and call it the *P-vocabulary* for "plain," though it is less a vocabulary than a set of clichés, idioms, and special constructions.

> She can twist him around her little finger.
> This hat really does something for you.
> Do you call that a hat?
> Don't try to put anything over on him.
> This knife won't do at all.
> He has what it takes.
> I just can't keep my eyes off her.
> He's not complicated; one can see right through him.
> Don't let them walk all over you.
> Farmville people always meet you at least half way.

It will be noticed how close these come to the vernacular or colloquial, if not outright slang. But this is not surprising. A second source of appraisive terms is slang itself and its near neighbors in the vernacular and the obscene. Examples are scarcely necessary. It is generally a trait of slang to function only for a brief time; its cutting edge is blunted with constant use and overuse. Even so, a good number of terms which have made their way into "respectable" English have their origin in slang, and they are often among the most expressive. The origin of particular slang terms is more often than not obscure, and the reason of their appeal hard to discover. But the striking fact about slang is the degree to which it is employed not for describing, but for purposes of appraising, using the term loosely to cover also all ways of emotive response, celebration and desecration, and judgment. In circles where slang is virtually the *lingua franca*, appraisal is unrestrained and emphatic; one does not conceal one's feelings out of considerations of "good taste" or couch them in "accepted" forms. The nature of this esoteric *lingua* is by its nature all too little known to outsiders. It has, however, a most singular importance because in it we see communicative language being born out of what were only moments before, as it were, nonsense syllables. It is one of the oldest theories of language to seek its origin in the expressive dimension. I would reiterate that the resort to slang in ordinary speech is largely for appraisive not descriptive purposes, but this could be confirmed only by an extensive empirical study. We shall speak of appraisive slang as the *S-vocabulary*.

There is still a third area in which we can see appraisive language take its rise. If the first was the use of ordinary communicative language and its transformation into appraisive language by subtle nuances and emphases, and the second the creation of new and extraordinary language for this purpose, the third is a kind of combination of these two: familiar words are used in extraordinary senses; in other words, metaphors are developed to convey appraisals. Once again, it would be idle to make authoritative declarations without empirical evidence, but one may be permitted to surmise that most metaphors are coined for appraisive, not for descriptive purposes. Virtually the whole range of animal metaphors developed for application to persons serves the purposes of appraising. We have excluded most of them here, with a few exceptions. But since language is deeply permeated with metaphor the effort to exclude them all would hamper if not immobilize our powers of expression. We may call this the *M-vocabulary*.

Looking beyond these sources of appraisive language there remains the body of explicit appraisives that are to be found in our present language-in-being. It is to these, the appraisive vocabulary or *A-vocabulary*, that we have here confined ourselves, and our reasons for doing so must now be fully set forth.

8   THE APPRAISIVES OF NATURAL LANGUAGES

It might be argued that the study of appraisal and judgment ought not to be tied down to the study of appraisives as they happen to appear in some particular or current language. What is authoritative about the distinctions made, say, in the English language? What reason is there to believe that any more than issues and habits local to speakers of English will emerge? We answer that it is of the utmost importance that we study the appraisives of a *living* language. But once we have studied English, we ought to resist quick generalization about other languages and instead encourage parallel investigations into them. It is both those languages that lie very near and yet differ significantly from English, and those that lie very, very far from it, that will afford us the greatest insight into the processes of appraising. We dare only one generalization, and even this is subject to confirmation, and that is that there is an appraisive dimension, division, or fraction of every known language, inasmuch as all men speak, and all men praise and blame, commend and condemn. Even if conclusions only about English-speaking people are in order here, the result will still be significant, particularly if the effort is made to compare the result with the appraisive systems of other peoples and other languages.

It is evident in this that we have thrown aside all *a priori* rules such as those which see philosophy as something which has nothing to do with empirical research. On the contrary, the present inquiry hopes to be empirical at every stage. It will be content to be identified with the Anglo-Saxon frame of reference or, if we like more pretentious terms, metaphysical standpoint, or *Weltanschauung*. Its only hope is that if it depicts this, it does so accurately.

But there is also a deeper reason for undertaking this kind of investigation with specific empirical reference to one language. I cannot, at this point, enter fully into the defense of the matter, to which we shall have occasion to revert again. The reason is this. A given language harbors appraisives which are solely its own. There is no such thing as the universal translatability of all appraisive terms. The present kind of investigation will have to be repeated in principle for every language because a significant part of the appraisives in a language are not translatable into other languages. When we speak of the way in which languages differ from one another we may have only very vague thoughts or impressions about their aesthetic characteristics, or about rhythm, sonority, frequency of certain consonants, vowels or phonemes, and so forth. These matters, of course, are entirely distinct from the semantic question as to whether languages are *intertranslatable*, where a well-constructed sentence S_e in English always has an exact equivalent S_g in, let us say, German. There is nothing whatever to choose between saying, "The children started to laugh" and "Die Kinder fingen an zu lachen." So far as the fact conveyed is concerned, the only issue will be whether to convey this information in the one form or in the other, let us say in London and in Berlin, in order to insure comprehension. Such sentences, I am supposing, raise no such issues as we are concerned with here since they merely record or describe a fact or an event. But when we have a paragraph of critical appraisal in English can we be certain that someone will be able to produce a rendition in German or something that evokes in German the same thoughts or feelings that are evoked in English, a perfect equivalent of it, so that again the one merely happens to be appropriate for a London and the other for a Berlin audience? Anyone who has ever endured the travail of producing the "perfect translation" of a poem or other literary effort knows without needing further examples that although he may succeed in reaching the heights of feeling of an original in a given language, he will have to confess even more often that such and such a passage is "virtually untranslatable." No one supposes that the matter of fact Baedeker is preferable in one tongue or another, so far as matters of fact are concerned. But why, for example, do German critical appraisals of art or literature or moral questions suffer such a sea change, why have they such a different "feel" merely by being rendered into English? In general, difficult or untranslatable passages are passages that are likely to contain appraisive terms or appraisive language in one of the forms described in the preceding section. One type of appraisive language, the P-vocabulary, generally will be the most elusive of all and the most resistant to translation. Similar things can be said of many metaphors that utterly defy translation, and of nearly all slang, which like **Kitsch** can be translated only by being taken over altogether.

Perhaps, one will say, the change is after all very little, and in these matters one mustn't be too fastidious: *de minimis non curat lex*. I agree that the differences are or are often minute and sometimes trivial for practical purposes, but the significant fact is that there *are* differences, and that they are completely irreducible by nature.

To say that any two linguistic items (such as words or sentences) or any two languages have irreducible differences is to say something like this. There is a large body of terms or expressions (A ------- N) which do *not* appear *identically* in all or most languages (true synonyms have each an equivalent with another subscript: A_e, A_f, A_g -------- etc., for English, French, German, etc.). There is rather only a union (a logical summation) of appraisive terms or concepts. That is, since they have few interlingual equivalents the "world stock" of them virtually consists of the totality of them in all languages. To be sure, there will be some which are closely congruent or identical. In other words, for one large body of terms there *will* be equivalents:

$$A_e, A_f, A_g ------------ A_z ------$$
$$B_e, B_f, B_g ------------ B_z ------$$

which, however, will all reduce simply to a kind of ideal type: A, B, C ---- etc. There also will be those which may have a family resemblance but remain irreducibly themselves in their several languages; and these will resist reduction to A or B or C, etc. What we are saying, then, is that a very large number of appraisives are of the latter type. If one were to seek to compile a universal dictionary of *descriptive* terms we would need only to invent the paradigms, A, B, C, D ----- etc., and then say that these can be expressed by A_e, A_f, A_g ----- ; B_e, B_f, B_g ----- etc. But with a large segment of the class of *appraisives* one could say only that there is a large body of families of terms, and a dictionary of appraisives would have to include *all* of the members of all the families: there would be no way to abbreviate it. We shall discuss other matters relevant to this below.

We can actually go further, as will become evident, and say that there are no synonyms among the appraisives even in one given language. Many are closely kin, of course, but essentially each "station" is occupied once only, or by only one member. *Here again it is the small differences that are significant.* Languages are more or less hospitable to the new coinages and creations of slang, metaphor and plain speech, but also to those "novelties" which they get wind of in foreign languages. The splendid good sense inherent in most languages has ever recognized this fact. Confronted with it, they simply borrow new terms from each other lock, stock and barrel. Having no real equivalents of **stigma** and **euphoria**, the English language simply borrowed them. Similarly, lacking the smart patness of **trounce**, **grudge**, **cozy**, **snug**, **qualm**, **squeamish**, and **smatter**, it took them over without asking their pedigree – which may very well be slang. And, of course, as has often been observed, *slang* is probably slang too.

The result then is not just that we have happened to investigate value theory and *couched our results in* the English language. On the contrary, we acknowledge explicitly that we have specifically *examined the body of appraisive terms which occur in* the English language. It remains for those who are bilingual or multilingual, so long as one of their languages is English, to see how far the categories adopted here, the interrelationships observed, the generalizations ventured, and the solutions offered apply also to tongues other than English. I have no doubt that very large parts of this will be readily comprehensible so that agreement and difference will easily be apparent. But again, the emphasis must be placed on the *small differences*. It is the subtleties of appraisal that show whether we are truly sensitive beings. We have thus arrived at the all-important question of the aim and purpose of appraisive language, that is, the uses to which it is put.

9 THE OBJECTIVITY OF APPRAISALS

We may begin our inquiry into the purposes of appraisive language by considering the familiar question of the objectivity of "judgments" of appraisal. The term 'judgment' must be stringently qualified as will be shown below.

I shall begin by replacing the idea of objectivity with the somewhat more concrete one of *detachability*.* When, for example, we speak of what we may call *information*, we readily see that *who* utters any statement or sentence about a matter of fact is completely irrelevant to the question of its reference or truth. (We may exclude all assertions about oneself or one's experience.) The facts of chronology (if not of history), of public records, of many other classes of information in an important sense are detachable from their

* Further discussion of the notion of "detachability" is found in (this author's) "Artistic Disclosure," *Studia Estetyczne* (Warszawa) T. 4, 1967.

authors or discoverers. No one can *own* them, and once their truth is established, no further reference to authors is necessary. All that is private about such information is the necessity for each person to understand the language in which the information is couched. It is perfectly possible to give objective rules for such languages. When we hear, or overhear, or share this kind of information we are not, as it were, asked to step behind the curtain and to meet the author. Facts, as we say, are cold. We may *use* them for purposes of enlivening or inflaming a conversation or a situation, but they are, by themselves, perfectly neutral, and they have no such causal properties as inflaming emotions unless someone deliberately employs them for such a purpose.

In this respect, appraisals or appraisive judgments show exactly the reverse character. When we hear someone characterized as dignified, vulgar, reserved, shrewish, or misanthropic, when language is said to be smutty, defamatory, belittling, or acrimonious, when people are said to be cowards, frauds, hooligans or sycophants, we at once tend to show as much interest in the speakers as in the targets of these characterizations. In a sense, we dare not think only of *what* is said: we must also think of *who* says it. Appraisive language is intrinsically *ad hominem*. When Spinoza says, what Peter says of Paul tells us as much about Peter as it does about Paul, and perhaps more, it is what we call appraisive language that he has in mind. And when we hear something characterized by the potent terms we have just mentioned, the first question that comes to mind is, "Who said so?" This is not mere idle curiosity. With every such judgment it is well to ask, "Whose is this image and superscription?"*

With description and information, questions of this sort have an altogether different purpose. Did Baedeker say that the population of Auxerre in 1910 was 16,971? We may be inclined to accept the figure if Baedeker did as a matter of fact say so, but Baedeker's asseveration is not what has made it true, in the sense in which we are likely to treat, "Sir, he is a fool" as a fair or reliable or apt characterization of someone because of the fact that it was, let us say, Dr Johnson or Mr Justice Holmes who said it. Only the facts, such as census rolls, will be thought to confute or confirm Baedeker. But if we want to know whether "fool" is a *fair characterization*, not a *true judgment*, of A, we shall have to take an interest *both* in A *and* in Dr Johnson or Justice Holmes. For part of A's being a fool consists in just this, that A has precisely the kind of effect on someone, such as these worthies, that evokes just this kind of characterization. If, on the other hand, we learn it is someone else who has said this of A, his valet, his housekeeper, the postman,

---

* Matthew 22:20.

we may think the situation to be considerably different. Valets and house-keepers operate at close range, but may also be petty, vindictive, and perpe-tually dissatisfied with their pay. The postman may be amiable for the most part, but also obstinate or resentful. Characterizations of "Fool!" may be strengthened or weakened by such close range observers; is there any way to tell whether they are fair except to examine the situation carefully and *use one's judgment*? That is the kind of advice we are most likely to get, if we ask how we are to appraise these appraisals.

Many philosophers are, however, inclined to turn a deaf ear to such advice. They will not cease asking, is the judgment *true*? I shall leave for later the explanation of the mistake that is involved here. In what follows we shall not speak of the truth or falsity of appraisals or appraisive judgments, but rather use only such terms as "fair" or "unfair characterization." The pursuit of a question such as, "What makes value judgments true or false?" rests on a total misconception of the "appraisive situation." We will show that "fair characterization" is apt and not just a surreptitious reintroduction of the notion of truth.

There is no way to "break out" of this situation. Our inclination to accept the "authority" of Dr Johnson or Justice Holmes can itself only be formulat-ed in further appraisive terms. It is no accident that we have had to resort to such terms as **petty, vindictive, obstinate**, and **resentful** in offering reasons why we may not want to trust the judgment of the valet, housekeeper, or post-man. These appraisives supporting other appraisives will inevitably have to be respected in order to decide whether to respect the judgment of Dr Johnson and Justice Holmes.

Is it not possible in the end to come to some *factual* resolution of this seemingly endless series of appraisives? I do not wish to suggest that this question is foolish, but it is not one to which we can now address ourselves. We shall, however, before the end have considered some possible answers. We shall now consider a more fundamental question whose answer bears on this matter.

10 THE REALITY OF VALUE

In our age, ideals of one sort or another are as likely to be excogitated and enacted by naked actresses as by sages or pontiffs. It is obvious that morals are in flux, and that we live in a time of moral crisis. There often appears to be a loss of nerve when it comes to decisive judgments of right and wrong, good and bad. We hear of a loss of support for morality or even a defiance of it, as if one could ignore or defy morality, and not just this or that morality.

At the same time, there is no dearth of moral judging: fanaticism and

demagoguery abound. We have extremes of moral skepticism and fanaticism
that always characterize ages of violent transition. Many are blind to the
blazing reality of the demagogue's kind of moral standards and their vast
remove from those of the past. Or they not only contravene but express
indignation at standards honored through long ages. We hear anti-heroes
and malcontents urging violence, hatred, and racial slaughter, or praising
indolence, idleness, and self-indulgence, which are all characterized as
highest goods in defiance of traditional virtues such as brotherliness, tolerance, thrift, effort, and self-denial. Or again, "tolerance" is the watchword
and is proclamed as if it were newly discovered. So the virtue is confused
with some manifestation of it. It is curious how anyone can think that it is
only now, under a new banner of anarchy, that we have come to enshrine
tolerance as a virtue, merely because of a newfound inclination to tolerate
such habits as homosexuality and irreligion.

What is astonishing is that an age which is often morally sensitive to an
acute degree should hear that morality is at an end, as if there were some
kind of Morality writ large and not just morality A which might be replaced
by morality B. So the filmstar tells us, "Good and bad, right and wrong,
these are children's words." Among psychoanalysts and social scientists, the
phrase 'value judgment' often names a kind of intellectual sin. We must not
make moral judgments, nor "moralize," must not exalt our values, nor
perhaps should we even think in terms of value at all. This tiresome story
could be richly documented, but perhaps mere mention of it will suffice.

It will, of course, be a commonplace to philosophers that there can be no
end of morality, of value judgment, of decisions, of 'ought,' 'good,' 'better,'
'bad,' 'worse,' and all the rest of the appraisive vocabulary. It is not difficult
to detect the re-introduction of moral judgments and standpoints in the
move to exclude them. It is true that in another morality the restraint of
sexual impulse we characterize as chastity and the restraint upon expenditure
we characterize as thrift may no longer be considered virtues, and this
morality will have as good a claim to the name as any alternative to it. The
question is, could we do without all moral concepts, all appraisals, all
judgments of value? Or we may ask, do human beings have a "moral
dimension?"

We answer by saying (1) that we have a reason for believing that man has
a moral dimension to his being and a grasp of "moral phenomena" because
he has a distinct form of language for valuation, (2) that this form is not to
be assimilated to any other, and (3) that there is no reason to believe that
he would have such a language if he had no proper use for it. We are making
so bold as to say that in the case of evaluative language we can infer a
reference for the language because in fact we speak it meaningfully – frankly

an "ontological argument," of sorts. We are interested in this argument only to insist that unless it is valid no other more exalted form of the "defense of values" is conceivable. The reason such an ontological argument can be entertained is that unlike the classic form of these arguments where one pretends to infer existence from essence (to put the matter in the briefest terms), here the "reference" that is inferred from essence (meaningful evaluative discourse) is not assertions about existence or facts but an application of value concepts to a range of subjects in the form of characterizations that may be apt or fair and moral judgments that may be just or right.

The "ontological" aspect of this is that we do not simply have a body of pre-existent moral facts or realities awaiting formulation in moral truths or concepts, but rather that moral and appraisive concepts wholly determine the moral reality or "phenomenon." Things are good because we have a power to characterize them; they are right because we have a power to justify the moral judgments we pass on them. In plainest terms, this means we can make evaluative discriminations because we command evaluative concepts and discourse; the command of a vocabulary is a necessary condition of evaluative intelligence.

We are moreover denying that value sentences are statements *about* feelings, emotions, or attitudes; or meaningless utterances to *express* or to evoke feelings; or imperatives, more or less in disguise; or wishes or resolutions. The essential appraisive vocabulary is one for the purpose of characterizing a subject, not of describing either one's own state or the state of anything else. None of these things, facts about oneself, feelings, emotions, attitudes, inclinations, evocations, imperatives, or wishes, real and relevant as they may be, makes up the reality of value. It must be sought in another quarter.

One of the strongest "threats," as we might say, to the reality of value heretofore has proceeded from the side of just these feelings, inclinations, and so on. At its most hopeful, the school of ethical naturalism has supposed itself able to "reduce" moral "propositions" or "facts" to genuine propositions or facts about such feelings and inclinations. The best one can say of this program is that if it succeeds, it fails, for it cannot possibly represent any kind of moral reality. We shall review in some detail the body of responses that may attend appraisals and judgments. In no case can any necessary relation be established between them.

If the "reduction" of moral and appraisive concepts is a threat from the side of the theorist, there is another threat from the side of the "average man" who falls into moral scepticism as he becomes aware of a great variance and conflict of appraisals and judgments and concludes that moral ideals must be illusory. (This view may be accorded somewhat greater attention here since it is not taken up again. The preceding position will be more or less continuously under review.)

We observe first that morals must not be equated with mores. Since morals are inherently ideal in nature, actual practice may mislead altogether the observer who confines himself to what he sees his subjects doing and never reads or listens to their appraisive language. Of course there may be large-scale convulsions in practice but these do not necessarily represent the repudiation of prevailing standards of evaluation. Our best clue to these is to observe the manner in which practice is characterized.

Suppose, for example, that Western society should in a matter of years or decades abandon its more combative, belligerent, and competitive practices in favor of those that are more subdued, if not passive. Actually this would represent no profound change in moral concepts or standards. For a study of our tendentive and sociative language shows that we have a greater store of appraisives designed to discredit conflict, combativeness, and aggression in every form than of almost any other kind of behavior; and we have ample means to bring credit upon irenic concourse between people or upon the use of force that is motivated solely by a restoration of accommodation between them. On the other hand, there is no way to praise cruelty or aggression in our standard moral vocabulary: we characterize our *own* resort to force as a staunch, unremitting resistance to evil, or as a resolute defense of justice. Of course we can find every known vice praised for the purpose of paradox or comedy or of promulgating some revision of our practice. Such intent is not always evident on the face of the matter. It may be misread as a repudiation of a moral standard when it is only a variant application of it.

Variance in actions and in the application of the moral vocabulary may be as conflicting as we please: it is not this that proves a conflict in moral criteria. On the contrary, it is more generally the case that the very same criteria are being employed and that the variance is only in application. But this is not a matter of calling what is true false, or what is false true: the conflict is really one of a quite different order. What we need here is a clearer understanding and awareness of how we are characterizing what we commend and discommend.

In our time moral awareness has actually deepened in many respects. Many things are combatted as cruel and obscene which in the past we thought we would have to tolerate forever. On the other hand, some things are declared innocent which we were in the habit of thinking shameful. Changes such as this are inevitable, later if not sooner. But how can they possibly show that we are no longer morally alert to cruelty, obscenity, and innocence?

It is an error to tie down moral consciousness or moral standards to particular practices and to particular applications of these standards and an even greater error to suppose such awareness is diminished by every variation in social practice.

But are not the actions of the Gestapo and the SS from 1939 to 1945 a refutation of this? During this time the extermination of a whole people must have seemed a morally blameless action to at least some of the executioners. But on the foregoing account was this any more than a change in application of moral concepts? Surely, it will be objected, no account of morals is correct if it does not entail the unreserved condemnation of persons and pratices such as these. How can one merely acknowledge it as a variance of particular moral judgments?

This is partly to be answered by saying that some of the guilty persons were clearly pathological personalities, while others may have acted under stress from superiors, but neither of these offers a sufficient answer to the objection. The fact is these persons were clearly not in proper command of moral concepts, of a moral vocabulary. It is clearly and definitively cruel in the extremest degree to inflict pain and death on persons for no reason except that they have been born and have grown up among their folk or kin. Moreover no real effort was made at the time to justify the action; it was kept virtually secret, considering that it involved the disappearance of some millions of persons. Later, the actions were disavowed and various self-exculpations were offered, for example, at the Nuremberg Trials – a clear recognition of the horror of the proceeding. To this extent the validity of the received moral order was recognized, even though it was defied. The alternative to this is even worse and is perhaps a more likely explanation of what happened. The moral order was not defied but simply fell from sight: the concept **cruel** disappeared from the thought of the *Herrenvolk*. (We may add that this applies also to the Allied generals who decreed the destruction of Dresden.)

If one is in command of a concept such as **cruelty**, one is capable of seeing instances to characterize by means of it, and one accepts the obligation to prevent or rectify it. One commands a moral vocabulary only by using it. It is not conflict, even severe conflict, that threatens a society so gravely as losing, or not having, the conceptual means for making moral and appraisive distinctions. For as long as these are before the mind a rationale for the just termination of conflict prevails.

Moral practice and moral realities are determined by the possession of moral concepts and a moral vocabulary. If we do not possess a given moral concept we cannot recognize the corresponding moral phenomenon. The variety and subtlety of the appraisive vocabulary determines moral sensibility and defines the "moral dimension" of man. This is the reason why the study of value theory must begin with the vast resources (at least in Western languages) of appraisive discourse.

It is fairly safe to say that there are no languages without appraisives. We shall also defend the stronger thesis that there can be no appraisals or appraisives outside of language. What kind of appraisals we can make is determined by the very lineaments of the language we speak. This thesis is but a variant of another more general thesis, largely associated with the name of Whorf in recent decades. If we have doubts about whether our metaphysical schemata are determined in the manner Whorf suggests, there can be little doubt that systems of appraisal are. This of course needs to be argued further. For the present we shall simply address ourselves to some of the broader aspects of the thesis.

11 DEFINITION AND THE UNDERSTANDING OF APPRAISIVES

In one of his essays Hume says: "That people who invented the word *charity*, and used it in a good sense, inculcated more clearly and much more efficaciously the precept, *be charitable*, than any pretended legislator or prophet who should insert such a maxim in his writings."* Hume's thesis that the very presence of a word such as **charity** in our language has a didactic or preceptive power more effective than any explicit command or exhortation can be extended to all appraisive language. To use it is to understand the implied precept if not actually to embrace it.

The first question we ask is whether there may not be conflicting commands of this sort. Surely, we say, a fully developed language is a system that enables us to express our own thoughts in any direction we please. Can we not praise the opposite of charitable thought, conduct, and speech? What we now find is that language seems not to permit us full freedom of expression. When we attempt to go against the grain of standard concepts and expressions the result appears paradoxical or even pathological.

The richest store of examples of this is to be found in Section 11.0 below, which is devoted to the "sociating" relations, both accommodating and conflicting, among persons. The very first sub-section (11.1) shows us that although we can speak in a neutral manner to describe a conflict (using the descripts listed), we can really only speak appraisively of conflict in a negative fashion: the appraisives are all discrediting. In the next sub-section we learn the vast number of ways we can appraise acts of contending. Here the stock of terms is virtually all negative or discrediting, but a few may be used to credit, provided the protagonist is being praised for his tenacity or courage (**paladin, champion**). The following sub-sections show us how we regard those whose contention is really contentiousness in word and deed; the

---

* Hume, "Of the Standard of Taste."

terms are nearly all harsh and severe. Judging from the standard vocabulary, there is no way to praise deception, defamation and derision, even if we present these in entirely descriptive terms. Sub-section 11.2 shows us how we may speak of the person who has achieved mastery and ascendancy. He must be anything but the Marshal Goering sort: he must be heroic, masterful, proud, but with dignity and a sense of justice and responsibility. The craven is discredited, not because he submits but because of his servility and sycophancy. If some will rule, others must obey: hence there are negative crediting characterisms for those who submit or defer, again with a sense of dignity. The following section shows us how we may speak of compromise, rapprochement, or as we have titled it, accommodation. This mode and the modes of covenanting or compacting with others, offer a kind of ideal culmination of social relations.

In our investigation, appraisive terms have simply been laid alongside one another, like with like, and a great effort has been made to turn up virtually the whole of the standard appraisive vocabulary in order to allow for all of the possible appraisive stances and postures. The result tends to confirm what Hume suggests: our language embodies exhortations and it is, so far, a surprisingly consistent exhortation, virtually pointing toward a kind of ideal man and ideal society. We have deliberately refrained from drawing the profile of this ideal. It is sufficient for the present that it should suggest itself. The degree to which it is consistent can best be judged from surveying the whole body of appraisive terms.

We may now turn to some of the problems raised by the foregoing. We may confine ourselves to two related questions: (1) how we in fact resist the kind of "determinism" imposed by the prevailing system of appraisive language, (2) whether the understanding of standard appraisive terms necessitates our accepting the implied precepts.

(1) The first question concerns the revisability of the system of appraisive concepts. For this we may turn to other languages and other cultures. All natural languages borrow from one another but not always as readily as we may suppose or wish. In fact changes in customs and pressures to effect change are ceaseless and eventually affect the character of language. Language exercises a restraint in a conservative direction, but this can eventually be overturned. We may look to some of the various areas of characterization to observe the forces at work. All that can be attempted here is a rapid survey; much more on the subject will be said later on.

Beginning with the appraisives of *intelligence*, it is apparent that the term is itself a kind of appraisive to be contrasted with stupidity, want of acumen, and so forth. It is, however, imaginable that such values should cease to attract mankind. Suspicion of "knowledge" and "philosophy" are

evident in the ancient Hebrew and early Christian Literature.* There are
those who urge a rejection of rationality in our time. Certainly we can imagine alternatives to it. The personal traits that have been characterized as
stupidity and simple-mindedness have not always received the discommendation now implied in these terms. Who can say that a serious retreat from
intellectual values may not develop significant proportions in the future?
The gap between celebration and observance of values is notorious in
nearly every culture, and changes are ceaselessly under way. The virtues of a
society reflected in its standard language may inevitably offer an over-
idealized picture. The paradoxes of "Christian civilization" during two
thousand years offer a comparable example. Gandhi might well have replied
in the same manner about this as he did when he was asked what he thought
of Western civilization: "I think it would be a good idea."

Turning to the appraisives of the body and *behavior*, a picture of an
active, strong, agile, well-dressed person emerges, not given to gluttony or
other excess, and preserving a certain seemliness at all times. But of course a
society consisting of persons with significantly different figures and habits is
readily imaginable. This century has witnessed great changes in the demands
and expectations about the body and its behavior. It has become totally
visible at times; sport, exercise, and physical display have become commonplace. Progressions and regressions now move at a quickened rate, and there
are alternatives that beckon from the pagan and primitive past. All of this
leaves its mark on appraisive language even though it has as yet had little
effect on the core vocabulary we are studying. But what effect does such
language itself exert? Have terms like 'propriety' and 'seemliness' any power
at present?

Diathetic appraisives such as those we have drawn from English of course
deeply inhere in the fabric of our attitudes and respondings. Since efforts
at translation readily reveal to us the non-congruence of diathetic appraisives
in other languages, there is no need to think of our own stock of terms as in
any way necessary or inevitable. Here as elsewhere we must ask how and
whether the actual conditions that are or have been appraised in terms of the
vices can now or eventually come to be *credited*. To be sure, we cannot
without linguistic impropriety or paradox try to say that ill temper, lethargy,
diffidence, vanity, affectation, vulgarity, and frivolity (all presently diathetic
vices) are good. But we can cease to condemn what has been condemned
heretofore in these terms, and we can even cease to use the terms altogether.

---

* Ecclesiastes 1:18, "He that increaseth knowledge increaseth sorrow." Colossians 2:8,
"Beware lest any man spoil you through philosophy and vain deceit, after the tradition
of men, after the rudiments of the world, and not after Christ." Also, 1 Corinthians
1:18 ff., and 2:13.

Sex-related appraisives offer a striking example of mutation under the impact of changes in actual practice. Judging from the appraisive vocabulary alone, sexual union in and of itself, that is, apart from ensuing fertility, has never enjoyed the endorsement of English-speaking society. Aside from the Biblical **enjoy** and the heretofore shamefaced or ambivalent **voluptuous** no standard term has served to praise sexual acts. From this we can gauge the limits of the conceptual determinism discussed above: we can observe both the strength and weight of tradition and the strength of the forces needed to alter social patterns including patterns of appraisive discourse. This "determinism" is obviously not insurmountable.

Tendentive appraisives may sooner or later exhibit the extent of the assault on the gospel of hard work, achievement, commitment to enterprise, acquisition, and kindred qualities associated by the intelligentsia with the "Protestant ethic." Even apart from this, the interpretation of the tendentive virtues has fluctuated in an almost contradictory fashion. For example, differences have sometimes been thought to reveal themselves as we pass from East to West or North to South. The Bavarians are "lazy" in comparison to the Prussians; so also the Calabrians in comparison to the Tuscans and Piedmontese. And what of the Tuscans in comparison to the Bavarians considerably to the north of them?

The remaining areas of social appraisal exhibit comparable tension and strain as the power and direction of social change vary.

(2) Our second question concerning appraisives is whether the precepts they seem to express are actually necessary to their sense or meaning. We see that Hume regards **charity** as inculcating the precept *be charitable*. If we now learn the term can we really learn it or learn it correctly if we do not accept the precept contained in it? I think it is fairly certain that we do sense an intention to advise or warn when, particularly here and now, terms such as **charm, generosity, self-confident, humiliation, mawkishness, parsimony, pugnacity, reckless, ribald,** or **turgid** are used to characterize subjects that are of some interest or concern to us. We may consider the question of implied precepts in fairly representative examples.

Many exquisite things were destroyed by the Barbarians during their invasions of Europe in the Dark Ages. Let us suppose their language had an equivalent of **exquisite**. One of their European prisoners is allowed to talk frankly to his captors. He asks, "Why do you destroy exquisite things? The artists were endowed with consummate talents. Such things should not be wantonly destroyed." The captor might say, "If they were indeed exquisite we would not wantonly destroy them. We simply do not find them so. "This is no doubt deplorable, but it is a reasonable answer, under the circumstances. The captor acknowledges the precept involved in **exquisite** but applies it to different examples.

Let us alter the example somewhat. The captor's language has no such term as **exquisite**. He is again met with the prisoner's complaint. But he must first be taught the use of the term **exquisite**. The captor will have to begin with examples other than the things just destroyed. The question is, could the captor be brought to the point where he truly understands the meaning of the term (he has been shown many examples and has done at least as well as the average speakers of the captor's language in picking out the ones that he thinks will be called exquisite by such speakers) and yet says, "I do indeed understand what you people mean by this term, but I am not in the least inclined to honor the precept to preserve exquisite things at all costs." Should we say he deceives himself in saying he understands what the term means? I am inclined to say that he deceives himself. I can understand how he could fail to agree with the captor's choice of examples, but I do not understand how he could apply the term as the captor does and then go on to destroy exquisite things, wantonly, that is.

If this is the correct conclusion to draw, we have a rather surprising result. We cannot, if this example is decisive, reasonably say we even *understand that* a term is in a language unless we acknowledge its imperative force over us. But what of the terms apparently for virtues and vices in our language which are not acknowledged by a large number of speakers. For example, blasphemy, one of the most fearful crimes in the Middle Ages, is regularly practiced and encouraged in the Soviet Union. Is it that the Soviet officials simply do not understand the meaning of **blasphemy**? Do they not know that uttering such and such remarks, acting in such and such ways in Christian churches is regarded by Christians as wicked, and is condemned by them? Indeed, they do know this. Is it simply that they do understand the term, but apply it differently? No, they do not acknowledge that anti-religious behavior in churches, at least if officially sanctioned, is wicked or reprehensible, although their treatment of Lenin's body, relics, and teachings cannot fail to appear to have something of a religious character to outsiders.

In this situation perhaps we may simply decide to separate the meaning of the term from the precept. We shall then be able to say that the Soviet officials understand the term but decline the precept. I think Christians, however, might well be thoroughly dissatisfied with this solution. "If you really understand what blasphemy means," they will say, "demeaning and befouling sacred and divine things, you will not want to destroy them. Otherwise you simply cannot understand what **blasphemy** or **sacred** means." I am fairly certain this is what the remnants of the Orthodox clergy must think in Russia. The crime of their rulers must, therefore, seem to them to be a lack of understanding. If *they* are right, we cannot accept the solution that the officials understand the precept but decline to follow it.

Evidently appraisive terms are rather hardy perennials. Although blasphemy and the defiance of chastity may be widespread, we seem to be unable to say that the protagonists of these modes of conduct either do understand what the terms mean (if they did understand what the religious mean by **sacred** and **pure**, they would not support such conduct) or that they do not (they understand them well enough to know what practices they wish to suppress or defy). What then is the solution to this dilemma? I suggest the following.

I think we must give up the idea that we can understand these terms without accepting the implied precepts. It is better for the atheist to say that he simply does not understand what religious people mean. It is indeed more honorable of him to say that he regards such ideas as meaningless and that that is why he ignores the precepts and exerts himself against them, than it is to say that he understands them but defies the precepts. On the other hand, the attitudes of the religious would be better served by this attitude. They can then pray for the enlightenment of unbelievers. This, in fact, is quite literally contained in the words, "Forgive them, for they know not what they do." If this is so, I should think the atheist should be given pause for taking up the cudgel against something he does not even understand. He ought not to pretend he understands when quite obviously in the religionist's sense, he does not understand at all.

We may not be altogether happy with this result. We seem to be permitting a potentially large number of terms to inhabit the English language, let us say, which we may not find at all meaningful, and indeed we may be forced hereby to contemplate alternative dictionaries for Christians and non-Christians, believers and infidels, and so forth. But this is only if we construe the term 'understanding' with the greatest rigor. Dictionaries are not treatises on theology or metaphysics or art or engineering. They can only speak rather briefly on each subject. What the religious understand by **sacred** or **sacrilege** is obviously far more than Webster can describe. At most he can point us in the right direction for finding out. I would rather say that I cannot understand what the "aficionados" see in bullfighting and be tolerant or intolerant of it depending upon what consequences I see from it, than to say that I understand (it would be a mere pretense) and yet condemn it.

We have to accept the fact that our language may harbor among its appraisives a certain vocabulary which many can no longer understand and whose precepts they can no longer follow. But understanding cannot be thought to have eyes only in the back of its head, so that we understand only what we can translate into language we already know. There must be a creativity of understanding in which truly novel meanings burst upon us. This is the problem of creativity in appraisal, to which we shall next turn. The creator of meanings in a sense also creates his audience. The inventor of **charity**, or any such appraisive, seeks an audience which is prepared to understand and to embrace its precept.

The task of moralists is then enlightenment, which is more inspiring than that of redemption. If the concept and the precept are indissolubly connected, the enlightener's task is simplified: once his concept is understood, his precept has been accepted.

12 APPRAISIVE CREATIVITY

Hume refers to the "invention" of terms such as we are studying. Since little or nothing is known about invention or creativity in any area that borders on the poetic or aesthetic, we can at most point only in the broadest way to this process. We have something of an opportunity to witness the origins of appraisives by observing the genesis of slang and metaphor, processes ceaselessly at work. But just what is involved in this and just how appraisives develop out of descripts, nonsense syllable, metaphors and other sources is known only in the sense that etymologies may have been traced. An account of the process at once theoretical and empirical is yet to be undertaken. We do not know what the differences are, if any, between a "standard" appraisive A vocabulary such as we have set forth here and the S, M, and P vocabularies. Nor do we know what role a determinant such as emotion plays in the process. The philosophical apriorizings of the emotive theory are altogether insufficient on this subject.

We can, however, see that times of greatest appraisive creativity are those in which there is the greatest mobility, contact, and friction between persons, classes, ethnic and age groups, and occupations. The world of popular entertainment, films, and periodicals is productive, though with little or no knowledge of the processes involved. Certain classes or ethnic groups have contributed more than their share of linguistic novelties.

The contribution of Jewish, Negro, and other cultures in America in this direction has been recognized at least as far back as H. L. Mencken's *The American Language*. We are here by-passing this area altogether, solely in order to concentrate on the core appraisives of classical English. This is the only way we can hope, for the present, to learn the grammar and logic of appraisives generally. This may then be extended to cover the M, P and other vocabularies.

We have already alluded to the fact that philosophers in the past, from Plato to Kant, had a far deeper interest in the question of appraisive terms and the ideas of the virtues and vices than has been manifest in the past century or more. One other name deserves particular mention, that of Locke.

An important contribution to the logic of appraisives is to be found in the second Chapter of Book II of his *Essay Concerning Human Understanding* in which he introduces the notion of *mixed modes*. This is quite clearly the area where appraisives belong, and it is not surprising that the examples Locke adduces are of this sort, for example, **adultery, ambition, glory, gratitude, hypocrisy, justice, murder, obligation,** and **sacrilege.** The point about a mixed mode is that it is entirely of our own making. We do not need to conform to what is existent in nature as we do with substances, where we are obliged to take empirical account of the properties which things have. We must not attribute feathers to a fish or scales to a bird. But we are free to invent names and mixed modes if we turn aside from the world of substances. If we see fit, we can characterize by some one word designation the act of depriving the sister of the brother of the cousin of your aunt of her life with little more ado than there is in speaking of the murder of your father as patricide. We must not suppose because mixed modes are not conformable to reality that in speaking of murder we are speaking of a fantastic kind of thing, like a feathered fish or a scaly bird. The point is it simply makes no sense to ask whether murder *exists* or not. If the term *is used* to characterize certain things, actions, states, or relations, it has a reference: it is meaningful If we ask whether some act *is* murder, we are asking whether the ascription of the term is justified, not whether it is true. I shall explain this at length below (in 5.0).

We are thus obliged to regard virtually any and every appraisive term as meaningful. Its coinage is possible because someone, anyone, has seen fit to characterize certain things by this term. It is thus scarcely to be wondered that the largest area of creativity of language lies here. On the other hand, the discovery of really new facts, new classifications of facts, new relations of things, new properties of substances and so forth can ensue nowadays almost nowhere except in rather limited or circumscribed areas under the expert guidance of the research scientist.

We come finally to the most significant and perhaps interesting of all the species of appraisive creativity, namely poetry. Poets do everything with words that anybody else does – describe, argue, commend, exhort, remonstrate, celebrate, dedicate, pray, invoke – it is an even longer list, and it must also somewhere include appraising and judging. Such appraising is done with the most subtle and elaborate means: a mere word, a pause, even a comma can have effects much more affecting than might be expected from such slight causes; or a comparison may be developed line after line (one thinks of Donne) to make one grand metaphor celebrating the poet's love or despair or regret. Of all the poet's arts I am interested now only in his ability to extend the meanings and functions of mostly familiar words simply by

juxtaposing them in new contexts and watching their extraordinary unpredictable results. All this can be and often is guided by the purpose of
expressing a response, an appraisal, a celebration, or a judgment of things and
people and places. The result is that what can in other hands be altogether
ordinary transactions are here completely transformed. He does not merely
say, "I loathe the Establishment, the purveyors of war and hatred, the rich,
or the stupid," or "I love the past, this very moment, my sorrow, or you," or
or "I curse (or he, she, or it curses) the brutal waste of life, time, and effort in
trivial doings," but he loathes, loves, curses, condemns, commends *so*, in the
very words of this poem and in no others (and scarcely even any others translatable into these). No doubt poets are all egotists. They are not content with
saying, "I love you." "You" no doubt occupy their thoughts, but they are *pre*-
occupied with themselves and their love. Do I love him or her so, or so, or
only so? "Let me count the ways." Of course, 'love,' the word, is not enough.
It is what every fool says. And if the poet should use the word somewhere, it
undergoes a transformation; it is no longer what the fool says, and even the
very word may not sound the same. The moral is that if one concentrates
thought upon exactly *how* one appraises something, ordinary appraisives
will seem flat and dead; and if one has any gift at all, some better way to say
exactly what this emotion or response or judgment here and now contains
may yet come to mind.

   The essential point about poetry, in the aspect of it that we are concerned
with here, is that it is the natural resort of those who cannot feel content
with language as it stands to express themselves. This means that the body of
appraisives we have collected here is but a mere skeleton. For each of our
appraisives of the modes of responding, appraising or judging there may
well be some hundreds of variants that one might collect from the poets of
all times and places. We see why there *must* be resort to the alternatives to the
P-vocabulary, to slang, metaphor, the vernacular – and poetry. It is ordinarily
foolish to stop to think of alternative expressions for "fire" if the house is
afire, or for "I need a shoe, size nine," or "the carbon atom has six electrons
in two shells." But there must be some word besides 'love' that expresses
my love, not yours, or his, or hers. This summons the poet out of every
person.

   We may think of the simple theme that forms the appraisive core of a
poem such as Keats' "On First Looking into Chapman's Homer." This is,
in some sense, a "book review." Or Tennyson's "To Virgil": "I salute thee
Mantovano, / I that loved thee since my day began, / Wielder of the stateliest
measure / ever molded by the lips of man." This is "praise?" Is there
no better word? Moral argument and deliberation are transformed as
they emerge from the hand of Sophocles – even in English. So Antigone

reflects on life and death, and on what is done and left undone in life:

> And before my time
> If I shall die, I reckon this a gain;
> For whoso lives, as I, in many woes,
> How can it be but he shall gain by death?
> And so for me to bear this doom of thine
> Has nothing fearful. But, if I had left
> My mother's son unburied on his death,
> In that I should have suffered; but in this
> I suffer not.*

Poetry is an integral part of the subject matter of any complete study of appraisive language. The difficulty is that it extends the subject matter so vastly that it is literally impossible to know where to begin, and we do not know where it will take us in the end. Appraisive language is an ever shifting sand under our feet, but it shows the creativity of language.

It seems to me, therefore, that the fixed and final form which J. L. Austin claimed to find in language is insupportable. In his "Plea for Excuses" he wrote:

Our common stock of words embodies all the distinctions men have found worth drawing, and the connections they have found worth making, in the life times of many generations: they surely are likely to be more numerous, more sound, since they have stood up to the long test of the survival of the fittest, and more subtle, at least in all ordinary and reasonably practical matters, than any that you or I are likely to think up in our armchairs of an afternoon – the most favored alternative method.**

Of course he might have made any number of qualifications to this to save the quantity of sane advice it no doubt contains. But he made no such qualifications and left it standing in full generality. And in full generality it is as unwarranted as such sweeping pronouncements must always be. What is "our stock?" The stock as it stood in the middle fifties? There is no reason, to take this era as any culmination. Nor is there reason for taking any other. It might have been said in 1056 as well as 1956. In that year, an Englishman could have written aesthetic criticism with a vocabulary including **askew, awkward, awry, bauble, deft, drab, garish, jangle, lissom, lithe, scraggy, stunted, couth** and **uncouth,** or words closely resembling these – certainly a forceful and expressive vocabulary. But he could not have used such elegant appraisives as **amorphous, chaotic, coherent, dainty, euphonious, exquisite, glamor, grand, magnificent, monotonous, refulgent,** and **sublime.** They were not, of course, dreamed up in an armchair but they were unavailable to the average Saxon and others more remote. When such speakers tried to get the

* *Antigone*, p. 145, translated by E. H. Plumptre.
** J. L. Austin, *Philosophical Papers*, "A Plea for Excuses," p. 130.

hang of them, or other such notions not in their "common stock," they might well have thought them violations of sound thought. In many languages foreign appraisive notions can be rendered only with difficulty or not at all. But it is absurd to adhere to linguistic commitments which make acceptance of them impossible.

Languages are not eternal Platonic forms. The changes in them often show the hand of people who are ignorant of grammar, etymology, logic, and rhetoric, devoid of "good taste," and given to barbarisms, vulgarisms and faulty constructions. But if the devices hammered out by illiterate speakers fulfill a need they remain in the language so long as useful. We live in an age that may even now be developing a tongue that by present standards can only be thought an incongruous mishmash. The last Roman patrician, whoever he was, might have feared the same result. If he had had *his* way, we would never have heard Dante, Tasso, or Leopardi.

The appraisive and other dimensions of a language depend upon the actual historical fortunes of the language and its speakers. But the process is reciprocal. The life of man is in part determined by the appraisives he uses.

PART ONE

PROCEDURES OF APPRAISAL
AND JUDGMENT

PART ONE

INTRODUCTION

The subject matter of Part One, as already explained, is a vocabulary in which we speak variously of acts, actions, procedures, processes, conditions, and states of persons responding to their world, involved in its concerns, and engaged in the evaluation of it. What we present is actually an essay on valuation. Enjoyment, emotive and appetitive response, appraisal, assumption of commitments, and moral judgment are distinct subjects of the exposition.

The vocabularies that are presented at the head of each section have a different significance from those in Part Two. The center of our interest is at all times the appraisive terms that are there set forth. Thus, even if we had no such terms as those in 3.0 (q.v.) we could nevertheless perform all of the acts mentioned there. We do not need **appraise, regard, accept, prefer, countenance, choose,** or **advocate** in order to be able to appraise, regard, accept, prefer, countenance, choose, or advocate. The terms are useful abstractions, but there is no real blood in these turnips; what is needed is to study the actual employment of the vocabulary by means of which we appraise, regard, accept, etc. The terms in 3.0 serve largely a descriptive purpose and may well be duplicated in other languages. As already noted, this may not be the case with appraisives themselves.

The situation is somewhat different in 1.0 and 2.0. Enjoyment and response, appetitive and emotive, are real aspects of our being, involved in but not identical with our commending, appraising, and judging. We need the vocabularies set forth in 1.0 and 2.0 in order to be able to talk about ourselves, our states and conditions. They appear here, therefore, in order that our account of valuation may be as complete as possible within the limits of our inquiry. We can of course have or exhibit responses without referring to them by means of the terms in 2.1, 2.2, and 2.3. They are not, however, abstractions like the concepts in 3.0. We often respond (in the manner of 2.1, 2.2, 2.3) by using just these terms in the first person. "I am fond...," "I'm appalled at..." report or describe my state but also show it; and the description helps to make what I am trying to show more clear and distinct.

According to J. L. Austin some of the terms appearing in 4.0 are necessary to perform designated acts.* Without entering into a discussion of this matter, it is sufficient to note that even if this were true, it would at most apply to first personal contexts and that in all other cases the terms serve a purely descriptive purpose. The most critical issue regarding 4.0 is the reality of implicit commitments, which by definition have not arisen from "performances" with these terms. For the rest, there are obviously many ways in which what persons do or say may *amount to* solemnizing, eulogizing, or welcoming (4.3), or authorizing, sanctioning, or rescinding (4.2), or swearing, committing, or subscribing (4.1) without even a suggestion of these terms.

In 5.0, the situation is varied. The terms under Moral Affects in 5.1 designate affects and are thus similar to those in 2.0. The Moral Involvements in 5.2 are in most cases not strictly necessary to the acts designated. We do not need **protest, denounce, reprimand, confess, absolve,** and so on, to protest, denounce, reprimand, confess, absolve, and so on, but the terms *are* usefully employed in such actions. Certain terms among the Outcomes are used formally in pronouncing decisions. The real necessity, however, is not for the performative use of just these terms but for the appropriate use of the Justificatory Appraisives (5.32), **right, wrong, just, unjust.** These parallel the ultimate, general appraisive terms, **good,** and the like in 16.0. The rather complex significance of these terms is explained at length in 5.0. We may postpone until later the discussion of matters such as the interrelation of appraisal and judgment.

To sum up, we may say that our purpose in Part One is to survey the whole of the process of evaluation but from what is sometimes a necessarily abstract standpoint. The real center of all the issues lies in Part Two, since it is to the concepts there considered that we must turn from the general and ultimate appraisives of Part Three and also, to a considerable extent, from the justificatory appraisives in 5.3.

---

* J. L. Austin, *How to do Things with Words*, Harvard, 1962. "In these examples [referring to sentences in which a ship is named, a marriage vow is taken, etc.] ... to utter the sentence (in, of course, the appropriate circumstances) is not to *describe* my doing of what I should be said in so uttering to be doing or to state that I am doing it: it is to do it," p. 6.

1.0 SATISFACTION

enjoy, enjoyment
gratify, gratification
satisfaction, be satisfied

The beginning and the end of our inquiry have a close connection with one another. In 1.0 we think of ourselves valuing something, possessing it or taking satisfaction in it. In 16.0 we think of something distinct from ourselves that deserves to be valued. The relation between these has stirred up a problem over whether things are valued because they are valuable, or are valuable because they are valued. We shall consider this question only to the extent that a study of the language of valuation, of commendation, characterization, and judging may enable us to throw some light on it. (Cf. 2.1.)

When we ask what it means *to value* a subject, part of the answer will be formulated in the vocabulary of 1.0 or some approximation to it: we take satisfaction in it. So far as reasons for our satisfaction can be found they must be sought in the particular way we characterize the subject. This refers us, when human subjects are concerned, to the resources of appraisal explored in 6.0 to 14.0, to which recourse can and must be had.

We can only be referred to the same source if we ask what it means for something to *be* valuable (16.0). This, like other notions in Part Three, must recur to the characterizations of Part Two. The differences between 1.0 and 16.0 are sometimes only verbal.

Enjoyment or satisfaction and its alternatives are the beginning and end of all valuation. The finality and ultimacy of enjoyment is readily seen in the phrase 'enjoy a woman'. But if it is to serve as the anchor to all our thought about value, we must not confine it to its sensuous modes, to mere stimulation and gratification of the feelings. It must comprise also our most momentous and solemn concerns where something has been possessed, lived through, *erlebt*, where it has solved a problem, answered a question. This will include the outcome of agonizing decisions as well as the fulfilment of inclinations, so that we can say not only of food or drink, but even of the outcome of a moral situation that has evoked our judgment, it satisfies. If it strains usage or credibility to say of Abraham in his moment of decision to slay Isaac that he enjoys the moment, or situation, or decision, we must yet be able to say that however heavy of heart he is he has yet a satisfaction in what he has decided, considering the burden that God has laid upon him. He knows his mere feelings must be defied, and from this standpoint he has no enjoyment, but he has certainly realized another kind of satisfaction.

These concepts serve to indicate the goal and culmination of all concern with values. They are not in themselves rich or colorful, but here as elsewhere one has resort to any number of other devices, including even poetry, to make more expressive the idea of the possession or the absence or loss of value. One of our expedients is, of course, the consultation of equivalents in other languages. **Satisfaction** may thus be compared with the usually suggested equivalents, **Befriedigung** and **Genugtuung**, in German. The first of these, of course, is close kin to **Friede**, peace. The second brings out the **enough** **(genug)** which is implicit in the Latin root *satis* of satisfaction, but which is now heard in English at most only by the learned ear. Although **Friede** is deeply expressive, it is somewhat passive and lacks the vigor of the English **joy**, in **enjoyment**, and this is likewise communicated to **Befriedigung**. The more one turns these so-called equivalents over in his mind the more apparent their differences become, both in the meanings they convey and the feelings they suggest or evoke. Certainly one would need more evidence than this to conclude that German and English satisfaction differ, but there can be no doubt of the difference in the interpretation of them that is evident in the concepts employed. And this we shall have numerous other occasions to observe hereafter.

2.0 RESPONSE

Effectively our study of the processes of appraisal or valuation begins here: enjoyment or satisfaction (1.0) is not a mode of evaluation but the goal and termination of it.

The order in which topics in 2.0 are taken up is as follows. We first try to gain some understanding of the processes of appetition which are in a plain sense animal, visceral, or motor and then proceed to emotional or direct responses involving the active participation of the feelings in reaction to an environment of persons and things. We conclude the section with a study of what we call Responsional Characterizations. These involve a vocabulary employed particularly to characterize the emotive responses of other persons. In contrast to the preceding, these are indirect or higher-order characterizations, as explained in 2.4.

We here presuppose intellectual powers, the truth- and fact-seeking capacities of human beings, and the whole apparatus of language or communication in order to direct our attention wholly toward the language and the processes of valuation. (The unique values of the domain of intellect are presented schematically in 6.0 and in Appendix A.)

One would like to avoid terms like 'process' in talking of responding, judging, or appraising; 'mental act' scarcely improves matters. In all things it would be best to avoid as many higher order abstractions as possible, yet it is impossible to do without them altogether. What is necessary is that we keep our investigation concrete, being specifically cognizant of actual appraisives and appraisals. These constitute the hard data, the explicanda of our subject. We shall, however, take the risk of developing abstract classifications, and sometimes of coining new terminology, since we shall never be far from the data to be explained.

2.1 APPETITIONS

(a) **appetite for**
crave
desire
hankering for
hanker
longing

predilection
want v.
yearn for
(b) **inclination**
proclivity
propensity

(c) **aversion**
revulsion

(A) *The Role of Appetition.* Before we consider appetitions in detail we may turn to the question of their unique importance in the development of theories about man as well as the theory of value.

It is difficult, even if not self-contradictory, to think of animal beings as devoid of appetitions. Animals of any complexity at all are capable of motion from one place to another, which we interpret as efforts to satisfy drives or wants or urges toward food or reproduction or escape from harm, and the like. Appetition and its satisfaction appear as links of kinship between animals simpler than ourselves and the basic animal stratum of our own being. It is therefore not surprising that philosophers have often been tempted to universalize the role of appetition in the interest of explaining the nature of man. This is but a variant or an application of a more general procedure of materialism, which, with its alternatives, was already in full development among the Greek philosophers. It appeared to them that either man is "really" that which *identifies* him with the rest of creation, or he is "really" that which *differentiates* him from it. The culminating form of pre-Socratic philosophy, atomism, propounded the first; the culmination represented by Aristotle, the second: man is animal, with the differentia of rationality. In flattest form, these are the alternatives, by some said to be decidable by more scientific knowledge, by others only by metaphysical investigation or fiat; by still others they are condemned as meaningless verbiage.

In the past century, the sciences of man have taken an interest in appetitions and revulsions because they have seemed likely to yield knowledge of laws of human behavior. For this purpose, man first has to be entirely "deracinated," torn from his context and from his history. Then by concentrating on what is left, laws about basic responses may be developed, "stimulus response arcs" out of which higher forms of "behavior" will appear to be constructed. Somewhere below the level of thought and judgment, man, it is thought, is attracted and repelled by certain definite patterns of stimuli, much as opposite magnetic poles attract and like repel. Attraction and repulsion appear here in the form of appetitions, inclinations, and propensities: but since these are too "subjective" they must first be, as it were, behaviorized.

Some of what these sciences say about man is, of course, plausible and confirmable. Doubtless there are certain basic regularities in the appetitions underlying man's conduct that are as fully expressive of laws as is his metabolism or his digestion. What is scarcely as plausible as this is the program of accepting only certain mechanical or physiological sequences as paradigms of explanation and the reduction of all higher order conduct to these. But it has proved hopeless for candid observers to declare the pure "reductive" program a failure, and it never ceases to renew itself: in "research" nothing succeeds like failure.

The relevance for us of behaviorism and similar scientific procedures is that their philosophical counterparts seem to bring with them a certain kind of philosophy of value that would, in effect, stop at the "level" of appetition and revulsion and declare that the rest of the processes of value, such as appraisal, judgment, and commitment, are but the same thing over, only in somewhat more complex form. This view tends to treat all alternatives as not merely mistaken hypotheses but as obscurantist ideologies. But in fact it has itself tended to become a creed rather than a theory. Since creeds make no assertions, they also permit no refutation: one can only swear to them or ignore them. Even if the choice is not one of creeds, the reductive method, as we may call it, fails when it seeks to carry out its program and having failed, asserts that what was to be reduced was after all nothing but delusion. But this is scarcely defensible. It is absurd to find fault with the analysanda when analysis fails; one should re-examine the methods he is employing. It is even more absurd to pretend that the subject matter does not exist or that it will simply vanish of itself if one simply does not talk about it.

(B) *The Ingredience of Appetitions.* We turn now to the consideration of appetition itself. It appears in something approaching a pure form in expressions beginning "I want," "I crave," and the like. We can consider appetitions also as ingredients in other acts or processes. Besides the distinction between *pure* and *ingredient*, we can make a further distinction between appetitions as *manifest* and *subliminal*. We shall consider appetitions first as ingredient and then as subliminal and manifest.

By the ingredience of appetitions I mean their occurring as accompaniments of more complex processes such as appraising or judging. It is evident that appraisive outcomes (3.13), such as disfavoring, prizing, or tolerating may be accompanied by feelings or appetitions, such as revulsion against, or desire, or certain more or less nameless "mixed feelings." But it is not all necessary that they accompany them: in general all of the appraisive outcomes are logically distinct from feelings or appetitions. In the cases under 3.13 we ask, does it follow from 'A is averse to, approves of, accepts, countenances, disapproves of, prefers x' that 'A feels appetition a or revulsion r'? And in each case, the correct answer is that it does not. Approvals and disapprovals are fully conceivable in the absence of feelings of appetition or revulsion. If we are correct in this it suffices to dispose of the necessity, though not the possibility, of the reductivist thesis. I do not, of course, deny that these or other feelings *may* be ingredients. We must not succumb to the temptation to identify being an ingredient or accompaniment with being a necessary consequence of or being identical with. We shall postpone consideration of the effect of the ingredients on one another until we take up more complex processes.

(C) *Subliminal and Manifest Appetitions.* What we may call subliminal appetitions appear to occupy the same region that Freud and the Freudians call the *id* and are in part identical with what they call the *libido.* The idea of subliminal "agents," both of perception and of appetition, goes back at least to Leibniz. There is no good reason to deny their existence. As subliminal they may be at work both in pure form and as ingredients in other appetitions. Although psychoanalysis represents a determined effort to provide something like a system of laws of human conduct, its method is exposed to distortion and error mainly because the role it assigns to the libido and other subliminal processes tends to prevent it from giving a true account of conscious life. Without denying the existence of subliminal functioning, it is necessary to reassert the autonomy of conscious life, particularly as it manifests itself in the processes of appraisal and judgment.

Simple manifest appetitions are most likely to appear in expressions beginning "I want," "I loathe," and the like. Scarcely anything we say of ourselves is capable of being said with more conviction and confidence. And no conviction seems more firmly based than that of the man who says he wants something and, moreover, adds, "I know what I want." We seem to be our own ultimate authorities on all such questions. Like assertions about sense data, assertions about one's own appetitions can easily be presented as "incorrigible."

Yet it seems we can sometimes be mistaken. It does not follow from the fact that A has said, "I know what I want," or "I know that I want x" that A wants x. We are certainly ready sometimes to stand corrected about what we want or wanted. Perhaps the reason is that the verbs in 2.1(a) are not for reports of happenings or *events* like seeing a red flash, which we are generally sure about, but *states.* To discriminate the state of anything takes some time and is subject to correction. The time implications of these verbs are rather different from those of verbs used in connection with sense reports.

The consequence of this is that if there is no absolute certainty (whatever this may mean) in the domain of appetitions, it is to be found nowhere in the area of valuation, except of course enjoyment. (It is even less likely in the remaining areas of 2.0, the responses.) This is not because complex appraisals (A is pigheaded, B is obnoxious) are more problematic but because only appetitions and enjoyments are in any sense the subject of *reports,* capable of truth or falsity, in this area. Commitments, enactments, judgments and appraisals are still less to be regarded as reports and cannot be declared in any sense certain, or even true or false. We shall see later on what character comparable to *certain* or *true* should be predicated of them.

All of the foregoing terms for appetitions can be employed, in suitable form, in the first person. But if we ask which we are most likely to use about

ourselves, I think we shall not hesitate to name the strong Saxon terms:
loathe, crave, want, hanker after. Aside from **desire** ("I desire" is a little stiff),
and **longing** (slightly poetic or epistolary), the other terms in (a) and (b) are
most likely to be used when one regards himself with a certain degree of
objectivity and detachment as a kind of subject of investigation. The objective stance is inevitable if one is talking in the first person in a past tense, for
this bears a resemblance to using the third person. We are not likely to
speak of our propensities, inclinations, revulsions, and appetitions in the
first person except, if at all, to offer the result of a process of reflection on
ourselves ("I have a propensity to ..."). These are technicalities of psychology
and do not suit well to candid reporting of what one feels.

We must not, however, exaggerate the importance of these distinctions.
All language, whether in one person or another, represents a certain degree
of reflection. Only spontaneous shrieks of fright, screams of delight, and
similar *res gestae* are altogether exempt from this. But since they are not
really a part of language we must not confuse them with terms for appetition.

(D) *The Value of Appetition.* Appetition is basic to all valuing since it is
apparent we would never take the trouble to make appraisive discriminations
or judgments if we were appetitively indifferent. But appetitions and appraisals are logically distinct from one another for we subject appetitions to
appraisal (AR), both our own and those of other persons. We can also
respond to them (R^2); thus we may loathe our own addictions although
there seems to be no unique vocabulary for this. (These symbols are explained below in 2.4.)

We can also ask generally about the value of appetitions. This leads us
directly to the question, as old as Plato's *Euthyphro*, whether anything is
good because desired, or desired because good (**Good** is the subject of considerable study later on, and what is said here applies only to desire and
other appetitions, not to appraisals.) On that question, I think we must say
that there is always a presumption in favor of the goodness of responses such
as these. In their elemental form, they are simply natural "forces" like light,
water, or wind, and share the essential goodness of these. Hence we answer
the classical question by saying that that which is desired is good because in
fact it is desired: desire is itself a good. But in any human situation there is
always vastly more to consider than mere animal drive and desire. *If* we
could reduce moral or human problems to this or if they involved only this,
their solution would be easy. But despite the propaganda of modern moralists, we can neither construe human situations in terms of such a reduction,
nor may we expect human life to reduce itself to mere animal functioning.
Desire, as an elemental force, is engaged by civilized men to human ends,
exactly as other forces of nature are engaged, and it is subject to judgment as

part of the total economy of life. It is also subject (in another sense) to two pathologies: morbid distrust and blind reliance. Appraisal and judgment are precisely the skills of escaping these alternatives.

(E) *The Object of Appetition.* We must now ask just what is the object of our appetitions. Should we say that it is pleasure? It may be asserted that pleasure and nothing else is the object in both 1.0 and 2.0. It is difficult not to make the separation of the object of satisfaction from pleasure seem altogether artificial. Perhaps, however, a clearer understanding of pleasure itself may help clarify matters. We must be aware that pleasure is a difficult topic to do justice to either from the side of psychology or of the theory of value. Although we must be brief on this subject, the following points are necessary to advance our inquiry.

There is curiously no proper place for pleasure in the system of value. It cannot be placed in 1.0 although that is where everyone who thinks of himself as following Epicurus, or at least Bentham, must place it. We can say with certainty that the object of our appraisive as well as appetitive and responsive efforts is satisfaction, but there is no such certainty attaching to the assertion that their proper object is pleasure. Benthamites have acted as if they could make it so simply by saying it with sufficient emphasis. Yet pleasure can be the object of our total appraisive effort only if 'pleasure' is made synonymous with 'satisfaction'. In this event, hedonism offers us only a verbal novelty, for then 'pleasure' must be made to serve many more uses than naming the body-centred datum that it is when we speak of the pleasures of food or sex. When we do confine it to these it is simply one given feeling among others, and then it *may or may not satisfy.*

Pleasure is a curious hybrid among experiences. It is a datum that is both like a sense datum, and not. It is like a sense datum because it involves the body and the senses, permeating these in whole or part. But it is unlike a sense datum because it can never be brought distinctly under scrutiny or isolated for inspection, like a whiff or a pain or an after-image. It is fairly certain that there are no sense organs for pleasure as there are for pain. The result is that pleasure is either integrated, or "localized" to use the technical term of psychologists, with particular sense data, as for example, tastes of food or sexual sensations, or it is diffused vaguely but more or less palpably over the whole body or person.*

If now someone seeks pleasure, as we say, he can only seek it by pursuing the sense data it is localized with. It cannot be found in independence of them since it is at best a kind of epiphenomenon of our sense data. Not only that,

---

* For various experimental findings about pleasure and other feelings, one may consult Woodworth, *Experimental Psychology*, Holt, New York, 1946, pp. 234–241.

but desires and involvements are always directed toward things far more complex than mere sensations and this is true even of the most ardent devotee of *la dolce vita*, and particularly true of him. We cannot possibly pursue pleasure in and by itself – it simply does not exist in that form. If it is particular sense data that are desired, then these are legion and in any event only part of the complex field of competitors for our approbation.

If we now seek to "liberate" the notion of pleasure from this sense-localized connotation for the purpose of seeing it as something common to all satisfactions, the cause of hedonism in the received sense is lost: there is no common *experience* that links love of truth, mystic revelation, fame, fine wine, victory over one's enemies, and erotic consummation. Whatever it is that these do have in common, it is certain it is not pleasure.

This then shows why we cannot simply assimilate pleasure to satisfaction in 1.0. How then should we think of pleasure? I believe we will not distort its nature if we regard it as the result of processes functioning in a manner that we may risk calling "normal." That is, good food, in the sense that it tastes good, is food that stimulates the body in a manner to make the process of eating run through a cycle proper to it from appetite to satiety, never overstepping limits of over- or under-stimulation at any point. Such a cycle is describable in terms of physiology. 'Pleasure' will thus simply be the term properly used to say that the cycle has in fact run, or is running, its course, yielding the unique sensations of water or food, or whatever, to a person *with an appetite for them*. Pleasure itself is nothing over and above all this. There is more than a grain of truth in the old saw that hunger is the best sauce. Pleasure is the particular form that satisfaction takes if and when we can consider a particular sensuous want by itself, from its origin to its end.

We return then to our original question about the object of appetition. Can it be pleasure? For reasons given we cannot say that it literally is for when we concentrate attention upon it, its distinct entity proves to be illusory. Yet there is no reason why we should not continue to say that such and such gives us pleasure. What is needed is not a reformation of our manner of speaking but a better understanding of it.

We may either seek to identify pleasure with satisfaction in general, in which case we only propose an alteration of our language that ignores the strangeness and paradox of declaring all satisfactions to be pleasures, and not only Abraham's satisfaction in his decision to slay Isaac, but also love of truth and satisfaction in seeing justice done; *or* to identify it with a particular datum of sensuous gratification, which, however, proves to be either illusory or indistinguishable from sense-experiences themselves. The result is that as a sense-experience pleasure is *literally nothing*, and it behooves us to cast about in other directions to find out what it is. This is not the first occasion when we have been erroneously induced by the presence of a noun to look for palpable substance, property, or relation.

The purpose of the term 'pleasure' is something else. It has no place as a synonym of a term of such generality as 'satisfaction': it is a term that needs to be confined to sense-experience. Here its function is to say that a train or cycle of limited shape and duration, such as gustatory or erotic experience, taken by itself, having been initiated, has run its course in accordance with the body's inherent physical possibilities. But the senses and their satis-factions occupy only a part of the person's whole functioning. This is said in defiance of the Freudian notion of the unlimited extent of subliminal libidinal causality, and in defence of the autonomy not only of other functions (in-tellectual, aesthetic, and many more) but indeed of this one as well. The whole of them is still subject to appraisal – it is absurd to suppose that our appetitions can or do perform this task for us, and it is false that 'pleasure' and 'revulsion' mark the outcome of appraisal.

The object of appetition is whatever it is we have appetites for. The nearer this approaches to a purely sense-experience the more nearly its success can be measured in terms of pleasure. But as we have seen appetitions are more often complex than simple. In the *appraisive* process pleasure is eventually simply an irrelevance. It would be difficult to find a more egregious irrele-vance to appraisal and judgment than Bentham's formula about maximizing pleasure.

2.2   DIRECT RESPONSES

2.21   SYMPATHIC RESPONSES

admire	have [regard for
adore	rejoice at
have [affection for	be, or feel sympathetic to (11.3)
appreciate (3.11)	
delight, delight in, at	
be [fond of	
glad that, to	
like v.	
love	
be [pleased at	

2.22   DYSPATHIC RESPONSES

abhor	be [aghast at
abominate	be [angry at
be [against	be [annoyed at

be [appalled at	dismay, be [dismayed at
care nothing for	be [displeased at
chagrin	have [distaste for
deplore	hate, hatred
despise	be [irritated
detest	be [loath to
be [discontented with	misprize, misprision
disgust	be [vexed at
dislike	

(A) *Appetitions and Responses.* Perhaps one of the most evident differences between appetitions and direct responses is that we would not call any of the appetitions emotions while this designation seems to fit the direct responses, particularly the dyspathic. Appetitions originate within us from causes ultimately instinctive and unconscious that are not easy to identify and understand. They are active and outward in direction and are most intense when unfulfilled. The interest they manifest is self-directed; the value of the subject is the degree to which it satisfies interest; aside from this it has no intrinsic attraction. The subject is in a sense an object of consumption.

Emotive or direct responses are very different from appetitions, though built upon them. An interest is taken in the subject itself. It is not just a means of satisfaction, but *concern* is shown *for* it. It is recognized as having a life of its own not as an object to be consumed. It is apparent that persons are the prime subjects of such responses. A familiar distortion of personal relationships occurs when persons are treated as objects solely of appetition and revulsion, that is, as having a relation only to someone's desires. This is evidently a worse distortion than indifference.

There is a comparable degree of concern underlying the dyspathic responses. To abominate or detest, to be angry, annoyed, or irritated at a subject is not just to find him or it to have thwarted our appetitions, but to have disappointed our sense of what the subject ought to be. The subject disappoints a concern we have for it.

What we have in mind then in 2.2 is the feelings or emotions. The sympathic responses are often comparatively mild. Of course love (which particularly involves concern for the subject of the emotion) and many of the other emotions are scarcely anything so simple as what is suggested by the mere titles. It is apparent that the negative or dyspathic responses of whatever intensity are all emotions. In 2.4 we shall find some further terms from the emotion vocabulary. These are, however, characterizations. The present vocabulary is one that may be used for the purpose of reporting and describing, particularly one's own feelings or emotive responses. (The reason for calling emotive responses "direct" will be made clear when we contrast them with the responsional characterizations in 2.4.) They also help to *show* our emotions although this calls for more than uttering such words.

We may now consider some of these responses more closely. One of the more difficult of the basic notions among the sympathic responses is **being pleased at.** At least two other places may be suggested for the notion of pleasure: Enjoyment in 1.0 and Appetition in 2.1. But first, **pleasure** can scarcely serve in the terminating position of 1.0 alongside the other terms. We can ask whether pleasure satisfies, but it makes little sense to ask whether satisfaction pleases. Second, on the other hand, **pleasure** may be seen to be an ingredient in appetitions such as **appetite, desire, hanker,** and so on, as their literal object or aim.

Being pleased at in the present number is obviously a milder term than **pleasure.** When placed with other sympathic responses we see that it is not self-directed like the appetitions but other-directed. We are finding a satis-faction in the fact that *the subject* is what it is, has manifested a certain prop-erty, and in fact we can say that it pleases us just because it satisfies certain expectations we have had. We can thus have feelings of sympathy for the subject, particularly when it is a person. We wish to see the subject maintain an identity, not to see it consumed.

In the same way the dyspathic responses are imaginable only under the condition that I and the subject perceive ourselves as relevant to one another. I have expectations that are frustrated and hopes that are not realized. But the center of emphasis is the subject who disappoints though it is myself who is disappointed.

The modes of 2.21 are all in principle realizable apart from both emotional and behavioral manifestations in the sense that all of the terms may properly be used by a person speaking of himself even when he neither feels any "emotion" himself nor manifests those outward symptoms that often accom-pany such feelings.

The series appetition, emotive response, appraisal may be regarded as one of progressive development. Thus emotive responses, as described, develop as the awareness of individuality both of the self and of others emerges. The person can conceivably remain indefinitely at this level. The decisive step beyond it is taken when subjects are appraised through characterization and thus reasons are produced to support what have up to this point been merely emotive responses. This in turn has the effect that the subject has to survey and characterize himself, and it opens the way to notions of involvement and responsibility. If conduct is left at the level of emotive response, there is never any hope of a solution to moral conflicts: indeed the conflicts are not even moral.

(B) *The Vocabulary of Emotion.* We turn briefly to a question that has already been raised in the Introduction. Since the core vocabulary of emotion words does not seem very extensive, the question must arise whether it draws precise lines and whether it is at all exhaustive. These questions are of particular relevance here since we are dealing with what are virtually "natural phenomena," the emotions, which all persons and peoples may be expected to feel. Here the question of interlingual congruence is relevant, though it is much more acute with the characterizations of Part Two. We shall take the matter up now for the emotion vocabulary, but much of what we say will be relevant throughout the sequel.

One important point is to be noted. The terms in the present section are essentially *descriptive* in intent: we are not *appraising* feelings. (Such appraisal is encountered in 2.4.) When we talk about the meaning of appraisives, the distinction between sense and reference applies if at all only in a qualified manner since there are strictly no referents for appraisive terms as there are or may be for descriptions.* But emotions are essentially natural phenomena and terms for emotions are descriptive. The designation of emotions is a factual, not an appraisive question.

We may first point out that the issue about alternative descriptions or characterizations is one that is real quite apart from the alternatives offered by other languages. We frequently make extraordinary efforts to find alternative expressions for emotions in our own language. And as before we may have resort to the usual alternatives to the core vocabulary in poetry, poetic and picturesque turns of speech, "objective correlatives", figurative language and figures of speech, metaphor, slang, and yet others, because in fact the standard vocabulary is at most only a core of resources. The poet is discontented with the emotion vocabulary not so much because the terms are imprecise externally, that is, in relation to each other, but because they are internally vague as to content. They fire too crude a projectile. As to exhaustiveness, this is the area where we must consult foreign tongues. There is no reason to believe that any language exhausts the possibilities of our emotions, certainly not English.

Let us pursue these questions further in particular reference to the response terms we have under consideration. In a typical selection from this vocabulary, the following seem to be obviously close in German and English: **anger – Zorn; annoyance – Ärgernis; despisal – Verachtung; disgust – Ekel; hatred – Hass; vexation – Verdruss; love – Liebe; pleasure – Vergnügen.** But we need only ask ourselves whether they are as similar as *stone* and *Stein*, *dog* and *Hund*, *street* and *Strasse*. They are scarcely that. If you are a German

---

* *Translations from the Writings of Gottlob Frege*, edited by Peter Geach and Max Black. 1952 ("Über Sinn und Bedeutung") pp. 56–78.

traveling in England *hatred* will be the best expedient for you if you are going to speak of **Hass,*** but in this and in other such cases, do not be surprised if your audience then fails to behave exactly like a German audience. The most we can say is that while **hatred** certainly fires in the same direction as **Hass**, it may evoke different results: but of course evoking results is what such words are for. And if our traveler is a Japanese in Cairo or Panama, there may be even greater differences in result. This is what we have meant by saying that an exhaustive vocabulary of the emotions can be approached (but only that) by a *union* of all the emotion terms of all languages.

We may think also of another selection of terms from 2.21 and 2.22, for example: **admire – bewundern; adore – anbeten; delight – ergötzen; have regard – ansehen, achten; abhor – verabscheuen; abominate – verabscheuen; appalled – erschrecken; deplore – bejammern.** These are standard equivalents that may be found in any reputable English–German dictionary. We should now turn them over in our minds, savor them, and ask ourselves if one term really can do what the other term does. Beginning with **admire**, we note that the **wonder** of **bewundern** appears also in the root of **admire**, but unlike the German, the Latin root in English does not emerge into any but the pundit's thinking of this word: whatever "imagery" one has in **admire**, it certainly is not influenced by **wonder**. Then there is "praying" in **anbeten** but no hint of it in **adore**, except etymologically. There is the suggestion of a heathen idol (*Götze*) in the spelling though not in the etymology of **ergötzen**, but no trace of it in **delight**. **Achten** marks one's esteem just a notch or two higher than **regard** or even **respect**. There is more than a trace of influence of **scheuen** and **scheu** (**be embarrassed** or **shy**) in **verabscheuen**; the English is far stronger. And so on. Yet all of these are in some sense usable replacements for one another in translation. The point is that terms for feelings are not the same even in two languages no farther apart than German and English.

Translations are inherently makeshifts. Yet the writers of bilingual dictionaries appear to convince not only the average language student but a part of the learned world as well that languages except in certain minor details are all alike, that there are "equivalents" and "translations" of every language into every language. Looking up such equivalents is much like going to a merchant and being told that a requested item is not in stock but that here are several others, "just as good." While this may be true for the names of many substances, qualities, and relations, it is emphatically not

---

* R. B. Perry at the beginning of his *General Theory of Value* (p. 2) quotes Ernst Lissauer's "Song of Hate," a propaganda poem of hate of England of the First World War. One gains an insight into the contrast of affective terms from two languages by comparing the translation with the original, "Hassgesang," which is more fierce in feeling than the usual equivalents of translation can render. (It is said that Lissauer died between the wars – in England!)

true of most of the vocabulary of the emotions, feelings, and responses, still less of characterizations and of appraisals and judgments.

2.3 SITUATIONAL AFFECTS

2.31 AFFECTS OF CAUSAL INVOLVEMENT

BENIGN	MALIGNANT
agog at	(a) feel [anxiety over, for
confident	be [anxious to, about
hope	be [apprehensive that, lest, at
reliance, rely	scare
trust v.	worry (v. intrans.)
	tremulous
	trepidation
	(b) dread
	fear
	be [afraid of, that
	fright, be [frightened at
	foreboding
	premonition
	presentiment
	redoubt
	(c) horror
	consternation
	panic
	terror

2.32 COGNITIVE AFFECTS

astonishment	disappointment
astound	
awe	
surprise	
wonder	

The preceding section comprised concepts of responses which are directed largely toward persons as accusatives. One can, of course, also *admire* the view from the North Rim of the Cañon, *adore* small animals or dolls, *abhor* or *abominate* English food or the English climate, and so forth. But it is scarcely rational to vent much emotion or emotive discourse on targets that are either inherently incorrigible, or incapable of appropriate reciprocal responses.

The concepts of the present section, in contrast, are oriented in the first instance toward the inanimate. Although one can certainly have these responses toward persons – one can feel anxiety over them, or what they will do, and likewise, fear, dread, panic, and hope – the terms owe their principal power to the fact that there is a *course* of events that is impersonal and goes its own way, most often regardless of our desires. Such affects have probably made their way into the human mind, in its long process of development, from the fears and expectations felt by earlier men toward natural forces and processes.

Psychiatrists have remarked on the complementarity of guilt and anxiety, one for the past, the other for the future. But, of course, although these may be equally poignant, they are, even in the sheer feel of them, utterly different. Guilt, being a moral affect (5.1), has a moral dimension absent from anxiety; it is personal and is felt for what one has done or has been involved in. Anxiety is felt toward what may be done to us, what may involve us. Guilt is intensely personal and generally with a vivid recollection of what has prompted it. Anxiety is broad ranging and may more easily be felt toward "one knows not what." The appraisive element that is so strongly present in guilt leads us to ask whether it is absent from the situational affects. Let us see what necessarily enters into them.

There are two principal sources of the power of these affects over us: the *causation* of events and the *imaginative anticipation* of the future. Causation appears in the situation in the form of whatever the person knows or does not know about the outcome of the situation. But what anyone, even if he is in some sense learned, knows of the shape and unfolding of human events is far more often a matter of rule of thumb and guesswork than of any expert knowledge. The inherence of ignorance in the situation gives emotions about the future a character quite their own. The person, therefore, may feel himself caught in the grip of "iron necessity" or the "web of circumstance," or turning to different clichés, feel subject to the "bludgeonings of chance" and the "caprice of events." The resort to imagination in the "construction" of the future stems obviously from man's ignorance, his inability to predict or to forearm himself against "outrageous fortune," and the like. If there is in even a well regulated man-made environment a real element of chance, this will insure the persistence of anxiety. Curiously, the same phenomenon will preserve hope, as witness the attractions of gambling. Imagination may be thus both man's comfort and his curse.

In addition to causation (or at least the presumption of it), and imagination, we must also take the *evaluation*, appraisal or at least direct response to the awaited event, as part or as cause of these effects. We may take the notion of evaluation or appraisal for granted here, since we are begging no questions by this somewhat anticipatory use of it. We may consider briefly its place in the genesis of these affects.

We define this class of concepts as affects deriving from evaluations of prospective consequences which are thought likely to involve the appraiser as participant, interested spectator, beneficiary, or victim. Three groups may be distinguished. First, anxiousness, anxiety, apprehension, worry are felt toward negatively appraised consequences as yet not known to be certain of realization. Second, dread and fear, together with the pseudo-cognitive notions, foreboding and presentiment, are felt toward fairly certain consequences appraised as untoward. Third, horror, consternation, panic, and terror are felt toward the immediate or inescapable certainty of the maximum of such consequences. One could arrange the affects in this ascending order: apprehension, worry, anxiety, fear, dread, horror, consternation, panic, terror.*

The vocabulary of these affects is potent but not rich. When we look to the side of the positive appraisals, little more than hope appears. It would seem to stand approximately opposite the first of the preceding groups. With hope, uncertain consequences are appraised as benign. Or we could define it as the awaiting of a benign consequence not yet known to be probable. Reliance, confidence, trust and indeed hope itself appear to be only weak affects but have an evident strength not readily shown at the surface.

The corresponding German vocabulary may be less ample, but contains some concepts of possibly higher potency than English. **Angst** is evidently stronger than the closely related **anxiousness** and **anxiety** (from the expressive clash of four successive consonants?). It has readily been taken over by the psychiatrists. Of the remainder **Bestürzung** and **Entsetzen** (both lying toward the upper end of the fear series set forth above) have a unique power deriving from the vivid roots, *-stürz-* and *-setz-*, to crash and to put or place. Thus, **Entsetzen** is close to unseating (cf. the colloquial "rocked off my perch"). There are other divagations too numerous or subtle to pursue here.

The cognitive affects (2.32) represent satisfactions or frustrations that fill the present. But the terms also have other uses. A thief has no satisfaction in being surprised in the act, and horrors of war may be awesome or fill us with awe. The positive (or benign) affects characteristically give unexpected or gratuitous satisfaction that entirely fills the present. They lie close to the aesthetic. Disappointment on the other hand derives its character from a previous hope, a systole not followed by the satisfaction of a diastole, a

---

* We may remark in passing that at least four of the terms, *consternation, panic, terror,* and *tremulous,* would generally not be used in speaking of oneself in the first person present but might well be applied to others. As will be explained as we proceed, the terms may, therefore, often have more of a characterizing than a descriptive use.

dominant not resolved in a tonic. German **Enttäuschung** hints even at a kind of deception or "surreption" (learnedly *subreption*), since in the outcome represented by a disappointment, the expected is replaced by something untoward (*tauschen* is to exchange). Both terms are powerful, the German somewhat more vivid. This may be expected in all languages preserving living roots, unlike the deceased Latin roots in English.

The emotive responses of 2.2 and 2.3 are oriented in time. Those in 2.2 are directed toward what is present or effective in the present. The responses of 2.31 are pointed toward the future. They have, therefore, a kind of rising inflexion. **Disappointment** in 2.32 implies a history of expectation frustrated in some present. But when the satisfactions of the present exceed the expectations in the past or appear as gratuities, the result is surprise, astonishment, and the like.

Are there comparable responses to the past? As already mentioned, guilt is obviously oriented toward the past, but being heavily moral in tone it is far more than a mere emotive response. There is, however, one bittersweet emotion, largely free of moral overtones, **nostalgia,** that looks at the past with some degree of aesthetic disinterestedness, though this is not quite the right term (if there is any), since one cannot but be disinterested toward the past.

We have, then, a range of concepts for responses attached to the whole gamut from past through future. What remains to be said of them is that these are emphatically responses, not appraisals or judgments. We must now refer back to what was said at the beginning of this section regarding the ingredients in these responses: causation, imagination and evaluation. We must consider the third of these somewhat further.

The expected, or intended, subjects that the imagination encounters in these responses must themselves be in some way appraised in order for fear or hope, surprise or disappointment, to be meaningful. Only if they are thought malignant or benign will we think them deserving of fear or hope. Such an apprehension of the idea of good or evil of the projected object or event can be a fully developed appraisal or nothing more than a sympathic or dyspathic response (2.2) which, of course, being "direct," can be experienced without any extended process of thought. But in either form, the thought of the projected event is a material necessary condition for feeling (in a psychological sense of 'rational') *rational fear* or *rational hope*. Otherwise, a psychopathological state prevails in which one fears something but does not know *why*, or an even more serious one in which one does not know *what* or *why*. The *why* need not be a reasoned appraisal or judgment of the outcome, but there must be some response to the outcome or its properties. Similarly, hope must have an object and an appraisal or response to it or its properties, in order to be rational.

The conditions for the present set of responses can and must be distinguished from the responses themselves. Accordingly even reasoned appraisals which help condition hope or fear are not part of hope or fear themselves. The three components or conditions of the response R (fear or hope for example) toward subject M are these:

(1) Projection of M and its lively presence in imagination.
(2) Response S to (or appraisal of) M.
(3) Inference of a certain degree of causal probability but not certainty of M.

Imagining (1) alone to be totally absent is a little difficult, but sometimes we do causally infer things without forming much of an image of them.

If (2) alone is absent, we would simply have a situation such as prevails when a biochemist has an expectation of the occurrence of M, but sees it as appraisively indifferent and neither hopes for nor fears its occurrence. There are degrees of this in ordinary situations. We should also allow for the possibility of a groundless or ludicrous appraisal of M.

Lastly, if (3) alone is absent we have just a case of daydreaming. It is certainly not a typical case of fear or hope.

We can easily imagine (1), (2), or (3) each obtaining independently without suggesting or implying the occurrence of R. This exhausts the possibilities.

It seems obvious that it is always irrational, though also very tempting, to base one's negative appraisal of M on one's fears of it or a positive appraisal on one's hope. The latter is akin to the situation popularly known as "wishful thinking."

These are the principal modes of our responses under 2.3. The states of mind under 8.12 below, which I have designated, *La Condition Humaine*, may well be thought of in conjunction with the affects of the present section.

2.4   RESPONSIONAL CHARACTERIZATIONS (See 8.3, 8.112)

POSITIVE (Cf. 11.3)

be well [disposed toward	**idolize**
be [enthralled by	**take to**
enthusiasm	**show [tenderness toward**
exult in	

NEGATIVE

be [agitated at, or over	**show [apathy toward**
show [animosity toward	**look [askance at**
show [antipathy toward	**feel [bitterness toward**

bridle at	**grumble at**
bristle at	**be [ill disposed toward**
chafe at	**be [incensed at**
contemn, be	**be [irate at**
[contemptuous of	**be [miffed at**
disdain, be	**be [nettled at**
[disdainful of	**be [piqued at** (using F. **se piquer** as basic)
in high [dudgeon	**scorn**
rage, be [enraged at	**spurn**
fume at	**be in a [temper, fly into a [temper at**
fury, be [furious at	**take [umbrage at**
bear a [grudge against	**vent [wrath upon**

OPERATIVES (Cf. Appendix G.)

access of (e.g., rage)	**paroxysm of** ( )
attack of ( )	**spasm of** ( )
fit of ( )	**throes of** ( )
outburst of ( )	**transports of** ( )

Being characterizations, the terms of the present vocabulary are strictly speaking out of place. They belong in Part Two among the diathetic characterisms. Accordingly, number 8.3 is designated as the logically proper place for them. The reason for their exposition here rather than at 8.3 is first, in order to round out the whole problem of response and not postpone the characterization of it too far beyond the analysis of emotive response in 2.1, 2.2, and 2.3, second, because there may be some question exactly where to draw the line between the response vocabulary itself and the appraisal or characterization of it (does *disdain* name a response or characterize a response?), and finally, because it may thus be possible to show in a preliminary way the nature of characterization, to which all of Part Two is devoted. (There is an ample exposition of characterization at the beginning of Part Two which is relevant to the present section. Also, Appendix H directly bears on it.)

The characterization or appraisal of a response is an example of a higher order appraisive, where the scope of appraisives and responses is compounded. If we signify responses by R and appraisals by A the following are possible:

$$R \times A, \text{ or } RA: \text{a response to an appraisal,}$$
$$A \times R, \text{ or } AR: \text{an appraisal of a response,}$$
$$R \times R, \text{ or } R^2: \text{a response to a response,}$$
$$A \times A, \text{ or } A^2: \text{an appraisal of an appraisal.}$$

Our language may not, however, provide ready means for expressing all of these possibilities.

The present class of terms seems to be a class of appraisals, not of responses. If so, the terms are either AR or A². But what is being appraised is pretty plainly responses. They are therefore to be regarded as AR. (Consideration of other possibilities appears in Appendix H.)

Sometimes the terms of the present vocabulary would be said to be "emotive." But regardless of what the speaker may be feeling, his language certainly shows a certain effort at objectivity and is at a certain remove from direct response. He is at the same time of course a participant. If K says L bridled at, was incensed at, bore a grudge against someone or something, K is not himself thereby *responding* emotionally to or at L, although he may in fact be experiencing some kind of emotion. He is characterizing or appraising a response (AR), not responding to a response (R²).

Or, if I characterize your attitude toward M as one of disdain, or characterize your spirited behavior and your angry departure with the remark, "He left in high dudgeon," I am indicating my appraisal of your response to the situation. What I have said is certainly not a neutral description of what has transpired. I could have availed myself of the "colorless" language of description, like a camera. "He was red-faced, raised his voice, uttered an oath or two." The point is, to be a witness to such a situation almost invariably is to be a part of it, and to be a part of it is to be not content with a mere description but ready with an appraisal of it or with a response to it. Unlike the situation where we have just an appraisal of a thing or person (couched in such language as "He is a braggart," or the Viennese jest, "The situation is hopeless, but not serious" which are first order responses to persons or to situations) an AR is an appraisal of a response.

The negative modes of 2.4 are thus neither descriptions nor expressions of response. What we have called *operatives* seem to have the same character: **attack, fit, outburst, paroxysm, spasm,** and **throes** are not just concepts available to the absolutely impartial or photographic spectator or the beholder of a scene. They one and all indicate someone who is part of the scene, a participant, a partaker, a *Teilnehmer*, even if only in a mild sense: one does not have to try to restrain someone caught in an outburst to be a participant; and also, to do nothing in such a situation is to do something.

The mythical photographic observer need not, of course, be distinct numerically from the participant. We must, if a court so rules, remove ourselves from the AR stance and become detached observers: it is presumed that we *can* do this. In that event, only descriptive language is appropriate.

Are the positive characterizations, including the positive operatives, such as **transports of joy**, likewise AR? One does not naturally use these terms to

characterize oneself, at least in the continuous or progressive present tense:
I am exulting in, showing sympathy for, feeling tenderness toward, being
well disposed toward, idolizing A. Since appraisal and characterization call
for a certain participation in an event and also a certain elevation above it,
it is obviously difficult to be a perpetrant or participant and also the recipient
of criticism of this sort, even if favorable, particularly from oneself. In the
past tense, the situation is changed, for here the difficulty of being critic and
perpetrant at the same time is effectively removed. There is also less difficulty in suppressing our *amour propre*. We can characterize our "past selves"
as bridling at, enraged at, bearing grudges, being miffed at, and the like, and,
of course, we can look back and say we exulted in, felt tenderness toward,
idolized, and the like. If it is a kind of modesty that prevents the expression of
these positives in the present, it is, of course, a unique kind of modesty, a
kind that even obnoxiously forward persons can have.

The rejected negative formulations in the present may be called *self-
stultifying characterizations*: to be able to characterize one's behavior in this
present moment as bridling at, enraged at, being miffed is in a unique sense
incompatible with the behavior so characterized. What this sense is will
engage our extended attention in Part Two where we are principally concerned with such characterizations.

The corresponding positive expressions such as **exult** are perhaps less emphatically characterizing. We shall call their application to oneself in the
present tense *self-applauding characterizations*. The "innocent" use of these
in the present would generally be accompanied by terms of behavior or
phrasing to acknowledge the impropriety (e.g., an ironic, exaggerated, or
self-deprecatory remark).

It is interesting to observe that the negations of these characterizations are
neither self-stultifying nor self-applauding. Although I may not say I am
bridling at, bristling at, or I am exulting in, feeling tenderness toward x, it is
entirely in order for me to deny all these in the present tense: I may say if
accused, perhaps angrily, I am *not* bristling at, I am *not* exulting in x. Such
denials, especially angry denials, show us something about these "accusations." I repudiate your negative characterizations of me ("you are fuming
at x") because I never, in the continuous or progressive present tense,
characterize myself so, because they are, in fact, fingers of accusation pointed
at me. If indeed all this is *now* transpiring, I cannot be expected to accept the
justice of this accusation, although a moment later I may feel shame and
acknowledge my transgression or lapse of taste or decorum. The same
considerations as to tense, person, and affirmation-negation apply also to
utterances with other appraisives, e.g., most of those in Part Two.

We may now consider somewhat further the question whether it is responding or appraising that is implied in the second member of these responsional characterizations (AR or A^2). In the first place, I think it is evident that if K is uttering, "You are merely venting your rage on us," or "Spare us this paroxysm of rage," or "You fly into a temper at the mere mention of this matter" to L, that K believes L's stance is here one of a mere *response* of feelings. Let us say K and L are two aldermen in a public quarrel. If K wants it to be thought that L has simply made a *faulty appraisal* of some matter before them, he certainly ought not to use this form of words to express himself about L. Part of what offends L is, in fact, that K is implying by his very choice of terms that L is caught in a merely emotive response. If L were addressed with the words, "Your appraisal is in error (or unfair, or unjust)," L (assuming even a minimal climate of calm deliberation and good will) would certainly be bound to reply with an even-tempered refutation, or a similar return. K's choice of just these words, that is, the vocabulary of 2.4 (negative) shows that what he is condemning in L is, as he sees it, an emotive response. Of course, this is not at all to say that K is fair, or right. It merely says what the nature of this vocabulary is in typical instances of use. I believe little argument is needed to show that the same may be said of utterances in terms of 2.4 (positive). What is being characterized here (showing sympathy for) is even more obviously just a response. The use then of 2.4 is for the purpose of directing an appraisal toward a response (AR).

Of course, in reference to the above quarrel between K and L, I do not wish to say that K ought not to have spoken as he has about L, nor that responsional characterization should be avoided. This would be to elevate mere politeness to a moral obligation. There obviously are times when we must not only say, "you are bearing a grudge," but even, "you are lying," nor should we retract the words.

With this we conclude our survey of response and turn to the acts, processes, and procedures of appraisal. Of course, we shall not be altogether finished with response until the very end.

3.0 APPRAISAL

Scarcely more than a glance at vocabularies 2.0 and 3.0 should suffice to convince us of their fundamental and irreducible difference. As we shall have repeated occasion to observe, this difference has often been contested for programmatic or tendentious reasons. Appraising, it is thought, simply has to be construed as merely responding since naturalistic commitments elsewhere make it inconvenient to permit a differentiation of them. It is sufficient to respond to this in what follows by letting the facts speak for themselves.

We begin our study of appraisive language by remarking on certain similarities and differences between 2.0 and 3.0. The processes of 2.0 are, as it were, complete in themselves; those of 3.0 are significant only as ways of generalizing about our ways of employing actual concepts and instruments of appraisal (especially Part Two). So far as it goes, the vocabulary of 2.0 is sufficient for reporting or describing our emotive and kindred responses; a poet may not be satisfied with its limited resources, but, of course, poets rarely confine themselves to their responses. One does not appraise or evaluate simply by saying, "I am evaluating such and such;" but "I hate him" may be an actual part of my hatred and suffice to communicate it.

Unlike 2.0, the whole vocabulary of 3.0 is in a very important sense superfluous. In the conduct of our affairs what we need to do is first of all to appraise, not to speak about our appraising. 3.0 is therefore entirely void without actual appraisives such as are to be found in Part Two. What is said in 3.0 is not to be taken as at all sufficient in itself.

On the whole, the terms in Part One are largely descriptive rather than appraisive and find cognates in other languages, though not always perfectly congruent. This can be seen by looking at 3.11, for example, which comprises descriptive terms to designate the processes and procedures of evaluation. Most languages are likely to have equivalents of most of these, and some languages other than English may even have a more extensive vocabulary. Subject to qualifications already taken up, the same may be said particularly for 1.0 (Satisfaction), 2.1 (Appetitions), most of 2.2 (Direct Responses), 3.13 (Appraisive Outcomes), 3.2 (Appraisive Sequels), and parts of 4.0 (Enactment) and 5.0 (Moral Judgment). In Part One, it is principally the concepts of 2.4 that will be bound to show differences in other languages, for these are already, in effect, appraisives: they are, as we have seen, best thought of as appraisals of responses. The concepts of Part Two will, we anticipate, show greater incongruences or inequivalences from language to language, and also within given languages. We may again encounter a considerable convergence among languages with the general appraisives that are taken up at the end of Part Three.

Thus the acts or processes indicated by most of the vocabularies in Part One are likely to manifest themselves in all cultures. But the means, devices, or instruments which different peoples invent in performing those acts, as shown in the vocabularies of Part Two, are the work of their own genius, work which will be "unfinished business" as long as they survive.

3.1 GENERAL

3.11 PROCEDURES OF APPRAISAL

(a) **appraise**   **prove**
appreciate   **savor**
assess   **value** v. (=**appraise**)
consider
criticize, criticism, criterion
deem (archaic in this use)   (b) **gauge** v.
diagnose   **grade** v.
estimate   **rank** v.t.
evaluate   **rate** v.
judge v. (=**appraise**)   **sample**

3.12 APPRAISIVE INTEREST

interest (3.13)
regard (3.13)
be [sensible of
be [sensitive to

(A) *The Garnut of Appraisal.* The vocabulary of 3.1 represents the process of appraisal from several sides. The terms in 3.11 can be used for designating *probative* acts, acts which are seeking the value to be placed upon something and also for communicating the *verdict* or result of such an effort. Both of these will come under review, the probative and the verdictive.

The concepts of 3.12 (Appraisive Interest) perform, in a sense, both probative and verdictive functions but they are weaker in both respects than the preceding class and convey rather the sense of a detached and noncommittal survey. Appraisive Interest may provide an introduction to the problems of the other acts or processes of appraisal.

The use of **regard** in the imperative mood is probative. (The French **regardez!** is somewhat stronger.) This is true also of "I am regarding," which, though perhaps rare and a little awkward, preserves the idea of a kind of neutral conning. When the term is used as an imperative, the subject addressed is expected to have an attitude of receptivity, of taking in everything that is before him. *What* he is to make of the scene before him is expected to occur to him in the course of regarding it. **Sensible of** and **sensitive to** can also conceivably occur in such imperative contexts, but this is rare. They are employed mainly to draw attention to specific effects. I am **sensible of** your great faith and confidence in me; I am **sensitive to** his innuendo and sarcasm; and so, one may be sensible of a benign environment, sensitive to what is untoward. But there is no obvious limit to what I might become sensible of or sensitive to: here conventions of use are not rigid. Another use of these two is less in the direction of a posture of probing for whatever the situation may turn up, as in **interest** or **regard,** and more in attending to or looking for some definite quality or event in it. These terms are not as colorless as **consider** in the main list of 3.11 which could also be put under Appraisive Interest. All of them serve the purpose of expressing the capacity for alertness to the environment, an absolute precondition of the functioning of all the processes of appraisal and judgment.

Before we begin our consideration of 3.11, we may observe that the vocabulary in 3.11 reveals very little of what the process of appraising or evaluating is like. We must resist the temptation to make generalizations about the "process of appraisal" simply from a body of terms that are used to designate it. The full nature and significance of appraisal cannot be appreciated until, in 5.0, we examine the processes of judgment and justification, and in Parts Two and Three, we come to take up the actual instruments of characterization and commendation. We can, however, venture some provisional generalization if we confine them to the vocabularies quoted here.

In 3.11, the subgroup (b) has certain suggestions of "objectivity," as compared with the concepts in (a). Concepts such as **grade, rank, rate,** and **sample** are very commonly employed in making certain necessary discriminations in industry and various economic fields. In these contexts their use is almost an "objective" or factual matter. The rating, ranking, or grading of food or of coffee, tea, or wine is largely determined by the demands of a market. By length and depth of experience, the merchant knows what his clients want to eat or drink. He comes to know or to sense the trends of the market and what adjustments of his stock are necessary for him to maintain his place financially. The abilities of tasters of beverages and spirits have long been celebrated for their subtlety. But they are certainly not employed merely to say which is good, better, best, bad, worse, or worst among the teas or wines they taste. There are very precise data of sense involved in these occupations, together with an interesting set of conventions for designating them. *Good* and *bad* may become merely a final *je ne sais quoi* character among others. Once these discriminations are recorded, the entrepreneur is in a position to bring his skills as a merchant and vendor into play. A series of steps that may be traced from the consumer *as purchaser* (his act of consumption is largely irrelevant) through the merchant to the expert mark the factors that determine this whole particular phenomenon. In all of this what is truly idiomatic to grading and ranking has disappeared in a series of steps of economic "iron necessity." Only the consumer at the end *may* be in a position to make discriminations outside this iron framework, although students of the economics and psychology of marketing have shown us how difficult it is. We are not saying that there is no "real" grading or rating in this process but rather that much that could be called evaluative grading or rating is irrelevant to the economic process.

The principal use of **appreciate, value,** and **deem** is as verbs to give verdicts or results. They, therefore, reappear in 3.13. But each of them has another, now obsolescent use as a probative term. This is regrettable in the case of the excellent old verb *deem*, the only one in the list that antedates Middle English: nearly all the others are late, being Latin derivatives.

Prove is likewise no longer a strong probative, but it preserves this sense, as anyone schooled in the New Testament will know, in St. Paul's, "Prove all things, hold fast that which is good."* The far commoner use is, of course, the one it has in logical, mathematical or legal contexts. (See Appendix A.) The probative aspect of *prove* is better preserved in **probe**, which is of identical origin in Latin.

Diagnose is now largely restricted to medicine and so retains very little of what we have said is idiomatic to appraisal, since it refers to ascertaining very specific symptoms and to making inferences about states, possibly pathological. However, the term has a very strong probative character and is, perhaps, unfortunate in being surrendered wholly to medicine. It can also appear as a verdict, particularly in the form **diagnosis.**

Gauging as meaning measurement properly falls outside our list. It serves mainly a verdictive function and connotes an ability to set the value of something at a definite place in a scale. Therefore, it may best be bracketed with **ranking, rating** and **grading.** Its use for appraisal is perhaps slightly pretentious and pseudo-technical. It raises no interesting problems for us.

Estimate and **assess** are likewise heavily marked for technical use in

---

* 1 Thessalonians 5:21.

science, commerce, and industry. **Estimate** is unique in connoting a certain degree of hazard, guesswork, "intuition," or "judgment." There is, however, no real limitation of the term in such a way as to exclude it from designating appraisals of persons or their character, for example.

Savor finds occasional employment in areas other than the appraising of ingestants. Since it is directly derived from the exercise of subtle and powerful body-localized senses, its employment elsewhere carries over something of the grasp of tangs and aromas, even if only metaphorically. The mere use of such a term where it is ordinarily not expected is a powerful stimulant to awareness: for example, savoring a slum, opening night at the opera, the atmosphere of a carnival, and so on.

The majestic connotations of **judge** fit it for appraisal of situations that seem instinct with serious, perhaps dread, consequences. In this area, because of the gravity of the circumstances, mankind has in every culture developed elaborate institutions to formalize the processes of judgment, among them the occupations of judges, juries, prosecutors and the like, as well as codes of laws and ordinances. **Judge**, therefore, is best used where such institutions are in being, or where something like equivalents of them are agreed upon as in the formal judging of competence in art, music, architecture and the like. We recur to the study of **judgment** in section 5.0 at the end of Part One. We will also encounter it repeatedly elsewhere.

The colorless and noncommital **consider,** the eternal refuge of academics and lawyers, deserves little more mention than that it is absolutely indispensable – occupying a position something like Voltaire's God.

(B) *Appraisal and Evaluation.* The concepts **appraise, criticize** and **evaluate** play a major role in all that follows. Of these, **criticize** often falls naturally to the special area of the aesthetic enterprises. We must also take note of its strong tendencies toward ambiguity: it is being subjected constantly to tensions that draw it into a censorious and negate its probative or neutral use. Popularly, at least, **criticize** and **criticism** are always thought of as censorious in nature, and this connotation is often in conflict with efforts to use these terms in the probative sense which we are taking to be primary in 3.11. The censorious sense, being verdictive, virtually removes the concepts to the area of the outcomes of appraisal in 3.13. The effort to retain **criticize** as a probative verb bespeaks a real need, but since it is too often necessary to specify that one is using it in this neutral sense, recourse is better had to other terms, such as **appraise** and **evaluate.** These then survive as best representing the task which one undertakes in trying to determine the value of things, processes, and persons. But this will not, of course, remove the others wholly from our attention.

There is actually very little that can be or needs to be said by way of an analysis or extended explanation of **appraise** and **evaluate** at this point in our discussion. Terms like these have a purely utilitarian and dispensable character: they are not functionally necessary for us to be able to appraise or to evaluate. Their only significance lies in referring us to our actual appraisings. The scope and character of appraisive discourse is what we have to explain and this is represented by the vocabularies that are presented for study in Part Two. Our generalizations about appraisal will, therefore, be of the briefest sort serving not to analyze this process but rather to show how this notion is being treated. We may summarize this as follows.

(1) We distinguish between **evaluation** and **appraisal** by using the former term in a more general sense and the latter as a particular mode under it, along with **judgment**, that is **moral judgment**. We shall have no great need for **evaluation**, except as the broadest designation for the topic we are studying. Judging, I should say, as when one condemns or exonerates, is a kind of evaluation.

(2) Appraisal is here treated as being what we call *characterization* and is thought of in Part Two as exercised in some eight large subject matters, with various subclassifications. What we mean by 'characterization' is amply discussed later on, particularly in the Introduction to Part Two.

(3) Characterization is not decided by *standards*, principles, commitments, or values. Understanding the unique terms of the process of characterizing, which are called *characterisms*, is all that is needed to apply them. Characterizations stand altogether on their own feet. They are the ultimate sources and originals of all valuation.

(4) Since, however, the subject matters of Part Two take on a tone of increasing moral seriousness as we approach the social and communitive sphere, some characterizations will also reflect or remind us of *moral involvements*, and thus also of standards of commitments that are in general not implicated in characterization. For these, moral involvement simply adds a kind of further dimension.

(5) While not all characterizations point toward accepted or fixed standards of value, all of them can immediately point a way toward some kind of *action*. For example, there are no standards by which we can judge whether A is credulous, squeamish, glib, careless, dissipated, ostentatious, bellicose, miserly, vulgar, or malevolent (to select a few negative characterisms virtually at random) but in each case an appropriate action for dealing with the subject of characterization is already suggested, if not dictated. In this way characterization provides a kind of transition between *is* and *ought*, or perhaps as much of a bridge as we can hope to find. Morally oriented characterizations are the only ones that point *both* toward principles and actions.

(6) Finally, although characterization inherently cannot be analyzed into

descriptive determinants, it can in every case be coordinated with some property or some set of describable properties that is *being* characterized; and we can characterize parts and aspects as well as wholes or substances.

Further specification of appraisal and characterization will be left to the exposition in Part Two.

3.13 APPRAISIVE OUTCOMES:

FAVORING

> **abide (=tolerate)**
> **accept**
> **acquiesce in**
> **appreciate**
> **approve of, approbation, approbate**
> **concern, be [concerned about**
> **countenance** v.
> **deem** (an auxiliary appraisive verb, e.g. **deem worthy**)
> **esteem** v.
> **favor** v.
> **be [for**
> **take an [interest in** (3.12)
> **pass** v.t.
> **prefer**
> **prize** v.
> **have [regard for** (3.12)
> **tolerate**
> **value** v. (=esteem)

DISFAVORING

> **be [averse to**
> **depreciate**
> **disapprove of**
> **disesteem**
> **disfavor**
> **disregard**
> **be [dissatisfied with**
> **have [misgivings about**

The concepts now under consideration are very different from the previous. They do not appear to be processes at all, and if they can be called acts we should not think of them in temporal terms. They are simply, as the title indicates, the outcomes or trends of processes of deliberation, of weighing considerations which may have occupied a certain length of time. The termination of these processes is their most important aspect, their excuse for being.

Outcomes are not to be confused with the allocutive sequels to appraisal set forth in the next section, 3.2. It is not logically necessary that outcomes be couched in words, hence they are not allocutions, whether pro or con (3.221 and 3.222). I may approve or disapprove, accept, be concerned about, esteem, prefer, or tolerate something (3.13) without uttering a word or formulating a specific thought.

Neither are outcomes identical with sequels in action (3.21). If I approve or disapprove of something (3.13), I *may* proceed to avoid or eschew, to promote, elect, or select, but none of these is *necessarily* a part of approving or disapproving nor is any of them a necessary sequel to them. They are, however, intimately related, as we shall see in 3.2.

Approvals and other outcomes are not to be thought of as "performatives," "verbal acts." My accepting, approving, or disregarding something does not wait for my saying that I accept, approve, or disregard it. I can, however, *signify* my approval by saying something: "aye," for example.

We must compare outcomes with the processes already discussed in Part One, since they are sometimes assimilated to them. Outcomes are often close to or indistinguishable from satisfaction and other goals of valuation in 1.0 and no firm line needs to be drawn between them. It is, however, possible in certain cases to favor (3.13) what one really is not, or is not entirely, satisfied with (1.0).

Taking appetitions (2.1) next, it is clear that outcomes are in fact quite other than cravings, likings, and longings: what we are craving, for example, is in fact something that we can approve, accept, be satisfied with. Moreover, these short term appetitions occupy our attention sometimes to the exclusion of everything else, for considerable periods of time. The long term appetitions (propensities, proclivities) may not make so insistent a claim on our attention, but they also obviously occupy tracts of time, unlike outcomes.

The next class perhaps makes the strongest claim to be able to absorb the outcomes, or be absorbed by them, that is, the sympathic and dyspathic responses (2.2). If I am averse to, disapprove of, or disfavor something, how can this differ from abhorring, abominating, being appalled at, being displeased, disgusted, or vexed at, in some degree or other? We should notice the essentially unemotive or unemotional character of the first group of terms as compared with the second. I can disapprove of or disfavor without raising my voice, so to speak, but I cannot really mean what I say and yet not be in a state of noticeable emotional warmth a significant part of the time when I say I abhor, abominate, am appalled at, and so forth. An outcome is the termination of something and stands apart from the previous proceedings.

We must not confuse the outcome with the emotive tumult that frequently characterizes responses and that may even accompany an outcome, along with other things. We cannot infer the existence of emotional states (2.2) from the fact that someone approves of, accepts, tolerates, favors, disfavors, disregards, esteems, prizes, or countenances some act or state or condition in his environment. Nor on the other hand, can we construe appetitions, desires, enjoyments, hankerings, discontents, disgusts, dismays, loves and hates (2.0) as the termini of appraisive processes.

Finally, these outcomes have no necessary relation to dreads, hopes and other situational affects (2.3); nor are they to be confused in any way with the charges and countercharges of the responsional characterizations (2.4).

Statements of approval and disapproval may sometimes serve as generalizations about our patterns of choice or about the direction our deeds will take in the future: they can make a kind of commitment (I don't countenance acts like that; I favor higher taxes). When this is not just the individual speaking for himself but society speaking for itself, it is easy to see how these verdictions can lead to the next step, the enactment of values (4.0).

Two important terms among the outcomes, **interest** and **regard**, have in one form already appeared under Appraisive Interest in 3.12. They are now, however, thought of in the verdictive rather than the probative sense. **Regard for** and **taking an interest in** are not the same as probative **regard** and **interest**. As verdictive, **having regard for** and **taking an interest** are based on presumed or previous processes of appraisal and probation, and responses, especially emotions, are also involved. But matters are only confused if we treat **regard** and **interest** as themselves responses. The effect of accompanying emotion is to lend depth to them. This gives the concepts an extraordinary strength as compared with other outcomes such as **accept, appreciate, approve**, or **favor**.

Concern for is somewhat stronger even than **regard for** and has a similar emotional dimension. Although **interest** is not necessarily self-serving, since it may be virtually identical with **concern**, it is most often true that I am interested in x because, as it may be said, x is to my interest. **Concern** has oftener a more "objective" character: we should be concerned about some things even if they are not in our interest. We can and should show concern for our environment even for such reaches of it as we shall not live to see. **Concern** is one of the strongest of the appraisive outcomes. To be concerned is to have appraised any subject – including oneself – in whatever counts as an objective manner and also to have some responsive and perhaps moral involvement with it.

We may now return to the question raised at the beginning of this section, whether **approval, concern, favor**, and the rest must be manifested in action or expression to be real or genuine. Certainly, to hear it said that A approves, favors, or prefers x may lead us to expect this. But an expectation is no necessity. Sequels (3.2) are quite distinct from outcomes. If A says he prefers something, this may, of course, be indistinguishable from a favoring allocution (3.221). But in general a sequel in action or allocution is neither a necessary nor a sufficient condition of an appraisive outcome. Some will say that to say of A that he favors or prefers x is nothing more than to say that he is about to undertake appropriate actions in support of x, and that if he fails to undertake them he does not in fact prefer x. I wish to deny this flatly. Outcomes and sequels are neither identical nor logically interdependent. We can prefer x and not choose or support x; we can support x and not prefer x. If someone says he prefers x, he is certainly likely to lead someone to expect him to support x. Alas, or fortunately, such an inference may be groundless.

It is for such reasons that we must say that outcomes, although verdictive and inherently favoring or disfavoring, are also indeterminate as to the scope or character of their application. We need, in certain circumstances, to ask whether someone's actions in support of something do really represent his real preferences and approbations. There is no reason why we must, accept some form of neo-behaviorism that renders such a question meaningless.

It is evident even from our sketch of some of the issues, that outcomes, particularly **accept, approve, favor**, and **prefer**, play a central and critical role in valuation. Since they are closely bound up with sequels we shall turn immediately to these and continue our discussion of outcomes in connection with them.

3.2   APPRAISIVE SEQUELS

3.21   ACTION

choose	**avoid**
decide (5.22)	**demote** (U.S.)
promote	**eschew**
select v.	**reject**
	relegate to

3.22   ALLOCUTION

3.221   PROLOCUTION

acclaim	**applaud**
advocate	**cheer** v.

commend (15.0)	**laud**
demand	**plaudit**
encomium	**praise**
extol	**recommend**

3.222 OBLOCUTION (Cf. 11.121)

condemn
damn
decry
deprecate
derogate
discommend (15.0)
disparage
dispraise
stricture, –s

The preceding sections have emphasized the logical independence of the processes of appraisal from other acts or states and the further independence of the outcomes of appraisals from the probations that issue in them. We now proceed from the appraisive outcomes to their sequels. These are, of course, related to appraisive outcomes but we cannot infer one from the other. Allocutive sequels are generally *meant to express* outcomes and indeed they do when the person is honest. Since no one will wish to deny the possibility of lying in this situation, we cannot infer one from the other, although we must still recognize a connection between them.

The situation is perfectly interpreted by Abelard, who says, "God considers not the action but the spirit of the action."* He is the *inspector cordis et renum*. That is, from some ideal standpoint, it would be possible to see the true relation between a sequel and the appraisive outcome it expresses. But *we* have no such "privileged access" to others. As Abelard goes on to concede, men, unlike God, can only look to deeds. Words *lead* us to expect deeds, and deeds are readily referred to preferences.

There are numerous problems about relating thoughts, words, and deeds in the present connection which must be left to ethics itself. Our main purpose, it must be remembered, is to articulate the language of valuation. We see that favoring or disfavoring outcomes may or may not issue in

---

* Abelard, *Ethics, or Know Thyself,* "Sin consists not in desiring a woman, but in consent to the desire, and not the wish for whoredom, but the consent to the wish is damnation." Ch. III. "God notes the soul alone, not its external effects, and counts what comes from our guilt or good will." Ch. VII. etc.

properly corresponding actions or allocutions. Our awareness that they may not is, apart from the evidence of language itself, the principal reason for insisting on their identity against all objections that they are shadowy and illusory entities, like intentions. It may be that actions (sequels) alone and not Abelard's "spirit of the action" or Kant's "good will" should be the subject of ethical appraisal.* Such a result still does not make outcomes any the less real. All of these concepts are needed in valuing; what is necessary is that we understand how each of them functions.

A considerable mystery has sometimes been made of what preferring and approving (3.13) "really are." But when we sort out the various "operations" that enter into valuation and discriminate the purpose of each, we find no reason to pursue preference and approval as if they were mysterious inner processes (they are just feelings, it may be suggested – a total misidentification; or attitudes – obfuscation can go no further). The only *processes* that have gone on are deliberation, appraising, or characterizing. Their goal is to terminate in commendation or discommendation and in actions in support of them.

Commendation as the formal goal of appraisal is expressible in such terms as **good, better, bad, worse,** and so on (15.0). When commendation, or more precisely, discommendation reveals also that basic commitments are involved and violated, moral judgment is brought to bear: actions not only of rejection or eschewal (3.21) but even of punishment (5.0) are set in motion. We may, however, confine ourselves for the present to **commendation** apart from judgment. It is the most typical allocution.

Commendation may be defined as a sequel that adequately verbalizes a favoring appraisive result. Its vocabulary (**good, bad**), as we shall see, is entirely formal. The matter or content of it must be found elsewhere. We gain a view of this content from the language of characterization (Part Two) in the particular and most significant case where we are commending persons. To prefer or to approve is therefore to be prepared to commend, and to commend is to be in command of a body of characterizations. Commendation or discommendation is thus simply the explicit direction which our characterizations have taken.

Thus, the vocabularies of 3.13 and 3.2, like so much else in Part One, are significant only in terms of the actual instruments of appraisal, the vocabulary of characterization: only in the actual use of it by appraisers is it significant to speak of "acts" or "processes" of appraisal. Referral to that vocabulary provides the best possible answer to the question as to what approval or valuing "really is."

---

* Kant, *Grundlegung zur Metaphysik der Sitten*, Erster Abschnitt.

3.3 HIGHER ORDER APPRAISIVES (Cf. Appendix H.)

fair, unfair
overestimate
overrate
underestimate
underrate

The present section points back to 3.11 but it also has wider implications. The subject is the appraising of appraisals or the revision of them. All the acts in 3.0 may themselves be the subject of scrutiny and evaluation. Appraisals and estimates may appear to be too high or too low; approval may be amended to disapproval, and vice versa. Similar considerations apply to the appraisive sequels.

What standpoint must higher appraisives occupy in order to pass judgment on lower? This is not a troublesome problem. All of these "processes" or "acts" have to do with the revision of appraisals; hence anyone who is in the process of appraising, is *ipso facto* involving himself with the question whether he is appraising the subject "too high" or "too low."

The present section raises no such arduous questions as the AR's and R^2's in 2.4 (Responsional Characterizations), where we had to decide whether the stance was a response or an appraisal at both levels. Clearly the present case is simply one of the revision of appraisals.

It is instructive to note that Webster (1934) records what must approach some two thousand compounds beginning with 'over-.' A vast proportion of these are also properly appraisive terms, and if our aim were exhaustiveness they would alone virtually double our vocabulary in Part Two. (And this is but one such prefix.)

Since the vocabulary of appraising (3.11) lends itself in various connections to probative and verdictive uses, we may particularly note that it is verdictions that we revise or correct. Probations are not corrected although they may be gone over again. The present higher-order appraisives are thus verdictions, or re-verdictions.

We have regarded outcomes (3.13) as essentially verdictive. But we must take careful note of the fact that the prefixes 'over-,' 'under-,' 're-,' and the like do not at all apply to appraisive outcomes (**abide, accept, prefer, tolerate, reject**). A preference or tolerance is not anything that one can overdo, underdo, or redo, for as we have pointed out, it is not *done* at all. One can only alter the degree of one's preferring.

The higher order appraisives also point in another direction: we may take an interest in them not just as revisions of former appraisals, but as evidence of a person's want of ability in appraising: he may be thought to set the mark too high or too low. The commendation of persons must consider habits and patterns of appraisal and skill, or want of skill, in appraising, evaluating, characterizing. The over- and under- terms recognize this variable and corrigible aspect of these abilities. This will be considered at somewhat greater length when in 15.6 we pursue the recursion of the commendation of persons back to the appraisive acts and procedures of 3.0. (Reference should also be made to the discussion of higher-order appraisives in Appendix H.)

Finally, the key terms **fair** and **unfair** deserve very special consideration, but this must be postponed until we have a much better view of the vocabulary of characterization. The terms are taken up at length in 15.0.

As already noted, the vocabulary of 3.0 serves to remind us of the terminology for appraising, but it throws little light by itself on the nature of the process of appraising. For this we must turn to the instruments of appraisal in Part Two. The next step to be taken is to consider commitment to values and other acts connected with this. Such commitments may be thought to grow out of appraisals. In fact, however, when appraisal is regarded narrowly as characterization it is seen to be autonomous, independent of commitments. Only when it is thought of as moral judgment is it necessarily connected with commitment: judgment presupposes commitment to values. Indeed it presupposes also the capacity to appraise and characterize. The latter, therefore, occupies a central position in all valuation, as will be made abundantly clear as we proceed.

We now turn first to acts of commitment and then to the states and processes of moral involvement and judgment.

4.0. ENACTMENT

All of the concepts we have collected under Part One represent evaluative concerns of various kinds: to enjoy, appraise, approve, long for, admire and love; to despise or abhor, dread or hope for, disdain or idolize, avoid or select, acclaim or abuse, and many more. When we collect a large number of such concepts and examine them closely they begin to show family likenesses too unmistakable to be ignored. In this way, we have seen how some of them represent direct emotional respondings, others acts of selection, still others explicit deeds, and so forth.

Speaking in very general terms, we proceed now from the discernment to the establishment of values. This appears to involve certain acts and these of a somewhat contested nature. According to some philosophers, verbs for these acts are not used to *inform* us that acts are being done or have been done, but are themselves used to *perform* the acts spoken of. These are the "performative verbs" that Professor J. L Austin identified and subjected to such careful study. Among them are the concepts found particularly under 4.1 and 4.2. We may concede that they ought properly to be segregated from others whether we accept Austin's theory or not. They obviously have a rather special use.

The first group of concepts we shall examine are the concepts of *commitment*, or acknowledgment of duties, of swearing allegiance to ideals or to standards of conduct, and the like. The second group is composed of concepts which signify the establishment of rules for others, ourselves, or our communities. We shall call these *ordainments*. There is also a group of acts which are often ceremonial or *honorific* in purpose. Here we elevate for particular attention or veneration persons or things or even abstract qualities which may then play an important role in moral judgment. A final section on *appraisive outlooks* takes note of our commitments at work or in action.

I have undertaken what may seem an artificial separation of the idea of covenance in section 11.4 from that of commitment, for special study. As I conceive the matter, covenanting or promising is a fairly narrow concept covering the agreements and contracts which persons make *to one another*. This brings various virtues and vices to light that are connected with the keeping and breaking of such contracts. Concepts of the present section have a more fundamental connection with morals and values than those of 11.4. Indeed, if I am right, values cannot exist without them.

4.1   COMMITMENT

4.11   ACTIVE COMMITMENT

adjure
swear [allegiance to
commit oneself to
subscribe to

4.12   IMPLICIT COMMITMENT

owe [allegiance to
be [committed to
owe [fealty to

(A) *Meaning of Terms.* The use of the term 'commitment' to signify an act of pledging, engaging, binding morally or legally is recognized, for example, by Wyld, though not as the first meaning. The primary sense is to entrust or consign. Here one commits something of his own to a certain purpose or service or destiny. One commits the body to the deep or the soul to God. The principal use for us is the reflexive where one binds oneself to devotion or to a certain purpose, idea, ideal, or code of conduct. This is the way, I think, holy orders are to be construed, an act of "giving over to," "giving oneself up to" – a move by no means confined to religious dedications and donations. Although what one is giving himself to may appear vague or difficult of formulation, there is no reason for doubting its reality or effectiveness: not every commitment is as palpable as committing or giving oneself up to a life of vice, drink, or crime.

Some of the terms in 4.0 may appear to be used performatively, but although the commitments in 4.1 and the ordainments in 4.2 (such as **annul, ratify, rescind**) may be acts, we are not committed to accepting the performance theory for them. **Subscribe to** is probably not even an act; we use the term merely to publish our beliefs in the first person (and we can do so without the term) and to make comparable assertions about others in the second or third person.

One important question we shall have to deal with is whether we can really be implicitly committed (4.12) if we have never taken any formal or even informal steps to indicate commitment or allegiance. This will be discussed under Generic Commitment in (C) below.

(B) *Commitment and the Explanation of Conduct.* When we ask why a man has done some deed, we may be asking for a psychological or psychoanalytic explanation or some physical or other causative explanation, or about the motives he had, what his ends in view then and there were, or again what kind of cognitive survey he had of the situation he was in, how he saw himself and his environment at a certain time, or we may be asking what his feelings, attitudes, habits, and proclivities were, and there are still other families of explanation of human deeds. Now I think we can know all of these things and yet have omitted something at least as important as any of them, and if we omit it we really cannot understand actions. What we need to know is to what if anything the person had some overriding loyalty, to what he had committed himself as guiding principles, what imperatives, if any, he heeded above all others, above his inclinations. Psychoanalysts locate part of this large body of obligations and loyalties in what they call the superego. We may note in passing that the superego is a way of answering at least the *de facto* question of how a person can be committed and even think of himself as committed without performing any act of commitment. He simply acquires loyalties in the course of experience, absorbing them from his community.

It is apparent that we must take account of commitments in order to understand conduct. Great works of literature, for example, *Othello*, enable us to observe their power.* With the greatest economy of effort, Shakespeare shows us fully what Othello cognizes of the scene around him, his feelings and the pattern of his attitudes and responses, his reasons for acting as he does. We need also to know the kinds of imperatives that he seems to live by and that would for him fully justify his deeds. Even if we had all of the full detail of his cognition or assessment of his situation, and knew in vast detail the character and pattern of his emotions and attitudes, and knew both of these as well as he did, we still should not know either what he was going to do, or having done it, why he did it, unless we also knew *what he thought he ought to do* in a situation of this or that kind.

At the last moment, before Desdemona is smothered, Othello hears her put the interpretation of murder on the act she knows he intends to commit. This surprises him. The description *he* has accepted of her recent behavior has convinced him that as a man of honor he must or ought to do her to death. But since he has deeply loved Desdemona, the decision to deliver her up to death seems to him not murder but a sacrifice. He is willing to sacrifice her because honor and all its train of imperatives are more to be prized than even the satisfactions of having a wife. This is how he sees the situation and how he appraises it. When at the last moment Desdemona, who has a cognition of the situation that happens to be true, unlike Othello, since she knows herself to be innocent, declares his deed to be murder, Othello concludes that she is even more wicked than he had thought. "O perjur'd woman," he cries, and does the deed.

* Cf. this author's "The Roots of Conflict and Action," *Inquiry*, Vol. 7, pp. 245–67.

Shakespeare has provided us with everything we need to know to explain Othello's action. And the play has detailed not only what Othello knows about his situation but what he thinks he knows, not only his emotional responses, something of his past habits and physical make up, and the like, but also what his overriding loyalties are that lead beyond his present feelings, attitudes, impulses, and motives; in short, what ends he is committed to or acknowledges.

It should be made clear that there is a difference between *motives* and *commitments*. When we inform others about our motives we speak of the intentions behind our actions usually in such a way as to justify them. The harder we are then pressed in our justifications, the more we may begin to speak of our commitments. It is not uncommon for the greater generality inherent in our commitments to issue in vagueness. We are usually expected to know what our motives are, although we may lie about them. With commitments, it is just possible that others may know more about us than we ourselves do. Some think questions about motives should only be raised if there has been some untoward or malignant result. But a person's commitments are in force all of the time, and enter into the explanation of all his actions, whether these are benign or untoward, and whether they spring from clearly discerned motives or not.

A person's motive for, let us say, depriving a brother or sister of an inheritance may be to "get even," "out of spite," "because they are lazy, worthless people," "to keep the family business intact," and so on. Commitments run a good deal deeper than this and are not always easy to expose. Religious creeds or ideologies often serve this purpose. For this reason the final part of 4.0 introduces some of these implicit and explicit commitments under the title Appraisive Outlooks. Commitments are also the natural domain of fanaticisms. One need only think of a selection of notable revolutionaries of the past sixty years to be able to judge of this. Ideological commitments dominated their lives, organized their emotions, and determined even their opinions as to the facts.

(C) *Generic Commitment*. Sometimes we have little idea of where the obligations we are said to have arise. If we have not committed or obligated ourselves, how can we be committed or obligated, or have a duty? Duty often seems something that rises to meet us out of a mysterious hidden quarter. Freud's super ego and Kafka's trial situation are effective images of this mystery.

If I have not committed myself, may I nevertheless be committed? If I have not obliged myself, may I nevertheless be obligated? Our vocabulary under 4.1. is divided specifically into active and implicit commitment. We might be tempted to regard committing and being committed as no more than a harmless logical or grammatical transformation from the active to the passive voice. The situation is far more complex.

In addition to acquiring a commitment by committing oneself, a person may be committed by virtue of N, where N is something like "being a man," "being the kind of man he is," "being what he is," "having the kind of position or office he holds," and so on. We may call this *generic commitment*. It reflects a standpoint no less influential than that of Plato, on the side of the moral theorists. On the practical side, it would be very close to arguments which common sense offers itself and seems entirely satisfied with.

It is unnecessary to document in detail the assertion that it would be compatible with Platonism to affirm that A is committed or obliged by virtue of N, if A were a person and if N meant something like the nature of A as a human being. This view concentrates attention upon the discrete division of persons, if not the universe, into types and the classification of instances under each type. What are your duties – you being known to be a child, a female, a pilot, a night watchman, a doctor? We try to discover what the definition, and thus what the nature, of each such class or occupation is. Each action of a person is the action of someone *qua* something, i.e., as having some role or occupation. Find this out, find out its nature, essence, or definition and you have the answer to what norms should guide his actions. If, of course, we cannot convince ourselves of this neat organization of things or any acceptable semblance of it, we shall have little reason to accept a Platonistic explanation of duties, obligations and commitments.

It may be thought that it is *not* reasonable to believe in "forms" and hence that the Platonistic moral theory is untenable. Perhaps so. There might, however, be a kind of limited Platonism which would offer a defense of forms or types to accord with a rather common sense derivation of duties and rights. It would argue that while we may not be prepared to accept Plato's metaphysic of forms as universal, in the area to which we confine ourselves in the study of morals there can be no doubt of the reality of persistent patterns. Thus organic species have each a distinct character, and the character persists. If the species change they do so by regular laws and by discrete steps. Such comparative fixity of species is suggested even in the inorganic world (the periodic table of elements, the typology of the history of stars, and so on, and there are other evidences of its reality at certain levels higher or lower). Moreover, the possible explanatory use of the "formistic" or Platonistic theory does not depend upon its universal truth. In short, it may explain some things and not others. Now man is an example of a form. Our knowledge of him shows his immense variety in all directions, but also a certain unity within limits. This is sufficient to enable us to make a great many generalizations about him. Expectations about him soon lead to presumptions and demands. Support for a moral order of some sort will be claimed. It will be argued that a woman is obligated to provide constant and sufficient care for an infant *by virtue of the fact* that the child is her own; and any number of other examples of the same sort will be developed.

It is not my intention to defend such an argument, although determined Platonists might provide a vigorous defense of it. The point is that such a doctrine could enlist also a great deal of support from the side of what we may call common sense. Philosophically unlettered thinking is quite hospitable at least to the idea of generic commitment if not to the tenets of Platonism. One could get immediate support for the idea that the personnel of a vessel on the high seas are obligated to give assistance of a certain sort to any other vessel in distress which it happens to encounter *by virtue of the fact* that it is itself a sea-going vessel in the vicinity. If there is a vast disparity of type, the rule would be interpreted in a proportional sense: if Sir Francis Chichester had happened to encounter the *Queen Mary* in a disaster situation his duty might have been said to be little more than one of sending a radio message and taking a few passengers aboard the *Gypsy Moth IV*. Here a person would be expected to know who or what he is generically, or suitably to his situation, and to infer what he must do.

We should now ask what we can appropriate from this approach, or how we may gain the same ends without investing our intellectual capital in the Platonistic metaphysic. Since it is no part of our intention to offer a developed moral philosophy, we shall be brief in answering the question.

(D) *Self-Characterization.* Plato's problem is seen in its most merciless light as one in which one tries to proceed from what man is, his nature, to what he ought to be or do. There is little hope of a solution in this, for reasons it is unnecessary to detail. Plato's approach and almost any modern version of it, if it reduces to the idea of generic commitment, is too external. We must see, following Kant, that the solution must come from within. Kant's way of expressing this is that I myself must be the author of the moral law or imperative. But if this is not to be confused with simply subjecting oneself to his inclinations, the person must first make an effort at self-definition or self-discovery: he needs to know what he is. This is not to be represented in some budget of existential or indicative propositions about his history or physiology, but rather in the answer to the question, how do I see myself, what do I see myself as, how do I define myself, or what do I define myself to be? We have learned enough from psychoanalysis to see the importance of posing such questions. Before we can begin to cope with the imperatives society lays upon us, or rather, in just those contexts where we may clash with them, we must seek to give ourselves answers to these questions. Here we cannot be satisfied with accounts merely of our "station" or the classifications that may be imposed upon us by the ordinances of society. Something more searching is needed.

There can be no doubt of the power of such self-definition. The person must reveal to himself his role or identity. Why does a Sirhan Sirhan think himself obliged to kill Senator Kennedy? It is not enough to speak of impulses. One must ask about the role or identity he has assumed, how he sees himself, how he defines himself. Resolute action is not the result merely of recognizing obligations in the abstract but of seeing clearly what one is. The irresolute have no identity. Once they learn what it is, they can act.

There is thus an alternative to the Platonistic explanation of obligation and other such explanations by generic commitment. We are indeed committed by being what we are, but this has no force deriving from mere categories and classifications. Only if "what we are" is the outcome of a process of characterizing ourselves can it have the consequence of revealing to us our obligations. Our commitments are implicit in such self-definition.

What is said of commitments applies equally to imperatives that issue from sources other than ourselves. The natural response to a stark and bleak external command may be resistance. To obey it one must first see *himself* as the ground from which the dictated action may take its rise. We cannot find the *authority* of imperatives in others, in those who issue commands, no matter how much force they may bring to bear. Only to conform is not to obey. To obey is to embrace an imperative, not to be embraced by it. Even the Decalogue, which may appear to be a series of authoritarian demands, had to be and for the most part was "internalized" in this way by its people. The imperative style suited the social situation of a nomadic nation some fifteen centuries B.C. that was ceaselessly in danger of destruction or disintegration. A few dozens of mighty words, more than anything else, kept it alive. The code was obeyed because the people "saw themselves as" the children of the one true God. Similarly, what Socrates saw himself to be led him to obey the state and submit to execution. In the end, force can accomplish little without the aid of those it is exerted upon.

We may or may not wish to support Austin's view that obligations can be acquired by certain acts involving performative utterances in the manner described by him. But whether or not the obligations we acquire are acquired in this way, it is certainly not the only way in which we acquire them. And even if their acquisition is indeterminate, they may be none the less real. We must, therefore, seek to uncover ways in which we come to be aware of and to acknowledge commitments. We can do so, I believe, only by a process of self-searching self-characterization or self-definition.

Such a derivation does not proceed either by a frontal effort to drive obligative statements from inner or outer description of persons nor by a circumvention of this. It is possible because we are capable of characterizing our-selves as potential perpetrants of a variety of actions. Some of these appear in crediting, others in discrediting light. Our review of the possibilities reveals our values.

On or before the fifteenth of March in 44 B.C. Marcus Brutus seems to have considered whether he could or could not any longer live with himself as a senator and Roman patrician if he let his friend Julius Caesar live. In so doing he revealed or could have revealed to himself what his political and other values were. The Brutus who would let a dictator live seemed discred-itable – certain values dear to him were revealed to be threatened by such a course of action, or inaction. Accordingly he chose another course. After the defeat at Philippi, he found he could no longer continue life if he was to be a captive of Augustus Caesar. If we could have assembled and documented a number of such decisions we could have determined what this man's values were, and he could have made the determination himself.

What the person wishes at all costs to avoid is to be the recipient of cen-sorious characterization, particularly from himself. He avoids every form of self-stultifying characterization, and he can see that self-applauding charac-terization is void of authority. In dwelling on contemplated actions, the thought of both these is vividly brought before the mind. Moral sensibility and sensibility in other critical directions consist precisely in reviewing a selection of characterizations of ourselves that we see as being inevitably applicable to us if we elect one action or another. For what reasons has so and so acted as he has? The ultimate answer lies in finding an answer to how he characterized himself, how he characterized doing or not doing certain actions. Was he aware that acting in such and such a manner would lay him open to a censorious characterization? Did he tentatively apply such a characterization to himself before he acted? And if he did why did he not refrain from the act? And so on.

Suppose we ask, can I be content to think that I am properly and fairly characterized as jealous, spiteful, sullen, domineering, fainthearted, reckless, or what not, and yet persist in an action which I know deserves such charac-terization? I think not. I may be willing to undertake some action in spite of the bitter criticism and obloquy of others so long as I am confident this is really not fair and applicable to me. Indeed, if I embark on a course of action where such judgment is likely to ensue, it will be foolish of me not to have confronted myself in advance with all such charges and to have given myself a satisfactory answer to them.

It is only by such a process of self-characterization that we can come to see what values we are devoted to and accordingly what actions are suitable for us to undertake. If we undertake a sufficiently searching examination we may eventually be able to discover all our commitments, although of course this would be a more lengthy and complicated process than most persons would generally care to undertake. In most cases, it will be easier to acquire the services of a pastor, confessor, or other moralist to persuade us what our commitments are.

Shakespeare has given us in *Hamlet* an opportunity to observe a person who reveals the process of self-characterization. Hamlet senses an obligation to act, he considers various courses of action, and engages in lengthy self-criticism of his motives and values, and of personal difficulties that stand in the way. His soliloquy beginning, "O, what a rogue and peasant slave am I!" in Act II affords us an opportunity to observe such self-examination. Hamlet sees himself as someone unable or unwilling to proceed to act upon a duty he has already solemnly undertaken and characterizes this inactive Hamlet as a "dull and muddy-mettl'd rascal" who is "unpregnant of his cause." Once he has brought him before his mind he sees what such a person is likely to deserve in the thought and at the hand of others:

> Am I a coward?
> Who calls me villain? breaks my pate across?
> Plucks off my beard, and blows it in my face?
> Tweaks me by the nose?

All this such a Hamlet would deserve, being truly "pigeon-liver'd" and lacking "gall." Or if this is not so, why has he not ere now

> fatted all the region kites
> With this slave's offal [?]

But then follows a remarkable second level characterization in which he sees his rage at Claudius in the shrieking lines

> Bloody, bawdy villain!
> Remorseless, treacherous, lecherous, kindless villain!

as merely a kind of substitute for the needed action. Here he characterizes the very response and characterization he has just indulged in. Like a whore, he says,

> I unpack my heart with words,
> And fall a-cursing, like a very drab,
> A scullion!
> Fie upon't!

The result is an evident repudiation both of his indecision and inaction and of his substituting a satisfying indulgence in rage for action itself. The projected self has afforded him a glimpse of what his duties, commitments and values are.

A second episode to illustrate our point occurs in the next act. Hamlet chances to find Claudius at prayer, evidently penitent for his crimes. Hamlet's first thought is to kill Claudius at once. But as soon as he thinks this, he contemplates himself as the projected perpetrator of the deed: "That would be scann'd," he says, and thinks the matter over. If he kills Claudius at that very moment, Claudius goes to Heaven, since he has been seeking forgiveness. But then Hamlet has dispatched to Heaven the murderer of a man who

> took my father grossly, full of bread,
> With all his crimes broad blown.

The elder Hamlet must suffer untold agony in Purgatory or even Hell since he died without extreme unction. No, says Hamlet:

> Up sword; and know thou a more horrid hent;
> When he is drunk asleep, or in his rage,
> Or in th' incestuous pleasure of his bed!

Then, he says, he will trip Claudius,

> that his heels may kick at Heaven,
> And that his soul may be as damn'd and black
> As Hell, whereto it goes.

One can call this "turn about is fair play," "compensation," or "eye for an eye": Whatever it be, it shows us what guides Hamlet's decision, if not ostensibly, then at least effectively.

Finally, in one of the greatest soliloquies, Hamlet formulates his rationale of action in both explicit and general terms:

> Rightly to be great
> Is not to stir without great argument;
> But greatly to find quarrel in a straw
> When honour's at the stake.

The occasion is one where Hamlet sees himself in an apt comparison with young Fortinbras, "a delicate and tender prince" and yet a man of resolute, unhesitant action who proposes to lead his army across Denmark against the Poles to conquer "an egg-shell," "a patch of ground" his own officer regards as scarcely worth five ducats. Hamlet falls to musing:

> What is man,
> If his chief good and market of his time
> Be but to sleep and feed? a beast, no more.

If there is more than this worth dying for, it is honor, and if so, Hamlet can no longer stand waiting:

> from this time forth,
> My thoughts be bloody, or be nothing worth!

Even from such fragments a picture of Hamlet's values may be clearly seen.

Hamlet affords a particularly apt opportunity for us to see how the projection of negative self-stultifying characterizations can reveal to the thoughtful mind what it wishes to avoid. The more observing and deliberate such a review is, and the soliloquistic method in *Hamlet* is especially favorable to this, the clearer the picture of the values of the person that emerges. Of course, positive self-characterization also plays a part but the negative form of it evokes stronger feeling and acts as a more potent determinant. We can thus see how scrutiny of the language of appraising can reveal commitments that may be implied in accepting and repudiating these characterizations.

(E) *How we Discover Commitments.* If we are seeking the sources particularly of implicit commitments, we must study modes of expressing judgments and appraisals. We can discern what the values and commitments an individual and a community, so far as they are united by a language, regard themselves as possessing by studying the paradigms and patterns of their evaluative vocabulary and its uses and implications. Such language not only mirrors reality, it is virtually the reality itself.

What are our values? We must begin by asking, what kinds of acts do we credit and discredit? The core vocabulary considered here is not an infallible guide to these values, but it is the first place we must turn to find out. It is not by itself infallible because we have also several other vocabularies, and we must study discourse not only paradigmatically but also in its actual applications, in the heat and fire of all the degrees of commendation and invective of persons concerned about themselves, their affairs, and their environments. Do we wish to know how we think we ought to address ourselves to our undertakings? The answer is if we address ourselves with vigor and energy then our effort must deserve to be characterized as intrepid, plucky and resolute, not foolhardy, rash, or reckless; if we proceed slowly we must be cautious and circumspect and not shirking and vacillating. We deserve discredit if we maltreat or molest others, if we slander and slur them, if we are arrogant and domineering, and so on. We recognize our obligation not to undertake courses of action that deserve such characterizations. When we refrain from actions which we ourselves would characterize so, we then and there exhibit what the nature of our obligations or commitments is as we see them. We need, therefore, merely to become completely aware of our appraisals and characterizations in order to discover what our commitments are.

It may be supposed that we can escape self-inculpations simply by ignoring them. But then we show, either to others or perhaps to ourselves at a later date, just as fully what we feel committed to or not committed to by just such actions and inactions.

The result, then, is that we must turn for information about our obligations to our habits of appraisal as these are exhibited in our evaluations. It will come, in general, as a surprise to persons to make such discoveries about themselves. The method of self-discovery was first practiced by Socrates, and it has scarcely been improved upon since. Before we set out in pursuit of new goals, or abandon old ones, or try to convince ourselves that we are cheerfully free of all such "moralistic" incumbrances, we do well to examine ourselves by some such method as that practiced by Socrates. Fully compatible with this and indeed in part identical with it is studying ourselves also from the standpoint of our discourse. If we are told that we need to revise our commitments, it is only ordinary wisdom that we learn first of all what we have been submitting ourselves to. We begin to understand this in surveying the huge resource of characterization set forth in Part Two.

4.2   ORDAINMENT (Cf. 11.4)

(a)	authorize	(b)	abrogate
	decree		annul
	enact		interdict
	establish		proscribe
	institute v.		repeal
	ordain		rescind
	promulgate		
	ratify		
	sanction		

The vocabulary of ordainment, drawn wholly from Latin, reflects the grandeur of Roman legal and political institutions. Most of the terms retain their ancient significance, and the vocabulary could be expanded from the same source. They have also a limited informal use, but so far as modern languages are concerned they have always been technical terms. They are probably the most "objective" we shall deal with, exhibiting virtually no trace of the emotional, moral, and intellectual processes that lie behind them. The hopes, fears, inclinations, appetites, sympathies and antipathies that are all in lively interaction in the progress toward the formulation of commitments and ends finally subside in unequivocal formulations of the law. Yet the ultimate foundation of the law can be nothing but these commitments.

But if law rests upon commitment, commitment is but a phantom unless it is expressed in action and in law. It is impossible for men to keep their commitments to themselves and yet think of them as relevant to conduct. Since commitments and obligations are virtually bound to touch even more on others than just on the self, and on strangers as well as kinsmen, it is not surprising that formality develops and evolves into law. The details of such development are, of course, scarcely even hinted at by a mere handful of legal terms such as we have here. We would have to go far afield into history, religion, poetry, folklore as well as law, and much else besides to give an adequate account of it.

What our experience of our past has taught us is that the holding of ends and values by the individual is scarcely significant, even as a mere hope, without a fabric of custom and law, however rude or imbued with superstition. In earlier societies it is not even "I" who properly exist apart from the group and who harbor my own hopes and values; only "we" are real. Holding to long-range aims (or any range beyond the absolutely immediate) is not, therefore, a prescribing of myself to myself, with a possible clash between myself and yourself, or themselves, but rather ourselves prescribing to ourselves. Individualism or individual rights in such "states of nature" are virtually nonexistent.

The ordainments we have under consideration are most likely to flourish under an advanced social order in which an equilibrium prevails between the social corpus and the individual. Society prescribes laws to itself in which the social conscience reflects more or less adequately the individual. There is sufficient threat of deviance to justify making the law but also a confidence that it will prevail. Such a society is content with the order it has set up, and it can absorb enormous shocks, as in war, without disintegration, since they do not really threaten this order. We have seen such an order in command in Europe from the end of the seventeenth to the end of the nineteenth century.

Such a society, however, has what one might call the safety of small numbers. When this is vastly exceeded in mass society the revolt and alienation of the individual is inevitable. Such ailments would not exist nor even be comprehensible to fully collective societies, ancient or contemporary. In order for there to be alienation of individuals there must first be individuals. Our way of thinking of moral conflicts typically in terms of individuals having values at odds with those of society is only our style of moral thought, appropriate to the way we see ourselves, and what we see in ourselves. There are strong disintegrative or centrifugal tendencies in such a society. The identification of value with what is absolutely individual and idiomatic may prove to lead to a sterility far more severe than that of a monolithic *Urgemeinschaft*.

If generalizations on history are somewhat safer than predictions of the future, we may claim at least to have learned that if the individual is significant he is so in virtue of a context that lends substance to his hopes and provides a system of significance for what he expresses. But the context is only the reflection of the commitments of its members.

4.3 HONORIFICS

(a) **ennoble**
glorify
solemnize

(b) **enshrine**
eulogize
pay homage to
honor
panegyrize, panegyric
venerate

(c) **celebrate**
commemorate
congratulate
greet

(d) **hail**
salute
welcome

(e) **dedicate**

(f) **anathematize**
censure

DEVOTIONARY ACTS (Cf. App. B 1.1)

(a) **beatify**
consecrate
hallow
sanctify

(b) **ceremony**
benediction

(c) **votive** a.

In our time there seems little patience or inclination for celebrations or ceremonies. We seem to see a fundamental cleavage between the act, value, or person being honored and the outward form the honor takes. We may feel that what is being honored truly deserves honor, but we cannot really accord much deep respect to the outer form the honoring takes.

At the opposite extreme from this attitude lies the celebration of the mass in the Roman Catholic Church. This is obviously no celebration in the degenerate sense the term has acquired, nor is it thought to be a "ceremony" or a "commemoration" of the Last Supper and other such events. It is thought to be itself an encounter with the value it celebrates. The idea of such a direct encounter has been reinforced by the doctrine of transsubstantiation: the substance celebrated is directly before the communicant, who cannot fail to be affected by the power said to repose in it, given that he is mentally and spiritually prepared for the encounter. I am not interested here in denying or affirming these claims. Such a rite is an elevation and glorification of a value such as was intended in all ancient religions. The value had to *be* present in order that there could be a proper honoring of it. There is, then, no longer an outer husk and an inner kernel.

This is the most potent, but certainly not the only, form that honoring a value can take. Rites which concern themselves with the same historic events but treat them in symbolic fashion may succeed equally well in glorifying the value in question in the communicant's mind. But they summon a different act, or an act with a different content, perhaps no less arduous than that of believing that the wafer is the body and wine is the blood. Here the communicant is asked to contemplate the original scene of the Supper and the Crucifixion in a certain manner and to derive therefrom the unique benefit imputed to it. With this form of the rite it is easy in time for the wafer and wine to become incidental symbols. The contemplation of the original event may, then, be detached from the symbols. Indeed, the communicant is advised to have this event always in his thoughts, so that every moment may possess a real or potential sacramental significance.

Scepticism about ceremonial and celebrative acts inevitably arises from the separation of the thought of the value from the present celebrative episode or spectacle. If attention is distracted to the sights, sounds and even aromas of the spectacle, and if yet the rite is thought to retain its intended power, the sceptic cannot but regard this as sheer superstition, as belief in magic. And if thought of the value appears even more vividly present without the spectacle, the latter cannot but appear wholly dispensable. The outcome of both *may*, however, be that the value vanishes from the mind, since, if there is a spectacle, it may be a distraction, or if there is none, there will be nothing even to remind the communicant of the value.

Everyone has observed the fate of the days that, in years past, have been set aside to honor events and persons. Scarcely even the name eventually remains where once there had been a physical display and earnest reminders of their significance. This is not a new phenomenon. The "Christian Year," as it was once called, celebrated or celebrates a saint every day of the year, most of them now virtually forgotten. With the passage of time the effectiveness of the spectacle is first discounted and the thought or value behind it is then rightly exalted as the inner essential. But since values themselves are first of all expressed in abstract words, the capacity of average minds for the contemplation of such significance is limited. Hence the divorce of concrete exemplification from the significance spells the end of contemplation, or at least its limitation.

The same may be said for the limited appeal of Ethical Culture, Humanism, Unitarianism and other similar movements. A large number of propositions enunciated by them deviate not at all from the classical Western religions, however deeply they may disagree with orthodoxy on other doctrinal and on social matters. But they refuse, perhaps out of grounds of "good taste," to take any steps to illuminate or inflame the values they honor, and so out of choice, they content themselves with enlisting the support of the few who can keep their thought on the value without the spectacle, rather than the many. In contrast to this one may recall that even Puritan Protestantism never neglected the power of imagery even if it broke up the images in the churches. American Puritanism may have appeared to the eye to be austere, but it relied on powerful imaginative reconstructions of scriptural history to help convey its message and its values. Any sermon of Jonathan Edwards will illustrate the point.

There is no reason whatever to believe that there could never again be mass participation in the celebration of values with vivid concrete and inflaming symbolism. This century has witnessed it in the rites and spectacles of totalitarian states. But no one can predict, even on the basis of vast experience of centuries past, what kinds of forms will possess such magnetism.

The personification of vices and virtues in ancient religion yielded to the Christian idea of the incarnation of the supreme values in an historic person. Both of these suggested effective ways of bringing their values before the mind. When we come now to the present scene we encounter the conviction that we do not need an apotheosis of values to do them honor: exemplification is sufficient. The present age is in a way reaching toward an effective symbolism for this. The form this takes may not be religious in the received sense at all. Values, in fact, now are in process of being brought out from under the sole guardianship of religion, for although religion certainly is likely to survive, it may continue to decline in effectiveness. The demise of the values man has labored so hard to discover or invent would be a calamity worse even than the decline of religion.

We may now consider somewhat more narrowly what enters into honorific acts or processes. Theologians are no doubt best qualified to say whether there is a single act that is most basic and fundamental in religion and if so what it is. We have ventured to say that it is a votive act, an act of surrender, submission, acknowledgment. This may be a submission or dedication to a being of some superpersonal sort, to an ideal, or virtue, or it can be an earnest resolve to emulate a person or being who embodies or incarnates this value (Cf. Appendix B).

The classical metaphysical scheme for this, which evolved in time although it was present from the beginnings of history, discriminated a character of the holy or the sacred, something set aside and apart from everything else, a quality such as could never be descried by the organs of the body nor, apparently, even by the highest rational powers. The potency of the holy was said also to be found in or could enter into certain human persons and places. These would then in turn be set aside and apart from all other things, persons, and places. Because of the power they derived from communion with the holy, they were necessary links in a sacred chain of being. With their aid one could hallow and sanctify mundane things, could consecrate persons to imbue them with sacred power, and indeed everything could be transfigured by a proper concourse with the holy. Even the fortunes of the dead could be affected. The development of the idea of God, signifying that the source of the holy is a transcendent person, illimitably enlarged the scope of interpreting the presence and absence of sacred quality. This now could be ascribed to a being who knows, wills, and controls all or some of man's world in palpable acts. With the aid of a person of this sort, values could be thought to issue as commands, demands, laws, exhortations, pleas, and wishes together with every other rational and emotive mode of thought. It is obviously easier to make a votive act intelligible if it is thought of as being made to a kind of person.

We may now draw a comparison between ancient religion and the acts designated in our honorific vocabulary, particularly secular acts. If we think of the award of a medal to a military hero, or the conferring of knighthood on a poet, can we say that this act is exhausted entirely in attitudes of approval, sympathic responses, and positive commendations? It may be difficult to suppose that there is more than this. But considering just the phenomenology of the situation we must not lose sight of the fact that there is a celebrative act here. One has not merely contented himself with his own reactions to the hero's deeds and the poet's verse, noting how one has felt, responded, and commended it. Nor do we think of the celebrative act as merely increasing the pleasures and satisfactions of the recipient. The reason we do not is that we believe we have genuinely found or encountered something that appears to have a power of its own, something which it is an honor to honor. This is how things holy or sacred seemed to ancient man. What he found, or thought he found, in all its idiomatic distinctness did not just deserve appreciation and approval but homage, veneration, and consecration.

We do not lose or divest ourselves of attitudes like these as easily as we may think. Any genuine celebrative or dedicatory act is the mark of encountering and "discovering a value" which appears to possess an objectivity independent of our commendations and of "our poor power to add or detract." If we do not have this sense of an encounter we cannot for long go through the motions of celebration.

I believe the entire vocabulary of 4.3 exhibits this sense of a genuine confrontation or encounter, including, of course, the simple and genuine complimentaries. We should notice also that all but one of these concepts is positive; all are ways of honoring a found value, and all inherently imply a certain formality and solemnity (the only exceptions, indicating a warmer and more personal air, are the Anglo-Saxon **greet, hail** and **welcome**). Only one important negative (**anathematize**) appears. The ostensible purpose of an anathema is, of course, the expulsion of a heretic (one thinks of Vanini and Spinoza). But it is not the act of a congregation that really feels in danger of collapse; rather, it is the occasion of a triumphant ceremonial reaffirmation of the faith. We must regard some acts of censure by legal bodies in the same light.

It is plain that the rest of the negative vocabulary already considered prior to 4.3 really does not belong here. One may look back at 2.22, Dyspathic Responses (**deplore, detest**); 2.4, Responsional Characterizations (**disdain, antipathy**); 3.13, Appraisive Outcomes (**disapprove, disfavor**); 3.222, Oblocution (**contemn, disparage**). Clearly an anathema is none of these, being highly formal, dignified, and objective, as these often are not.

A few further technical characteristics of the 4.3's may be observed. All of the terms, except possibly **glorify**, may be used to **describe** certain acts. Their specific differences are matters of lexicographical interest only. The term **glorify** is used ritually ("We glorify thy name") and in order to characterize but not, I think, to describe, an act. Other terms that can be used to make characterizations are **compliment, ennoble, eulogize** and **panegyrize**: these generally would not appear in the first person present. The terms most naturally used in the first person are **congratulate** and **salute**, and the Old English derivatives **hail, greet**, and **welcome**. All but these three go back to Latin or Greek, showing how much our rituals owe to the formality and grandeur of ancient civilization. The Greek terms are concerned with honoring the dead and condemning heretics. Of all the terms, I should say only **dedicate** could conceivably have what Austin calls a performative use.

4.4 APPRAISIVE OUTLOOK

activism	**moralism, moralist, moralize**
asceticism	**nihilism**
Christianity (many forms)	**optimism**
cynicism	**pacifism**
egoism	**pessimism**
hedonism	**puritanism**
humanitarianism	**quietism**
idealism	**radicalism**
individualism	**realism**
liberalism	**sentimentalism**
libertarianism	**stoicism**
meliorism	etc. etc.
misogyny	

We have tried to maintain a sequential, presuppositional order of development in the topics so far treated, while hoping not to succumb to the temptation to impose more rigor than the subject allows of. The place of the present vocabulary might be here or later. It is not obvious that it deserves to stand closer to moral judgment than to appraisal. There is also a question whether outlooks such as these determine our appetitions and responses or vice versa. And there are untold issues about the degree to which even what are on the surface highly intellectual orientations are really conditioned by physiological and anatomic processes and structures, and the whole train of causes deriving from personal psychic history. We are, therefore, in a situation where no matter how much we say in treating these topics, it will not be enough, or how little we say, it will still be too much. But we may recall that brevity is more often a virtue than a fault.

Even aside from its placement, this vocabulary presents rather a different aspect from all the other vocabularies under Part One. Here we have nothing to do with what we have ventured to call acts and processes, such as appraising, hoping, fearing, approving, and the rest. We again seem to be concerned with the characterization of valuations, or the trend or pattern of valuing, not altogether unlike Responsional Characterizations (2.4). To call someone a legalist, a defeatist, a moralizer, or a pessimist is already to characterize not only him but also the judgments, appraisals, and responses he has had toward persons and things. The terms thus serve as higher order appraisives.

It happens that most of the terms end in 'ism', though this is no qualification for appearing as an outlook. Not every such ism appears here, and there may be isms and *Weltanschauungen* that are unaccountably absent.

We repeat, then, that these outlooks may be conditioned by our responses or vice versa. What, then, are the outlooks themselves? Do they or do they not, in the end, analyze exhaustively into patterns of appraisal, response, and the rest all taken together? The question *what* these are begins with the appearance of Hegel's *Phenomenology of Mind* and is by no means exhausted today. We cannot presume here to answer the question whether the stoic and the sentimentalist judge matters differently because they are cognitively attending to different things or different aspects of the same thing, or because they have differing "ontological commitments" that are neither the foregoing nor merely differences of temperament but are metaphysical propositions incapable of verification, conditioning every turn of thought. We can only say what presumptions we are making in reference to these questions. This may be put as follows. The entire vocabulary of valuation as treated here is taken to be in itself neutral as to its use by anyone occupying one or more of these standpoints. It may or may not be possible in practice to occupy an appraisive stance independent of all of these, but whether it is or not it should be possible to decide what is *meant* in our judgments and whether the judgments are *just* and *fair* or not independently of the stance taken. There is not one justice for stoic and another for hedonist, but if we have reason to believe that a man is speaking as one or the other, this is a clue to what he is intending to say, what we must interpret his judgment to mean. But it is not relevant to the justice of the judgment any more than these or other categorial or ontological commitments are relevant to decisions of matters of fact (unless in fact, of course, they are themselves facts or generalizations about facts rather than the "categorial" generalizations they are put forward to be). In a word, we interpret them as clues to meaning, not as bunkers and pillboxes that house impregnable "perspectives."

Considering them in this light we can point to some significant differences and similarities among them. Some of the terms will be used most commonly to indicate negative characterizations, for example, **defeatism, egoism** or **egotism, legalism, nihilism, pacifism, pessimism, Puritanism, quietism, radicalism.** Of these, **defeatism, egotism,** and **legalism** would not be used to designate a perspective anyone would embrace. If anyone is declared a defeatist, in the appraiser's opinion he is first, conceding too much to the inevitability of defeat, or second, giving in too easily to a feeling of discouragement, rather than looking frankly at the facts. An egoist is, of course, something like a philosophical sophist or idealist and thus falls outside our consideration. An egotist suffers from an inapt appraisal of himself. A legalist is unduly impressed by what the law says. These "standpoints," then, can be explained with merely a level-headed attention to the facts and to a reasonable understanding of human feelings, and their frailties. All the others will often be employed as large-sized volleys to fire at various enemies, and are significant only if they are simply encapsulations of more precise, accurate and detailed appraisals. Each of these, however, can be a rallying point of defense. "Pacifist, pessimist, Puritan, radical – and proud of it!" Even **nihilism,** as also **anarchism,** can serve a positive and significant purpose. Consider Nietzsche. Some of the list serve as historical identifications of standpoints in metaphysics and ethics, such as **Christianity** (together with Christian philosophy and theology), and **Stoicism.** These will obviously be the most significant of our outlooks, since historically they made the greatest effort to offer a complete view of life, both a theory of value and a careful attention to whatever was needed to provide a metaphysical support of it. If we now also add some others such as **hedonism (Epicureanism),** we are dealing with a classic situation of seemingly irreconcilable outlooks. Some of our terms will be concerned mainly to recommend alternative patterns of conduct such as **activism, iconoclasm, quietism.** Some will suggest programs disagreeing in the degree of participation of individuals and groups in enterprises of various kinds, **asceticism, egotism, individualism**. The apparent alternatives, **optimism, meliorism** and **pessimism**, should stimulate us to some questioning. Either the two extremes merely exaggerate the prevalence of the quality they are interested in, or they are merely looking at instances of these and not at their contraries; and the remedy for each of these is obvious. Or they are tending to make things look better by buoying up the spirit, or the contrary by the contrary, in which case one may get nearer to just appraisal by simply abstaining from the stimulant or depressant that is recommended. Sometimes similar things need to be said of **defeatism, sentimentalism**, and **stoicism**, and probably **idealism** and **realism** too, in this their popular and unphilosophical sense.

This will give a suggestion as to what strategies we might pursue in more detail in order to deal with the apparent problem of the conflict of outlooks. But at this point it can be no more than a suggestion. I do not wish to imply that problems of immense difficulty may not be concealed here. We have not even begun to suggest the possibility of great differences in outlooks stemming from different backgrounds: of ethnic group, of culture (from national to regional and local differences), of historical tradition, of relation to nature (temperate and tropical zone habitancy), and above all of linguistic resource, as well as still others.

With the appearance of ideologies and other outlooks on the scene it is fully evident that we enter into or submit to commitments because we confront the serious and inescapable business of action, and not in order to indulge in moral or intellectual luxury. We must urge decisions and make decisions, act for and against. We feel offended at certain actions, we judge and condemn offenses in the name of our values, we forgive, expiate and rectify them, and we seek to justify the outcome. Since our very survival may hang on this train of responses, its course is not left to chance or the inspiration of the moment: durable institutions, particularly legal institutions, are developed. But before such institutions can come into being, moral institutions must already effectively, if often informally, exist. The outlines of the scheme of moral judgment and justification must therefore be considered next.

We shall conclude the ensuing section with a discussion of the concepts **right** and **just** although general concepts such as these rightly belong in Part Three with other commendations such as **good**. We do so because it is difficult to separate acts and procedures of moral judgment from the conceptual instruments with which these are carried out. We have separated the acts and procedures of response and appraisal (in previous sections of Part One) from the instruments of evaluation (in Parts Two and Three) only for reasons of exposition already adequately explained.

5.0 MORAL JUDGMENT

All the previous acts or procedures in Part One are involved in moral judgment, but it is principally the next preceding acts under enactment (4.0), that is, commitment, ordainment, and the celebration of values, that set the stage for it. Matters which are of the greatest moment to us are the subject of commitments pledging us to maintain a certain loyalty, whatever contrary attractions may arise. In judgment we seek to exact obedience of ourselves or others to just these commitments.

Appraisal, in a narrower sense of the term, and response are concerned mainly with the good, commitment and judgment with the right. But the good is the culmination of all the modes of valuation. The just and right have their end in the good; the good does not exist for the sake of the just.* We must be careful in drawing lines between the right and the good. Commendation of a person must often recur to the pattern or character of his moral judgments [cf. (G) under 15.6], and on the other hand, although what we judge is principally actions (the assignment of virtues is not judgment), our opinion of a man's character and virtues enters into judgment of his actions (Cf. 11.112).

We shall restrict the phrase 'moral judgment' to concern with the just and the right as these are defined and analyzed in 5.3. In general we avoid the expression, 'value judgment,' since this is too loose a designation and would obscure the difference, for example, between moral judgment and characterization. Of course, tradition can be invoked for the use of 'judgment' for any and every assertion so that one has judgments of fact as well as judgments of value.

Although this usage is avoided here, there is an important link between the two. The term 'judgment' should be reserved for the application of general rules to particular cases. There are at least two forms of this, moral and intellectual. A value judgment or, as here restricted, a moral judgment is the act of referring a particular case, such as an action or decision, to a moral rule, prescript, or commitment. The term 'judgment' unqualified, designates an act of the intellect applying general scientific laws or truths to specific cases. The appraisal of intellectual judgment is taken up in 6.2; the subject there is the person judging and his use of his judgmental powers.

* For a contrary view on this celebrated question one may consider Sir W. D. Ross's *The Right and the Good.*

Most of what concerns the appraisal of moral judgment is taken up in the present section, 5.0.

For our purposes it is of far more moment to keep appraisal, and in particular, characterization distinct from moral judgment than it is to distinguish the two areas of judgment. In judgment one has a standard to conform to and the standard dictates the use of the vocabulary in our moral involvements 5.2, and acts of justification, 5.3 (the ultimate source of the standards is the commitments already studied, 4.0). In characterization, on the other hand, the characterism or appraisive concept is in a fairly evident way its own standard. When we characterize we have no supreme commitments or standards that may be appealed to: characterization produces its own *originals*. Here we "suit ourselves," we do not judge. Characterization points ultimately toward virtues and vices, toward the commendation or discommendation of subjects and indeed provides the "premises" on which such commendation rests.

Taking man as our subject, we find that characterization and moral judgment preserve their identity and difference except to some extent as we enter the social areas of characterization (11.0 to 13.0). Here we have man as a subject of both characterization and judgment, that is, some appraisals will prove to be governed by prescripts or commitments (e.g. **breaking faith** and **theft**). But in all cases characterization is more fundamental, for our prescripts have ultimately grown out of characterization, and not the reverse.

Moral judgment, therefore, has a limited scope. This tends to vary over periods of time. What has appeared to deserve stringent moral judgment at one time or place is exempted at another. What was sexually immoral at one time may eventually become a matter of tolerance or indifference. Once the doctrine *cuius regio eius religio* prevailed; a later age regards restriction of thought or expression as virtually immoral. But these variations do not affect the basic reality of moral judgment.

We shall now proceed to examine the vocabulary of moral involvement and of the processes of judgment and justification that arise out of it.

5.2 MORAL INVOLVEMENTS	5.1 MORAL AFFECTS
5.21 JUDGMENTAL PROCESSES	
REMONSTRANCE	
complain, complaint	
grievance	
protest	
remonstrate	

ACCUSATION

    accuse
    blame
    censure
    charge with an offense
    hold culpable
    denounce
    impugn
    inculpate
    indict
    tax with

CORRECTION

    admonish
    advise
    chide
    correct
    rebuke
    reprehend
    reprimand
    reproach
    reprove
    scold
    upbraid
    warn

INTERCESSION

    intercede
    supplicate

INCULPATION

    make [apology, apologize
    confess
    acknowledge [guilt
    recant
    repent
    self-reproach

feel [indignant at
feel [outrage
rankle
resent
(loathe, loathsome) (14.01)
    (15.2)

feel [anguish over
be [ashamed of
compunction
feel [contrite over or about
feel [guilt, guilty
be [penitent about or over
qualm, qualms of
regret
remorse
feel [shame
twinge of (e.g. remorse)

EXCULPATION

absolve
condone
exculpate
excuse
extenuate
forgive
gloss, (-over)
indulgent
mitigate
palliate
plead (also used elsewhere in 5.21)
self-righteous (discred.)
   (=self-exculpation)

5.22   MORAL OUTCOMES AND
          SEQUELS

OUTCOMES

DESERT

deserve (16.0)
merit v.
warrant

DECISION

decide
doom

REPROBATION

condemn
convict v.
reprobate v.

REMISSION

acquit   **bewail**
clemency   **feel [grief at**
exonerate   **lament**
forgive   **have [mercy**
leniency   **pity**
pardon   **feel [sorry for**
remit
reprieve

venial, veniality
vindicate

SEQUELS: PERFORMANCE OF DUTY
RETURN

chastise
penalize
reward v. & n.
give short [shrift

RETRIBUTION

avenge, vengeance   **gloat over**
lex talionis   **vindictive**
inflict [punishment   **vengeful**
recriminate
requite
retribution
revenge

RECTIFICATION

make [amends
atone, atonement
expiate
compensate
rectify
restore
restitution

(A) *Moral Involvement and its Context.* Moral judgment is essentially concerned with the pathology of conduct, with misconduct. Assuming that there are agreed upon or at least operative loyalties or commitments, we may expect to find conduct that ignores, contravenes, or defies these loyalties. One cannot say which "comes first," loyalties or the system of judgment: judging makes sense only if there are commitments; commitments seriously held must be enforced or at least in force.

The vocabulary of 5.2 presents those acts which show our serious moral involvement with other persons. Assume there are recognized commitments. When we find someone to have contravened them, we may expect some or all of the moral involvements to be set in motion. We may *remonstrate* with the apparent offender or present an *accusation*. We may then seek to *correct* the offender in one of several degrees of seriousness, *intercede* for him, hear him *acknowledge* his offense or seek to *excuse* or deny it. With or without formal institutions, *judgment* may be passed, the action *condemned* and a suitable *outcome* decided upon. Possibly *punishment* is inflicted. There may be *retribution*, or even *reward* under certain conditions. Some of these involvements or procedures are also formalized in courts of law, but they are by no means confined to formal legal institutions. All of these steps may be accompanied by unique appropriate turns of feelings, the moral affects (5.1). These must not be confused with involvement or judgment.

The family of processes of involvement forms the general context of moral judgment. More narrowly, judgment is the *outcome* or doom of the person involved; it is the justice that is meted out *de facto*. There is also a quite different process that runs concurrently with the foregoing and may continue subsequently: the process of *justifying* the doom that is decided upon. It addresses itself to the question whether the doom is just and whether actions that were anywhere involved in this or brought into question are to be judged right or wrong. This involves a relationship between the judgment and original commitments. (This is considered at some length in 5.3.)

There is no issue of moral judgment that arises over "good men" or even "bad men," as such. There must be an offended loyalty, covenant or commitment, or the danger or accusation or question or temptation of offense. *Good* is not the outcome of a judgment but of a process of appraisal, through characterization and commendation, something very different from judgment. Of course, the "good man" is characterized in the older moral idiom of the Bible as up*right*, *just*, or *right*eous. These terms actually refer to character; the person is being represented as having certain critical virtues. (This is set forth in detail at the end of 14.0.)

This may suffice to present in outline what is meant by the involvements here. We may now observe how judgment fits into the context of appraisals and the responses of feeling that have already occupied our attention in Part One. We shall consider the relation between moral judgment and its affects in (B) below.

The cognitive grasp of a situation involving persons as subjects may occasion a responsive reaction. Such a response, for example annoyance, is concealable and not inherently manifested in behavior, but it may readily lead to appraisal and characterization of the subject and in this instance to discommendation. In the appraisal, the appraiser gives himself a reason for the discommendation, and not only himself: he expects others, even the offender, to pay heed. The appraisal is a necessity here; a mere report of annoyance would not be enough, for it might leave the offender entirely indifferent. A negative characterization in an idiom the offender understands reaches through to him to undertake a valuation of his own. Such a move can count on striking home, because the subject is characterized in a way in which he will refuse to characterize himself, at least in the present. (A favored counertechnique in such an exchange is to dismiss the appraisal as merely "emotive;" it is of course certainly not *inherently* emotive.) It is possible, of course, that the offender may come to agree with the appraisal and make amends. If he does not and the appraiser thinks the matter serious, he may go on to make an accusation which involves commitments which he believes the alleged offender to be bound to observe and to have offended. If he does, we open up the possibility of a whole series of moral involvements such as we have already surveyed.

(B) *Moral Affects and Involvements.* Judgments must be kept distinct not only from response and appraisal but also from the moral affects which are much more close at hand. Moral affects have a family resemblance to the responses, but they differ from these for the same reason that judgment differs from appraisal: their special character derives from the subject's concern about commitments. Confining ourselves to the negative, we may say that the moral affects are the fever that goes with any injury to our values. We feel, let us say, outrage, an affect, and enter into a moral involvement through accusation; we feel remorse and acknowledge our guilt; we feel pity and forgive; and so on.

We may observe that several modes of moral involvement seem to have no corresponding affects *in this vocabulary.* Names of affects do not come readily to mind corresponding to exculpation, decision, correction, and the assignment of rewards and penalties, although informal or improvised resources of language may always be drawn upon. It is unnecessary to look for a close correspondence between the affects and the involvements. Indignation, outrage or resentment may well be felt not only when we accuse but also when we remonstrate, accuse, correct, or intercede; there seem to be no "ready made" remonstrative, corrective, or intercessive affects. Grief and pity may be felt not only with remission but with exculpation: it may depend upon the degree of guilt. It is not the correlation of particular affects with the involvements that raises questions so much as the paucity of the moral affects themselves, or rather of designations for them.

The affects stand toward moral involvements as the responses (2.0) stand toward appraisals (3.0). We have said that appraisal and response must not be identified, and that in fact, they are not inferrable from one another. I think we are less likely to identify the processes of judgment with their affects because judgment by its nature, although it may be prompted or swayed by affects, such as pity or mercy, is a matter that everyone recognizes ought in principle to proceed with an eye only toward fact and principle, toward commitment and ordainment. It is in short a solemn matter to accuse, reprehend, repent, intercede, excuse, condemn, or pardon, far too serious in possible outcomes and sequels to be left for the affects to decide. There may be conflicts of commitments between doing justice and showing mercy, but justice properly considered should include provision for degrees and occasions of mercy within itself.

All of the involvements may be adverbially qualified by affective processes, expressed in appropriate language, but it is not difficult to separate one from the other. We may, therefore, say that the judgments inherent in moral involvements in general proceed, and are intended to proceed, in independence of the affects. For the affects, on the other hand, we may with fair certainty infer that corresponding involvements are either present or contemplated.

This is the context in which the moral affects inhere. They are evidently much more complex modes of being affected than are the sympathic and dyspathic responses where only sensibilities and feelings are involved. Take, for example, the *inculpative affects*, the most poignant of all moral feelings, such as anguish, shame, guilt, penitence, regret, or remorse. Such feelings are something other than mere dismay or vexation at myself. In regret I see myself in the larger framework of my commitments. I contemplate my past behavior, live it over, and would do it over, if I but could. I condemn it, by my awareness of how far it is inconsistent with what I think is proper to me. I tell myself that certain behavior is called for by virtue of my being…, and I supply the blank with what I think myself to be. In such experiences I seem to see what I am, what my commitments are, and how I have offended them.

This is even more evident when we consider the *accusative affects*, indignation, outrage, resentment. The reader will recall the place Plato accords these in one of the three distinct faculties of the soul, the faculty of spirit. The spirited man is indignant at wrong; it does not merely displease or disgust him, it offends him. He marshals his energies of intellect and every other power to strike it down. In indignation the subject or target is generally someone other than ourselves; more than feelings have been violated; it is something to which not only we are committed, but also the subject. Therefore, we rise to the defense of it.

Similarly in the *remissive affects* we feel not only dismay or some vague "unhappiness" at someone's misfortune. A subject lays claim to our pity because we recognize in him a value to which we also are committed, even though it may be dimmed by various faults. We may say his was a venial sin, one which could earn remission, pardon, leniency.

We must then observe important differences between mere dyspathic responses and moral affects. Responses such as disgust, dislike, and dismay may arise without commitments being threatened or violated or even brought to mind: here I am only preoccupied with what is present before me and with the painful and negative feelings I am experiencing. I am not concerned about long-range interests and responsibilities stretching from the past into the future.

Some of the terms we have placed under the moral affects differ from the foregoing. **Vindictive** (and perhaps some others) is not a predicate one will apply to himself in the present. It is a higher order valuation; one person's indignation at another is being characterized as an aggression. It has an evil reputation as a singularly un-Christian vice. Yet it too can show a kind of concern about value, for he who is vindictive may be not only dyspathic or aggressive towards others but unwilling to tolerate the thought that enemies of his *values* are at large. Similarly **rankle** and **gloat over** are characterizations of responses as much as they are names of affects. These terms are analogous in basic respects to the Responsional Characterizations of 2.4 and 8.3.

Which are "prior" or more fundamental, the affects or the processes of judgment and moral involvement? It is possible though perhaps unlikely that we might feel anguish, indignation, or pity even though we might not be able to formulate verbal expressions (5.2) of repentance, censure, or pleas for forgiveness. It is certainly possible that we might feel anguish, indignation, or pity even without any command of just these terms (5.1) for them. In this the affects resemble feelings and responses and differ from the appraisals considered in Part Two, which can be made only because appraisive language is available to us.

What of the reverse possibility? May the involvements and all the processes of judgment proceed without the affects? To this we must also assent. Certainly the involvements are not merely verbal expressions for the moral affects. Moreover, and more importantly, accusation, blame, censure, indictment and even denunciation can be expressed by persons who are in no sense *feeling* indignation, outrage, or resentment at the same time. One can confess, recant or repent without feeling anguish, shame, contrition, or remorse. The independence applies in both directions. One can work wholly on the level of emotions, seeking out of pity or grief to evoke in other persons the same emotion in order thereby to gain exoneration or pardon or excuse for oneself or other persons. Or one can argue the justness of exoneration, pardon, and excuse, regardless of feelings.

The primacy of the affects would be particularly affirmed by sentimentalists or by anyone who would go so far as to say that all guilt deserves mercy. But certainly if there is any point to our commitments in the first place it is absurd to abrogate them at the moment we encounter instances to which they apply. Mercy (the act, not the affect) should be argued like any other involvement. The granting of clemency should be countenanced only when it enhances justice or makes it even more effective. The involvements must be able to proceed of their own momentum.

Despite all this, the fact is that the processes of involvement would not even be set in motion if it were not for the affects. It is conceivably the same with the aesthetic affects and aesthetic judgments, and other respondings and their corresponding appraisals. The fact that there are moral affects is a material or causal condition for their being judgmental processes. If these affects were to disappear from man's thought, so probably would all thought of right and justice. We must be cautious in interpreting this primacy of the affects since it applies only in a general sense. That is, no particular judgments are necessarily conditioned by any of the affects. Legal history is full of instances where judgment has proceeded in an impersonal and heartless manner: laws have often remained in effect even when they no longer respond to any human sentiment or feeling of need such as may have prompted their initial enactment.

Material conditioning of the judgmental process by the affects is a constant source of confusion between the two. There are those who take an accusation as founded from the mere fact that they are so deeply offended or outraged, just as there are those who take depth of enthusiasm for an art to be a certain evidence for talent in it. But there is no other single fixture that defines a civilized society better than the capacity for a total segregation of affects from judgments. All that depth of indignation indicates *at most* is that there *may* be ground to make an accusation.

It is interesting to note once again the far higher proportion of terms here drawn from Latin-French sources than from Old English, particularly on the side of the judgmental processes. But those that are drawn from the latter source are exceptionally powerful, e.g., **chide, scold**, and **doom,** and they also seem less easy to use in the "objective" manner that characterizes the Latin and French derivatives. The preponderance of the latter befits a vocabulary that at the outset was largely at the service of courts of law. Our interest in it is, of course, far wider than this, since all the terms have an informal use before they serve the technical uses of jurisprudence. Moral deliberation and judgment may eventually lead to decisions about what was right and just in accordance with the methods outlined in 5.3. What we call the outcome of the judging process is expressed first of all in judgment which states what the subject deserves, merits, or warrants in accordance with the conventions of bringing-to-justice and seeking-justice, and with commitments as interpreted and applied in a present case. This is usually expressed in the vocabulary of decision in 5.22 ranging from reprobation to remission. In some instances outcome and sequel will be virtually identical, for example, where a reprimand or censure is the doom handed down. But in most cases the sequel is a more concrete and literal act of penalizing, avenging, restoring, and so on. It is in the area of the sequel (whether identical with outcome or not) that the person will be said to have done his *duty*. I believe this notion should be used only when and where one may speak appropriately of thoughts, acts, and responses such as are detailed in 5.1 and 5.2; that is, where someone has been morally involved in a situation in the manner of accusing, correcting, interceding, and so on. Simply to have performed some action or other without such involvement is to have done what is more or less irrelevant to duty. We turn next to the more precise meaning that may be attached to the language of judging.

5.3   JUSTIFICATION

5.31   JUSTIFICATORY PROCESS

adjudicate
adjust
judge v.
justify
predicament

5.32   APPRAISIVES OF JUSTIFICATORY PROCESS

judicious, in-
just, unjust
justice, in-
justiciable
partial, im-
right, wrong (14.01, 15.6)
rightful

The principal notions of the present section are the **right** and the **just**. For the uses of these we may be referred to the OED, as also for the uses of the terms akin to them, such as **righteous, rectify, justice, justify**, and so on. What is needed, however, is not definition but an interpretation of certain facts about language and the role these concepts play in valuation.

Of the two terms, the **right** is by far the older in use among English-speaking peoples, including the speakers of Middle English and Old English. The whole vocabulary of the just (we may call it the J-vocabulary or simply J) **jural, juridical, jurisdiction, jurisprudence, jury** and **justice** are contributions of Middle English, and apparently not very early Middle English. The right (the R-vocabulary, or R), on the other hand, has scarcely changed at all since it was spelled *riht* or *reht* in Old English. It evidently goes back to the very dawn of the northern languages being parallel in origin to Latin *rectus*.

At the same time, J, of course, is equally ancient in Latin. Many of the details of the etymology of J and R are of no particular significance for our purposes and may be left to philology, history, and jurisprudence.

The terms of J and R are, to begin with, entirely distinct from **law, legal,** the Latin *lex.* **Lex** (L) is specific while **jus** is generic, but more important, **lex** must, in the end, rest on what is right or just. Therefore, we may set the whole L family aside: the law itself cannot make anything right or wrong, just or unjust.

J apparently has sources or cognates in two verbs which are of great significance to us, *jubeo, jussi, justum,* and *juro, juravi, juratum;* the first means to order or command, the second, to swear, to take an oath, and even to conspire. These two amount to the *imposition* of an obligation on others, if based upon something other than force, and the *assumption* of an obligation by oneself. The sources of all acts under J may be traced back to obligations and responsibilities thus taken or imposed. The force of the imposition is, of course, nil (except under duress) if it is not correspondingly assumed by the recipient of the command. The basic act, therefore, is the assumption of an obligation: J is built principally around *juro.* Such ideas appear to have changed but little through many centuries. The durable structure of the Roman legal heritage has contributed most to this, but Saxon legal institutions have proved equally durable.

I will now state my principal thesis regarding R and J and then show its consequences and significance for the theory of value. The thesis (T) is this:

> **Right** and **just** are concepts without essential content serving a
> purely formal and adverbial purpose in assessing the derivation
> of present decisions from supervenient obligations.*

An examination of the facts of usage and of practical affairs will, I think, clarify and confirm T.**

Of the two families, R is in my opinion the more basic. First of all it is older in English and even more deeply embedded in thought and language than J. But a weightier consideration is that the right may serve as a ground to which we may wish to appeal even beyond the just. Notions of the just may vary in time and place partly because J must always be in some degree

---

* Cf. below 15.6, particularly (G).

** Without intending an appeal merely to authority, the following definitions from the Introduction, Section IV of Kant's *Metaphysische Anfangsgründe der Rechtslehre* may yet be found to present an important precedent for views in this section: "A deed is right or wrong (*rectum aut minus rectum*) insofar as it is in accord with or contrary to duty (*factum licitum aut illicitum*); such duty may be of any kind on content or origin." "Duty is any action to which someone is committed (obliged, *verbunden*)." "That which is right according to external laws is just (*justum*), and what is not is unjust (*injustum*)."

associated with L. Beyond these, only R serves as an appeal. That is, its inherent purpose is to lead us back directly to our commitments – where alone conflicts can be resolved, if at all. I shall, therefore, confine attention for the present to R rather than J.

When we examine the R terms in their various forms, as substantive, adjective, adverb, and even verb, we find that there is no suggestion of anything but a formal sense of them until at least the seventeenth century. *Right*, according to NED, signifies safe, advantageous, appropriate, desirable and even something or some principle of which one approves. The term may serve the following purposes. As a *substantive*, R may first appear as "the standard of permitted action," but no indication of what the standard permits or forbids is given; it may also be what is "consonant with equity or the light of nature." Equity, however, does not terminate the search for further specification; it may again be used to designate conformity with fact; or it may be used to indicate "justifiable claim on moral or legal grounds." As an *adjective* R may signify "being put into proper condition or relation or order," or being "disposed to do what is just or good," or "agreeing with a standard or principle," or "fitting, proper, appropriate," and the like, or "normal, sound, and whole," or "correct in opinion, judgment and procedure." The *adverbial* form is the most instructive of all as will immediately appear.

We cannot fail to be struck by the formalism of R that emerges from all these definitions. There is no reason to believe that the definitions are in error or lack specificity. If the concept of right is completely formal in nature, we must next find out what formal purpose it serves. The result, I suggest, is this. When we use the concept, we are presuming for purposes of present application some principle, P, of far-reaching consequence in a *commitment* we are bound by, a *prescript* we accept, an *imperative* we agree to obey, a *creed* we have pronounced, a *resolve* we have taken, an *obligation* we see as suitable to ourselves as certain kinds of beings. The use of R is innocent of any questioning of the foundations of such principles or imperatives. The purpose of declaring anything right is to say that its derivation from P has been or can be made in a direct, correct, and not in any deviant or evasive manner. The proper route has been taken and every stage of the journey from the present maxim or decision to the supervenient principle has been traversed in due course and order. The line, therefore, is right, *rectus*, direct, correct. All this is to say that R has served an *adverbial* purpose, saying *how* the stages of connection have been traversed. (I am not, of course, "reducing" *right* to *rightly*, or literally talking in terms of a part of speech.) In general, then, when someone declares an act, maxim, or decision D to be right, he is not making a material assertion about D. He is saying that D is or has been related to a supervenient principle P, and that D is consistent with, or possibly an instance of P, or in any event that the derivation of D from the P that is presupposed is direct and logically correct.

We are thus interpreting the processes of courts of law as a kind of formal model for judgment in general, seeing that their purpose is to insure that obstacles to justice shall be overcome and some semblance of an ideal reached. We have, however, no need to investigate details of the procedure of courts. The whole process involves just two essentials of interest to us, which may be called the *dicastic* and *defensive*.

The dicastic function in judgment is to reach a result, outcome or doom on the matter at hand: the person's behavior may be declared incompatible with some fundamental obligation or commitment that is held to be in force. His action is declared wrong, not right: it is declared to have violated a commitment.

The defensive function is involved in the foregoing, yet distinct. Here an assessment which we call justification is undertaken, the purpose of which is to prove that the doom *is* proper and correct.

The dicastic aspect, as the term implies, is the judgment of a person, that he is guilty of a wrong. This aspect falls to R.

The defensive aspect is the defense of whoever judges, that he has been just. This falls to J.

Thus, the more fundamental character of R as compared with J derives from the fact that J is a kind of second order appraisive, but of a much more complex sort than those we have encountered before. J, however, is by no means "incidental" to R. We can say, "There is nothing right or wrong, but *judging* makes it so," in the sense that that is right which can be justified: the right is the justifiable.

The two processes, the dicastic and the defensive, are concurrent in any civilized judging situation for this merely means that in arriving at a pronouncement on R the judge has been circumspect and careful to examine his own posture and procedure in arriving at it. (The two, however, can scarcely be confused, for one takes the "accused" as subject, the other takes the "judge.") If we think of Anglo-Saxon courts of law, we remember that it is the function of a judge to keep J constantly in mind, for he is the president of the court and responsible for the conduct of its proceedings. In all courts, with their vast funds of tradition and experience of written and unwritten laws, of safeguards to insure relevance, the whole process of derivation has been, or at least has appeared to be, formalized. It is never, however, formalized to the extent that arguments are converted to symbolistic form and tested by rigorous logical methods. Informal procedures serve well enough – there is no reason to be more rigorous than necessary. It is the "unwritten laws," the "cases in equity," the ultimate and inevadable concern with human values that summon the abilities of not just legal and legalistic minds, but minds sensitive in a moral direction. Decisions, judgments must be reached, but in civilized communities they must also be justified. That is, one must show that the way from the judgment to basic values is direct, unbroken, and not evasive. **Rectify** in 5.22 goes even beyond **justify** in that it involves an *action* that is taken in order to bring about an accord between a principle or obligation and a present situation. In our scheme it should take the form of a *sequel* to the judicial process in which one may endeavor to right a wrong, to alter an existing situation in order to bring it into accordance with principle.

We should be careful not to allow our symbols J and R to signify more than the two distinct processes we have described nor to identify these too closely with the J and R vocabularies. The vocabulary for justificatory process (5.31) is in English drawn almost wholly from J which is more "formal" or technical then R. In German on the other hand, the act of judging is *richten*, thus making specific the idea of proceeding in a *right manner*.

We can now see how much hangs on the commitments we sought to isolate earlier – literally everything. It is assumed that every one who is addressed shares and possesses these commitments, even though he may not himself be able to excogitate exactly what they are. It is assumed also that although this value, that is the subject of the obligation or commitment, may be subject to lapses, infractions, deviations, defiances, and endless false applications and derivations, it maintains its being-in-force. J and R, however, say nothing about whether for all mankind there is only one set of P's or values to which all acts, maxims, and decisions must be reconciled. They merely affirm that the derivation has been rightly made from a principle that is here and now presupposed. What is needed is a better understanding of what our commitments are and to this the study of evaluative language can make a contribution.

CONCLUSION OF PART ONE

We have now surveyed the entire range of the acts of valuation for which common language supplies specific designations. We have used the term valuation, for want of a better, for all of the ways in which we come to accept or to reject what we find in our environment ranging from those that lie near instinct at one end to those that may be thought to be virtually sacred at the other. We may offer a brief review of these at this point.

Standing apart from all other acts or states is the enjoyment and possession of value. This may cover anything from enjoyment of food to mystic vision. If we were unable to have, to lay claim to values in this way, we could not even begin to think of man as a civilized being, as anything other than another organism. What now is contained in, what lies behind our enjoyments and revulsions, into what acts and facts do they articulate themselves?

There are essentially two culminations in the realization and the coming into posession of values. The first of these is what we have called appraisal. The second is moral judgment. Each of these arises out of, or since this is open to misunderstanding, let us say emerges in, a context of animal processes that we know commonly as feelings. These are, on the one hand, the appetitions and sympathies, or their contraries, that lead ultimately to appraising, and on the other, the moral affects such as indignation, regret, or pity which lead to moral involvement and judgment.

It is the human capacity not only to respond dyspathically but with a sense of offense that is basic to judgment. And with offense goes defense: a desire to hold and preserve something intact. This is the source of commitment, of dedication to values. Some things are to be held to at all costs, some acts may not be done, ever. With the projection of a sacred dimension of the environment and the idea of transcendent but personal beings, a rationalization (here in no invidious sense) of all that has gone before is at once possible. What is rejected is forbidden by someone, something else is sanctified and beatified, and a regimen is imposed on life from beginning to end, and perhaps even beyond the end.

The regime thus instituted, with its elaborate system of moral and civil law may be purged from time to time of outworn or inessential formalizations and rationalizations, but it may also retain them far longer than they are needed. The system of moral judgment is in our time in a condition of reexamination. The question of its continuance, however, needs scarcely to be raised. Just as the processes of appraisal arise out of the context of responsive feeling and are bound to continue so long as the feelings persist, doubtless forever, so the processes of judgment arise because there is a body of complex moral affects which we seem unable to allay, assuage, extirpate, exorcise, or give satisfactory solutions to except by the elaborate processes of moral decision and justification. Could one exorcise them by other means? Undoubtedly, pharmacology may only be in its infancy! But it remains to be seen whether guilt and compassion are so easily dealt with.

What is immediately of more interest to us is the question whether men in every other culture really share the pattern of our responses and appraisals, of our affects and judgments, and thus also share our particular need for cures and solutions. The present study hopes to help diminish dogmatism on that subject.

PART TWO

THE CHARACTERIZATION OF MAN

INTRODUCTION

(A) *Explanation of Terms*. After lengthy consideration of the acts of valuing, we may turn now to the actual resources for these acts in our language. Part Two comprises the heart of our appraisive vocabulary. If we ask for the judgment, appraisal, or evaluation of something we do not simply want an ultimate *Good!* or *Wrong!* any more than the real lover of sport wants to know only the final score of the game or match. It is, therefore, the real working vocabulary of valuing that we now undertake to explore.

What we are valuing or evaluating in man is what man is and what he does. Man exerts himself in various ways and in various directions, and these exertions, enterprises, undertakings may be classified in any number of ways. I think the present classification (from 6.0 through 13.0) can claim a certain authority because it has begun from the actual data of appraisal, the vocabulary, and worked up to larger classifications, rather than allowed an *a priori* classification to determine the placement. This, to be sure, is a matter of degree, since in either event the categories of classification have to be invented or appropriated: the data do not bear marks showing what the classifications are under which they are to be classified. A great deal, however, depends on the direction in which one works, either (from above) developing categories and arranging the data to fit them, or (from below) observing the data carefully to excogitate categories to order them. Our emphasis steadfastly has been the latter: better to have a profusion of categories to accommodate the differences in the data than a neat and logical scheme with innumerable forced marriages and identifications.

We now turn aside almost altogether from questions about the nature of evaluation and judgment in order to explore a vast area which provides rather the reasons for, the "premises" on which evaluations and judgments are based. The statements which constitute these premises are *characterizations*. Our immediate task is to introduce this notion and to explain it in a general manner, with the understanding that the study of the immense vocabulary of characterization extending virtually to the end of Part Two will itself afford the best clarification of the term.

The term 'character' has had a varied history and has always had an important moral significance. To the character of a person have been attributed the ultimate springs of his action. It has appeared a stable and unifying centre, the very essence of the *self*. Extending out from this centre, the locale of the person's virtues and vices, are his behavior and certain of his relations to the world around him. Even at the present time, an important part of European psychology turns around the idea of character. What American psychologists term personality seems, from that standpoint, simply the outer form of an inner entity designated as character. For the present, we shall not be concerned about the errors or shortcomings of either European characterology or American psychology of personality. We merely observe that we are now in the midst of the area that is the subject matter of such studies.

We notice first that the term 'character' has come into the language by the route of metaphor. The Greek term χᾶρακτήρ stood for an instrument for marking or graving, and for an impressed mark, as on a seal or coin. In modern languages it then came to signify a feature or trait and then the unique mental, but especially moral, constitution of the individual person. The vaguely implied idea of an agent who produces this unique stamp or pattern has fallen away of course except possibly where the verb form 'to characterize' is used.

Besides 'character' there are also cognate terms that need to be discussed: 'characteristic,' 'characterize,' 'characterization,' and 'characterism.' A characteristic is distinctive mark or distinguishing peculiarity; it is like the *differentia* in the Aristotelian logic and metaphysics, that which is unique either to a class of things or to an individual. What is characteristic of man among the class of animals? His rationality, it is said. What is characteristic of Phipps among men? Either some single trait he alone has or the constellation of many distinguishing marks, mental, moral, and physical. Other persons might separately have these marks, but such is the bounty of nature, no other individual is likely to have in fact this particular constellation of them.

Any property a thing has *can* also be shared by other things, that is, being of a certain color, size, form, etc. Obviously, however, not everything has a *given* property like, let us say, being red all over, or being a rhomboid. We are therefore able to find what we are looking for by concentrating on properties that some things have and other things lack. In practice we have no need to take note of what *may* be the fact, namely that every intrinsic property and every constellation of such properties, as against relational properties, may be duplicated and multiplicated in other individuals. The *fact* is we live in a world where there are innumerable uniquely different but also resembling things. Our language is built around this fact, reflecting the class resemblances and differences of things. What we find then is that while the particular properties of things are multiplicated and multiplicable, the constellation of them in particular things in fact is not. This is fortunate. The resemblances enable us to gather things together into kinds and classes, ignoring the differences. The unique constellations enable us to select a particular object for some special purpose, either because it has a given property that is rare or is in fact possessed only by this thing, or because it has an unusual or unique combination of, in principle, multiplicable properties. We can speak of what is characteristic of Arabs, operatic tenors, and suspension bridges, or of what is characteristic of Colonel Nasser, Enrico Caruso, and the Golden Gate Bridge. Of course, in these cases the characteristics are not the same.

Here we must be even more careful to distinguish the term 'characteristic' in such situations, where it simply means a property, from 'being characteristic of'. Colonel Nasser, for example, had the characteristic of being an Arab, but since there are some millions of Arabs it was not characteristic of him. But the vertically inverse ogive arches of the tower of Wells Cathedral, forming a unique hour-glass figure, are characteristic of that church.

It is important to emphasize this point since it may be tempting to say that the characterisms we are going to explore are characteristic of their subjects. But we must avoid this. For anything to *be characteristic* of something, it must first of all *be a characteristic* of it. But being pigheaded is not a characteristic or property at all.

We must also be careful in the use of 'characterize'. As already observed, because of what seems an odd grammatical convention, we do not cite characteristics, such as being an Arab, when we characterize someone. We do not characterize Colonel Nasser as an Arab; he *is* an Arab. We could, however, characterize him as obstinate or perhaps as resolute, depending upon our politics.

We come then to the result that characterizing has nothing very much to do with characteristics. What it does have to do with is talking about subjects in such terms as **lazy, obstinate,** or **credulous.** These we call characterisms and we avoid almost wholly the term 'characteristic' in talking about them in what follows so as not to be led off toward properties or descripts.

One of the terms most significant for value theory in this family of terms is still another, namely 'character'. First, and of least importance, is the use of the term as a kind synonym of 'characteristic'. Here it will simply mean a property, or even more commonly, a collection or constellation of properties that are unique to an individual or a class. Of far greater significance, of course, is the use of the term to speak of what appears to be the inmost core of personality, especially, if not exclusively, of human persons. In the end appraisal depends heavily on this notion. It is a fixture of everyday thought and of many parts of moral discourse, but it has fallen afoul of the objections of psychologists and so lies in a kind of academic or subacademic limbo.

We shall here bypass explicit study of the idea of character, which in any event belongs almost wholly to ethics. We shall, however, consider the vocabularies for virtue and vice at the end of Part Two; in this way, we may be able to make an indirect contribution to the study of character since of course virtues and vices lie very close to the heart of this idea.

A typical account of character in a familiar sense may be found in René Le Senne's *Traité de Caractérologie*, 1957.* The term, he says, "signifies the ensemble of inborn dispositions forming the mental skeleton of a person." He distinguishes in it three elements: "Character is not the whole of the individual, but what he possesses as the result of his hereditary traits .... It is solid and permanent assuring the structural identity of the person through time .... It is the skeleton of psychological life, situated at the common border of the organic and the mental." Of course Professor Le Senne has much more to say on the subject than this, but I cannot help feeling that these explanations hardly suffice even as introductory definitions. I do not offer a direct alternative to his approach here only because I believe our investigation of characterization may be the best way to help to prepare the way for a study of character itself.

We may now briefly summarize our use of the family of terms touching on character since some of them are of critical importance in what is to follow.

(1) *Character.* (a) This common term, referring to a kind of abiding moral core of the person which is often cited to help explain his good and evil deeds, has little standing at present among moral philosophers and less, as we saw, among psychologists. The notion may still be serviceable if too great a strain is not placed upon it. We have used it occasionally, mainly to paraphrase commonsense moral notions but have avoided assigning it any explanatory functions. (b) The term is also often used to sum up a body of descriptive traits belonging to something and sometimes it may mean simply a single property.

(2) *Be a characteristic of.* This is another way of speaking of a single property and thus may coincide with part of 1b.

(3) *Be characteristic of.* For any trait to *be characteristic of* something or someone it must first of all *be a characteristic of* it in sense 2. What it adds to this is the notion that it is the differentiating mark of a class or a member of a class. The former is like the Aristotelian notion of a *differentia*, and the latter is either a single unique property or a constellation of properties that makes some individual or particular comparatively unique.

(4) *Characterize.* Our problems begin with this verb. To characterize is,

* René Le Senne, *Traité de Caractérologie*, 1957, pp. 9–10.

in the usage I have adopted, not concerned with "existential" or "descriptive" traits at all, and thus not with 1b, 2, or 3. But it is obvious that the verb *is* often used for just these, and I do not propose to "revise" such a usage at all. I do, however, think that when we ask someone to characterize something or someone or ask for a characterization of it we are *most commonly* not asking for 1b, 2, or 3. What we are asking for is a characterism.

(5) *Characterism.* What we wish to hear is something in an appraisive vocabulary such as Part Two is devoted to, for man, and as is to be found in some of the appendices for other things. A distinct term is needed to distinguish appraisive predicates from descripts. 'Characterism,' I suggest, will serve this purpose and has respectable etymological credentials for the purpose both in Greek and English.

(6) *Characterization.* Finally we use this term in the present context for sentences whose principal purpose in employing some part of the appraisive or evaluative vocabulary is to appraise, judge, or evaluate. I have thought it wisest to attempt no extended account of the 'value' family of terms. The term 'value' simply serves as an umbrella for the notions and procedures I have discussed at great length. Further definition or some kind of reckoning with what others have meant by the term seems to me unprofitable at this point.

(B) *Characterisms.* We now address ourselves to *characterization* and the verbal devices, *characterisms*, by means of which we characterize. I shall be brief on this subject because it is more important for us to acquaint ourselves with the conceptual materials of characterization themselves.

Each characterism in Part Two may be the answer to the question we often have occasion to address to each other: how would you characterize him (or her)? Our answers might run: he is physically robust or even portly; his movements are somewhat awkward; his speech is a kind of drone; his bearing is august and sober; his presence is one of courtliness and charm; his temperament is equable, and so on, through the many possibilities set forth in Part Two, and far beyond that. Characterizations of this sort are the very lifeblood of all our evaluations, appraisals and sometimes, judgments. To characterize is to survey the properties and behavior of a thing or a person, or even a part or aspect of these, not simply to report them but to "sum up" the subject in a unique way.

We now ask what this "summing up" is and how it proceeds.

Let us pursue for the moment the original idea of character as one of in-graving a pattern. Certainly the appraiser has not literally worked an affect on the subject, but more nearly the subject's reputation. In this sense a servant is "given a character" and bears it with him (perhaps to his next job) as what may be an even more palpable reality than his physical presence.

Yet it is not a description of him and the key terms in it do not refer to public and verifiable properties. The appraiser clearly speaks for himself and yet wants to imply that what he has said of the subject is rooted in the subject's being. Some moral theorists deny that appraisals of this sort can have any foundation except the appraiser's attitude, perhaps also his feelings. His "judgment" may be said to embody these feelings or attitudes. We shall avoid explanations which involve reference to the *attitude* of the characterizer, to an alleged *emotive tenor* of appraisive language, or to the *embodiment of emotion* in such language: first, embodiment is something like a fossilized metaphor long since hardened into a mere manner of speaking which resists any decoding such as metaphors usually yield to; second, it is simply false that one can infer that a speaker using such language is in any particular emotional state. The language can be spoken and can be interpreted without any such emotion, though nothing here *prevents* there being emotions. The speaker does not somehow feel an emotion for or against the subject appraised and then bottle it into appraisive language. If anything, he may have an emotion because such and such appraisals or characterizations seem apt, fair, or appropriate to him; his emotion does not, and neither can it in any sense, justify the use of a given form of appraisive language. For this would be to say to the appraised subject (if this is a person), "Your discourse is fatuous (scurrilous, contumacious, palaver, eyewash, ranting), you are impudent (pompous, officious, stubborn) because I feel emotional offense at your speech and personal bearing." The proper answer to this is, "Your emotions are your own and a matter of no concern whatever to me." If on the other hand, I say, "I hate you and shall take every step necessary to prevent your persisting in this course of action, because you (and your discourse) are impudent, pompous, officious, disdainful and so on," I will really have given you something to think about: the "accused" must now make a trial of applying these terms to himself and find either that he cannot see them as applicable to himself (and to be applicable they *must mean something* more than that the adversary has negative emotions toward him) or he will fall in with such a characterization of himself, or his immediate past self, and take some appropriate step to remedy the situation according to the conventions of his time or society.

We shall leave this as a mere sketch of some of the "moves" and "gambits" of the "game" of characterizing one another. For the present, two aspects of characterization must be brought out, since they are basic to what follows. There is first of all a subject of appraisal, some person or some aspect or action of his, or some other kind of accusative to whom or which the appraisal or characterization is applied. Second, there is the appraisal proper or what is being said in appraising or characterizing the subject. The first of these is occasionally referred to here as the appretiand (the *appretiandum*, or what is being appraised). In general this can be specified in considerable detail. It should be noted that the predicates by which this is done are entirely descriptive or at least not themselves appraisive. Using an example that recurs below, if we try to teach a child, say, what the word **dignity** means we must first of all be certain that the child is clearly aware of *what* or who is the subject of appraisal. For this we do not say only "Mr. Potts" but rather we draw attention to various *appretianda* (what is being or what is to be appraised), namely the way this person walks, talks, sits, stands, moves, responds to others, the speed or slowness with which he acts, etc. Keep your eye on these, we say. We can make this as detailed as we like, and let us suppose we are restricting our remarks to the subject of appraisal and are careful to avoid using any appraisives the child already knows. In so proceeding we do *not* teach him "what the appraisive means"; we teach him what in detail and precisely is the subject of the appraisal. These steps are not in any sense necessary and sufficient conditions for the use of the appraisive terms. The only further steps that can be taken are first, to be even more precise in specifying the subject, and second, to resort to other appraisives the child already knows, and try to make distinctions in them. The first, of course, repeats or adds to what we have already done, the second is merely an expedient that does not really solve any problem, because (as we contend) there are really no fully synonymous terms among appraisives, and even if there were we would still have to explain how we learn them, and because one must, by this method, already have the knack of appraising: we are not teaching it, nor teaching the appraisives.

Dictionaries are instructive on this matter. If we take a representative sampling of appraisive terms we find that dictionaries simply resort to "synonyms," *to other appraisives*, to convey the meaning of given appraisives. But this is clearly only a makeshift. Dictionaries tell us with more or less accuracy what words mean but they do not explain to us how we learn what words mean. With appraisive terms, dictionaries are at their weakest, and there is no remedy for this situation, since they cannot, and no one can, cite the descriptive conditions that suffice for the use of appraisives. At best dictionaries can draw attention to, can try to specify in descriptive terms the subject of appraisal, but such a specification, as explained, is by its nature *not* appraisive. If we look up **gawky**, some dictionaries will say "applied to a tall, overgrown person." Here if we allow the phrase to be regarded as descriptive, we are merely being told to look in a certain direction, but we are not being told, nor *can* we be told, what to look for, that is, the definitive conditions of being gawky. For being tall and overgrown applies also to basketball players, who seldom deserve to be called gawky. If we do not allow this (and I incline to this side), *overgrown*, if not *tall*, is already an appraisive. This is now used as a kind of creel to help us "catch" what is meant in the English language by **gawky**.

We can take a random sampling from the following sections and see what the problems are when we try to learn or to define appraisive terms. One should ask what, in detail, are the properties of subjects of appraisal for these appraisives, and then how a subject is characterized by them. In these cases we either accumulate descripts or else various pseudo-synonyms. These may, however, somewhat advance our understanding of the terms; little else does.

The following terms may particularly reward reflection regarding the points raised in this section:

fatuous	6.11	**merry**	8.111	**browbeat**	11.2
nebulous	6.13	**impudent**	8.22	**kind**	11.3
finicky	6.22	**pompous**	8.22	**tawdry**	12.1
palaver	6.311	**staunch**	9.22	**waste**	12.1
glib	6.32	**aplomb**	9.3	**prig**	13.1
preen	7.12	**nag**	11.11	**tyrant**	13.4
smirk	7.33	**furtive**	11.13	**desperado**	13.71

Dictionaries have little time to draw our attention to descriptive traits that are being appraised; they devote their effort to citing a constellation of other appraisive "synonyms" from which we may somehow catch the new meaning. In neither case are sufficing conditions cited. This condition is irremediable and is the first thing we must learn about appraisives, particularly characterisms.

The two points in our exposition that should be kept in mind are thus the *subject of appraisal*, and the *appraisal proper*. These will be before us constantly in sections 6.0 through 13.0, and of course also in other sections.

It should be remarked in passing that etymologies are particularly important for characterisms. The origins of descriptive terms are generally not of decisive significance in any present use; so far as the world of origins is concerned we can say, *pereat mundus*. Value concepts are very different. They do not detach themselves from their origins or their speakers, as factual concepts do. One must often pursue them to their roots or even to their trunk, leaves, or surrounding "atmosphere."

To complete our preliminary account of characterization we may summarize our discussion and add some further observations.

(1) Characterizations are always of a *subject as a whole*; they are overviews. They are not meant to report some discrete properties among other properties of substances. We may talk of Phipps as portly, or Phipps as

stupid, or Phipps as a boor; in one case, it is the physical Phipps, but Phipps as a whole, that is being characterized; in the next, Phipps is thought of as nothing more than an intellectual being, whatever we may have in mind by that; in the third case, Phipps in his social setting, with friends, enemies, strangers, equals, and so on, occupies the whole of our interest. In each case, he may have virtues or vices in other respects, but we are ignoring them. All the traits that are being drawn upon in this portrait of the man, or that are in any way thought of, are related back to this one key to character. The appraiser is staking everything on one throw of the dice.

(2) One of the most decisive features of characterisms is their *inherent positive or negative character*. One might call it a valence. A descript on the other hand simply names a substance, quality, event, or relation, e.g., *red, conifer, translation, shoe, birth.* Of course, this valence derives from the use of characterisms, that is, they credit or discredit the subjects they are applied to. The terms themselves seem to acquire a certain character because they are involved in what is loosely called the expression of feelings.

The terms preserve their valences with remarkable consistency, but they are on occasion capable of shifting from one valence to the other. There are also occasions where the valence is varied for the purposes of humor, paradox, or defiance of convention. The positive or negative character of these terms is perhaps their most distinctive trait, enabling one to select them easily from a series such as appears in a dictionary. The actual properties or relations of things characterized can be neither positive nor negative, unless in some altogether different sense.

(3) Whatever it is we are saying of a person in characterizing him, we are deeming it for the moment *essential* and of greater gravity and significance than anything else. It is as if we had somehow arrived at his essence. The present characterization tends to obscure all other things we may know of the person or to subordinate them to this. It is for these reasons, in fact, that we speak of *character* here. It may be a myth, but it is a myth that dies hard, that there is an inner core to a person (and indeed of any and every thing that can be *characterized*), that it is the ultimate inner determinant of all that is unique to such an existent or person, and that all traits and properties of this as an acting being are related to it. This is the kind of thing we are prone to think when we speak of character and characterization.

(4) Characterizing is *not judging*. Judging supposes that there is a standard in terms of which we judge. We either rightly derive the judgment from a standard or commitment or we do not. A characterization may itself be characterized as cruel or flattering but it does not have a standard to conform to. Its function in appraisal is original not derivative. Characterisms and characterizations are not rule governed and in the sense in which

descripts may be defined, they are essentially indefinable. Some efforts can, however, be made as may be seen from our discussion of "substitutive definitions" in 6.0.

(5) The content of the characterization shows the detectable *effect* of the subject characterized *on the speaker*. We are always led back to this speaker. When the arrow strikes we look back toward the bow and the archer. It usually affords an insight of some degree into his thought or feeling. It is not, however, in any narrow sense merely traceable to some alleged emotive source in him, nor does it somehow merely express his emotion. Theories that confine themselves to this in their study of "attitudes" are oversimplified precisely at the point where analysis is needed.

(6) Finally, no trait is more definitive of characterisms than that they are *not used* in the first person active present tense *with the intent of self-applause or self-inculpation*. This has already been set forth in a preliminary fashion in 2.4. Generally, when we are in doubt as to whether a term is being used as a characterism or as a descript we may appeal to this rule in appropriate fashion. The following conversation from Thackeray's *Book of Snobs* will vivify the point:

There were eleven more dinners hustling one another in my invitation-book. "If you eat two more, you are in for apoplexy," said Glauber, my medical man. But Miss Twaddlings is to be at the Macwhirters' on Thursday, I expostulated, and you know what money she has. "She'll be a widow before she's married," says Glauber, "if you don't mind. – Away with you! Take three grains of blue pill every night, and my draught in the morning – if you don't, I won't answer for the consequences. – You look as white as a sheet – as puffy as a bolster – this season you've grown so inordinately gross and fa– "

It's a word I can't bear applied to myself.

6.0 INTELLECTUAL CHARACTERIZATION

We begin our study of the appraisal of man by considering intellect, since it is the key to understanding many other abilities. Obviously it is not the key to all of them, since for some tasks we may be perfectly content with a man so long as he is honest, brave, amiable, or good at tennis, even if he is not very clever or subtle.

The first thing that needs to be made clear is just what aspects of intellect or intelligence enter into personal appraisal. It is pretty obvious that verbal abilities are intrinsic to both of these or are manifestations of them. The exercise of such abilities produces results in the direction of knowledge or information, of the grasp of significance, of the capacity to carry on processes of reason or inference. But the appraisal of a person capable of exercising these abilities is something different from the appraisal of the product of these abilities such as statements, which are appraised as true or false, or arguments, which are appraised as valid or invalid. Appraisals of the latter sort are of no direct interest to us here. I have sketched out their main outlines in Appendix A simply to show what they are like.

At the same time, if our interest extended to the effort to make apparent what it is we mean by each of the intellectual appraisives of man that are considered particularly in 6.1 and 6.2, we would have to go into matters such as those in Appendix A in some detail. That is to say, if we are asked what we mean by saying that a person is acute, ingenious, or perceptive, we eventually have to spell this out by giving examples of how he reasons and precisely what kind of mistakes he makes, how he handles problems of the meaning of words and the errors he makes, how capable he is at amassing knowledge and the kind of ignorance he manifests in what directions. In short, the meaning of terms in 6.1 and 6.2 eventually must be resolved, if anywhere, by actual knowledge, understanding, and reasoning, and the analysis of these inevitably takes us, for example, into logic, a small but important part of whose vocabulary is offered in Appendix A.

It may be worth pausing over the matter of the nature of intelligence just a little longer. When we ask whether a man is intelligent and ask for more than the usual vague but apparently sufficient assurances, we must, in the end, observe him doing something, solving some problems, or showing what kinds of problems he has solved. We may give him intelligence tests and see where he stands with respect to others. We have now substituted a technical and mensurable performance for whatever it was we were seeking when we asked about intelligence apart from such tests and trials. We could devise a kind of test for each of the appraisives we have listed: for example, there might be a test (in fact there *are* such efforts) to show what level of creativity and imaginativeness he could achieve, and so also subtlety and wit. Tests and trials of this sort are essentially substitutions, and provide what we may call a *substitutive definition*. They are not, for example, tests of intelligence but of something that we call by the same name or are taking the risk of asserting is the same thing. Of course, there is no particular harm in this if we are careful to distinguish the original and perhaps vague but nonetheless more decisive preanalytic notion of creativity of intelligence or wit from the machine-tooled, scientific, postanalytic notion that we choose to call by the same name. The first of these is more decisive, since in the name of it we can always express a dissatisfaction with the second because the latter does not conform to what we expect. We give A a creativity test in which he ranks high, but we may not give it much credence because, in fact, we have never had the slightest reason to be impressed by the creativity of any of A's productions apart from the test. It would be stupid to go on insisting that A really was creative, simply because he had ranked high in the test. But the world, especially the learned world, is replete with such stupidities. In all of this, we must demand a clear understanding of what one can and cannot do with tests.

The significance of this is that of the hundreds and hundreds of appraisives we are about to examine, a very great many might be the subject of tests (of course, even the thought of this is repelling) in exactly the same way as intelligence is. It is unlikely that the results of any of these tests could become truly *definitive* of the concepts in question, though many "testers" are obviously tempted: "intelligence is what intelligence tests test." But efforts to supply something precise in place of these concepts, perhaps even by tests, is not inherently absurd, so long as the original preanalytic and perhaps even "intuitive" use is recognized as *in the end* decisive in all ordinary contexts.

The distinction between intelligence and judgment is one that has an uneven history. Some of the best things on the subject appear in Kant's *Critique of Pure Reason* and his *Critique of Judgment*.* In the first of these, Kant undertakes to separate what he calls the *understanding* as the capacity

* Kant, *Critique of Pure Reason*, Transcendental Analytic, Book II, Introduction; also Transcendental Dialectic, B, The Logical Employment of Reason. *Critique of Judgement*, Introduction IV, and passim. Also relevant to the moral aspects of this is Kant's essay, "Concerning the Maxim: That May be Correct in Theory, but Does Not Hold in Practice" (1793).

for arriving at the laws of nature by the road of the sciences, from *judgment* as the capacity to explain a given phenomenon by reference to (he tends to say, subsumption under) the laws of nature that have been determined by science. This use of the term is admirably conformed to common speech. Conceivably, someone may have a great command of theoretical physics but be helpless when it comes to devising a method for lifting a heavy weight under complex conditions, or to explaining a given complex phenomenon. Kant suggests that such a person is gifted in the direction of understanding but is deficient in judgment. Again, a person may be ever so ignorant of general principles and yet be extremely clever and gifted at devising precise and workable solutions to problems presented to him. Such a person shows ability in the direction of judgment rather than understanding.

Sooner or later, all of us tend to resort to this distinction. A person particularly gifted in showing good judgment may often earn praise for his "intuition," as if there were still a third kind of intellectual ability. I believe intuition, that is, the ability to make complex inferences rapidly and accurately, without having to resort to piecemeal, step by step procedures, can generally be resolved without residue into judgment.

In accordance with what we have said earlier in this section, the foregoing must be tempered by the fact that in the end we shall have difficulty in establishing someone's competence and knowledge of general principles (understanding) except through his capacity to solve particular problems (judgment). In this respect, the difference between the two appears to be less one of quality than of degree. Probably, however, there are other factors. For example, the highly theoretical mind may simply be impatient with whatever appears to it to be a host of trivial particular cases which it could solve if it but chose to do so. From this standpoint the judgment needed to solve such cases is irrelevant to the creative development of theories. In the end, the distinction is best made by reference to the appraisive concepts themselves that have fallen to one side or the other in 6.1 and 6.2.

In the case of intelligence and also of judgment we have appraisals of powers and of performance. Judgment must not be thought to be simply the exercise of intelligence. The defining characteristic of judgment is the making of decisions between live options where there is a compulsion to act and where there may be grave consequences either way. Performance under intelligence on the other hand means, as the subtitle indicates, "character of thought," the character of theoretical explanatory structures or the capacity to invent them to make things intelligible, understood. It has no choices to make directly affecting human acts. Intelligence, the understanding of the world, reflects, in these vocabularies, the life of reason, the career of Aristotle's theoretical man, or in our time, the career of pure science and pure research.

This is the character of the conceptual framework. Of course, we may choose to think that thinking on a "purely abstract" level is somehow a bad thing for scientists. But how scientists distribute their time between developing explanatory structures and the solution of particular, and perhaps practical problems has no bearing on the distinction between these two in themselves.

6.1   INTELLIGENCE

CREDITING CHARACTERISMS	DISCREDITING CHARACTERISMS
6.11 GENERAL	
SUBSTANTIVE	SUBSTANTIVE
genius	(a) **addlepate**
savant	**boob, booby**
	crackpot
	crank
	dolt
	dotard
	duffer
	fool
	idiot
	ignoramus
	imbecile
	lunatic
	moron
	nincompoop
	(b) **bluestocking**
	pedant
	pundit
ATTRIBUTIVE	ATTRIBUTIVE
able	**anile**
bright	**cracked**
brilliant	**crazy**
gifted	**crotchety**
intelligent	**daft**
original	**deranged**
rational	**eccentric**
talented	**fatuous**
	irrational
	naive

senile
stupid
unbalanced
witless
mad (=disturbed in mind)

6.12   ACUITY
SUBSTANTIVE

precisian

SUBSTANTIVE

blockhead
dotard
dunce
dunderhead
dullard, dull
numskull
obscurantist
simpleton

ATTRIBUTIVE

acumen, acute, acuity
incisive
ingenious
insight
keen
perceptive
perspicacious
perspicuous
subtle
wit, witticism, witty

ATTRIBUTIVE

obtuse
dull

6.13   TENOR
ATTRIBUTIVE

creative
deep
imaginative
profound

ATTRIBUTIVE

inane
inscrutable
nebulous
obscure
shallow (14.11)
smatter, smattering
superficial
trifling
trivial
vacuous

The appraisives or characterisms comprised under intelligence fall into a number of different types, often based on the imagery of light, space, or acuity. Others are more general.

General. The metaphor in **bright** and **brilliant** recalls the ancient image of the light of reason. It is not likely to lose its effectiveness and stands in no need of analysis.

Characterisms such as **able, bright, gifted, talented,** and **genius** are altogether general. Others which may occur to us in this connection seem on closer consideration really to belong to judgment: **adroit, apt, dexterous, expert, quickwitted.** We may therefore begin with the former.

Talented, gifted, and **genius** need not be confined to intelligence.* The touch of indeterminacy in them serves to remind us that there is much that we do not know about human abilities or that most commonly we do not know how these abilities are acquired. We have them as "gifts" from anonymous "givers." Until they are reinforced by illustration of actual achievements their use to characterize persons is almost wholly uninformative. Yet it must not be supposed that they are equivalent to the substance of these illustrations.

The term **rational** has a very narrow use among philosophers that removes it, in that context, from the characterisms. Its use by psychologists is usually technical. **Irrational** will be vaguely assimilable to other negations of intelligence, when it is not used appraisively.

The negations of these general terms are sometimes not easy to segregate into the classes of unintelligence or intellectual incompetence, and of irrationality or mental incompetence. We may consider these briefly. When we ask after the contraries of **intelligent** and **rational** we receive answers in several different directions. If a person is not rational or mentally competent, this may, for example, derive from his calendar age. Terms like **anile, dotage, dotard,** and **senile,** particularly the first and last, may receive fairly accurate substitutive definitions. In this manner they are removed, at least in the new context, from use as appraisives and characterizations. The same may be said of **moron, imbecile, idiot,** and **lunatic,** and of **irrational** and **deranged.**

On the other hand, terms like **addlepate, boob, cracked, crank, crazy,** and **daft** have never seemed to deserve analysis or substitutive definition. They remain, therefore, as characterisms with various degrees of power to evoke

---

* It is likely in fact that the opinion of many persons would incline in the opposite direction echoing Kant's well-known view that genius appertains only to art and not to science, to Homer but not to Newton: "In science, the greatest discoverer differs only in degree from the most tedious imitator or pupil, but he differs in kind from him to whom Nature has bestowed a gift for fine art." *Critique of Judgment,* § 47.

emotions, whether of derision in the application of them to certain subjects, or of resentment in the victims or their sympathizers.

It may be worth saying that most of the out and out technical terms of psychology and psychiatry are instructive but of no immediate significance here. Being technical lifts them at once out of the area of characterizations.

Fool is one of the most ancient and powerful characterisms in the language and one could devote a great deal of space to it and its "synonyms" in other languages. What appears to be unique in it, among other terms of this class, is its strong moral force. It can be used not only to deprecate someone's intelligence but even more his moral judgment. The fool who has said there is no God is thought to be deficient not only in knowledge or intelligence but also in moral insight. **Fatuous** appears not to be so strongly moral as **fool**.

A somewhat specious norm is implicit in these concepts. All of them imply in some way a threshold between normality and subnormality. (We could also speak of supernormality with a term like genius.) The moron, idiot, and imbecile fall below a threshold of intelligence, the daft, deranged, and the like below another kind of threshold of mental and perhaps social competence, the senile descending a threshold at still another point or in another way. A person can of course be thought of neutrally as falling below the threshold in a way that is neither emotive nor patronizing. If this is now done by means of an appeal to a more or less objective scheme, the terms are not being used as characterizations or appraisals. Of course, the analyst may, *at the same time*, have compassion for such persons, but their placement itself is not a matter of emotion or compassion. Most of these terms in common discourse are not being used with any cognizance of or in reference to a technical substitutive definition. They are being used, therefore, as characterizations. In fact the terms are most commonly applied to persons who would *not* be placed below the threshold by a technical expert e.g. **idiot**.

The appraisive use of the negative terms is often cruel, particularly when the terms are applied appraisively to those definitely below a technically devised threshold. On the other hand, if they are applied to those definitely above, it is cruel to assimilate them to those who are ill-endowed. Thus a pretty problem arises. If we are all above or below the threshold (assuming none is exactly on it) all appraisals in these terms will be cruel. But we must not be cruel. Therefore, etc. This is about as conclusive an argument for courtesy as one could hope to devise.

Perhaps, however, we are taking these too seriously. Have they indeed any content? Are they not merely abusive and for that reason to be avoided? I think one more defense should be offered for the vocabulary, namely, that the terms can be used in a metaphorical sense. If A is characterized as an idiot the principle being followed is not unlike that which operates in saying he is a donkey or a chicken. In these cases, we are invited to excogitate some property or quality that the donkey or chicken has that is shared by A. It makes not the slightest difference that we would be hard put to say what the property is, and of course even the person who has said, "Donkey", may not be able to help us. In a similar manner, when A is called a lunatic or an idiot, he rarely is one by any substitutive or technical definition, but a heavy hint has been dropped that he shares *some property or other* with "real idiots." This is what is likely to be meant in our day when people know that **idiot, imbecile** and the like have technical definitions. For them the non-technical use is a metaphor. For those who know nothing of such technicalities, the terms are often little more than broadsides of abuse.

But what is more important is that in characterizing persons by means of these terms, as against classifying them so in order, let us say, to prepare them for some kind of therapy, the speaker is leaving *his* mark on an image of them he wishes to convey. In the ordinary nontechnical contexts of the use of these terms, none of them is being used to designate a property that is there for everyone to inspect. They are like the bullet in the corpse: it is not just an interesting phenomenon but immediately stimulates interest in the angle from which it was fired and who was holding the weapon. This does not mean that they are nothing more than broadsides or that they are merely marks of aggression coming from a certain quarter. It means that *who* has said it makes a difference. Characterizations are always indefeasibly *ad hominem*: *who* has uttered them is a large part of the key to their meaning and to the question of their appropriateness. It may be of the utmost significance that it is A that has characterized B, that it is, let us say, *Churchill* who has characterized Attlee as a fool, or Mussolini as a jackal. And we do not only ask who has spoken, but what his status is, what his speech habits are, whether he is merely a cruel but witty phrasemaker, how serious he is, whether he is often moved to speak with just this degree of force or emphasis, to whom he said it, etc.

Tenor. We may conveniently consider the appraisives of tenor (6.13) before those of acuity (6.12). The term tenor is meant to suggest the rather "geometrical" dimension of intelligence that is to be discerned in some of these characterisms. In a sense it is of course impossible to speak of intelligence in any but its own abstract terms. The abstract, if it *is* anything, is by its nature at a maximum remove from the physical or perceptible world. It is therefore noteworthy that the resort to metaphor to express intelligence goes so far toward the very concrete: light, the sword, the dimensions of space and what fills them. We may observe immediately that the characterisms under space or breadth are concerned with the *products* of intelligence, that is, ideas, theories, hypotheses, constructs of various sorts; those under acuity (the sharp instrument) pertain to the intellect as a faculty or *power*.

Under the metaphor of space we have the characterisms **profound, deep, shallow, superficial, vacuous,** and **inane**: thought reaching the depths or ascending into nothingness. There is no need, nor any temptation, to "precise" these terms or to demonstrate their aptness, but we may wish to add to them a dimension of breadth. Profound theories very often provide threads or roots of connection among elements that lie scattered to the eye.

Closely related to these images are the characterisms **inscrutable, nebulous, obscure, trifling, trivial.** The first three seem directed particularly toward the logical integument of theories or intellectual constructs and the difficulties which beset the mind in trying to comprehend them. **Inscrutable** has an unusual origin. *Scrutor* is Latin for search or examine, but *scruta* is rubbish or trash! Thus scrutiny should raise up the image of a collector looking over discarded materials to find something of value. When the term takes on a figurative sense, we finally have inscrutable, that which one examines carefully but which then fails to yield up its valuable secrets.

Trifling and **trivial** remind us that we are often confronted by a void where we were expecting something substantial. The highly expressive **piffle** conveys the same response but with greater forcefulness. It dismisses the pretensions of constructs by assimilating them to mere noises of the wind. We shall encounter this device of "relegation" again and again among characterisms. **Smatter** and **smattering,** whose origin is obscure, and thus may be slang or onomatopoetic, rely either on what the sound suggests (perhaps grain or sand spilling or spattering on a floor) or on certain outright conventions such as the idea of want of information or knowledge and negligence of effort to acquire them.

Savant is somewhat corrupted by its heavy journalistic use. In that context the term has a touch of patronizing indulgence. The far stronger **pedant** has an ancient standing as a characterism, but its origins are obscure.

Acuity, the last large class of characterisms pertains to the power of intellect and is built around the notion of the knife or anything that is sharp or cuts. The terms closest to literality here are **acute (acumen, acuity)** and the negative, **obtuse.** The capacity of intelligence to penetrate is the capacity to show connection where none had been suspected. Here we are more concerned with the intellect as an engine or instrument than we are with the products of it, as with the spatial characterisms treated above, **obscure, nebulous, inscrutable.** One might also place **keen** here since we tend to think of it as first of all the sharp and cutting. The term has an interesting history. It began as a term applied to intellect and in its Old English form meant wise. Also, it had the sense **bold** (cf. German **kühn**), and from the might, power, and fierceness of the warrior, or from his sword, came the application finally to any physical thing besides swords that could cut. Our use of it in application to intellect is now a metaphorization from this physical use. The term therefore has gone through a metamorphosis from the intellectual to the physical and back to the intellectual.

There follow a pair of terms comparing the intellect to the powers of the eye, **perceptive**, **perspicacious**, and the product of the intellect to something the eye can see through, **perspicuous**. Similarly, **stupid** derives from a comparison to senses that have been deprived of, or impaired in, their function. **Blockhead** and **numskull** rest on a similar comparison.

Ingenious, from being merely the recognition of inborn powers, has become more specialized in use to indicate inventiveness or capacity for invention.

Subtle derives from Latin *subtilis*, but even more instructively from *subtextilis* implying fine weaving, which is easily understood in the present appraisive. **Subtle** and **ingenious** may also appear under judgment.

There remain the self-explanatory substantives **ignoramus** and **simpleton** and the much more important **wit**. It is safe to say that no ready explanation of wit, either as applied to persons or to discourse or to intellectual power, is available except in general terms. The etymology is straightforward but not instructive since the elusive quality that makes up the capacity to say witty things generally is expressed only by further characterisms: **"quickness** of intellect, **liveliness** of fancy, **apt** expression," (NED) etc. We shall leave it to literary people to analyze further. There is also a rare and interesting substantive in **precisian**, the origin of which is apparent.

There remain finally one or two characterizations which are not uniquely applied to intelligence but which provide a large subject for speculation when they are applied to it, namely, **imaginative** and **creative**. As noted earlier, we are much more inclined than formerly to concede that *creativity* in mathematics and science is very likely the same capacity as that which artists, poets and composers possess. In fact we may be forced to concede this since, as compared with the triumphs of science, technology and mathematics, those of contemporary artists are neither numerous nor may they prove as significant. It is apparent that in either direction creativity is more than novelty. Current artistic practice that prides itself on its progressivism is more likely to think that it has supplanted tradition because it sets out to destroy it than because it has proved its capacity to take its place. It *tries* too hard. The scientist merely does what has to be done, and every now and then some stupendous step needs to be taken. When at length it is taken, it is rightly marked a creative stroke of genius.

We should now point out some of the problems of what is in effect the logical dependence of characterisms on instantiation, particularly those of intelligence which have just been considered. In this case what is necessary is that we give such characterisms interpretations in terms of real episodes of intellectual activity of the person characterized, or in terms of his expressed and stated product of thought. With characterizations every application of appraisive terms amounts to a definition or contributes a necessary part of it. We can at best only produce exemplifications, and this method of explication should be distinguished sharply from providing definitions where we give necessary and sufficient conditions for the application of terms. Aside from hints provided by near synonyms, which have the same logical character, examples must define the characterisms: we need to find out exactly what it is that is being characterized. Specifying 'determining' conditions is merely a kind of sign pointing in a certain direction toward the area that is being characterized, but it does not tell us how to characterize with the aid of a characterism. As we have seen, further guides to the use of such terms may come from the fact that they are often metaphors, and there will be other hints.

The uniqueness of characterisms is apparent from the fact that these terms have a use only for individual cases, for example, persons, their intellectual deeds, the episodes of their thinking, inferring, and speaking. They can have little or no standing as parts of theory or any status as parts of a general science of human nature, although, of course, they are parts of the subject matter of such a science. (Cf. 13.2)

It is instructive to observe, at the very outset of our study of characterisms, the contrast between the foregoing approach to them and that of the method exhibited in the shorter Platonic or Socratic dialogues. The ideas which Plato has there under review are either virtues, which we shall examine at the end of our study of characterisms, or characterisms themselves. It will be recalled that the interlocutors almost invariably answer the Socratic request for a definition with *examples*, which are immediately and often repeatedly rejected, since they are not general and will not enable Socrates, or anyone else, to decide what in fact are to be considered instances of the idea. Our approach repudiates this aspect of the Socratic method insofar as it implies that we can find general definitions of such terms that will enable us to recognize "instances" of them. The fact is, the best we can hope for is that the "examples" we apply them to are fairly characterized by them. 'Instance' and 'example' themselves are misleading, since they suggest classification and membership in a set or class, which are completely foreign to characterizations. The model of set membership is wholly inappropriate. What we are saying is that the perhaps naive but healthy habit of the interlocutors to produce "examples" when they are asked for definitions may deserve greater respect than Socrates appears to accord it. We should observe, however, that the dialogues nearly always end inconclusively, and the definitions that are demanded are rarely forthcoming. I think it would be too ingenious an explanation of this fact to say that what Socrates or Plato is trying to tell us by this inconclusiveness *is* that these ideas are really indefinable. But it is possible.

We may remark finally that to describe characterisms as indefinable might however be misleading, since it would suggest there is a strange "intuitive" process at work here. We shall have sufficient opportunity in what follows to dispute this notion.

6.2   JUDGMENT

CREDITING CHARACTERISMS	DISCREDITING CHARACTERISMS
6.21 CRAFT	
astute	(a) **befuddled**
calculating	**bemused, bemuse**
canny	**chump**
circumspect	**credulous**
clever	**fool, foolish**
cunning ±	**gullible**
discreet	**sucker**
gumption	(b) **eclectic**
infallible	**fallible**
shrewd	**sophistry**
smart	**suspicious, suspicion**
	(given to suspecting)
6.22 DISCRIMINATION	
delicate	**captious**
exacting	**cavilling**
fastidious	**finicky**
meticulous	**hairsplitting**
nice, nicety	**pernickety**
sensitive	**quibble**
	squeamish
6.23 ARBITRAMENT	
balance, balanced	**arbitrary**
consistent	**bias, biassed**
disinterested	**dogmatic, dogmatism**
dispassionate	**opinionated**

equitable	**prejudiced, prejudice**
impersonal	
judicious	
liberal	
objective	
reasonable	
scrupulous, scruples	

6.24   COUNSEL

sagacious
sage
sapient
wise
wiseacre ±

We encountered judgment previously under the moral involvements of 5.0. There, decisions and judgments were themselves being thought of as subjects of evaluation. Such evaluations are efforts at justification: we wish to know whether a given decision can rightly be derived from commitments. The present subjects of evaluation are the judges themselves, rather than their decisions. We are seeking to characterize them as exercising judgment or to characterize the habit and pattern of their judgments.

Judgment is always concerned with action, and in fact we judge out of the necessity to act. This is at least true if judgment is thought of as decision, as I think it ought to be. If we think of a judgment as the same as a statement, as it was in formal logic at the turn of our century, we fail to avail ourselves of a very useful distinction. There are several other terms besides 'judgment' we can use for registering, or taking note of, or asserting, or entertaining facts and what appear to be facts. Judgment, we shall say, is the election of courses of action and inaction. It may also be selection and predilection. We are not particularly concerned about its verbal form. This may be whatever it is. In fact, one may even concede that we are somewhat vague about *what* it is we are saying is sagacious, meticulous or judicious. This does not mean that we need have any hesitation in saying A is sagacious.

I think what we have said about judgment covers all of the recognized fields of its application from moral judgment to intellectual judgment that issues in actions in the sense of the application of theories, and to aesthetic judgment. In the latter case it would be, and too often has been, misleading to speak of every episode of enjoyment as a judgment or even as involving a judgment. The term ought to be reserved for decision even in this case. I do not mean just actions such as buying a picture, but more generally two others which will catch them all, namely, deciding to prolong or to terminate episodes of aesthetic experience, and deciding to encourage or discourage the experience by furnishing or denying the means for it.

The actions we are concerned about are done either out of some interest we have or believe ourselves to have, or out of some obligation we believe ourselves to have, whether this accords with our interest or conflicts with it. We shall consider first the characterization of judgments that are most commonly concerned with actions done out of some explicit or apparent interest.

Craft. Characterization of judgment taken in the pursuit of one's interest is to be distinguished from the characterization of tendentive traits and powers of personality that are also involved in this. The latter are particularly considered under 9.0; examples of such characterisms are **wary, stamina, reckless,** and **adroit.** The characterisms under judgment now in question are exemplified in judgments of craft: **astute, calculating, canny, cunning, shrewd.**

We should observe immediately that these are fairly obviously extern characterizations. We see this even more plainly in the negative characterisms of this class: **befuddled, bemused, chump, credulous,** and perhaps **foolish.** Normally we can see the futility of self-applauding characterization, and we are too full of self-esteem to use the corresponding negatives. These are obvious facts of our nature: in general we do not judge or decide upon an action in the present and in the same moment characterize it in censorious terms. Characterization of ourselves is about our past actions, and the characterization may then enter into an outright judgment, perhaps a condemnation. Without wholly confirming the Socratic opinion that all men always act for the good, this may yet confirm or corroborate it as far as it can be. Every deliberate action seems to be taken in the present conviction that it is good: if it is done on a felt compulsion, one may characterize and later condemn it in the most extreme terms. The striking fact about these characterisms, as about those in many other classes, is that it is not the norm that earns characterization but the extremes. In order to characterize the "normal" man one may, in fact, have to upgrade or downgrade the extremes: he is "no fool," or he is "rather cunning."

The pursuit of interest must not, however, be construed too narrowly. It is not necessary to confine characterizations of this sort to application to those who act only in their *very own* interest. History is particularly replete with men who are disinterested in the qualified sense that they identify themselves with causes that are far greater than themselves yet fall far short of universality. These are the patriots whose passion is not themselves but Athens, Rome, England, the working class, the white man, and so forth.

Possibly such a patriotism could be exemplified also by the head of a corporation on its behalf.

Discrimination. A second family of characterisms also reflects the individual's pursuits of his own interests and satisfactions as seen from an extern standpoint. This is shown in the characterisms of discrimination: **fastidious, finicky, pernickety,** and **squeamish**. Such terms are also often used in slightly different contexts, for example, those of eating habits. But they have an important place here as appraisives of judgment. Negations of these would most commonly include **coarse, crude,** and **insensitive**. There are also terms which seek a middle ground, crediting the subject with having made proper or nice or meticulous discriminations, or shown the right degree of sensibility, or delicacy. It is often difficult to distinguish this from the use of these terms to characterize perceptivity.

Arbitrament. We now ask about the manner of characterizing the powers of judgment of persons who are, or claim to be, or are credited with being completely disinterested in their judgment. The arbitrative characterisms are directed toward the exercise of fairness in judgment. The minimum standard to be observed is obviously consistency so that even if the law being enforced is unjust it is, if possible, to be no more unjust in one direction than in another. Above this, it may be demanded that, regardless of content, the judgment be unmoved by irrelevant determinants (appeals to passion) and that it maintain balance and objectivity. These and the other characterisms of judgment can be applied as often to the process of justification as to the persons participating in it. That is, we shall speak of reasonable and equitable persons if their decisions and judgments themselves are reasonable and equitable. The first term (unless used as another way to say dispassionate) will indicate that the derivation of the present judgment from the commitment is according to reason, and the second that where no precise commitment exists, the present case nevertheless has been decided in a manner that accords with other existing commitments (cf. 5.3).

Counsel. Finally, we come to the most important of the characterizations of judgment, those expressed in giving counsel: **sagacious, sapient, sage** and **wise**. Of these, **sagacious** seems somewhat closer to **cunning** and **shrewd** than to **wise**, and thus may be reckoned an intermediate characterism between them. Setting **sapient** and **sage** to one side as somewhat literary versions of the same idea, the most significant of all of these is obviously **wisdom**.

Wisdom in practical use is not far from prudence. Its kinship with this deserves respect and is more instructive than the often highflown connotations attributed to it that remove it to the level of an all but divine attribute. It may indeed have such connotations, but it is, to begin with, more humbly related to the familiar problem of weighing means toward ends.

I wish to suggest, contrary to Plato, that **wisdom** is not an appraisive of ends. It is an appraisive of choices and decisions which are imbued with a concern for our most comprehensive ends. But choice among ends is not a matter of judgment any more than it is of intelligence. No "faculty" can specifically decide among commitments or ends. The complexities of this decision are such that we can know at most that it has no simple solution, such as, comparatively, the doctrine of Ideas or Forms proposes for it. Commitments must stand wherever they stand. What we ask of the wise is less to undertake to judge commitments themselves than to judge courses of action in terms of our most comprehensive commitments.

6.3   COMMUNICATION

6.31   CONTENT OF EXPRESSION

CREDITING CHARACTERISMS	DISCREDITING CHARACTERISMS
6.311 SIGNIFICATION	
make [sense	(a) **babble**
	chatter
	gab
	gabble
	gush
	jabber
	prattle
	(b) **ballyhoo**
	blarney
	gibberish
	gobbledegook
	nonsense
	rigmarole
	senseless
	(c) **balderdash**
	bilge
	bombast
	buncombe, bunk
	claptrap
	drivel
	eyewash
	flapdoodle
	flimflam
	flummery

fustian
humbug
obscurantism
piffle
twaddle
(d) badinage
banter
palaver
persiflage
rodomontade
(e) bathos
lugubrious
lurid (= sensational)
pathos ($\pm$)
rave
turgid
(f) cliché
trite
(g) farrago
obfuscate
preposterous
(h) garble

6.312   VERIDICTION (v. 11.13)
candid, candor
frank
honest
probity
truthful
truth-telling
veracious

bad faith
canard
cant
cock and bull
dishonest
equivocate
evasive
exaggerate
false witness
fib
fictitious
lie, liar
mendacity
misrepresent
perjury
prevaricate
sophistry
tergiversate

6.32   MANNER OF EXPRESSION

CREDITING CHARACTERISMS	DISCREDITING CHARACTERISMS
ATTRIBUTIVE	ATTRIBUTIVE
(a) concise	(a) anfractuous
laconic	blatant
succinct	garrulous
terse	glib
	harangue
	longwinded
	loquacious
	prolix
	rambling
	verbiage
	verbose
(b) eloquent	(b) ambages (=equivocation)
forthright	grandiloquent
magniloquent (−)*	jargon
orotund (−)	rhetoric
	sententious
	stilted
PROCESSIVE	PROCESSIVE
[declaim[	maunder (7.32)
	pronunciamento
	rant
	tirade

6.33   INFORMANCE

PROCESSIVE	PROCESSIVE
enlighten	(a) air v. (=divulge)
[inform]	bare v.
	bruit
	noise v.

* We frequently need to add slight qualifications to the classification of concepts as crediting or discrediting. We may put the matter by saying that the characterisms of Parts Two and Three, except the descripts, which are marked in brackets [], appear in discourse always either to credit or discredit their subjects, but that they sometimes shift from a crediting to discrediting valence (though they are rarely ambiguous) sometimes with ironic or humorous intent. When necessary to recognize possible shifts of this sort, characterisms are marked (+), (−), or (±). Care should be taken to distinguish the positive-negative pairing of characterisms (e.g. *vivacious* and *quiet* in 8.21) from the credit-discredit pairing (*vivacious* and *lazy*). The latter is also sometimes talked about as positive or negative, or as valenced.

own v.
reveal
scoop
trumpet
unbosom
unfold
(b) **blab**
blurt
tattle
(c) **eavesdrop**
pry
spy

SUBSTANTIVE	SUBSTANTIVE
	informer
	talebearer
	tattletale
	tipster
	tout
ATTRIBUTIVE	ATTRIBUTIVE
	exposé
	gossip
	rumor
	telltale
	tittle-tattle

Communication as the revelation of thought and personality is a constant subject of evaluation and characterization. Scrutiny may be directed toward the form or the content of expression. The present section presents the most general characterisms of expression. There will also be subsections devoted to tendentive expression (9.5) and expression employed in contention and aggression (11.12). Still further areas of expression come under our survey only if there are specific vocabularies of characterization for them.

For convenience, we may consider the characterisms in respect first to their content (signification and veridiction) and then the form or manner of expression. At first sight, the characterisms of 6.311 seem too trivial for very much attention, but they are powerful when suitably employed, and the source of this is not altogether easy to reveal. I believe they are something different from what the emotive school of ethics or value would make of them. They may be and often are uttered in moments of emotion, excitement, or stress, but they aim to convey a thought. They are not merely of the order of "Bah!" or "Oh!" Characterisms of group (a) in 6.311 are concerned with the content of expression like the others, but the speaker's appraisal of this content is so severe that he pretends it has no more significance than a murmur of voices heard at a distance. There is scarcely any greater insult that can be devised of someone's speech than to assimilate it to a mere noise, such as popping or crackling. However, there are some subtle differences in (a) worth a moment's attention. **Prattle** and **babble** are fairly mild compared with **gabble** and **jabber**. These are used most characteristically not only of ways of speaking of persons for whom contempt is probably felt. **Gab** and **gush** are somewhat less severe. There is a touch of amusement in them at the speaker's effusiveness.

Group (b) takes notice of the kind of talk that issues from sources that know how to size up their audiences and get desired results – the talk of salesmen and advertisers. It may include "officialese" and other strange "–ese" tongues. The point of the characterisms, of course, is that the stratagems have been seen through and are thenceforth declared ineffective in some part of the audience that has been addressed. I have placed **jargon** under manner of expression, but it may as easily fall under the present class.

Group (c) appraises talk that may not be designed actually to mislead but is nevertheless of wholly nugacious content. **Drivel, fustian, piffle, humbug,** and **twaddle** appear to mislead speakers as much as they do the listener. Again the appraiser serves notice that he has seen through and has "defused" the confusion or the stratagems. Of course some of these characterizations, as well as the others, can on occasion be used in jest. There are various other interesting differences among these which we shall pass by.

Group (d) characterizes in a much gentler vein. The talk is conceded to have an excuse since it is entertaining. On occasion it may be used to chide in a mild manner.

The rather pretentious and literary **rodomontade** seems to spoof itself as much as it does the accused. It deserves a slightly special place for this reason as also for the fact that it singles out boasting and blustering discourse. This may sometimes be characterized as **bombast.**

Discourse is perhaps garbled most often because of confusion in modes of communication, though this may also be ascribed to inattention or to more serious mental or intellectual vagaries.

Comparison should be made between the account of Significance given in Appendix A 1.0 and Signification in 6.311. Although the titles may not adequately denote the difference between them a distinction must nevertheless be made. In the present number we are concerned with the intellectual habits and capacities of persons rather than of the sentences or statements they utter. In Appendix A 1.0 we presume that sentences themselves can be well constructed and that there are principles underlying such construction certainly in formal and to an approximating degree in informal languages. Yet a person, even if he uses well constructed sentences, can fail to make sense (6.311, Crediting) and can be guilty of all the other communicational "crimes" (6.311, Discrediting). The distinction in question has perhaps most often appeared in the past as one between logic (including what we now call semantics) and rhetoric. It is evident we must be able to exclude communicational, rhetorical (and psychological) matter from logical and semantical without in any way denying their relation to one another.

Turning next to the appraisives of veridiction, we may observe that no terms of appraisal are likely to exceed those of 6.312 in sheer moment. Their gravity derives from the fact that it is persons whom we are appraising, although we use most of these terms equally of persons and their discourse. The same considerations apply throughout 6.0. It is obvious that deception must involve persons: no proposition of itself lies or speaks truly although sheer truth or falsity applies to propositions themselves. Lying and telling the truth are a certain employment of truth and falsity by persons. To count as a lie a proposition must first of all be asserted, uttered, put forth as true, *by someone.*

It is always a source of offense or chagrin to find ourselves to be dealing with not-x or y when we had thought ourselves engaged with x, whether x be a tool, method, subject matter, or as here a proposition. But our offense increases immeasurably when we find it is not the proposition that is responsible through some inadvertence or surreption but a person. Thus the appraisives of 6.312 are properly placed under the Characterization of Man rather than Ponence (Appendix A 2.0).

(In order to make the reference to persons clearer we may be forgiven the coinage *Veridiction* for this subsection. We might also have resorted to *Verilocution*, if not to *Etymology* (Greek ἔτυμος, true), if this term had not been pre-empted. *Veracity*, we might add, is rather more properly to be regarded as the virtue corresponding to veridiction.)

We must now observe that this is a vocabulary strictly for characterization. Philosophers are largely in agreement in accepting the Law of Excluded Middle according to which every proposition is either true or false. It would seem offhand that veridiction is a no less clearcut matter. But in fact the veridictiveness of some person A is "indeterminate" in precisely the same way as every other characterization. We have to decide whether a man who tells only one falsity, or *n* falsities, deserves to be called mendacious, and whether a man who tells only one truth, or *n* truths, is veracious. There are no necessary and sufficient conditions for such terms or for **candor, probity, exaggeration, bad faith,** and **sophistry** as characterizing persons. Here as elsewhere we should be careful not to think of characterisms simply as ponents inhabiting a limbo between truth and falsity, like the infinite number of rational numbers between 0 and 1.

The veridictions, and their opposites, are revelatory of more than traits or distinct properties of their subjects. The characterizer also is involved. In accusing you of telling me a falsehood, I may also reveal the extent of my knowledge of the corresponding or relevant truth. For you to say that I am honest involves your particular range of acquaintance with my assertions. I may never deceive you about money but totally falsify to you my family background. But since you and I only encounter each other as economic agents, I can count as honest in your book. Again, my honesty may be a function of the number of times I have been tempted to lie. And how many times are necessary to prove me honest? It cannot be said, and it is not a question of an indeterminacy about the truth. Such characterizations, like all others, are neither true not false; they are fair or unfair.

What is perhaps most important about this vocabulary is to see that it is one of characterisms. We may also observe that the terms are in a sense higher order appraisives, but of a considerably more complex sort than others we have considered.

Beginning with the characterisms in the area of Manner of Expression (6.32) and Informance (6.33), we introduce a classification that will be employed with increasing frequency as we proceed: attributives, processives, and substantives. Roughly speaking they divide the nouns, adjectives, and verbs, but their purpose is not merely to divide predicates, whether grammatical or logical. Characterizations in these three directions distinguish themselves as trying to say, in the case of substantives, what character a thing or person really has, what that character really is, or even "what it really is," of attributives, what a thing's "traits of character" are, of processives, what the real character of its functioning is. These explanations will be sufficient for the time being.

The attributives of 6.32 seek to present the "real character" of discourse, for example when it is said to be a harangue or pronunciamento or to be jargon, verbiage and rhetoric. (Of course, there are also important respectable uses of **rhetoric**.) In all these cases, the appraiser finds the discourse to be resorting to unnecessary devices to convey thought and to be in danger of conveying little or no thought at all from preoccupation with these devices.

Conciseness and prolixity are, of course, matters of degree. What they are a degree of depends upon the persons addressed or of the speaker. There is obviously no objective standard of length for the expression of a thought. Hence, if B characterizes A's discourse as prolix or verbose he is saying something about his own powers of comprehension and expression. He is saying something to the effect that he would or could, if motivated, express A's thought in fewer words without loss of meaningfulness. Or if he praises it as succinct he is saying that *he* would add no further words to A's discourse to convey the thought. To characterize it as terse adds just the suggestion that the discourse is almost too brief for the thought, or that it has made no concession to those who might ask that more be said.

In such cases, we see displayed the unique feature of all characterization, the reference back to the appraiser himself. We learn something about the subject, here an expressive discourse, but also something about the appraiser. But more than this, the appraiser is presuming to say something not just of what he has immediately before his eyes or ears, but what the inner "character" of the thing is. Thus, looking to 6.32, we can learn something of what it takes to impress or to bore the appraiser, by attending to what he has characterized as eloquent, glib, sententious, or stilted.

Processives are often the most powerful of the several types of characterisms. The appraiser appears to be confronted by the subject of appraisal in its active and acting capacity, not speaking of its outer traits or guessing at its inner character. The characterisms therefore have a kind of active force. The target of criticism noises or bruits information or misinformation about, or bares, unbosoms, unfolds, airs, ventilates, and trumpets it abroad. The effect on the appraiser's spirit is almost palpably felt. With **own** the appraiser evidently takes satisfaction in seeing what may be his enemy compelled to acknowledge that he has said or done what he has been accused of.

The discrediting characterisms (there is only one that credits) are used to characterize what appear to be undignified ways of revealing information, or discourse that tires and irritates. **Pry** and **eavesdrop**, of course, characterize ways of ascertaining rather than divulging information. For nearly all contexts, **spy** would serve as a characterism, but on some occasions it may serve as a descript.

Attributive characterisms are often used in a subtle and potent manner in interpersonal contention. To characterize S as rumor is to take a step toward discrediting S and to imply that S possibly ought not to be believed. Also it shows us that someone is professing not to be convinced by S, that he may be, or may want to be thought to be, a difficult person to fool, and so on. **Gossip** and **tittletattle** go even further in the same direction. To characterize an investigation as an exposé *may* both endorse the intent, method, and approach of the investigation and add further discreditation to whatever it is the investigation is studying. It is also just possible to think that the investigation is being thought sensationalistic if characterized in these terms.

To find someone to be a talebearer or a tattletale is to hold what he says suspect but also his manner of relaying his information or misinformation. Such a person usually uses these for purposes of aggression, though he may be acting only out of compulsion. Among the substantives, **tout, tipster,** and **informer** differ from the remaining two in the sense that they are names of occupations, of sorts. The informer, known as such, is, of course, highly disapproved of since he betrays those to whom he owes loyalty. The tout and tipster also follow despised occupations. To the degree that any of these are occupations with ascertainable properties they are not true characterisms. Perhaps only **talebearer** and **tattletale** are characterisms in terms of our general specifications. They tend very strongly to be used to injure the credit or repute of persons and particularly of the capacity here under consideration, the conveyance of information. All of the characterisms in use also reveal as much about the appraiser as they do about the target, the subject.

As we shall have further occasion to observe, the uses and misuses of expression are varied and numerous. The foregoing ample vocabulary shows how we may come to see that what has been proffered as information can be little more significant than a puff of air. The use of language to mislead, a serious offense, will engage more of our attention below when we consider the numerous modes of aggression in section 11.0.

These are the principal characterisms of intelligence. The lists could be further extended, of course. We could also move closer toward parallel fields such as the aesthetic in discussing communication, since many of the characterisms of communication would be hard to classify conclusively in one field or the other.

7.0 BEHAVIORAL CHARACTERIZATION

What we consider under "behavior" is the characterization of the body as it presents itself principally to vision. In the first two parts, on figure and motion, there is no inference to internal states that might be said to be expressed by these states and motions of the body. In the third part, on body response, there is probably a trace of such inference. We are interested in a truly *human* body, in no sense a mere "object" weighing so many pounds. Yet a great many of the characterisms might also find application to other kinds of animal bodies. Although they exhibit little that is commonly thought of as *character*, at least in any moral sense, these are nevertheless genuine characterisms.

We also come close here to the large family of aesthetic characterisms, which we are leaving almost wholly out of account in this study. The interest we show in a human body when we characterize it as alert, rugged, or puny, and so on, is not an aesthetic interest, although certainly these ideas can also enter into aesthetic experience. The application of many of these characterisms presupposes a close and penetrating scrutiny of persons and perhaps even a kind of "disinterested interest" (to appropriate a fitting phrase) that is not altogether foreign to aesthetic experience.

We may next ask how precisely we can distinguish characterizations from descriptions, and characterisms from descripts? The following are examples of description rather than characterization.

> In walking he first raises himself on the heel a centimeter or so before thrusting upward and forward.
>
> He rotates his trunk and upper body rather markedly in walking.
>
> His head has a marked side to side motion coordinated with his steps.
>
> In walking he seems to have little coordination; hands and arms seem to work in a system totally remote from his leg movements.
>
> He never lifts his feet off the ground when he walks.
>
> The child took three short steps and fell.
>
> He has a sallow complexion.
>
> He is taller than average.

Without trying at this point to make a one to one comparison between description and characterization, it would yet be easy for any of us to make observations of the foregoing sort and immediately suggest characterizations for each or several of these. We might say the person is awkward or clumsy in walking, that he shuffles or shambles along, that the child toddled and tumbled, and so forth. In all these and similar situations everyone could fairly readily "improve" on a mere description by offering what seemed an appropriate characterization.

The reason, of course, is that we are not devices for recording facts, like barometers. To live is to respond to and to enter into concourse with surroundings. We are never really indifferent to what we discern, though we may conveniently "bracket out" part of the environment. Responding to phenomena in such a way as to characterize them is the norm of response. Impassive registry is a kind of abstraction that is built on the model of the scientific observer – a rare kind of observer indeed. It is not just the limited class of what we have called elicitives (15.1) among the characterisms that shows how we may be engaged and involved with or responsive to the environment. All characterisms in an important degree, are evocative. Words like **fearful**, **enchanting**, and **stupendous** may of course appear to attribute to objects states which are more truly our own, such as fear, enchantment and stupefaction (an obvious exaggeration). But such attributions cannot really be convicted of the pathetic fallacy; they are not necessarily anomalies of response. Not just elicitives but most of the "constitutional" characterisms (7.0, 8.0, and 9.0), when applied to other persons may evince the vitality of our own attitudes and feelings.

Vitality and vivacity of characterization are close kin to the sources of poetic and other artistic efforts at expression. The vocabulary we are examining is one of familiar words which are sometimes fossils of poetic thought. Poets prize their success in devising unusual forms of expression, and in turn are appreciated by others who find a poem expressing not only what the poet thinks or feels but what they themselves think or feel. The use of the existing treasury of characterization and the enrichment of it with new coin is the very heart of human creativity. The characterisms of this section, and indeed of most of Part Two, are each and all marks of such creativity. The best of them were, to begin with, unexpected and unpredictable, and each stands as a kind of monument of imaginativeness. We may turn now to a brief examination of the vocabulary of 7.0, seeing it in this light.

7.1 FIGURE

CREDITING CHARACTERISMS	DISCREDITING CHARACTERISMS

7.11 PHYSICAL CHARACTER

ATTRIBUTIVE

(a) **bluff** a.	ATTRIBUTIVE
hardy	(a) **gangling**
rugged	**gaunt**
spry	**gawky**
sturdy	**haggard**
	puny
	skinny
	wizened
(b) **buxom**	(b) **fat**
plump	**flabby**
portly	**fleshy**
robust	**hefty**
slender	**paunchy, paunch**
stout	(c) **blowzy**
	frowzy, frowsty

PROCESSIVE

dally, dalliance	PROCESSIVE	
languish (–)	**dawdle**	**lurk**
loll (–)	**loiter**	**slouch**
	lounge	**tarry**

7.12 DRESS

chic	**bedraggle**
clean	**careless**
dapper (cf. G. **tapfer**)	**dowdy**
immaculate	**draggle**
neat	**frump**
preen (process.)	**grubby** (also fig.)
smart a.	**sloppy**
	squalid (and fig. 14.01)
	titivate (process.)
	unkempt

7.2 MOTION

7.21 MOVEMENT

agile	**clumsy**
awkward	**fussy**
mannerism	
nimble	

7.22 LOCOMOTION (largely discrediting)

amble	scamper
caper	scurry
dash	shamble
dodder	shuffle
flounder	stagger
lurch	strut
plod	stumble
poky (attrib.)	toddle
prance	totter
ramble	traipse
reel	trudge
saunter	waddle
	wobble

7.23 AGITATION (largely discrediting)

amuck,	hectic
run amuck	helter-skelter
antic, –s	hurly-burly
bedlam	pandemonium
berserk	pother
boisterous	rambunctious
frantic	restless
to a [frazzle	roister, roisterer
frenzy	rollicking
fidget	romp
frolic,	unruly
frolicsome	

The characterisms for physical character and dress show an unusual number of terms whose origin is obscure: **frowsty, frowzy, gawky, plump, spry, slouch,** and **tarry.** Some of these have an uncommon expressiveness. They have evidently risen from the ranks of unconventional and colloquial speech, possibly slang, and have survived simply because they have a genius for conditioning our way of looking at certain things. A very large proportion of these, and of the rest of 7.0, have been in the language in one form or another from pre-Conquest times.

A considerable number originated as metaphors. **Rugged,** not surprisingly, is related to rug, a coarse and rough coverlet. It has cognates in Scandinavian languages. **Buxom**, related to **biegsam** in German, begins with the image of a bow, something flexible and tractable, and thence moves toward health and vigor, and finally to ample, feminine fullness. **Plump** has moved towards the concrete rather than away from it, beginning in bluntness of manner and dullness of intellect, and evolving toward the fat, rich, and abundant. Similarly, **stout** has gone from a trait of the spirit expressed by **stately, proud** (it is related to German **stolz**), to fierceness, valiance, strength of the body and finally fullness and amplitude. **Haggard** is of obscure origin. It may have begun with a Norman word for hedge, that is, something wild, and then moved toward application to a body contorted by privation, anxiety, and terror, and one that has lost flesh in old age or sickness. **Unkempt** is simply uncombed, to begin with.

The processives show a similar tendency toward metaphorical origin. **Dally** begins in Old French *dalier*, to converse. **Dawdle** seems to begin with the bird (i.e., jackdaw) and then to gain application to the simpleton, and to the sluggard and the slut, both given to lazy ways. **Loiter** seems to derive from Middle Dutch **lateren**, to wag about like a loose tooth. **Lurk** has developed from a verb to shuffle along. **Loll** has come from the rocking or swaying of a child being put to sleep; compare lull and lullaby.

The characterisms of motion may be divided in the following manner: (a) *movement*: generally that of hands or body; often the context is specifically that of a body engaged at a mechanical task, such as sewing; (b) *locomotion*: purposive motion of the whole body principally in translating itself through space, often with various apparent difficulties and handicaps; (c) *agitation*: the body in an action that may be done with or contrary to other persons but without the formality of a march or dance or organized combat.

There is no one way, nor even a very limited number of ways, that a body can be performing its motions. At most, we can state rather hesitantly some broad limits within which the motions would most likely be performed. In a shuffle, the feet generally do not leave the ground, but this description also might include a fairly graceful skating motion on a smooth floor, hardly a shuffle. A nimble motion usually brings to mind a compact, resilient, flexible body. And yet pachyderms often almost force us to speak of them as nimble and graceful. How high should the feet be lifted in a prance? What are the extremes of motion, the least and the highest, that one might expect in bedlam or in motion that is boisterous, rambunctious, rollicking, or roistering? When do motions step over "familiar bounds" and become berserk or frenzied? If there is anything at all safe to be said, it must be that positive traits, *sine qua nons*, or sufficient conditions are virtually impossible to give. We succeed best perhaps in offering certain negative conditions.

Sauntering is not done at breackneck speed, like sprinting. But such rules are like specifying the location of a person as "Brazil."

Of course it is not an attractive outcome to learn of words that they are or border on the indefinable. Yet this is what, in any familiar sense of definition, we must say of characterisms. I believe a careful statistical survey would show that the "definitions" that lexicographers are professionally bound to offer of such terms are predominantly citations of other characterisms. If the purpose of a definition is merely to send us out on a treasure hunt in the right direction, then these definitions may serve their purpose. But we could never be content with "definitions" of this sort of *electron, prime number, axis of rotation, vacuum,* and *syndrome,* or of *blue* and *square.* Citing other characterisms is a makeshift, but it can be no more. New characterisms are coined for the very reason that we want to characterize things as they have not been characterized before. To appraise agitation as berserk or rambunctious we need **berserk** and **rambunctious,** *and nothing else will do.*

From this we again learn something that we shall see confirmed with every new characterism and appraisive: we do not have a "phenomenon" in search of a designation, but the designation is a condition of experiencing the "phenomenon." This accounts for the enormous magnetism and power of slang. Whatever it is that is the phenomenon (for want of a better term) that is referred to by **corny, square,** and **kinky,** it comes into being on the coinage of the term. To be sure, the "bourgeoisie" were already the available target for the purpose, but *what* one wanted to say of the bourgeoisie in calling them squares was not previously in existence. We must add immediately, nor is it in existence afterwards. Such terms have nothing to do with existence or non-existence, nor have they anything to do in the present case with perception and perceptual traits. It is not their purpose to furnish the means to describe something.

If perception and names are erronous leads to follow here, we should not resort immediately to vapid phrases such as "expression of feeling," "embodiment of feeling," "projection of the self," "taking an attitude," or "emotive meaning." Obviously we are not indifferent to our surroundings when we characterize things or persons in it as frowzy, haggard, puny, gawky, or unkempt, but to look for feelings *in* such terms is nonsense, and we cannot say that feelings necessarily accompany the use of such terms. Feelings are more likely to be had when one sees diamonds, or meets friends or enemies, or suffers humiliation, or gains honor.

What is needed here is a determined, extensive study of characterizing concepts and expressions. In the case of characterisms, unlike descripts, we cannot afford to ignore etymology. We must go back to the sources of metaphors, and inquire into the origins of particular slang terms. Only so can we begin to throw light on this fraction of life. If the present view is correct, it is all the more important because the most ultimate of our judgments in the end rest on characterization.

7.3 BODY RESPONSE (largely discrediting)

7.31 VIEWING

gawk
gaze
ogle
peek
peer
stare

7.32 VOICING

drone
fret
maunder (6.32)
mutter
peep
scream (7.36)
screech
squall
whimper
whine

7.33 FACIAL COMPORTMENT (7.36)

giggle
pout
simper
smirk
snicker
snigger
snivel
sulk
titter

7.34 COMMUNICANT GESTURE

ape
clown
leer
shrug
[wink]

7.35 INGESTING

(a) **starve**	**devour**
(b) **abstemious**	**engorge**
abstinent	**gobble**
(c) **cloy**	**gormandize**
crapulent	**guzzle**
glut, glutton, gluttony	**munch**
[satiate, sate]	**overeat**
surfeit	**voracious**
(d) **batten**	(e) **dissipate, dissipated**
bolt	

We must note first the difference between the present and the previous uses of the term 'response.' In 2.2 we were talking about the person's sympathies and antipathies, his feelings of liking and disliking. We were not concerned there with the characterization of those feelings. The appraising and characterization of feelings particularly in persons other than ourselves are the subject of the diathetic characterizations of 8.0. In the present section we are thinking of the person as actively responding to his surroundings through a more or less deliberate use of his body and of being characterized in his use or deployment of it. The body is involved in the person's cognitive or communicative enterprises, except in 7.35.

Viewing. We may consider this topic first from the standpoint of the difference between characterisms and descripts. *Look at, observe, inspect, con,* and *view* itself are representative examples of the latter. One does not use these to characterize anyone's viewing. Acts of this sort are not characterizing and show no individuality. This is partly because there is nothing concrete about them; they are not really part of behavior. One assumes that eyes or other sense organs are involved, but they call to mind the intellect and judgment rather than the body. These terms do not characterize the intellect or judgment, however. They are simply standard descripts.

The most patently characterizing members of the list are **gawk** and **ogle**. They are not rule determined: sufficient and necessary conditions for their use cannot be given; the characterizer's interest in and involvement with the subject are evident; the terms are used to call into question the subject's credit, in this case, in respect to good manners.

The other terms appear to be closer to being rule governed, but the rules themselves are likely to elude us. We cannot say how much longer a gaze, peer, or stare is than a glance. We will be hard put to specify the furtive or stolen quality of a peek or peep. Nevertheless, they are not very genuine characterisms. What makes them appear so is perhaps that staring and peeping. and sometimes the others happen to be socially disapproved of. But there is nothing inherently discrediting in them as there is in **gawk** and **ogle**. The peeping Tom is disapproved of because of the context and subject, but there is scarcely anything discreditable about viewing itself. We may repeat that 'viewing' simply designates an area in which characterisms are to be found; it is not itself a characterism.

Voicing. We may make the same kind of discriminations among characterisms in the area of voicing. *Talking, uttering, calling, shouting* and various other members of the family are plainly only descripts. Among the listed terms, the ones that are most definitely characterizing are probably these: **drone, fret, maunder, squall, whimper,** and **whine. Drone** is perhaps only borrowed from the aesthetic appraisives, or even aesthetic descripts. A drone bass is merely being drawn attention to rather than appraised, if we are told that it is part of what we hear when a band of bagpipers is playing. But it can be used to draw attention to an aesthetically offensive, because monotonous, quality. In this sense it is used as a characterism, let us say of a person's voice. All the other terms of this part of the list are used to discredit principally the human voice. They also draw attention to what is offensive aesthetically, or they are discrediting because they are really elicitives of a negative character. That is, squalling and whining offend because they elicit boredom, displeasure or even pain. **Mutter, peep, scream,** and **screech** may elicit similar forms of unease or they can be used in almost wholly neutral fashion as descripts. A peeping or screaming noise *may* not offend. Muttering is often offensive because of the content of speech, rather than because of the mere voicing.

Facial Comportment. There are many terms for facial expression, most of them very ancient in origin. One could name at least these: **frown, gape, glower, grimace, grin, scowl,** and **smile.** The first and last of these seem to me to be the best examples of what are definitely descripts and not characterisms. Opinion may, however, differ about these and also about whether to put certain others in one class or the other. Very definitely **blanch, blush, flush, gasp,** and **squint** would seem to fall much too far toward the side of reflexes to be of interest to us.

Once again we must be careful to distinguish those descripts that are accompanied by feelings of pleasure or displeasure from the characterisms, which are inherently crediting or discrediting. Of course we are probably always pleased by a grin or smile, and somewhat displeased by a frown or scowl, but there is no necessity in this. We may register quite objectively *the fact that* A has smiled or grinned and be mortally offended at his amusement at what we think a serious or solemn matter. Similarly, we may take A's frown or scowl as evidence that he agrees with a disapprobation of our own.

Moreover, it is not at all obvious to many people that smiling, laughing, and cheerful good fellowship are praiseworthy, and it is not just New England Puritans and Trobriand Islanders who have thought so. The story is told of the aged Goethe taking his place in the grandest stall of a theatre where a comedy was to be performed, turning to the audience in the hush before the curtain rose, and commanding: "Man lache nicht!"

With the foregoing in mind, I think it becomes plausible to say that the terms of 7.33 are all characterisms. I do not think we have much cause to be offended if A says to us, "I caught a glimpse of you and saw you frown (gape, glower, grimace, grin, scowl)" though A may be implying we are not in very ready control of our expressions. But we will not say of ourselves that we are now pouting, sulking, smirking, and so forth, since they tend to injure our repute or credit. What prompts us to apply characterisms of this sort has a profound bearing on our moral evaluation of persons. The conviction that someone smirks, snickers or sulks can be as firm as that he has some physical feature.

The paucity of this vocabulary is deceptive. There is nothing, rightly or wrongly, that is so likely to be relied upon in the prima facie judgment of character than facial comportment. The vocabulary, therefore, is endlessly augmented by further efforts at characterization in all of the available modes, such as slang, metaphor, and amplifying phrases, far too varied to be quoted here. Because of this we should keep the present section particularly in mind when we approach the decisive narrower questions of the moral characterization of man.

Communicant Gesture. The previous class of characterisms was based on what the person more or less betrays of himself, the present class on what he may wish to convey deliberately. It may be open to some doubt whether these are really characterisms. We can certainly describe gestures in fairly nice detail if we make the effort; certainly we can do so for a shrug or a wink, and it is fairly easy to describe aping. Clowning and leering are, however, much more difficult. I should say that clowning is positively not a descript, and that leering is subject to no rules whatever; it is obvious one can deliberately wink and shrug. One can also imitate and impersonate. But in the latter case, one would not say of his own imitation that it was aping. This, then, is a clearcut characterism which is applied to others when they seem to us guilty of imitating in a slavish manner because they lack the imaginativeness to do anything original. (Notice how our "definition" of one characterism involves us in others.) In the end, then, I would say **ape, clown**, and **leer** are definite characterisms, **shrug** is a borderline case (it can also be used slightly abstractly) and **wink** is perhaps a bit more descriptive than **shrug**. Others, however, may have reason to classify these in a different manner.

Wink seems to belong here rather than under the previous section on facial comportment because it is clearly subject to deliberate use.

Nothing affords quite so much evidence as these communicant gestures for the difference of body and spirit, the outer and the inner, or better, for the conviction of the reality of this difference. I think we err in thinking that this is merely lay or popular psychologizing. One should try to answer the following questions: Does this vocabulary imply the inner-outer difference? If it does, is there a fact of some sort conveyed by this implication? If there is, can the fact be conveyed in other than inner-outer terms (e.g., purely behavioristic terms)? If it can, how is it to be done and will it sound different from the present phraseology? Answers to these questions are not so easy to produce. Of all psychologies, behaviorism rides most roughshod over what laymen feel and think, or what they say they feel and think, whereas our whole effort from beginning to end is to be religiously faithful to just that. Any adequate psychology must recognize first the brute facts *and then* proceed to produce theories to explain the facts. Most behaviorisms are programmatically prejudiced from the start as to what the facts are. In this situation, we must be absolutely clear that one of the brute facts is the *conviction that* there is an inner-outer, or body-mind distinction, and this must be distinguished clearly from the use of these distinctions as theoretical, explanatory constructs. I readily grant that the latter is doubtful, or problematic, but it is surely impermissible to ignore the former. Theories of this sort are obliged to explain the fact of our convictions. A groundless conviction deserves as much respect from an explanatory theory as a valid one. We therefore return the problem of the explanation of this and other phenomena to the psychologists with this methodological exhortation.

Ingesting. The quantity, quality, and manner of the intake of food and drink have always been a most important topic in the characterization of persons. It is frequently thought to bear on the total appraisal in a limited but definite degree. It is imperative, therefore, that we give it at least nodding consideration. (Explicitly gustatory appraisives are considered briefly in Appendix E.)

As to *quantity*, we may point out first that there is obviously no norm that can be laid down as "proper." Each appraiser has to decide what quantity of ingestives shall be thought to injure, enhance or maintain the credit of the subject. It is obvious that social customs, varying from culture to culture, must determine the limits of quantity in the direction either of gluttony or its full alternative (whatever it is).

A serious question arises, not over relative quantities, but over the characterization of the extremes themselves. It is not only conceivable, but it is the fact that there are or have been societies so chronically undernourished that they have no term for gluttony, or if they have, it is not a characterism to be used to discredit the subject. Indeed, it might be something of a virtue to overeat (as *we* might say). In the Moslem view, Heaven is plenteously filled with refreshing water. It is obvious that no one can make a virtue of zero quantity of food, but what is actually thought about quantities at the other extreme is mainly a matter for empirical research. Its significance for us is that it raises for the first time the question of cultural relativism as evidenced in characterisms. This we shall encounter repeatedly, especially under such categories as aggression and sexual orientation.

The characterisms devoted to the *quality* or *manner* of ingesting appear to claim a somewhat greater authority than those of quantity. It is true that in some societies it is thought barbarous to eat with hands and fingers, while in others instruments of eating are little known. The fact is **devour, munch** and **guzzle** have little or nothing to do with such local differences. The supreme consideration is whether, within whatever limits it sets itself, a society has decided on a certain quality of seemliness and unseemliness, of propriety or impropriety in ingesting. Quite obviously considerations of this sort, like those of others already taken up in 7.3, always have a bearing on the total evaluation of persons. Matters of this sort will engage our attention again in the study of the particularly behavioral virtues and vices in 14.0.

7.36 RES GESTAE (7.33)

blush	**snarl**
frown	**tremble**
scream	**yawn**

A rather curious class must be added to the foregoing. The term *res gestae* seems to have several meanings, but the present use is one that is to be found in martial or naval law.

The point of these various *res* is that they are essentially and almost wholly involuntary or even reflexive yet they clearly "express" certain conditions of mind or emotion. Thus we blush from embarrassment, we yawn not only when sleepy but also when bored, we may scream or tremble from pain or fright, we may frown from disappointment, and in a certain sense, we may snarl when enraged in utmost degree.

The terms appear here only to round out our presentation of behavior. They are objective or descriptive in full degree but can be used to characterize when not literally applicable. In this latter sense application to oneself in the present would be felt as self-negating. One might, however, in appropriate circumstances say, "I blush (but not 'am blushing') to repeat what he said," or "I tremble to think what may come of this."

8.0 DIATHETIC CHARACTERIZATION

The two principal vocabularies of 8.0 may be distinguished as *moodwords* and *mienwords*. There can be no doubt of their difference, although opinion may differ about the classification of particular terms.

Moodwords are characterizations of the manifest emotional or feeling states of persons either as passing and episodic or as more or less continuant dispositions. The determinant source of feeling is inner. Moods as such are not responses to the environment nor determined from without. The person tends to feel as he does regardless of environing circumstances.

Mienwords may also reflect inner states of feeling but these are responses to prevailing or projected circumstances. They seek to characterize the manner in which a person comports himself especially in response to others. Their subject matter is other persons in their outer presence, but not as simply physical or "behaving" bodies. It is *persons* that are here in interaction with one another.

With both classes of terms the speaker occupies a standpoint where he seems only to need to open his eyes to confirm what he says. But is this enough? Must he not also reflect about himself, and is he not speaking about matters which only a subject can report of himself?

Here we again encounter a familiar move by the behaviorist. He either ignores what the speakers are saying or he offers a "behavioral interpretation" of it: when we say A is cheerful, dejected, merry, moody, or sulky this is said either to mean nothing at all or to mean nothing more than that he behaves so and so and so.

These are false alternatives. No doubt we are judging A on how be behaves (what can be more trivial than that assertion?), but there is not the slightest doubt that we are in some sense talking about his emotions and how he feels and we are presuming to be able to say something about him that at least resembles what we are able to say about ourselves.

What is needed here is that we make clear the distinction between reporting and characterizing oneself and others: we are reporting when we talk about ourselves, but we are characterizing when we talk of others. It is really quite trivial to insist that we cannot report the emotions of others. But the fact is there is no reason to believe that we are ever tempted to do so, and this fact can be learned from language itself. The vocabularies of 8.11 and all of 8.2 are not designed for making report either about oneself or others; they are vocabularies for characterizing others. We do not characterize ourselves in these terms. If we wish to report our own feelings there is a serviceable, if small, vocabulary for this that we have already examined, namely 2.2, the direct responses. This covers the affects, the states of being affected and of responding, though not the reports of, say, being happy or sad. The latter are characterizations of 8.12 that can be and very often are self-applied. The purpose of all of 8.11 (and of 8.3, or 2.4) is essentially characterization of the emotive states of others. This intent is not affected by our sources of information or misinformation about one another.

What we are saying can be summed up under four possibilities:

(1) *Reporting or describing our own emotions.* For this we have the vocabulary of 2.2, Direct Response, of 2.3, and other vocabularies, (e.g. Moral Affects, 5.1).

(2) *Reporting or describing the emotions of others.* We certainly cannot report the emotions of others. On rare occasions we may offer neutral descriptions of the manifest bodily states of others who we say are in emotive states. What is more likely is that we will resort to (4) below.

(3) *Characterizing our own emotions.* We do not characterize our own emotions in the immediate or continuant present. Characterizations are crediting or discrediting. Hence a present self-discreditation will be avoided as self-stultifying, and a self-creditation will be seen to be as worthless as giving oneself a diploma. A characterization is by nature a summing up in an extern manner, by others. (This needs qualification only in 8.12.)

(4) *Characterizing the emotions of others.* We can characterize immediately ongoing emotive responses of others by using the processive terms of the responsional characterizations, 2.4 (= 8.3); or we can characterize the moods of others (8.111) or their patterns of temper (8.112); or we can characterize their air, bearing, or manner (8.2), etc.

Once again, it would be well for the behaviorist to begin his inquiry by listening carefully to what persons are saying, what kinds of claims they are making and not making about themselves and others. No characterization claims to be reporting the emotions of others, nor does it occur to us to try.

Mienwords in 8.2 are characterisms whose subject matter is other persons in their outer presence, not as mere physical or "behaving" bodies but as persons. The present division seems plausible and without forced classifications. The separation of 8.2 from behavior, 7.0, is obvious with regard to all except perhaps the first subgroup in 7.11, a point considered briefly below. 8.2 emphasizes man as conducting himself in a social setting and role, whereas most of 7.0 is devoted to man in his physically distinct, if not private, role.

The term 'diathetic' represents a new coinage or at least a useful revival or revision, and is meant to designate the characterisms that set forth the constitution of man. We are now beginning to be concerned with character in a stronger sense of the term; there is more to come. There is scarcely a predicate that appears here that could not in some degree reappear as the name of a virtue or vice. It is the area to which Theophrastus in antiquity contributed some of his thirty characters. We could enlarge that gallery of portraits by constructing more substantives from the stock of diathetic characterisms: the placid man, the haughty man, the poised man, and so forth. Present day personality psychology usually leaves such devices behind as oversimplifications, yet it does return to them occasionally, as it sees ancient insights confirmed. It should however be unnecessary to add that the analysis of characterisms themselves in no sense necessitates any "platonizing" procedure toward these predicates such as may be found in ancient or early modern psychology and anthropology.

8.1 EMOTIVE TONE AND TEMPERAMENT

CREDITING CHARACTERISMS	DISCREDITING CHARACTERISMS

8.11 MOOD AND TEMPER

8.111 MOOD

cheer, cheerful	dejected
elated	downcast
exuberant	downhearted
gay	gloom
glee	glum
good [humor	lachrymose
jolly	maudlin
merry, merriment	mawkish
overjoyed	melancholy (8.13)
on [tenterhooks	moody
	mope
	morbid
	morose
	mournful, mourn
	nostalgia
	sad

8.112 TEMPER (see 2.4)

[calm]	crab, crabbed
equable	cross a.

equanimous	**embittered**	**repine**
gentle	**emotion,**	**sulk**
good-tempered	**emotional**	**sullen**
imperturbable	**fret, fretful**	**surly**
	fractious	**tantrum**
	grouch, grouchy	**termagant** (subst.)
	huff, huffy	**testy**
	ill-tempered	**tetchy**
	irascible	**touchy**
	irritable	
	misanthrope,	
	–ic, –y (14.22)	
	peevish	
	petulant	
	pique	
	querulous	

8.12   LA CONDITION HUMAINE

8.121   HAPPINESS

bliss	**joy**
content, contented	**repose**
felicity	**secure**
happy, happiness	

8.122   DESPAIR

desolate	**lonely, lonesome**
despair	**miserable, misery**
despondent	**nothingness**
disconsolate	**wretched**

8.123   AFFLICTION

affliction	**ordeal**
agony	**sorrow**
crisis	**tribulation**
distress	**trouble, troubled**
malcontent	**woe, woeful**

The characterisms of mood, tone, and temper afford a glimpse into the human condition if not human nature itself. The words themselves, apart from context and use, would seem to teach us little, yet when a considerable number of them is assembled they are eloquent and insistent reminders of the kinds of insights and judgments we have of ourselves and of others. They exhibit the modes of our sympathies and antipathies, our capacities and incapacities for understanding and sharing inevitable burdens, and hint at the heights of satisfaction and despair which human lives are capable of. All of these characterisms are directed essentially outwards; they are characterizations or appraisals of others. Yet each one of them as clearly points back toward the appraiser, showing how he has "taken" the situation and person or persons before him. This shows that these are tone characterisms, rather than descripts. Is A irritable, irascible, embittered, maudlin, elated? Then whom does he irritate, who senses his states as embittered, who is put off by his overripe emotive state, who senses the lift in his spirit? Once again we learn as much of Peter as we do of Paul, when Peter expresses himself in such characterisms.

In attending to another person's *moods*, we have a view of him as if he stood in isolation from his surroundings. Good or ill temper, on the other hand, is manifested in reaction to others or to the environment.

We may consider first the *moods*, which appear to characterize the subject as if he were detached from his context. His exuberance or gaiety seems to bubble up from somewhere within, and his moodiness and dejection seem to point backward and inward and downward. Moods may certainly have a cause or occasion in present or previous experience, but characteristically they lay hold of the whole subject as if they arose from within. Moods can of course sometimes be counterfeited or feigned, but perhaps not as easily as the counterfeiter supposes. The fact is that elation and dejection, or buoyancy and depression, in others are things of which we can be almost dead certain. We can detect the slightest tremor of hesitancy or dissimulation in others, and we tend to take our characterizations for objective descriptions. There is nothing that even a fool can be so thoroughly expert on as feelings. Elation, if genuine, tends to generate elation, and dejection dejection. Hence, if *we* are not quite elated we may hesitate to characterize a subject in these terms. Among the stronger characterisms here are the terms **maudlin** and **mawkish**. They appear to have a kind of ambivalent character suiting them for use about those who rather tend to wallow in and in a perverse way to enjoy their dejection, or who manage somehow to make their enjoyments unattractive.

If mood may stand in apparent detachment from surrounding affairs, temper is quite clearly a response to it. Accordingly under temper we characterize the manner in which persons relate themselves to one another or to ourselves. Once again we find here the familiar phenomenon among all characterizations, that good news is no news: good temper is much less likely to be remarked upon than bad temper and more likely to be taken for granted. Of characterisms of good temper we have here only three or four examples, of bad temper nearly a score. To be sure, the examples exhibit a fair degree of synonymity or near synonymity. Yet we find it evidently an advantage to have an extensive treasury to draw from in order to characterize the exact shade of ill-temper in others.

It should be noticed that these are not actual responses or characterizations of response. What we are characterizing is the established habits, long term or short term, of others. The emphasis is, however, on the short term. If we are said to be sullen, peevish, petulant, or surly this probably will be based upon actual episodes, which may then have a greater or lesser frequency. This does not mean that these characterisms are used to characterize actual episodes and transactions. We have our eye on the episodes without directly appraising *them*.

The less that is implied about an invariant or long-term condition, the less these characterizations will have to do with character. But no doubt, if it is felt we may always be on the verge of showing bad temper, even though somehow we do not, this may be thought to have some bearing on character.

Another aspect of the difference of what we are characterizing here from actual responses may be discerned by reference back to the responses considered in Part One. In 2.21 we had such concepts as **rejoice** or **delight**, and in 2.22 **annoyance** and **irritation**. But these are descripts. Their application to ourselves would not be self-stultifying; we would not hesitate to give a report of ourselves with the aid of them. It is not an evidence of ill-temper to show annoyance or irritation, since obviously if there is any reason to speak of values at all we must, on occasion, be irritated with negations of value. It is part of growing out of childhood to learn how to distinguish between the chronic grouch, for whom there is little or no excuse, and the persistent critic, for whom some day we may be thankful.

Another class that is likely to be confused with the characterisms of mood or temper is that of the Responsional Characterizations of 2.4. The difference here is the one alluded to, two paragraphs back. Responsions are actual episodes: one bristles or fumes at for a length of time, or at a certain time. Ill-temper, on the other hand, manifests itself in time no doubt, but it refers to how I am likely to behave, or have tended to behave: it is not itself a discrete process in time.

What we have called *la condition humaine* from its current and recent use by existentialists owes nothing to this school of thought except a convenient title. Certainly neither this nor any other school discovered that to which these characterisms make reference. What we are trying to get at here has an evident profound air, as if one had sounded the inner depths of personality. The characterisms themselves are neither shallow nor profound. They get whatever quality of this sort they have because they are used to characterize man in his extremity, having either achieved an impregnable security, or fallen into an infinitely menacing and hopeless void. The characterisms of the human condition are not merely for third personal use. They are used by all who can no longer disguise from themselves the horror of their situation or whose security can no longer be denied. Here the distinction between descript and characterism may seem to disappear.

We must distinguish between the characterisms of mood, (elation and dejection), and those of happiness and despair. While there remains a possibility under the former that the good or evil of something may be only the "opinion" of a bystander, even if it is an engaged bystander, the good or evil of the latter, happiness and despair, seems to be boundless. The reason for this is that in such situations *value appears a reality*. And indeed if the idea of value *is* meaningful then it must, in the end, have an exemplification. The series in which *a* is valuable in terms of *b*, and *b* of *c*, and *c* of *d*, and so on, may have no final member, but some state is *de facto* the last member for each of us. Inevitably it must fall either under one extreme or the other, or the series must appear to converge toward one of them. If none of these is realized this will have its own quantum of despair or happiness for us.

The third group of appraisives is not essentially different from the others, but allows for the characterization of man in his context, his relation to time and place rather than "in himself," as with the two preceding groups. Here again he finds himself in an extremity, and we must understand these characterisms in terms of the ultimate and the insoluble: the affliction, crisis, ordeal, tribulation, or distress must be hopeless and raised to an ultimate and inescapable limit.

All of these characterisms are paradoxically the most indefinite and vague of all those we have under consideration, yet they also are of an unparalleled meaningfulness and poignancy when there is no conceivable alternative to them in some agonizing situation. Therefore, we must accord them a place of first importance.

Of lesser interest are the additional characterisms **malcontent** and **misanthrope**. The misanthrope is in a situation of extremity out of choice rather than out of the force of circumstances. His place is here rather than under the moods or tempers, because he quite evidently looks beyond his own satisfactions and pains toward the end reaches of the human condition. Certainly Moliere's misanthrope does. If the malcontent is anything at all distinct, it may be because he takes a less universal view of things than the misanthrope. With this we complete our survey of feelings – the word can hardly bear the heavy traffic of the human condition! We must turn now to the characterization of man in his more public capacity.

8.13   TEMPERAMENT

(a) **choleric (irascible)**   shrewish, shrew
    phlegmatic (apathetic)   volatile
    sanguine (hopeful)   waspish
(b) **spleen, splenetic**   (c) **melancholy (sad)** (8.111)
    saturnine

In 8.13 we have a vocabulary of terms of older science persisting in use to the present day but with little present cognitive value. Some four of the terms go back to the theory of humors, **sanguine, phlegmatic, choleric, melancholy**. Four fluids, blood, phlegm, yellow bile, and black bile, were thought to determine human temperament, and to account for differences in these among men by the variance of their mixture in the physical frame. As mere designations for certain kinds of personality or behavior the terms retain an informal value. As such they have little use as characterizations, since they appear to be descriptive in intent. The terms **shrewish, volatile, waspish** and **splenetic** are more definitely characterizing; it is an open question whether they may not more properly be placed among the short-term characterisms of temper. The reason they are all placed here together is not unrelated to the persistence of the humoral predicates not only in speech but even in science. They represent an effort to see the human person as a whole and not dualistically as body and mind, and to seek for the ultimate foundations of personality and temperament in the physical body. It is only in our time that this, the essential lesson of Galen's theory, has been in any position to be studied objectively through biochemistry and psychology. We must await the outcome of such studies, but neither of these subjects can cover the field alone.

We must reiterate the descriptive (in intent) character of the humoral predicates. Only **shrewish, volatile**, and **waspish**, as we have noted, are more plainly characterizing. And in these cases, we have no sure guide to follow in placing them among the tempers or the temperaments. We can see the need of such terms from their unabated persistence in speech, but we are not very clear what we are saying in using them. The best counsel, therefore, is to await the outcome of empirical studies in this area.

We must distinguish between the explanatory and the typological phases of ancient theories. As Professor Allport says, "In the light of modern physiology and endocrinology, the list of specific 'humors' advanced by Hippocrates has been completely abandoned, but the principle of psycho-physical correspondence remains." * The typology of Galen and Hippocrates in some measure is reconfirmed, that is, the distinction into four, or sometimes three,

---

* Gordon W. Allport, *Personality, A Psychological Interpretation*, London, 1961, p. 63.

basic types of personality retains its meaningfulness and application, although the humoral theory has, of course, been wholly abandoned. He further states:

Although modern science has shown that the hormonal substances of the body are more numerous and complex than the ancients knew, still the happy guess that temperament, the emotional groundwork of personality is conditioned by body chemistry has been increasingly borne out in modern research .... The four patterns described by the theory fit neatly into almost any modern dimensional scheme for classifying temperament. It is true that the names of the temperaments have a qualitative flavor: choleric means *irascible*, sanguine *hopeful*, melancholic *sad*, phlegmatic *apathetic*. But these qualitative colorings ... are congruent with a logical and quantitative view of the possible dimensions of temperament.*

8.2   AIR, BEARING, MIEN, MANNER

The entire vocabulary of 8.2 is devoted to the extern characterization of persons. Although every such characterism may presuppose a conscious person, it is first of all directed toward the figure, pose, or posture such a conscious person presents to others. The popular or informal meaning of 'conscious' is sufficient here for the purpose.

We divide the characterisms into some five classes which are distinguished by their material meanings, rather than any formal character. Considerable effort was made to arrive at a division on the lines of the classes designated in the title of 8.2: air, bearing, mien, and manner. But this is unsatisfactory in the end for two reasons. First, these designations as handed down to us are themselves too vague to be precised, explicated, or supplied with substitutive definitions: unless there are some presumptive limits or delimitations initially, there is no good reason to try to refurbish the terms; one may as well invent new ones. Second, even if the terms can be precised in some formal way, the subject matter proves too complex to fit into the classes thus devised. Human behavior and conduct is simply too rich in variety to be encapsulated in formally defined classes.

One may not wish to yield quite so easily, however. Mien, for example, certainly appears to involve the face quite necessarily, and bearing the body. Thus the following are fairly plausible divisions:

BEARING:

august	**rigid**	**unbending**
demure	**sedate**	
dignity	**stately**	

* Gordon W. Allport, *Pattern and Growth in Personality*, Holt, Rinehart, and Winston, 1961, p. 37 ff.

MIEN:

grim	solemn
severe	stern
sober	taciturn

With these as a kind of suggestive or *exemplary definition* (a device we often are forced to use in spite of its question-begging character) we could now attempt to place some of the remaining predicates into the two classes and perhaps devise others. I confess that this has appeared to me to break down almost immediately. We cannot confine the area of characterization to the face alone or to the body alone. The purpose of characterisms is defeated if they are too restricted. The imagination is being invited to roam rather widely in the use of the characterisms and shows its creativity in this. I therefore offer the classifications of 8.2 in an entirely tentative fashion.

To this class are allocated all of the predicates under any of the four main headings guided by the idea of the characterization of the conscious person in meaningful response to an environment of other persons. The subject matter, therefore, is not motion of the body, as narrowly considered in 7.0, nor the person in the ban of various moods and tempers, as in 8.11, nor the person as involved in the complexities of sociative, sexual, economic or other relations to other persons.

8.2   AIR, BEARING, MIEN, MANNER

8.21   VIVACITY-PLACIDITY

POSITIVE CHARACTERISMS	+	NEGATIVE CHARACTERISMS
CREDITING		CREDITING
(a) alert		(c) placid
blithe, blithesome		quiet, quietude (App. E 2.0)
carefree		
ebullient		
exuberant		
exultant		
genial		
hearty		
jovial		
light-hearted		
lively		
pert		
radiant		

responsive
restive
revel
spirited
sprightly
verve
vivacious

$+$ ════════════════════ × ════════════════════ $-$

DISCREDITING	DISCREDITING (9.2)
(b) **flamboyant**	(d) **blasé**
nervous	**indolent**
tense	**lackadaisical**
	languid
	languor, languorous
	lassitude
	lazy
	lethargic, lethargy
	listless
	moribund
	slack
	sloth, slothful (9.22)
	supine
	weary

$-$

In 8.2, the first group, Vivacity-Placidity, appears to border closely on previous classes and so raises problems of classification. For example, 7.2 considers the motion of the body (e.g. **agile, alert, nimble**) yet it is only the motion of the body and not the whole person responding in a lively fashion to others. It is obvious that, for example, **alert, languid, lethargic,** and **lively** could well characterize the body's manifestation of energy in a perfectly behavioral manner, and one could easily place them under 7.11 or 7.2 if the body alone were thought of. Apart from this, they seem to deserve their present place.

It is also possible to think of 8.11 (Mood and Temper) as a possible destination for some of the class Vivacity-Placidity; and some of the mood-words certainly will have often been used to characterize air and bearing. Yet a thoughtful examination of the present class ought to dispel the notion that it is devoted to moods or tempers: **blithe, indolent, lazy, lackadaisical, lethargic, placid, pert, restive, radiant, spirited,** and **tense** are certainly neither mood nor temper words, and neither, I think, are the rest. In general, I should say the assimilation of some of these terms to behavior is much more plausible.

The vocabulary of 8.2 is one for characterizing persons in their immediate relations to one another. In 8.21 several terms seem to be somewhat more descriptive in function than the others: **alert, lively, restive, tense**, and possibly **quiet, weary**, and **nervous**. They have little or no implication for the subject's credit, one way or the other, and possibly fairly decisive rules might be developed for them. The rest of the positives are all manifestly characterisms. The characterizer will evidently be confessing to a certain lift of the spirit when he directly characterizes a subject in terms of the positives. A certain depression will be evident in the use of the negatives. Moreover, the subject's credit will appear to rise or fall depending upon whether he or she is thought, for example, to be vivacious or listless.

As in previous cases, a good clue to what we are trying to convey by the use of these characterisms is etymology. (We may set aside most of the Latin derivatives as terms whose origin lies too far afield.) Some of the more interesting are these. **Blithe**, now largely poetic, derives from an old stem, to shine and **flamboyant** similarly comes from O.F. *flambe*, flame. **Sprightly** traces directly to spirit, and so to a disembodied being. The family of characterisms is built on the idea of something light, bright and refulgent.

The negatives also show interesting origins. They approach the general idea of decline and passivity from a number of different sides. From Latin *placeo*, we get the idea of submissively pleasing or obliging (**placid**); from Latin *langueo* and *lassus* we get being faint, weak, exhausted (**languid, lassitude**); the **lethargic** is in origin the drowsy and forgetful; from *lay* with the addition of –sy, as in *tipsy*, comes **lazy**; **indolence** is of course from *indolentia*, freedom from pain; **slothful** is related to *slow*; **listless** traces back to absence of list or pleasure (cf. lust); and what is **supine** is sprawled helplessly on its back; **weary** is cognate with words in ancient languages for giddiness, faintness, and sleep (its physiological implications remove it to the periphery of 8.21). Yet none of the characterisms as it stands today merely describes what some ancient root or cognate may have been used to describe. The descripts for the passive postures that are being alluded to with these characterisms are fairly limited; the characterizations of passivity are literally endless, so that even now new coinages, mostly from metaphor, make their appearance. Metaphor, in one form or another, sires many of the characterisms.

The arrangement of the vocabulary is meant to separate the positive-negative distinction from crediting and discrediting. By means of the image of light and motion we characterize the subject as alert, pert, radiant, and sprightly; by the opposite image as languid, listless and placid. But it is possible to be overcome by the violence or intensity of motion or light, and to welcome the relief of relaxation. These are shown by **nervous** and **tense**, and in a more attenuated degree by **flamboyant** (faintly discrediting) which suggest that certain limits have been approached or overstepped, and by **quietude**, a negative or privative term plainly used to characterize its subject favorably.

We now introduce a four-square or fourfold arrangement of characterisms that will be increasingly evident as we proceed. As may be seen, the relationships run horizontally, vertically, and diagonally. On the horizontal we take note of the fact that both positive and negative characterisms can be crediting, and another pair of sets of them can be discrediting. A similar pairing of sets vertically is evident. These are the true opposites. Equally interesting are the diagonals. In general, upper left and lower right virtually intend the same result: one of them credits a condition and the other discredits its negation. Upper right and lower left correspond in similar fashion. The fact that we credit (or discredit) both positives and negatives has a slightly anomalous air. Perhaps, in the words of the Preacher, "To everything there is a season." More will be said of this presently.

It is with some diffidence that I suggest an alternative to Aristotle's celebrated tripartite division of virtue and vice as set forth in Book II of the *Nicomachean Ethics*. It will be recalled that Aristotle describes virtue as a mean between two vices. All of these in fact are opposed to one another: the virtue is opposed to each flanking vice and the vices are opposed also to one another. Is there a viable alternative to this scheme? What claim has a fourfold division to supersede Aristotle's? I shall pause briefly to consider this qustion.

Aristotle is dividing dispositions. To take some of his examples they may be schematically presented as follows:

Vice of Excess	Virtue	Vice of Deficiency
1. Rashness	Courage	Cowardice
2. Self-Indulgence	Temperance	Insensibility
3. Prodigality	Liberality	Meanness
4. Tastelessness or Vulgarity	Magnificence	Niggardliness
5. Irascibility	Good Temper	Inirascibility

Let us take one typical instance of our fourfold division, namely Provision under Economic Conduct (12.24) which attends to the same subject matter as the example of Aristotle's marked 3 above. Each of Aristotle's virtues appears in our scheme, but there is also a fourth, as follows.

Liberality   **Frugality**
Prodigality ✕ **Meanness**

The missing member in Aristotle's scheme is Frugality, which seems to have a good claim to being a virtue. Why then is this member missing?

I believe the answer lies in the fact that Aristotle is writing a book on, about, and in support of virtue, among other things. And this is where his effort differs from our own, which is about the concepts of value, including the concepts of the virtues. He is clearly urging us to support liberality as against the two vices, and of course it is quite clear that we ought to follow it and eschew prodigality and meanness.

But Aristotle has failed to consider the fact that as concepts, liberality and meanness are really one and the same: one commends a certain course of action and the other condemns the contrary of this course. The true and full opposite of liberality is not meanness but prodigality. If we now ask what commendable course of action corresponds to what is condemned in prodigality we see that it must be frugality, for this commends a course of action and prodigality condemns the precise contrary of it.

One might say there are two means between the extremes. Must we now choose between these? The point is that no general answer can be given. We must decide on each occasion whether to be liberal or frugal.

Similarly, the choice we confront with example 1 is between courage and caution. Clearly, no one should be either cowardly or rash. Surely it must sometimes be true that caution (discretion) is the better part of valor. We cannot say that valor is *always* better than discretion.

Aristotle seems to have elected to recommend liberality in general. As a partisan of a certain scheme of moral advice it is quite proper for him to do so. But we have left this question altogether open. The fourfold scheme simply shows us what the conceptual alternatives are. Aristotle's choice is actually not a mean. It clearly avoids the extremes: not by striking just the right balance between frugality and liberality, but by tilting a little further from meanness; this must then move him toward prodigality.

One may wish to re-examine the other Aristotelian virtues and vices from this standpoint. There are various other issues about the situation that will bear further examination.

8.22 CONFIDENCE-DIFFIDENCE (Cf. 9.3, 11.2)

POSITIVE CHARACTERISMS   +   NEGATIVE CHARACTERISMS

CREDITING

(a) **aplomb**
   composure
   [confident]
   cool
   flush a.
   sang-froid
   self-assured
   self-confident

(±) **brusk, brusque**
   crusty

CREDITING

(c) **modest**
   reserved
   reticent
   unassuming

(±) **bashful**
   coy
   gentle
   humility, humble
   self-conscious
   shy
   wistful

+ ═══════════════════ × ═══════════════════ −

DISCREDITING

(b) **bumptious**
   conceited
   consequential
   (=pompous)
   forward
   "fresh"
   haughty
   hauteur
   impudent
   malapert
   officious
   pompous
   pride
   saucy
   smug
   snob
   supercilious
   vain, vanity
   vaunt

DISCREDITING

(d) **crestfallen**
   diffident
   distraught
   forlorn
   shamefaced
   woebegone

−

Although, as we have explained, it is difficult to classify the appraisives of 8.2 among the four principal titles (Air, Bearing, etc.), we may venture to say 8.22 is more concerned with manner than the others. The title itself is not altogether accurate since it singles out a quality that is not always to be numbered among diathetic appraisives. It can fall as easily among the tendentives, or sociatives, and it is also a character of expressive activity. This, however, is only to say that it has a range of uses. Confidence, self-confidence, diffidence, and self-assuredness certainly are very often used diathetically, even if they are not so apt or imaginative or colorful as some of the others. **Confidence**, a descript, is a fitting title for the whole class.

As we have seen with the previous class, a figure or image, as the basis of a metaphor, is used to express our characterizations of one another's person. If there is any single figure or image lying behind the characterisms of confidence-diffidence, it is that of something thrusting itself forward or receding into the background. **Bumptious, saucy,** and of course **forward** present this image of self-assertion best. We have learned to identify the image **cool** with such self-assertion or courage, though it is not altogether clear why this image expresses self-control better than another. Other languages may here show significant variations. Indeed, one need go no farther than German to find **frech** and **Frechheit**, meaning impudence, to see an apparently different metaphor employed; this leads directly to the Americanism **fresh**, meaning much the same thing. The source of **fresh** (somewhat obscure, apparently) may lie in an ancient Germanic word for going or coming forth, thus conforming to the general image for this class of characterisms. Or again, what is fresh may come forward or strike us by its cleanliness. **Froward** may sometimes appear in this class in place of **forward.**

Some of the negatives not surprisingly derive from the opposite direction, that of passitivity or receptivity. **Bashful** derives from **abash,** and this in turn from shouting bah! at someone; thus the bashful man has retreated as if in the face of verbal aggression. **Crestfallen** explains itself. **Shy** is from an old Teutonic term for being frightened. The eloquent and subtle **wistful** is somewhat obscurer in origin; it is not particularly metaphorical but draws attention to the fact that in passive situations we can only think and reflect rather than assert our desires or egos. The woebegone person is surrounded or engulfed by woe. The modest man keeps himself within the bounds of measure (L. *modus*). The reticent man is, in origin, the silent man. Thus the negatives ring all the changes on the self as retreating or withdrawing within itself.

The foregoing pair of sets must now be extended, especially on the positive side, by a group of appraisives (b) which apply to persons whose confidence seems to derive not so much from inner strength as from being fortified by a sense of impregnable or unassailable position. So a person may have the air or manner of being haughty, officious, pompous, supercilious, smug, or snobbish. The basic image of thrusting forward or standing out or forth can be seen in all of this class. **Haughty** reflects French *haut* (exalted or high); the officious man is interfering and meddlesome; **pompous**, deriving ultimately from the Latin for a parade or spectacle, which is, of course by its nature, an outstanding occasion, could appear either here or in 8.23 with **conceit** and **pretense**, or in 8.25 with **stately** and **solemn**; **supercilious** traces to the figurative use of the Latin term for eyebrow to mean a brow, ridge or summit; smug is akin to German *schmücken*, which is to lend eminence by means of ornamentation; **snob** has had too varied a history to trace its progress accurately into the present class, though of course the snob obviously hopes to attain eminence simply by assuming it or by associating himself with the great or eminent. The vain or conceited person seems to rest his claim to eminence on the pretension to certain assets with which he closely identifies himself.

Corresponding to this class there is a set of negatives used to credit the subject (c); these include **humble, meek** and perhaps **gentle. Meek** traces back to an ancient form in Old Norse for soft, and humble to the earth itself, to L. *humus*. **Gentle**, of course, is **well bred**, and thus the manner of easy and unostentatious living which appeared to characterize the gently born.

Now of course these essential tenors of the metaphor are but the descriptive framework upon which the characterisms are hung. Coming forward and retreating are in themselves both obviously necessary modes of performance in the conduct of life. As such one cannot say that only forward motion is good and retreat is evil. On the contrary, we need to evaluate both modes both ways: forwardness may be praised as confident or cool, but there will be occasions also when it is condemned as bumptious, fresh or impudent, or is mildly tolerated as saucy or malapert; on the other hand, retreat will be praised when it is characterized as modest, reserved, or unassuming, or rejected (although with more or less sympathy) when the subject is diffident, woebegone, or crestfallen. We must remember that we are here concerned only with the air and manner of persons, which are not always easy to distinguish from their actions. We take these up under the tendentives, 9.0. There we will find even more positive lines of praise and blame when *enterprises* are declared bold or prudent, courageous or cowardly.)

The negations in 8.22 differ from those of 8.21, which they superficially resemble, in that the latter concern the innate vitality and energy of the spirit, while the latter concern the address of the person to what he undertakes and his defeats and retreats.

Turning to the appraiser's involvement in his subject, we see him rather more deeply involved when he speaks in concrete terms: when he says the subject is bumptious, cool, forward, or saucy, or that he is bashful, crestfallen, or woebegone rather than when, speaking in more "abstract" Latin terms, he says he is confident or reticent. One senses more of the sensuous impact of the subject on the appraiser and a greater liveliness in his response in the former set of characterizations. The tendency or intent to enhance or to discredit the subject is the more plain the more concrete the characterisms are. But they are not all universal in this use. As in many other situations, one and the same characterism may, in suitable contexts, be used now to enhance, now to discredit a subject. Such contexts are often created by the conjunction of other appraisives. For example, A, we learn, is cool and ruthless in his attitudes, while B is cool, calm, and collected. Some child is, say, saucy and impertinent, while some new automobile engine is (as only an advertiser would say) saucy and dynamic. The popularity of ironic turns of speech in our time can be documented endlessly: one praises something by saying it is mad, crazy, mean, insane, and so on, the habit of a bored and jaded age.

We have designated some characterisms as plus-or-minus ($\pm$), meaning that they may be used either to credit or to discredit, but of course not both at once.

8.23   SINCERITY-PRETENSION

POSITIVE CHARACTERISMS	+	NEGATIVE CHARACTERISMS
CREDITING		CREDITING
(a) **artless**		(c) (none)
bluff a.		
downright		
frank		
simple		
sincere		
straightforward		

+ ═══════════════════ × ═══════════════════ −

DISCREDITING		DISCREDITING
(b) **ingenuous** (+)		(d) **affected**
naive		**devious**
simple-minded		**disingenuous**
		meretricious
		ostentatious
		pretentious (13.2)

−

The title "Sincerity-Pretension" for this section indicates well enough the subject matter, but it may be a trifle more "moral" than is needed or appropriate to conduct, especially to something that here includes what we may call physical conduct. A rapid glance at the vocabulary quickly discloses that what is being contrasted here is simplicity, straightness, directness with complexity, indirection, deviance. A rather remarkable and surprising fact is the direct kinship of simple and sincerity through the root *sem (one). The simple is one or the once folded (plico). (One may compare the exact German equivalent **einfältig**.) **Sincere** has the same root but the second element (cere) is obscure. We may suppose, therefore, that the basic thought of this class is openness or transparency of insight into another as against twistings and turnings that obscure extendedness of view. However much they may have themselves offended by such obscuration, even scoundrels have admired the open personality, identical "outside and inside."

It is necessary to reflect on these matters, since we need some kind of explanation for the apparent preference for simplicity over complexity in human conduct and concourse. It certainly cannot be because we think we can "see through" and outwit the straightforward and open personality. The genuinely simple soul often triumphs, unless of course he stands in the pathway of a juggernaut like a totalitarian machine. Perhaps the answer is no more complex than this, that we have a primitive horror of suffering and ambush; we feel a respect for the straightforward person, since even if he is otherwise the most formidable of adversaries, we know at least what weapons he will use. Again, the devious and disingenuous person often has more to fear from this kind of person than he has from someone his equal in strategy and deception. This is not to say, however, that all forms of simplicity have such power: the mere fact that we have also the concept of the simple-minded shows that we praise simplicity only if it is accompanied by the virtues of good judgment.

These concepts inevitably begin to border on the tendentive (9.0) and the vastly complex family of concepts under contention and aggression (11.0). We should try to confine the present vocabulary distinctly to the area of bearing, mien, and manner, granting that there is an inevitable overlap with the field of palpable action.

The vocabulary of 8.23 contains simple terms like **downright** and **straightforward** which need no explanation, but also more complex terms. **Frank**, for example, along with **naive** and **ingenuous** introduces the idea of the free; the Franks were at one time the only free people in Gaul! In time the term came to signify the trait of free and open revelation of one's thoughts or feelings. **Ingenuous** (which may sometimes credit) is Latin ingenuus, that is, native, free-born, or noble, and thus is linked with **naive**, L. nativus. The oneness in

simple and **sincere** has already been remarked upon. **Bluff**, almost predictably, is obscure in origin, but immensely expressive. (Is it an ancient piece of slang?) We see, then, that the family of terms is built around the ideas of the free, direct, and uncomplicated. All of them can also be recognized as characterisms for expression and indeed all of them could be placed in a distinct class of this sort.

We turn now to the negative side. If we emphasize the actional aspect of the positive appraisives rather than the mien and bearing of the person, the negations obviously should be **deviousness, disingenuousness, trickery,** and the like. If, however, we confine ourselves strictly to mien and bearing the negations are those given here, that is, deceptiveness in the actual person with as little reference to action as is possible. At first glance a problem presents itself in **affectation** and **pretentiousness**. The person presents a front which, so to speak, reveals itself wholly. What is part of the person's bearing is either here or nowhere. But to represent these concepts must there not be duplicity (or several strata) as against the simplicity we have found in the positives? The affected or pretentious person reveals both appearance and reality, that is, according to the one who has so characterized him. But if he reveals them, where is the deception? The point is *we* claim to see through the façade while others may be taken in by it. The person may also be pretending or affecting but not doing so intentionally. He may simply have fallen into certain habits without knowing it. He may deliberately adopt a certain new mask or role and then fail to recollect what his real self is like. A male transvestite may begin by adopting the dress and mannerisms of a woman and virtually deceive himself, at least in public, that he is a woman; whereas an objective bystander may at a glance understand the game from the start. **Affectation** and **pretentiousness** are not only used of bearing, mien, or manner. Similar issues arise when these characterisms are applied to the manner and the substance of discourse, to the cleft of inner and outer, or word and deed. **Ostentation** raises similar questions wherever it approaches near synonymity with the foregoing terms. It may also signify a mere overstepping of certain limits in the conscious use of certain devices to gain effects and may thus not raise questions about deception. (The paradox mentioned above deserves further study.)

In all of the foregoing something of the moral use of these terms has inevitably been mingled, meaning by 'moral' a connection with or reflection of the social and communitive context, considered at length below. So far as possible, we should here try to see their primary use as confined to characterizing mien and manner. As such, most positives, except **simple** as meaning simple-minded, attribute credit to the subject. All of the negatives appear to deny such credit, though it is at least possible that we might devise means for giving credit to a subject in speaking of his capacity to dissemble (one thinks of Ulysses). But it is difficult to restrict this vocabulary to mien and manner in such a way as to rule out all reference to deception, hence aggression, and thus all moral implication.

8.24   PRESENCE (Cf. 13.1)

POSITIVE CHARACTERISMS	+	NEGATIVE CHARACTERISMS
CREDITING		CREDITING
(a) **charming, charm**		(c) **diamond in the rough**
civil, civility		
comity		
composed, composure		
courtly		
debonair		
gallant		
gracious		
mannerly		
personable		
poised, poise		
suave		
urbanity		
worldly, worldliness		

+ ══════════════════════ × ══════════════ −

DISCREDITING	DISCREDITING
(b) **namby-pamby**	(d) **awkward**
	boorish
	coarse
	crude
	gauche
	gruff
	hag
	slattern
	uncouth
	unprepossessing
	vulgar

−

As in previous cases, it is not altogether easy to keep one's eye on these characterisms solely in terms of Air, Bearing, Mien or Manner, or as we shall characterize this set, Presence. A person may also be awkward physically, crude, coarse, and gruff in his speech, a hag or slattern in dress, and so forth.

I have omitted **polite** and **courteous** from the positives and have doubts about **courtly** and **mannerly** because these are manifested in the manner in which certain deeds are done, whereas by presence we mean to abstract from actual deeds, though this cannot be wholly done. No doubt the sets will convey a distinct impression of certain ways of characterizing persons in their conduct and appearance among others, but not in specific acts or deeds.

If there is any single image that appears to underlie these characterisms it is perhaps that of roughness on one side, smoothness or sweetness on the other. But this provides only a superficial linkage. In terms perhaps as neutral as may be found for the subject matter of these characterizations, one may say that the positive characterizations concern the person who finds ways of accommodating himself to others, the negative the person who refuses to and ruggedly ignores what will make for easy relations with them. The modes of accommodation spoken of below in 11.4 are *deeds*. Here we are speaking more of the figure the person cuts in the *presence* or in cognizance of others. In the positive direction he takes their presence into account, thinking of what gives offense as being aggressive or unappetizing aesthetically, according to the customs of the place. In the negative direction, he ignores their presence out of the conviction that he is self-sufficient and need take no account of their feelings or preferences. None of this is *as yet* to praise or to condemn one or the other. We must see first that there are two poles of this aspect of personality.

Once these extremes are identified (and, of course, there are endless gradations in between) we can see that there must arise occasions where the other possibilities are exemplified. The accommodative person or accommodating conduct will be appraised as aberrant and characterized in appropriate discrediting terms. Whether there is an explicit or formal vocabulary for this or not, an appropriate expression can easily be devised. Or again the self-sufficient person may be thought to behave in a praiseworthy manner (c) regardless of the amount of offense he gives. Slang and colloquialism are particularly apt in all of the four possible stances of characterization.

Like other vocabularies of characterization, this one exhibits the appraiser's interest in the whole of the subject. Any or all parts of the subject may be relevant in such characterization, none can be wholly excluded. There is more than a suggestion with the negatives that failure to accommodate oneself to the sensibilities of others shows itself in the state or the habits of mind or thought of the subject as well as in his physical and social presence. (The greater the "extent" of the subject, therefore, the more difficult it is to locate application of the characterism.) When the subject is characterized as a diamond in the rough there is an implication that he may have tender and humane inclinations despite the external impression he makes. Positive characterisms, it is suggested, are to the subject's credit, so far as they go. They appear to imply only faintly that the subject's mind or thought also deserves favorable characterization. The characterization **namby-pamby** is a rejection of the whole subject, body and mind. There are other subtler aspects of this that could be pursued.

The effect on the appraiser is perhaps best shown by the rough-smooth image that underlies the characterisms. He feels the presence of the subject as an abrasive or as one of smoothness and ease. Not only the native stock of characterisms shows this but improvisations, figures of speech, figurative speech, and slang. The response of the appraiser is an indefeasible part of the characterization.

8.25   GRAVITY-LEVITY

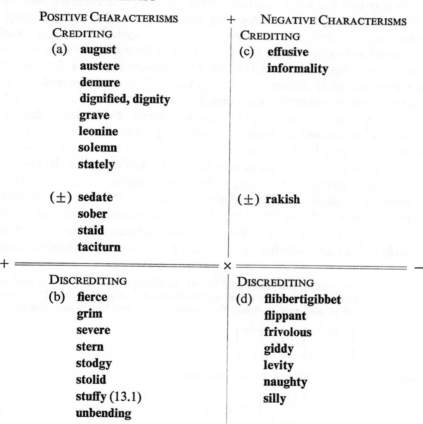

POSITIVE CHARACTERISMS	+	NEGATIVE CHARACTERISMS
CREDITING		CREDITING
(a) **august**		(c) **effusive**
austere		**informality**
demure		
dignified, dignity		
grave		
leonine		
solemn		
stately		
(±) **sedate**		(±) **rakish**
sober		
staid		
taciturn		

+ ════════════════════ × ════════════════════ −

DISCREDITING		DISCREDITING
(b) **fierce**		(d) **flibbertigibbet**
grim		**flippant**
severe		**frivolous**
stern		**giddy**
stodgy		**levity**
stolid		**naughty**
stuffy (13.1)		**silly**
unbending		

−

This class of characterisms, like some others in 8.2, illustrates the fact that the classes in the title (Air, Bearing, etc.) do not coincide with the subject classifications of the five subclasses. Thus, although many of the terms belong definitely under bearing, some of them, such as **taciturn, grave, grim, severe, stern** are definitely words for mien. All of them must obviously be placed under gravity and levity. The terms are also used in other connections, e.g., frivolous talk, stern discipline, etc.

The principal image that underlies this class, particularly the negatives, is that of something standing upright, which appears in **stately, staid** (=stayed, supported, sustained, held up), **sedate** (sitting up), **stolid** (from *stultus*, foolish, and earlier from a putative root,*stel,* to stand still), **stern**, and of course, **unbending.** The negative of 8.25 is close kin to the positive of 8.21, since the contrary image of the present (i.e. 8.25) positive side is the resilient, elastic, lively.*

We may now ask what descriptive traits are being characterized with the aid of these images. In general, they are the traits of something intact, possessing the fabric and structure of an actual physical body or a social institution and durability against the erosion of time or circumstance. The characterisms based on them have primary application to *persons* functioning in a social or public context. The title "presence," already employed, would not be altogether misapplied here, especially as pertaining, say, to group (a). The principal positive characterizations are **august, dignified** and **demure.** Since the implications of **august** are rather awesome, the term might in a sense be held in a kind of reserve for application to persons of maximum genuine dignity. **Dignity** is the central characterism of the group. Its origins, apparently of incredible antiquity, go back to a possible Aryan root, *dok̑-, to seem good,* which also yields *dogma* and *decent.* **Demure,** interestingly, shows that what is characterized here is not just a masculine trait, but that it can also appear in thoroughly feminine guise, although the term has now fallen into disuse, evidently from want of examples. The metaphor **leonine** shares

---

* It is hoped that what is being suggested here is something more than a merely curious exercise in diagramming. The point is that the lines between Gravity–Levity and Vivacity– Placidity are not always easy to draw. One alternative is therefore to combine them:

$$\left\{ \begin{array}{c} \text{Gravity} \\ + \\ \text{Placidity} \end{array} \right\} \text{---} \left\{ \begin{array}{c} \text{Vivacity} \\ + \\ \text{Levity} \end{array} \right\}$$

Another is to unite one extreme but not the other:

$$\text{Gravity} \text{--} \left\{ \begin{array}{c} \text{Levity} \\ + \\ \text{Vivacity} \end{array} \right\} \text{--Placidity}$$

In other words, the positive side of 8.21 is closely related to the Negative of 8.25. The reason for the arrangement in the text is that the other extremes (Positive in 8.25 and Negative in 8.21) are really not congruent, particularly in the discreditings.

something of the thought of **august** or **dignified**, but with a trace of humor.

At the other extreme from **dignity**, the idea of durability appears to have atrophied or mortified in subjects that are characterized as stodgy, stuffy, stolid, and unbending. Somewhere between the two we find **sober, staid,** and **sedate.** Here the subjects seem neither to attract the appraiser, as do those thought dignified or demure, nor to repel, as do those thought stodgy, stuffy or stolid. When we turn to the facial expression of grave or weighty thought, what we may tend to feel is not disdain (as with **stolid**) but fear. What we behold is, let us say, a person resolved, despite evident difficulty, to maintain intact a position or program. Of course, there are also grim prospects, tasks, and other subjects of these terms.

Turning to the contrary of **gravity**, what we have called **levity,** with more symmetry than accuracy, is the characterization of persons who at the moment are unconcerned about the maintenance of some firm social structure or façade. If we find such demeanor crediting, we may say it is lively, pert, sprightly or vivacious. If not, we may say it is giddy or frivolous; children may be scolded as naughty. Rakish behavior may be thought of as occupying an intermediate position between giddy and lively. Or it may associate with one or the other. Thus one may say A is rakish and pert, or rakish and frivolous; in the one case it is praise, in the other blame. Similarly A may be praised as stately, solemn and staid, or blamed as stuffy, stodgy and staid. All characterisms take on some of the traits of other terms in their contexts.

Terms under Gravity and Levity show typical traits of characterisms: they are based on a whole view of the subject, or the subject as a whole; no specific properties are invariably and definitively present; they are devised for the purpose of enhancing, diminishing or impairing the credit of the subject; and they show a detectable effect of the subject on the appraiser. In (a) the appraiser feels himself supported by the strength and firmness of the subject; in (b) they oppress him. In (c) his spirit is buoyed up by their vitality; in (d) their aimlessness and inconsequence dismay him.

8.3   RESPONSIONAL CHARACTERIZATIONS (See 2.4)

For the responsional characterizations we must turn back to section 2.4 and review its content. The reasons for placing these characterizations in 2.4 is there explained. Systematically their place is the present section.*

---

* The concepts of 2.4 deserve more than a merely nominal place in 8.0. As characterizations of distinct episodes of passion they belong in 2.0. But a pattern or accumulation of these certainly bears on character and helps to determine mood, temper, or temperament (8.11 and 8.13).

The three divisions of 8.0 have covered three areas of characterization: first, emotive tone and temperament; second, air, bearing, mien, and manner; and third, responsional characterization. A few final observations on the field so divided may be in order.

As we saw in 2.0 emotive responses (love, hate, hope, fear, awe) are themselves subject to characterization. The vocabulary of 2.4 (=8.3) surveys these appraisals of response (AR). Such responses are actual episodes of emotive reaction: outbursts, outpourings, transports, in short, onsets which, in some now, fill a subject's whole being.

The source of such onsets lies deep in the person, physically and psychologically, and is determined further by numerous influences in the environment. These have been allowed for in one way or another since ancient times and expressed in the vocabulary of temperament (8.13) and temper (8.112). Together with the vocabulary for moods, they furnish us the means to speak of more or less lasting responsive states or dispositions to respond. Their dispositional character sets them somewhat apart from the actual onsets of 2.4 already noted, but they can be applied also to present states of being. The deepest shape and pattern of personal tonality are shown in the vocabulary for the human condition (8.12): **happiness, misery, distress, serenity.** All of these modes can well up, or appear to, from the isolated personality himself. They appear to give a color to the world originating from the person alone.

Emotion, however, is rational only when it is responsive to the environment, especially the universe of persons. This is the source of the huge vocabulary of 8.2, devoted to devices for characterizing the public aspect of personalities in reaction to one another, **lively** and **placid, confident** and **modest, open** and **devious, civil** and **vulgar, stately** and **silly.**

This is the framework on which alternative and supplementing vocabularies to express the self-in-itself and the self-for-others are based.

9.0 TENDENTIVE CHARACTERIZATION

With tendentives we have taken an important step toward the moral appraisal of man. Our first three areas of appraisal (intellectual, behavioral, and
diathetic) for the most part concerned man in his individual person, though
often, if not always, as a being responding to his surroundings and to other
persons. In the next division, treating the sexual or sex-related, we shall be
concerned more explicitly with interpersonal relationships, in this instance
the most intimate conceivable of persons toward persons.

The tendentive, in general, represents the effort of man to assert himself,
to master the environment, to subject it to his wish. In the three remaining
areas of characterization this assertion brings him into direct confrontation
with others, leading both to aggression and accommodation, to economic
and political conflict and order. The tendentive, in traditional terms, is the
area of the will, but that term has no prominent place in the total economy
of characterization.

How necessary are tendentive characterisms? Are they present in all
societies and languages? Of course these are questions which can be answered only by empirical investigation. One would have to examine large
tracts of spoken discourse to see whether, and to what extent, characterisms of this sort are in actual use. In time investigations of this sort must
be undertaken. But there are also some aspects of the matter that can be
profitably speculated on or that may be the subject of hypothesis. Once our
own tendentives are assembled, we can begin to see what order they show
among themselves.

It is not surprising that the language of a society such as ours that is
devoted so wholeheartedly to work and the accomplishment of ends should
reflect so fully all of the logical divisions of purposive activity. There is first
the determination of the degree of *volitivity* of the action and at the end an
outcome in defeat or success. The intervening steps involve the person's involvement in the action itself. The first subject of characterization will be the
address to action, the manner in which the person undertakes a task. It is not
easy to distinguish this phase from the next which is the degree or manner of
engagement with a task. The orientation of our language community toward
the value of work and achievement is clearly reflected here. There are few
concessions to anything but resolute determination to get tasks done. This
does not, or would not, prevent this community from questioning such goals

or even of overthrowing them. Indeed, there are, and have always been, those who have questioned the implicit approbation of the ostensible ends of this society. But the body of characterisms reflects the trend that has been dominant for some centuries. From address and engagement we pass to the characterization of the *capabilities* or endowments of persons so engaged, and then of the manner in which *enterprises* have been managed. The devices of *expression* are, of course, marshalled in aid of the promotion of such enterprises.

One must not allow preconceived notions of the strength of the "Protestant ethic" and all it has entailed to determine what is to be considered here. It would be absurd to set up the tendentive in such a way that only the "ethic of striving" was reflected in it and then to conclude that everyone in this society subjected himself to such an ethic. Hence it is necessary to construe 'tendentive' in such a way that all characterization of acting and doing, including in principle what is called "doing nothing," are considered. In order to complete the portrait one would here have to look also at the less established forms of characterization, slang, metaphor, and so on. We may observe, however, that the first examples that come to mind reflect only the idea of the virtue of a *cessation* of work. So Walt Whitman, undoubtedly an idler by prevailing standards, could write, "I loafe, and invite my soul," but he had to state his value in terms of the negation of work. It has of course the piquancy of a denial of the prevailing ethic. (One will not, of course, forget Whitman's praise of the energy of the American enterprise in subduing a primitive continent.) One will also hear "taking it easy," "goofing off," *dolce far niente*. The first is again a negation, the second is largely disapprobative, the third evokes thought of the pallid and feeble sport of unenergetic persons. In due time a vocabulary of the positive characterization of passivity (to oversimplify the matter for brevity) may emerge. Indeed, the current cult of the retreat into drugs has already developed both the attitude and the vocabulary as well as the practice.

One may safely speculate that among the hundreds of languages and cultures of the earth there will be more than a few which have altogether different attitudes and different vocabularies of tendentives from those of European peoples.

9.1   VOLITIVITY

[advisedly]	[purpose]
[deliberate a.]	[studied]
[gratuitous]	[voluntary]
[prepense]	[willful]

There is no doubt that ordinary thought and practice unaffected by philosophic thought uses the vocabulary of volitivity in a confident and meaningful manner. Although it may not be the whole of the so-called problem of the freedom of the will, surely the most significant part of it turns on the question whether the confidence of common sense is or is not groundless. The effort to show that freedom must be real simply because common sense or ordinary language proceed as if they were will not be discussed here. The possibility of its complete illusoriness is not diminished very significantly by the fact that the tendentive vocabulary appears to rely on the, or an, idea of freedom throughout. Therefore, we maintain the meaningfulness of both the inquiry into freedom and the idea of freedom that appears to be presupposed by the tendentive vocabulary.

We could evade or avoid many of these questions by simply observing that 9.1 actually contains no characterisms. It is attached to 9.0 mainly for the sake of a completer picture of tendentive characterization. (The convention of brackets [ ] is used to mark non-characterizing terms.) As we have seen, no necessary or sufficient conditions are forthcoming for characterisms. But any court of law, in virtually every case that comes before it, will wish to satisfy itself conclusively as to the volitivity of the actions that are at issue and will recognize certain criteria as decisive. Moreover, with the exception of **gratuitous**, which is peripheral here and could actually also be classified elsewhere or as a characterism, the terms are not such as to be applied for the purpose of crediting or discrediting the subject. This is certainly true of **advisedly, deliberate, purposive,** and **studied**: these may be predicated either of creditable or discreditable actions. **Prepense** and **wilful** have a rather different use. They are not themselves discrediting, since they simply say that an action was not involuntary, but they are used only (it is fairly safe to say) in connection with actions which are themselves discredited.

What this vocabulary is mainly meant to remind us of is that human action sees itself as purposive, as aim- or goal-directed. It is important that we recognize this as a fact. Regardless of the outcome of behavioral research, there is no reason to believe that we will alter our manner of speaking of our enterprises. It is safe to assume that we use the volitivity vocabulary meaningfully and what we use it to mean is for us fact. The option to deny facts is not one that is open to the behaviorist any more than it is to any other inquirer. At most he is free to dispute and repudiate any and every "spiritualist" *explanation* of what subjects describe to themselves as purposive action. The denial of the *facts* is the gravest of scientific errors, graver by far than any error of theory.

9.2   ADDRESS AND ENGAGEMENT (Cf. 8.21, 8.22)

9.21   ADDRESS

POSITIVE CHARACTERISMS	+	NEGATIVE CHARACTERISMS
CREDITING		CREDITING
(a) **alacrity**		(c) **caution, cautious**
gusto		**circumspect**
intrepid		**wary**
nervy, nerve		
plucky, pluck		
resolute		**chary** ($\pm$)
spontaneous		
($\pm$) **impetuous**		
impulsive		

+ ══════════════════ × ══════════════════

DISCREDITING		DISCREDITING
(b) **foolhardy**		(d) **caprice, capricious**
hasty		**dainty** (also aesthetic
headlong		and other uses)
precipitate a.		**dither**
rash		**faint-hearted**
reckless		**feckless**
temerarious		**fickle**
temerity		**flighty**
		nerveless
		remiss
		shilly-shally
		shirk
		tardy
		truant
		vacillate
		whim, whimsy, whimsical

—

It is first necessary to observe that no firm line can be drawn between address and engagement. The distinction itself merely acknowledges the fact that we ordinarily find it necessary to distinguish the commencement and the conduct of an enterprise. When the distinction is itself immaterial, characterisms can be exchanged between the classes. A second observation is that many of the terms are employed as much to attribute characteristics to persons as to their enterprises. They therefore seem close kin to the diathetic characterisms of 8.0. They should be distinguished, however. The present

vocabulary is largely attributed to persons in their capacity as beings that
have undertakings and enterprises in hand. As the title indicates, while
the characterisms of 8.0 are directed to the inner constitution of persons,
those of 9.0 refer to persons in explicit response to external challenge. But
there is no reason to think that the foundations of 8.0 and 9.0 are remote
from one another merely because the distinction between them has a common
sense status. Such a matter properly belongs to the psychology of personality.

Negative discrediting terms may be applied to a person who enters upon
enterprises with no vision or resolution or who in fact fails to enter upon
them at all. He may be declared to be tardy, truant, remiss or to have shirked
or to vacillate or shilly-shally, or to be fickle or flighty. Or he may throw
himself into action with scarcely a thought and thus be declared to act from
whim or caprice. These characterisms are most often independent of other
considerations, such as ends or obligations, except for **tardy, truant** or
remiss. One would, for example, condemn vacillation and flightiness even in
one's worst enemy, although the results might yield us great benefits. There is
more than a little of the "sporting proposition" in this: we tend, at least in
our society, to admire a professionally competent performance. Most
commonly, it is the athletes and soldiers and less commonly politicians, comedians, artists, and perhaps boxers who behave so to one another.

9.22   ENGAGEMENT (Cf. 11.2)

POSITIVE CHARACTERISMS		NEGATIVE CHAR.
CREDITING		+ CREDITING
(a) **adamant**	**courage**	(c) **amusement**
aggressive	**derring do**	**diversion**
(= earnestly	**determined**	**dolce far niente**
engaged)	**devoted to**	**leisure**
ambition,	**devotee**	**pastime**
ambitious	**diligent**	
ardor	**disciplined**	
aspire,	**dogged**	
aspiration	**doughty**	
attentive	**dynamic**	
audacious,	**earnest**	
audacity	**[endeavor]**	
bravado	**energy**	
brave, bravery	**enthusiasm**	
competitive	**firm**	
[confident]	**fortitude**	
constancy	**indefatigable**	

indomitable	stamina		
mettle,	staunch		
mettlesome	steadfast		
moil	steady		
morale	strenuous		
patient	strict		
pertinacious	tenacious		
persevere	tireless		
puissant	toil, toilsome		
relentless	travail		
resolute	unflagging		
rigorous, rigor	unflinching		
sedulous	valor, valiant		
serious	vigor		
stalwart	zeal, zest		

(±) assiduous

    avid

    industrious

    inflexible

    perfervid

    plod

    stubborn

(±) potter, putter

    routine a.

+ ══════════════════════════ × ══════════════════════════ −

DISCREDITING

(b) cocksure

    craze

    drudge,

      drudgery

    fad

    fanatic

    headstrong

    mania, maniac

    pigheaded

    pushing

    quixotic (+)

    zealot

DISCREDITING

(d) dabble

    effete

    ennui

    fainéant

    flinch

    idle

    indifferent

    indolent

    insouciant

    lax

    lazy

    loaf

    perfunctory

    pusillanimous

    shiftless

    slapdash

slothful (8.21)
sluggard
timid
timorous
unnerved, unnerve

The obvious "imbalances" among the characterisms of engagement must immediately strike the eye. It is first of all difficult to find candidates in English for the logically possible category of crediting negative characterisms (c). It is only when one asks, what it is to be as free as one can be from engagement and yet to be praised or commended, that one at length sees that, if anything, it is leisure that fulfils the conditions. A few other characterisms, that are not really strongly crediting (sometimes even the reverse, if they are "mere"), may be added: amusement, diversion, pastime. No effort has been made merely to add synonyms to the original list, either here or elsewhere. Therefore, it is a fair surmise that the speakers of the language sense a greater need to praise being occupied than being free of work or effort. This is not surprising in a language that early appropriated and identified being busy and industrious with what we call business and industry. ("The business of the United States is business," said President Coolidge.) Business and industry are, to be sure, necessary, but are they therefore virtues, any more than digestion is a virtue? But these are only side issues. What the characterisms mean to say is, "whatsoever thou givest thy hand to do, do it with all thy might;" once a goal is decided upon, the pursuit of it is itself virtuous; it is of no credit to embrace the loftiest goals if they are not striven for.

This is essentially a pragmatic conception of virtue. Are there no alternatives? It is interesting that the European aristocratic ideal that has been in decline in the last centuries has been just the reverse of this. The grubbing for the realization of ends has been beneath it, but a brilliant stroke, unmistakable in its intent and significance, in defense of honor or virtue has always been acclaimed and has rallied the most astonishing feats of bravery. Life itself was a commodity of no significance if it served such a defense. The redemption of man celebrated at the end of *Faust* involves the draining of swamps; for Parsifal it could lie only in the pursuit of the Holy Grail. The knightly ideal involved not the litany of virtues of engagement but rather being "true," **treu** in German, being loyal and committed to an ideal, not merely to exert oneself, to show determination, "grit." *That* ideal is wholly compatible with regarding leisure, the negation of engagement, in crediting terms. Of course, an aristocracy could always take economic sufficiency for granted for itself – and who else mattered? We need go no further than our own tradition, therefore, to find alternatives to the achievement ethic. Though the aristocratic ideal is now in decline if not extinct, no one may venture to predict that other alternatives to our ethic may not arise.

I think we must make some distinctions within the body of (a) to allow for a difference in the kinds of goals being striven for. **Bravery, courage, morale, valor** may be and often have been applied to persons striving for quite earthly goals, perhaps even to gangsters or stock market speculators. Yet in fact we are all aware that the engagement of persons like these deserves to be distinguished from selfless devotion to altruistic causes. Where lies the difference? I believe it is at present impossible to discern a difference *from the vocabulary*. That is, one and the same vocabulary will be used for selfless and selfseeking deeds, and sometimes even with the defense that there is, after all, no difference between these. It is evident that the indiscriminate use of the same vocabulary for both reflects the general confusion as to where or whether a difference obtains. This is the present state of affairs. In the days of knighthood, no one would have confused mere stamina with **Treue** or loyalty. Indeed the stamina of Columbus, da Gama, Hudson and Cabot provided what seemed an alternative that even commoners were capable of. If this led directly to the swashbucklers and industrial robber barons, the thought of a higher alternative never altogether vanished. In the course of the nineteenth century, and of course our own, sport provided a framework in which something like the knightly ideal could continue its existence. The whole engagement vocabulary is exemplified in sport as often as it is anywhere at the present time, even despite current professionalism. It does not, of course, provide in the prizes that are won anything like the ideals of knighthood, unless the Davis Cup is thought to be a Grail symbol.

In the framework of the achievement ethic, the alternatives to the positive characterisms of (a) are provided more emphatically by the negative discrediting characterisms of (d) than by (c). Here a kind of (false) alternative is offered: if you are not brave, mettlesome, staunch, vigorous, and above all *active* in your efforts or commitments you will be idle, lax or lazy. But there is also another way to be "disengaged," as we may say here. Leisure time can be spent in a creditable manner. The achievement ethic was slow in giving this thought a hearing. Truly amateur team sport embodies the components of knightly war in the Middle Ages: stamina, loyalty (*Treue*), leisure, disinterest – all but the holy. In the nineteenth century the increasing affluence of certain classes, particularly in England, began to question the achievement ethic at the very time of its greatest appeal. The gentle (or pallid) **dolce far niente** (the art of sweetly doing nothing) made its way into the language. By the end of the century 'aesthetic' also had been acclimatized, not without whoops of scorn from the more muscular and "engaged" segment of the population; 'aesthete' evoked the vision of Bunthorne "walking down Piccadilly with a poppy or a lily in his medieval hand."

I am not subjecting the achievement ethic to attack. The point is that like every ethic it eventually becomes smug. There is, then, only the remedy to remind ourselves of the alternatives to it, of which there are several: the aristocratic, the athletic, the leisure-culture ideal, and still other ideals based upon sweet idleness, escape, withdrawal into comas of various sorts, and death itself. All of these are in a process of reconsideration.

The positive characterisms of (a) are subjected to a kind of mild criticism from within, as represented by (b). Pertinacity and perseverance can degenerate into fanaticism or pigheadedness. The causes they serve can become mere crazes or fads. Between these extremes lie terms which may be used either to credit or to discredit. One may praise or question resolute effort as plodding. Inflexible, perfervid, or stubborn effort may be creditable or not. Association of these terms with others in (a) or (b) is often decisive: inflexible perseverance; stubborn and pigheaded conduct. In like manner, he who potters or putters may be either enjoying a richly rewarding leisure, or wasting his time in idleness. Routine is a little difficult to place. It may belong in (a±) as a creditable, if unimaginative, form of engagement or in (d) as essentially lazy. It obviously cannot be placed in (a) or in (c).

Surveying the whole of Engagement we can see that it comprises true characterisms. In each case it is personal character that is surveyed and invariably as a whole. To speak of a person as lazy is not to identify a distinct property but for the moment to wrap all of him into one tidy parcel and ignore the rest of him. All of his other traits, characteristics, and properties are surveyed from this point of vantage. There are no rules for applying the terms **laziness, courage, steadfastness,** or **fanaticism.** We cannot be certain whether philately, change-ringing, or autobiography are work or leisure pursuits: in fact there is no such thing as being sure or not sure about this. In each case, we will not apply the discreditations or the most complimentary creditations to ourselves in the present. As before, the reason is that the characterisms reflect external responses, an effect or impression on others. We can only be a proper other to ourselves in the past or future. None of the vocabulary, especially from (b) through (d), is "neutral:" it reflects very strongly the nature of the speaker. Idleness is not merely something I attribute to *you;* to utter the term is to *reveal myself.* The characterisms in (a) also have this character, but some are obviously so close as to be almost indistinguishable from descripts: **energy, firmness, seriousness, vigor.** On the whole, however, they all have great empathic power. When I characterize your effort in such terms as **perseverant, relentless, staunch,** or **zest** I am virtually expending my own energy.

It is not difficult to detect further evidence of empathy in both Address and Engagement. If an appraiser takes the trouble to characterize address to or engagement in work (work is the typical case, though it may be war, sport, or other activity) in the present, he shows his involvement in the work, even if he cannot hope to derive benefit from it, or he identifies himself with the cause. Of course there are apparent exceptions to this. Generals praise the courage and pluck, or even the foolhardiness, wariness, or caprice of their enemies, and speak similarly of their degree of engagement. They often feel virtually insulted by the stupidity of opponents; it tends to bring the "art" of war itself into disrepute! Who can forget Hitler's astonishing remark early in the Russian war that he could easily defeat the enemy if only they were not "military idiots". More commonly we take the trouble, as we have said, to characterize enterprises because we actually do have an interest in their outcome.

9.3   ENTERPRISE: CAPABILITY AND MANAGEMENT

Positive Characterisms		+ Negative Char.
Crediting		Crediting
able	efficient	
adaptable,	enterprising	
adapted to	expert a. and n.	
adept	finesse	
adroit	gifted	
aplomb	pawky	
apt, aptitude,	precocious	
aptness	provident	
artful	prudent	
astute (6.1)	resourceful	
business-like	shrewd	
canny (6.1)	skill, skilful	
capable	stratagem	
careful	temperate	
competent	wary	
cool,	watchful	
cool-headed	wily, wile, wiles	
crafty		
cunning (6.21)		

$(\pm)$ expedient
     facile

+	×	−
DISCREDITING **opportunism**	**DISCREDITING** befuddled inept bemused incompetent careless intemperate chump makeshift clumsy maladroit dolt malapropos duffer neglect falter temporize inapt tinker	

The categories Capability and Management are presented together because of the obvious difficulty of trying to distinguish sharply between them or between ability and execution. Ability, we suppose, is the condition of significant execution, but only execution can show conclusively the degree of ability.

A significant number of the predicates under Capability are, for practical purposes, vacuous. We may say a person is able, adept, apt, capable, competent, gifted, precocious, or skilled, but taken by themselves these are nonassertions parading as assertions. Able at what, competent at what, skilled at what? Unless they are supplemented by the name of a particular competence, plumbing, schoolmastering, or even burglary, we have actually been told nothing.

There remain a number of more significant characterisms of capability: **astute, canny, cool-headed, cunning, self-possessed, self-reliant, shrewd, wily**. These are all sometimes characterisms of judgment (6.2) but are placed here to show their close involvement in action. They are meant not merely to attribute ability but to characterize the nature of the subject's comprehension of his situation. **Astute, canny, cunning, shrewd** and **wily** are meant to attribute an intimate knowledge of a situation, its yield of potential benefits and detriments, and a comprehension how to derive one and frustrate the other. The spectator who speaks in these terms is evidently affected by the sight of such knowledge and expertise and is in some degree in awe of them.

The discredits are rather vague. The chump is incapable of understanding even who his enemies are until it is too late. **Dolt, duffer,** and **chump** are the strongest characterisms among these, being substantives. These have the intent of saying what a man "really is;" they seek to speak of "character" as against what the subject may have happened to do (processives), or how he appeared (attributives). To have been duped is one thing, to be a dupe is another: the force of the distinction has little to do with *what* is being said. In general, many of these concepts strike fairly deep. Being inapt or inept or clumsy is not, if the charge is deserved, a shortcoming easily remedied, if at all. **Befuddlement** is perhaps discrediting only of a passing condition; if it proves to be chronic, severer characterisms will be applied.

Of the management vocabulary, perhaps only a few are in a very strong sense characterisms: **adroit, aplomb,** perhaps **stratagem.** The others will not appear to depart too far from propriety if self-applied in the present. **Adroit** and **aplomb**, however, indicate that a considerable impression has been made on the appraiser. They bear a hint of suspicion directed toward their subjects. They can even serve to discredit scheming enemies. The discrediting vocabulary is wholly characterizing, obviously unsuited for self-application in the present.

Considerations similar to those for the two preceding classes apply to Enterprise. Terms are applied principally to persons as a whole without thought of the terms naming particular properties the subject possesses. The strength of our interest in the enterprise and of the impression or effect the subject has upon us depends on the degree of our own identification or involvement with it; as already indicated one can, on occasion, take a kind of "professional" interest in enterprises of even our enemies and grant that they are shrewd or efficient. We go to the length of saying enterprises are managed by dolts or of regarding them as makeshift or tinkering if they are in some manner *our* enterprises. "O dolt," cries Emilia to the sheepish Othello after Desdemona is found dead at his hand, "as ignorant as dirt." She is identified with her mistress, and with service to her. What the speaker's expression primarily reveals is herself and the awareness that the enterprise she is involved in has gone awry. It is this rather than some mysterious "expression of emotion" "embodied" in the term **dolt** that accounts for the functioning of the characterism.

What remains, then, as the core of these characterisms is their reflection of the subject's conviction regarding the right or the mistaken conduct of tendentive enterprises, those in which individuals project themselves into the future. The appraiser, the whole of him, thought and emotion together, is involved.

9.4 SITUATIONAL AIDS AND IMPEDIMENTS

CREDITING CHARACTERISMS	DISCREDITING CHARACTERISMS
fortunate	**handicap**
lucky	**hapless**

opportune, opportunity		**mischance**
timely		**misfortune**
windfall		**mishap**
		pitfall
		risk, risky
		unfortunate
		unseasonable
		vicissitude
(±)	**adventitious**	(±) **perplexity**
	fortuitous	**predicament**
	inadvertent	

Except in one or two cases, the appraisives in 9.4 are not predicated of persons, but their entire significance is for man alone. What constitutes an opportunity is obviously not a condition in nature in itself but in relation to human wants, needs, or purposes. The same may be said of windfalls and also of risks, pitfalls, and handicaps.

The place of the concepts of 9.4 is made somewhat clearer by comparing them with situational affects in 2.3. The 9.4's resemble them in that both classes of concepts display our involvement in causal processes, in particular that part of them which we may not understand or which we cannot be certain of controlling. But in 2.3 we are dealing with affects, with actual emotional states that are engendered. These must be dealt with in ways appropriate to emotions. In 9.4, we are not explicitly concerned with situational affects, but with situations and processes themselves. We can only deal with these by seeking to understand them. The purpose of the vocabulary of 9.4 is that of characterizing in human terms the processes of nature that we suppose are governed by laws.

The term **perplexity** is somewhat out of keeping with the others. Yet it evidently belongs here and not among the situational affects, since, of course, it is not an affect at all. It is rather an intellectual state compounded of our knowledge and ignorance of the processes or situations around us that are appraised in the present vocabulary. **Predicament** indicates a difficulty for action; **perplexity** more a difficulty for understanding.

9.5   TENDENTIVE EXPRESSION

POSITIVE CHARACTERISMS	+	NEGATIVE CHARACTERISMS
CREDITING		CREDITING
(a) **actuate**		(c) **caution** v.
animate		

boost
buoy
cajole
champion v.
coax
egg on
elate
embolden
[encourage]
[endorse]
energize
enliven
excite
exhilarate
[exhort]
goad
importune
incite
inspire
inspirit
invigorate
quicken
spur
stimulate
[support]
sway
vitalize, vivify

+ ═══════════════════════ × ═══════════════════════ −

DISCREDITING   DISCREDITING
(b) abet   (d) check v.
    instigate   demoralize
    provoke   dishearten
    wheedle   dispirit
    [discourage]   hamper
    [impede]   hinder
    [inhibit]   killjoy
                                    stifle
                                    −

The length of the foregoing list is deceptive; many of the terms are quite plainly not characterisms and others are doubtful. To be characterisms they must do something more than state the fact that someone seeks to stimulate or inhibit action. There must also be evidence that some one is making an effort to enhance, diminish or injure the credit of him who stimulates or inhibits. From this standpoint the following may be suggested to be explicit characterisms in (a):

boost	**elate**	**egg on**
buoy	**embolden**	**goad**
champion	**energize**	

Among these, **energize** may be thought doubtfully characterizing, and **egg on** and **goad** may easily appear in (b). The (c) term **caution** may not be a true characterism. I believe all of (b) and (d) are such since by definition they are used to discredit, or to diminish credit.

With **boost, buoy** and **champion** the appraiser is himself somewhat caught up in the enthusiasm that is being manifested for the subject. In this instance, schematically A characterizes in terms such as **boosting** or **buoying** the activity of B, who is engaged in seeking to exhort or inspire C. These are somewhat similar, therefore, to the second order appraisives we encounter elsewhere. **Elate** and **embolden** appear most commonly in the passive voice, that is, A characterizes C as having been elated or emboldened either by some circumstance S, or by the exhortation of B. **Energize** seems slightly inflated, or at least metaphorical.

If one wishes to characterize the discourse of B negatively without discrediting it, one may say B has discouraged C, or impeded or inhibited him. These do not characterize but only describe his action. If we wish to diminish B's credit for his act of discouraging or inhibiting C, we will say he has disheartened, stifled, or demoralized C or that he has been a killjoy. These show fairly clearly the effect B's action has had on the appraiser. **Dispirit, hamper,** and **hinder** are rather weaker instances of negative discreditation.

Abet, instigate, provoke, possibly together with **egg on, goad, incite,** and **nerve** are rather clearly employed for the purpose of diminishing B's credit in his encouragement or exhortation of C. In these and many other cases, the characterizing power and function will be fully evident, but there are possible shifts across the line from crediting to discrediting or the reverse, according to context.

9.6 TENDENTIVE OUTCOME

Crediting Characterisms		Discrediting Characterisms	
(a) **achieve**	**fruition**	(c) **go[awry**	**miscarry**
accomplish	**work** v.	**botch**	

(b) feat	(d) abortive	(e) blunder
mastery	disappoint, (8.12)	bungle
success	futile,	debacle
	otiose	defeat
		discomfiture
		failure
		fiasco
		misadventure

The alternatives of 9.6 are obviously success and failure. The terms have, of course, great expressive strength, yet they are not highly characterizing, since in many enterprises to which they are applied there are altogether objective criteria of winning and losing, for example, a higher number on one side as against another.

The source of power of these characterisms is evidently the appraiser's own involvement in the fortunes of the winners or losers. Therefore, he will give much of himself in declaring an end result to be a debacle or fiasco, or in appraising a possible temporary setback as bungling or a blunder. In more restrained terms they are discomfitures or misadventures.

There is little that can be discriminated among successes unless there is a further specification of *what* has succeeded or failed: "many ways to fail but only one way to succeed." Success, though not failure, is an all or none affair, on this view.

We have thus surveyed the characterizing appraisal of man as agent. The entire vocabulary is built on the conviction that man is a being who sees himself as sometimes the creature of fortune, caprice, accident, alien power, and menacing evils; sometimes as capable of controlling his destiny within limits, spontaneous, adaptable, able to choose among alternatives; sometimes finally as whimsical, capricious, foolish, or heedlessly detached from his milieu while yet in the midst of it. I emphasize and re-emphasize the phrase *sees himself*. It is the duty of psychology and value theory to take how-man-sees-himself as a kind of datum and to offer explanations in several directions of depth. Such theory is invariably a failure, has missed the point and condemned itself to uselessness and futility if it sees all this as but something to be "explained away," to be reduced to something else, to be reliably accounted for only if this is done in "behavioral terms," if it aims only to replace what are thought of as the foolish vagaries of ordinary speech with the artificiality of substitutive definitions. It is particularly in the field of purposes that theoretical effort most often fails regarding man.

10.0 SEX-RELATED CHARACTERIZATION

It is a matter of importance that we set forth the reasons for the terms 'sex-related' and 'characterization' in the title of this section. We are not concerned with *sexual* characterisms or sexual morality or sexual properties or relations. We are concerned with the characterizing of persons as sexually differentiated, but not with sexual differences. For example, the words *male* and *female* are descripts and not characterisms, whereas **masculine** and **feminine** are generally characterisms. Vast tracts of information about this amply discussed subject are therefore of no interest to us whatever. We are interested in how the sexes characterize one another, how they characterize their sexual interest and their sexual roles. The term 'sex-related' must be construed broadly so that certain aspects of the family fall inside our area. The family arises out of the sexual order of nature in conjunction with other factors which are social and economic. One and the same person is therefore a subject of characterization from many sides. A woman can be *described* as a female, a mother, a daughter, a sister, a wife, a mistress, and in various other ways, but she will be *characterized* in very different terms. The term *prostitute* is a descript, not a characterism, since there are simple and objective criteria by which this occupation can be defined. What appear to be various "synonyms" for this term are often characterisms, not descriptions. Nowhere else in human life are touches of meaning and intention more subtle, and nowhere, we may add, are they more brutal than sometimes they are here.

We must next remind ourselves again that it is the existing or "natural" vocabulary on this subject that draws the boundaries of our inquiry. The endless improvisations, neologisms, metaphors, slang, figurative language and much else from the folklore of this subject must be set aside as too vast a field to be explored here. The result is that this section will have a curiously traditional slant on this subject, for the simple reason that it is the traditional sex attitudes and mores that are now enshrined in the language. It is obvious that human sexual patterns are always undergoing change, but perhaps more at the present time than for a long time past. To reflect these changes we would have to explore new language and new ways, if they *are* new ways, in which sexual behavior and sex-related facts or conditions are now appraised.

It is possible that the changes in the characterizing sex-related language far exceed that of the descriptive language on the same subject for the reason that most of the objective conditions are unalterably established by the order of nature, but there is no limit to man's wit and ingenuity in characterization. Sexual custom could, of course, alter radically in the future, as witness the possibilities of realizing Aldous Huxley's *Brave New World*, which are ever more palpable. It is precisely a time of change in actual practice that sees the most pronounced innovation in characterization.

We may suppose that every scheme of sex behavior, no matter how different from, let us say, the nineteenth century pattern, if it is more or less accepted and uniform, can enjoy a kind of "innocent" state. For example, the temple prostitution of antiquity had a kind of innocence in that it was entered into as an accepted order of conduct. For a woman to serve in such an institution or for men to patronize it could not have been anything like the situation of the professional and her clientele today, or the attitudes entering into this. Changing patterns of mores destroy states of innocence and always bring with them guilt and shame. There is every reason to believe that both the introduction and the downfall of sacramental prostitution was accompanied by severe affects of this sort. In general, such feelings will tend to occur when the sexual customs of a group are undergoing upheaval or when there is a lapse from conformity to the prevailing sexual norm. The present time is one of sexual innovation. Should sexual practice again find a kind of equilibrium, guilt and shame would be confined to the deviant, and sexual and sex-related language would display little novelty. Certainly much of our sex-related appraising and characterizing develop out of anxiety and guilt, so that if these were not real, whole tracts of discourse would cease to be of further interest or use.

But with or without the prevalence of feelings of guilt and shame, innovation in custom is bound to stimulate the growth of appraisive and characterizing language. The whole vocabulary directed against the homosexual could not but vanish if or when the homosexual gained social acceptance. Defenders of such a new order would then seek to discredit the user of a term like **fairy,** exactly as those who still use the term **nigger** are discredited at most levels.

What we are witnessing in our time is a considerable effort at the de-moralization of sex, the effort to remove it from the area of moral appraisal. The degree to which this succeeds will be reflected in the kind of sex-related language that is employed. It is not surprising that the received morality of the last century about sex should be reflected in the Oxford Dictionary. What is interesting is that the vocabulary of the subject, largely appraisive or characterizing, which was deliberately omitted as vulgar or obscene would reflect that morality even more, not less. The vocabulary that is omitted showed forth the fear, anxiety, guilt and dread with which the subject or the phenomenon was approached. But this did not stem somehow from the language *in itself*. What was condemned had been the routine English vocabulary for sexual phenomena since long before the Norman Conquest. The original vocabulary had been sinking in status since the middle ages. By Victorian times it had been relegated to a dark corner where the phenomena themselves were kept under cover. One could no longer look sexual phenomena directly in the face; only circumlocutions were permitted in society, except for certain fringes of it.

In our times the liberalization of sex attitudes has seemed naturally to bring with it a demand for the rehabilitation of the Anglo-Saxon vocabulary and its reintroduction into speech. But this effort often proceeds as if the rehabilitation of the vocabulary was a necessary part of sexual reform. It is difficult to understand why anyone should suppose there is any connection between these two. The vocabulary conceivably could come into use again under conditions of conservative sexual practice, or it might continue to be proscribed with an entirely revised sexual culture. Probably the vocabulary as having the meanings, implications, innuendos, and other subtleties of Victorian subculture could not survive in an age with such a revised sexual culture. Once the words were used again as descripts (if that is possible), they would lose their power as characterisms. To suppose that one could use the vocabulary freely and publicly for the purpose of abuse (its purpose at the bottom of the Victorian trough) would be thinkable only if abuse itself were to be made socially acceptable – but if socially acceptable, how could it be abuse?

What is likely is an increasing liberalization of sexual culture but without any large-scale re-entry of the Anglo-Saxon idiom into the language. If it is no longer necessary to obscure sexual phenomena it is unnecessary to use the vocabulary for it, ancient or modern, for the purpose of abuse.

The word **nigger** provides an interesting comparison and contrast for this vocabulary. In itself its origin is the innocent term for the color black in Latin, *niger*. The term was not a term of abuse for a long time, even despite slavery. It was the informal but accepted way to refer to members of African races. Only with the consciousness of the monstrous character of slavery did the term itself begin to appear abusive. Thereafter the two were inseparable, the actual abuse of the race and the abusiveness of the language. At length the conscience of the white man was stirred by the abuses, but instead of asking for a rehabilitation of **nigger** the term was almost wholly suppressed. If the term had arisen in the dung heap of slang, one could more easily understand this response, but, as we have said, its origin is nothing less than the august Latin language. What has happened is that the demand for a change of status necessitated a symbolic change in the language. It is not likely that **nigger** could ever be revived unless the Negro gained absolute equality in every last quarter of life and no longer felt his previous humiliation.

With the Anglo-Saxon vocabulary one has a parallel and yet a divergence from this situation. Here the sexual liberal proposes a rehabilitation of the old terms as a symbolic part of the rehabilitation of sex from Victorian discredit. In both cases the descriptive fact or phenomenon is restored to favor. But in the case of the Negro the association with the preceding state is too close, the sense of humiliation is too poignant to permit the effort to restore both the term as well as the people to favor. Such efforts, however, have succeeded in the past, where subject peoples have resolved that *their name* will one day be honored rather than abused. *Jew* is now undergoing rehabilitation. *Gentile*, which may once have served to characterize people outside the limit of Jehovah's favor, has long since become a mere descript.

The vocabulary of sex-related characterisms now installed in the established language cannot begin to display the extraordinary variety of other linguistic resources. It is therefore dealt with only briefly. Of all the main divisions of our subject, the present reflects perhaps least the nature of characterization currently. One could only hope to do justice to this subject by examining current slang, colloquialisms, and obscenity. Beyond this lie the resources of poetry and literature which provide a deeper exemplification of and insight into sex-related characterization. We shall consider now the characterisms that have become more or less part of the fabric of language.

10.1   SEX-RELATED DIFFERENTIATION

MALE CHARACTERISMS	FEMALE CHARACTERISMS
CREDITING	
(a) **boyish**	(a) **feminine, femininity, feminality,**
manly	**feminility, femineity**
masculine	**womanly**
virile	**tomboy** $\pm$

DISCREDITING	
(b) **effeminate**	(b) **girlish** $(+)$
womanish	**mannish**
unmanly	**unwomanly**

The characterisms in 10.1, like all others, are used to survey subjects as a whole; they do not record detectable properties such as primary or secondary sex traits. Clearly there are no sufficient and necessary criteria for the use of

masculine and **feminine**. Each use of the terms can be a novel and yet relevant interpretation. It is evident that the terms are used to credit or discredit the subject, to enhance or diminish his or her credit, and some have prominent uses in moral judgment. All of them reflect an effect upon the appraiser.

It is apparent that **masculine** and **manly** develop from *male* and **feminine** and **womanish** from *female* but they are not synonyms. We can say that some men are more masculine than others and that not all women are feminine without contradicting ourselves.

In the instance of male and female we have natural differences virtually as fixed as those of animal species. Cultures and conventions project additional differences. In time the boundary between nature and convention becomes vague with the result that everything associated, perhaps even remotely, with males or with females tends to be thought of as part of the irreducible nature of the one or the other. Thus an enormous luggage of conventional traits (style of dress or hair, occupation, etc.) is carried along with the natural physiological properties: a kind of "phenomenal construct," *man* or *woman*, is brought into being.

Occasionally we encounter contrasting cases which shake the construct and reduce the conventional content. It is generally restructured again in other directions. The natural and seemingly irreducible physical differences of male and female constitute a firm core for the construct and its firmness tends to radiate to the peripheral parts until a new convulsion occurs.* We can scarcely overestimate the power of such constructs, and this is the first fact to be reckoned with in considering the present vocabulary.

Certainly there can be no doubt of a core to such constructs which includes not only anatomical differences but also anatomically determined modes of functioning. Thus the manner of walking, the length of the stride, the motion of hands or arms, the strength of the limbs, the pitch of the voice may be little affected by cultural differences and so install themselves close to the core of the phenomenal construct.

As may be expected deviations from a construct with a core as firm as this are inevitably remarked, but they are more often deviations from the periphery than from the core. Restricting ourselves to the deviations that lie in the direction of the opposite sex, it is not surprising to find a verbal coinage that reflects the fact. A deviance toward the female in what is in core respects a man is *like-a-woman* or *woman-ish*.

But it is not just the observation of a resemblance. What is significant is that it is a *reproach*. The subject is in effect admonished to correct his devi-

---

* Like a thousand other "eternal differences," not only *masculine* and *feminine* but *male* and *female* may prove to be more conventional than we had supposed, with the advance of sex surgery.

ance. This, however, assumes that it is in the subject's power to correct it. If it is not in his power (thus an anatomical or physiological deviance), the admonition is impertinent and discredits the appraiser rather than the subject. If it is in his power and the deviance is without physical foundation, the reproach is entirely cultural in nature and must be met in an appropriate manner.

It is obvious that a good deal lies concealed beneath the exterior of these characterisms. It is not easy to rid ourselves of the habit of adding peripheral structures to phenomenal constructs like these or of supposing that conformity to the construct, periphery *or* core, has moral authority. The constructs bring with them a body of expectations, the expectations bring demands, and defiance or evasion of demands brings reproach.

But this is not to suggest that there are no defensible demands arising from the core or periphery of the construct. Thus, a proper use of the male characterisms would be for affirmations about a subject who has failed to discharge a duty he is clearly bound by; he is accused of being weak or unmanly. (The characterization can no doubt be elaborated upon.) The subject has not functioned as a male might be expected to in such and such a situation, has not, for example, resisted aggression when he had it in his physical power to do so.

For similar, rhetorically more effective reasons the reference to the opposite sex in **womanish** is discrediting to a man. But the reproach does not arise from an undesirable trait imputable to women as such. It has reference only to a comparative difference of the sexes in certain powers. The charge of **womanishness** may gain its significance from the fact that the non-resistance of a female to a particular sort of aggression would be no reproach to her but would be to a male in the same situation.

One can easily construct situations with comparable uses of **mannish** where a woman in a certain situation has done nothing inherently discrediting that is imputable to males but has rather unsuccessfully attempted to do what only a man could do properly, while neglecting to do just that which a woman could.

There is no need to decide in general the limits between the natural and the conventional. The point of drawing attention to this distinction is to remind us that in nearly all societies the conventions as to what is appropriate to men and what to women tend toward rigidity simply because there *is* a core of more or less fixed and unalterably different underlying traits. The core and the periphery tend to work in concert as one phenomenal construct.

We must now be careful to observe that the core properties and powers are decisive only where in fact they are present. Since deviance is as natural a fact as the norm, though more seldom, only that can be expected of the deviant that is possible to him. We must in short be prepared to recognize more phenomenal constructs than two; it is something of a triumph for our society to have transcended the standpoint that regards woman as a deviance from or a degenerate case of man. It remains to be seen how far our tolerance will exceed this.

In the light of the foregoing we may now consider briefly other individual appraisives beginning with the less serious terms.

Boyish is often used as a behavioral or diathetic appraisive to characterize the charming if awkward manner of an adolescent and is sometimes even used of young girls hovering below pre-adulthood. For no very apparent reason **boyish** is used in a crediting, **girlish** * in a discrediting manner, perhaps a lingering piece of cross-sexual prejudice. **Tomboy** often appears in contexts similar to those of **boyish. Feminine** clearly presupposes a kind of phenomenal construct and definitely does so in negative characterizations. Both natural and social or conventional traits (core and periphery) may enter into consideration, and there is a great deal of room for delusion and surreption when social and culturally determined traits are taken to be natural.

The remaining crediting terms, **manly, masculine, virile**, and **womanly** all lean heavily on a construct whose authority is thought to derive from nature and not convention. These terms raise interesting problems only when they are used negatively to offer reproach. This, however, merges into the unique issues raised by the discrediting terms.

The discreditings, as observed earlier, can properly be used only if they are based solely on nature. But we must be careful about what we regard as natural. **Not manly** for example can be no reproach if the substance of it is a natural deviance. A reproach must imply that the subject has choice and control. We may therefore say that subjects can be charged with a want of manliness or womanliness only if as a matter of fact their violation of a commitment arose from neglecting to exercise powers they actually possessed. The same may be said of the discrediting characterisms, **unmanly** and **unwomanly.** An unmanly person has simply not behaved in a manner in which our commitments lead us to expect a man to behave, assuming that he does conform to the physical norm *man.* If the terms amount to a serious reproach, we must allow for the principle that 'ought' implies 'can', and we should try to make certain that it is no mere conventional notion of manliness that has been violated. Thus a reproached subject must have the powers somehow

---

* One of my friends justly reminds me of the lines:

> April, April, laugh your girlish laughter,
> Then the moment after
> Weep your girlish tears.

Accordingly, I have modified the discredit of the term with a (+). It is likely that many more "counter-instances" of this sort will suggest themselves, though I believe the terms on *any given occasion* are *either* crediting *or* discrediting.

naturally proper to males but have failed to exercise them. The remainder of this issue may safely be left to ethics proper.

This leaves the interesting cross-sexual terms **effeminate** and **womanish** as applied to males and **mannish** as applied to females. I suggest that these arise by way of metaphor. For just as when we say, "Phipps is a cold fish," everyone knows it is false that Phipps is really any kind of fish, so here when we say, "Sir Philpott Phipps is an old woman," everyone knows that Sir Philpott isn't a woman at all. We are being invited to catch precisely the right strand of resemblance, just as we are told a joke and expected to catch the point of it. But if someone says Cassius Clay or Lyndon Johnson is effeminate, everyone knows that this is not even a metaphor. Metaphors are *interesting*, intriguing falsehoods.

When the terms of this vocabulary have a moral employment they must look toward core or natural traits, allowing for individual deviance; it is these traits that can most successfully support or negate moral demands because they determine function.

But not all uses of the terms is moral and in fact their primary use is simply for the purpose of characterization. In this capacity they have an authority that lies outside the area of moral commitments, outside the natural core of the constructs *man* and *woman*. Finding some convention of male dress effeminate can carry its own original conviction, but it cannot properly be declared a moral evil though this is often done by moralists. It is necessary to free terms like this, and perhaps the others too, from too close a connection with phenomenal constructs because the appeal to these is too often the refuge of moral dogmatists.

10.2   AMATIVE CONCERN

ATTRIBUTIVE	SUBSTANTIVE
(a) **affection, affectionate**	(b) **beau**
amative	**cavalier**
amorous	**flame**
infatuate, infatuation	**gallant** n.
jealous	**inamorata**
love	**lover**
lovelorn	**mistress**
lovesick	**suitor**
passion, -ate	**swain**
sentimental	**sweetheart**
tender	
uxorious ($\pm$)	

The present class of terms is meant as a contrast to the next section, 10.3 (sexuality). There we take up the ways in which the stimulus to explicitly sexual response is characterized. The present represents concern for a *person* though it is obviously not possible to draw any hard and fast line between sexual and nonsexual concern which, at the same time, is intersexual. The present subject is intersexual concern that is not necessarily or not always sexual. It seems evident that while these vocabularies may alter, along with alterations in sexual customs, there must always remain an area of nonsexual concern between the sexes. Parts of 10.2 seem slightly archaic.

Of the terms in (a), **amorous, infatuation, jealous**, and **passionate** are probably the most explicitly borderline cases towards 10.3. But it is possible to imagine a person who is, say, jealous only as regards affection or only as regards sexual expression, or one who is amorous, infatuated or passionate only as regards one and not the other.

It is obvious that the terms in (a) are not all characterisms. The most explicitly characterizing, I suggest, are **infatuation, lovelorn, lovesick, tender**, and **uxorious**. In (b) I would say all except **suitor** and **mistress** (in its sex-related application) are characterizing. Of the (a) terms, **infatuation** will be used to discredit (over a range of intensity, mild to severe) a relationship of amatory attachment or concern, **tender** will certainly be used as a crediting term, and the other two will vary according to the context. It is interesting to note that **tender** is probably always used in a sincere, non-ironic manner, and its range extends beyond intersexual concern to relationships of friends, and of parents and children. **Passion** and **passionate** obviously show the least kinship with terms for concern, since they suggest either a merely intense degree of feeling or possibly a self-serving concern with the amatory object. **Uxorious** is a genuine characterism. It expresses a detectable adverse effect on some appraiser of someone's involvement in marriage, and it is used to discredit this involvement. Obviously, it is safe to say if A is found uxorious he is the last person likely to designate his own person or situation this way. The term is thus not for first personal use in the present. It also exhibits the trait that, for the time being, the subject is being treated as if all of him could be reduced to just the capacity or aspect in which he is now being characterized. The decision that *so* much involvement in marriage (as A displays) is *too* much is the appraiser's own, reflecting what he thinks is a proper degree. Once again, as in 10.1 we see the prevalence of typological thinking at the bottom of this. But here there is much less of a natural type than **male** or **female** to appeal to: marriage may be ordained by God but whether it is ordained by nature is another question. Finally, **lovelorn** is mainly a humorous term and **lovesick** an exaggeration.

The terms of (b) have mostly a somewhat dated appearance. In this subject, nothing ages so fast as the terminology. Thus **cavalier, gallant** (which could also serve a heavier purpose elsewhere), **swain**, and **inamorata**, have little more than a literary use, if that, and **beau** and **sweetheart** are not widely used at the present time. **Flame** is a piece of somewhat dated slang from a fairly trite metaphor.

From the foregoing, one would never suspect that there is nothing in the whole language on which so much imagination and ingenuity are expended as the effort to characterize the mutual concern of the sexes. Only a canvass of current speech and colloquialism could demonstrate this.

10.3 SEXUALITY

POSITIVE CHARACTERISMS			NEGATIVE CHARACTERISMS	
CREDITING		+	CREDITING	
(none)			**chaste, chastity**	
			continent	
			decent	
			modest	
			proper	
			pure	

+ ═══════════════════════════ × ═══════════════════════════ −

DISCREDITING			DISCREDITING	
ATTRIBUTIVE				
bawdy	**naughty**			
bestial	**obscene**			
carnal	**orgy**			
concupiscent	**profligate**			
degenerate	**promiscuous**			
erotic	**prurient**			
immodest	**ribald**			
improper	**risqué**			
indecorous	**rut**			
indelicate	**salacious**			
lascivious	**sensual**			
lecherous	**sensuous**			
lewd	**smut, smutty**			
libidinous	**venery**			
licence,	**voluptuous** (+)			
licentious	**vulgar**			
loose	**wanton**			
lubricious				

SUBSTANTIVE

(a) **adulter, -ess**   (c) **cuckold**   **prude**
  libertine   (d) **pander**
  lothario   **pimp**
  masher   (e) **bawd**
  rake   **courtesan**
  roué   **harlot**
  voluptuary   **quean**
(b) **coquette**   **slut**
  flirt   **strumpet**
  hoyden   **tart**
  hussy   **whore** n.
  jade   (f) **pervert**

PROCESSIVE

  adultery
  deflower
  debauch
  incest
  lust, lustful
  erotomania
  nymphomania
  perversion
  rape
  seduce

We come now to the heart of the sex-related characterisms that are established in the language. The manner in which they reflect the sex attitudes of the speakers is evident from the nature of this vocabulary, but the attitudes themselves would have to be confirmed also from other sources. We shall forego such an effort here and leave the matter where such further confirmation would begin.

A further word or two may here be in order regarding the present application of our fourfold scheme for classifying appraisives in terms of two principal criteria: positive-negative, and crediting-discrediting. The first of these distributes the characterisms according to whether a phenomenon is present or not, the second whether it is thought to enhance, diminish, or injure the credit of the subject. As we have seen, the language itself *can* provide characterisms under all four heads. Thus, under confidence-diffidence in 8.22 we found confidence praised when it could be characterized as **self-assuredness,** but not when it was characterized as **impudence,** and we found the absence of confidence could be praised when it appeared as **reserve** or **modesty,** but not when it appeared in the form **woebegone**. (By 'confidence' as the property praised or dispraised here we mean, of course, the power of self-assertion.) In like manner, other phenomena can be praised and dispraised. In the present case, it is the phenomenon which in its most objective terms is the overt exercise of sexual instincts and whatever in a fairly narrow sense is naturally involved in this as a process in time. The positive side of this will be the exercise of the instinct, the negative the restraint or suppression of it. In principle, we can regard the *exercise* of it now as a credit to the subject and now as a discredit to him, or again we can regard the *restraint* of the same or other acts now as a credit, now as a discredit to the subject. We shall have, then, the whole range of stances that are taken toward sexual acts as these are reflected in the vocabulary.

There are some rather surprising results when we examine this vocabulary in detail. In other fields, the presence of the whole fourfold range of predicates shows that full resources for characterization are present and that it is up to the appraiser to select which of these best applies to the present subject. In the present case we see an extraordinary imbalance in favor of the discreditation of the phenomenon itself. There is scarcely a single characterism employable for the positive occurrence of the phenomenon, yet there are almost six dozen that can be used to discredit it, and there is only one mild characterism that may be used to discredit suppressive attitudes toward the phenomenon. On the face of it, one cannot but be astonished that the race survives among English-speaking people when their language affords no resources for praising the phenomenon that is absolutely necessary for survival. In qualification it should be said that the characterisms may be used in several different connections. They can be used to condemn not just sexual acts but also certain things connected with the sexual phenomenon, such as words, pictures, works of art, and sundry other objects that are often concomitants of or stimuli for the phenomenon.

But even so, the fact remains that neither the acts nor the verbal or other stimuli to them fare very well at the hands of established language. No distinction is detectable in the language itself as to whether it is to apply only to extra-marital acts, except *adultery* and the vocabulary for the occupations of prostitution and procuring; and there appears to be no ready way in which even those sexual acts that are sanctioned by society or religion can be praised.

We must remind ourselves, however, that one of the first commandments in the accepted tradition of Judaeo-Christian culture is "be fruitful and multiply" (Genesis, 1, 28). There would seem to be a conflict between this and the paucity of characterisms praising the act on which such fruitfulness depends. Perhaps a glance back at the Genesis legend will throw some light on this.

On the sixth day man is created, "male and female" and all living creatures, presumably also man, are commanded to be fruitful and multiply. There is an anomaly in that after all has been created and declared good, the writer appears to forget what has been said and relates the story of the creation of Eve from Adam's rib. But we may ignore this. Immediately after the creation of Eve, Adam declares, "This is now bone of my bones, and flesh of my flesh." It is also said that man and wife "shall be one flesh," an obvious reference to sexual as well as spiritual unity. Immediately thereafter follows the statement that Adam and Eve were naked and unashamed. The implication is clear that man in his innocence is a sexual being. None of the prudery of later centuries, therefore, has any basis in the Biblical source of our tradition so far as we are concerned with man in this state.

It is only after the eating of the fruit of the tree of knowledge that guilt and shame appear. With this comes embarrassment over nakedness, and pain now becomes the burden of childbirth. Thereafter, with various other sins already in being, the expulsion from the Garden occurs. The question is, is man truly man in the state of innocence or is he truly man only after he gains knowledge and sins? I believe the tradition in practice must have leaned in the latter direction. Therefore, it regarded nakedness as an unmitigated wickedness and thought that men never could regain the happiness of innocence here on earth. It had not the slightest authority, however, for thinking that innocence was necessarily equal to the nullification of sexuality, although it may have been right in thinking that innocence could never be regained, short of the after life. What we learn from this legend, then, is that there is actually far more good sense in it than in the tradition that has grown out of it.

I must abandon many of these issues to theologians and psychologists. Here we can speak only of the nature of the characterizing vocabulary. If theologians should say that only such sexuality as lies beyond the blessing of religion is discredited one could only reply that none of this appears from the vocabulary itself. It would be possible, in fact, to apply any or all of the discrediting vocabulary in 10.3 to persons blessed by the marriage sacrament for behavior wholly within marital limits. It is in any event indisputable that there exists in English no established vocabulary in praise of any aspect of sexuality except the issue of it. As may be expected, it confirms the sexual attitudes that have prevailed for centuries in Western civilization.

It must be made clear, however, that the existence of such a one-sided vocabulary must not now be interpreted automatically in such a way as to condemn traditional sexual attitudes. All that its character shows is that sexuality has been held in ill favor, but to show that the phenomenon deserves favor more is necessary than simply pointing to the attitudes or vocabulary against it. There are no words which do not condemn deception or murder but this does not show that we have been wrong about such acts all this time. If sexuality is to be "restored" to favor some material reason must be offered. There is no doubt that the present "pro-sexual" trend will, in time, coin its own terminology if the attitudes of society actually are changed. Language is always a barometer of such attitudes, as the present vocabulary so amply shows.

In examining this vocabulary, we must be careful not to exceed the evidence we have before us, particularly the discrediting characterisms in 10.3. Without exception, they are terms whose primary use is to be applied to various phases of sexuality. It is true, also, that many persons would regard most aspects of sexuality in these terms. Yet from another point of view the vocabulary may be construed as one which is only to be used in condemnation, not of all sexuality, but of certain deviant or abnormal aspects of it. From this standpoint the vocabulary falls into the following groups. First, there are terms for characterizing abnormal sexuality in particular instances (not generally, I believe) as **bestial, degenerate** or **lascivious**. Second, excessive sexuality or excess of ardor may be characterized as **concupiscent, libidinous, lubricious, wanton,** or **rutty**. Third, indiscriminate sexuality may be characterized as **licentious, loose, orgiastic, profligate,** or **promiscuous**. Fourth, sexuality and sexual discourse that for one reason or another seem simply out of place may be characterized as **improper, indecorous,** or **indelicate**. Now, none of the foregoing classifications is *inherently* an unreasonable ground for objecting to sexuality; that is, abnormality, excessiveness, indiscriminateness, untimeliness. I would think that the case for saying sexuality is itself a good would be compatible with saying that in particular respects it could also be abnormal, excessive, or indiscriminate. If so, then the vocabulary would of course survive efforts, so copious in this century, to "restore" sexuality to a public favor it had lost in previous times.

There remain, however, several other characterisms to be considered. These seem to derive from an outright rejection of sexuality itself, or at least a conviction of its inherent wrongness: namely, **bawdy, lewd, naughty, obscene, ribald, salacious, sensuous,** and **smutty**. In these cases the typical use would be, let us say, that some picture, discourse or action is bawdy, lewd, or obscene because it depicts or involves sexuality and for no other reason. Perhaps one can only appeal to people who have a deep sense of guilt or embarrassment about sexuality with songs or discourses that are explicitly ribald, obscene or salacious. This is a trite observation on this subject, yet true. Or perhaps this could be better put in another way: people with a sense of guilt about sexuality are most likely to characterize virtually any and everything with sexual import as bawdy or lewd. But I am not at all satisfied with the converse of this, that those who characterize anything as obscene or ribald

suffer from guilt or embarassment, although this is passionately advocated
by most sexual reformers. In short, it seems to me these terms should not be
repudiated wholly simply because certain people profess to be able to see
guilt and shame behind every use of them as serious characterizations. The fact
is we do not even now know enough about this phenomenon to say in general
that there is something wrong with people who condemn sexuality in one
degree or another. There is no subject which is so riddled and corrupted by
fallacious *ad hominem* arguments as arguments about sexuality. The psychoanalysts have contributed to this. For some of them, virtually no argument
questioning free sexuality is allowed to have merit, not because it is inherently
invalid but because the propounder is necessarily the victim of a state
which is neurotic in one degree or another. Hence his counter arguments are
inherently invalid! Yet no one ever seems to make any headway pointing
out such absurdities. It is hard to resist the temptation to reply by attributing
appropriate neuroses to the psychoanalysts.

It is possible that these characterizations do reflect the widespread suspicion or rejection of sexuality in many of its phases. They may, however,
survive and continue to serve a purpose even if sexual attitudes and practices
are considerably reformed.

There are two terms which deserve special mention. It is instructive that
we are hard put to find a general and neutral term for sexuality (other than
'sex' or 'sexuality') which can be used as a descript. **Amative** and **amorous**
are too closely tied to the actual manifestation of a certain kind of interest.
Erotic and **sexual** are too narrowly physical. In this juncture, terms deriving
from *Venus* might have offered certain advantages. The Greek form, *Aphro-
dite*, was appropriated for very special use in 'aphrodisiac'. The term **venery**
could have served but its adjectival form 'venereal' is unfortunately and
perhaps irrevocably ruined as a neutral term by its use in pathology. The
instructive fact is that one of the problems the sexual reformer faces is the
want of a neutral terminology for a phenomenon that embraces love, in the
sense of tender regard, and personal concern as well as physical sexuality.
The only term in our list that is more or less neutral is the substantive form
venery.

A second term that deserves a special mention is **voluptuous**. Its Latin
form (=pleasure) served both for the physical and the spiritual sense of
delight, but the physical alone has largely survived in English. However, it
is *almost* free of discrediting overtones (or the nearest to this on our list) and
thus deserves to be set apart from the other characterisms which either discredit, or if they credit, do so in an embarrassed or shamefaced way. Yet it
is not sufficiently crediting to deserve classification as such a term.

The substantive discrediting terms fall into several classes. First are the characterisms of the male, second of the female in the capacity simply of persons who pursue sexuality in some ardent degree. It is not easy or necessary, however, to segregate very closely the first two groups from the last, which comprises the most serious characterisms.

We need not pause long over the rest of the group. There are several terms which are names of occupations, but the occupations themselves have been so despised by society that scarcely any line can be drawn between descripts and discrediting characterisms for them. This holds of **pander, pimp, harlot,** and **whore.** The others perhaps are more characterizing. The application of them to persons *not* actually engaged in these occupations is, of course, a more serious instance of their use. To speak of a woman as a whore or a man as a pimp, in such an instance is of course to characterize them; the terms seem to display all the several traits we have identified in characterisms previously. It should be said, however, that there is some doubt of this, for some objective grounds generally will be found for using the terms. Thus to speak of a matron as a slut, tart, or whore while perhaps not an accusation of accepting a fee, will generally mean the more or less inveterate, furtive pursuit of sexuality outside marriage. Aside from this, it is not altogether easy to see why society in most languages has reserved its most violently scornful language for an occupation which has always existed and to which it has often even accorded legal status.

We learn little from the etymology of this class of terms. At least six are obscure in origin and thus very possibly derived from vulgar or even criminal slang: **bawd, hoyden** (from *hoit*, to be riotously mirthful, which is of obscure origin), **jade, pimp, slut, strumpet. Flirt** is thought onomatopoetic. **Harlot** at first is simply a lad, but then descends (like **knave**) to base fellow, and finally to base woman. The worst term of all, **whore**, derives from the same source as L. *carus*, dear! There are many other aspects of the situations in which these terms arise which must be the subject of material investigations lying beyond the scope of our analysis of language.

The processive characterisms are again wholly negative. The subject matter, of course, is sexual acts themselves. Traditional language draws a veil over all but acts which appear to deserve discredit: adulterous, incestuous, violent, perverse, and more or less frenzied acts. Even granting the rightness of such discreditation, it remains to be explained why there are no explicit terms crediting sexual acts. Perhaps the only term, and an expressive one, that can be mentioned here is the Biblical **enjoy.** This is a term with a more general use which is here "specificated" temporarily for a special use. It deserves mention, if only to balance the other half of the vocabulary.

The terms used to credit the checking of sexuality are not surprising, considering the long list discrediting its indulgence. Yet it would be entirely possible and likely that such a class of terms would be devised even if a sexuality were to be completely revised and a new language for it devised. For just as excessive ingestion of food and drink may be discredited, it is reasonable to suppose that there would also be a need for discrediting the excessive exercise of other instincts. What is, however, not so easy to explain from this standpoint is that the present terms credit only the total suppression of sexuality (**chaste, continent, pure**) or its virtual suppression. All such terms serve their purpose, but the range of terms is limited. The final term provides a more hopeful note in that the recognition of an excess of suppression is allowed for in **prude** and **prudery**.

The body of characterisms as a whole evidently provides ill for the expression of deviance from the traditional code of sexuality. Resort is therefore had to other devices by those who believe that this code is in need of revision. Should they succeed, language itself would sooner or later reflect the change.

10.4 FAMILIAL CONCERN

brotherly (also 11.3)	**matronly**
domesticity	**motherly**
fatherly	**piety** (filial)
filial, un-	

In accordance with our decision to construe the term sex-related in the broadest sense, we include also the characterisms that are devised particularly for relationships within families.

It should be observed first that these characterisms will not be repeated necessarily in every language. The attitude of devotedness of parents to children or children to parents, of brother to brother, of brother to sister vary from one society to another. Our own attitudes, so deeply stamped with the imagery of Judaic and Christian religion, are by no means repeated everywhere, as we can see from the customs explored so fully in Frazer's *The Golden Bough*, where so often sons to protect the sisters from the father rise up to kill him and seize control of affairs. Challenge to the Christian conception has also sprung up in European thought itself in the past century or more, in the ideas of the Marquis de Sade, Nietzsche, and various apostles of violence.

Brotherliness is often cited as the epitome of sanity and progress in social relations. Yet, considering the enormous differences that can obtain between actual or blood-related brothers, the term has force only if we ignore many real or potential differences. That the term is a characterism can scarcely be doubted. Actual brothers frequently are exhorted to treat one another in brotherly fashion, and this in no redundant sense. The source of the characterism seems therefore to be a metaphor. The listener is invited to think of some trait or relationship brothers have and to project this into other human situations, for example among nations or members of a lodge or school. Or the device may be one of singling out some approved trait or other and then asking that it be emulated: so fathers are asked to be fatherly. Of course, this has the curious result that a father is being asked to be a father in a metaphorical as well as a literal sense.

The application to the corresponding class (**fatherly** to *father*, etc.) as a characterism must remind us also that we are again invited to think in typal terms, as in 10.1 (**masculine, womanly,** etc.). What was said there about typal explanations will apply in almost equal measure here. The powerful hold of types on our thinking is nowhere more evident than in thinking of men and women as fathers and mothers.

This must suffice as an analysis of sex-related characterisms. If we were to try to give a complete picture we would be hopelessly seeking to complete a vocabulary that keeps increasing all of the time. Perhaps a framework for such a vocabulary has been set forth here. There are large tracts, however, that have been left unexplored, for example, the argot of obscenity. Where the standard vocabulary has little more than a few expressions to express its thought, the argot has many more. Also, we have not made any effort to explore the technical vocabulary of abnormal psychology, psychiatry, and psychoanalysis. Our subject matter is the core of appraisive terms in the natural language on all the subjects we take up and not technicalities of any sort.

11.0 SOCIATIVE CHARACTERIZATION

The area of human conflict and accommodation to which we turn next is already to some degree anticipated in the areas of sexuality and the tendentive. The latter forms a dimension of the person's asserting himself in the world through what has generally been called the will. He appears as a center from which power radiates in various degrees of strength. Inevitably, his power and inner energy lead to contact not only with the environment generally but with other persons. Through conflict and contention with others he may assert or overassert himself in aggression, gain ascendancy, acquiesce in defeat, or accommodate himself to an equilibrium of wills. Since all this is the very thick of life, it is not surprising that the vocabulary of sociative characterization that now presents itself is by far the most extensive of the several into which we have divided our subject. It is an encounter with the world of "others" that lies beyond the narrow circle of sexuality, an encounter with persons having similar concerns and similar hopes to affirm themselves.

The sequence in which the various areas of sociative characterization are presented already reflects a theory. One could begin with the more placid and peaceful modes and proceed toward disintegration and conflict. If we have begun with conflict and proceeded toward covenance, it is to recognize that conflict is natural and endemic to human kind, and that its aim in general is to establish or to re-establish order, even if it is fiercely autocratic. Conflict itself is *in order* when old orders are moribund. Ultimately, everything points toward covenance.

To speak of conflict as an irreducible feature of life is not, however, to say that aggression is. Persons may enter into contention without aggressing: their aims may be wholly defensive rather than offensive. We must be careful to distinguish between two current senses of aggressiveness. In one sense, we think of aggressiveness as praiseworthy. In this sense it means having a vivid sense of one's own worth and a capacity and will to assert oneself among others in the affairs of life. It is not meant to characterize a person who takes unfair advantage of others. In the other sense it is just such self-assertion together with a ruthless disregard for the rightful claims of others. It is the second, where aggressiveness amounts to aggression, that will tend to occupy most of our interest. Much of the first falls into the tendentive area since it is not thought of as exploitative of others but merely the rightful assertion of the self.

A differing mode of organization of the present set of characterisms is possible. Ascendancy, aggression, accommodation, and submission, together with some of the tendentive characterisms, could be organized into a fourfold pattern such as we have employed before. We could set up a division to contrast active and receptive modes of conduct. These could be distinguished as positive and negative characterizations, with further classifications into credit and discredit. The following is an illustration:

11.01   SOCIATION

POSITIVE CHARACTERISMS	+	NEGATIVE CHARACTERISMS
CREDITING		CREDITING
(a) ASCENDANCY (11.2)		(b) ACCOMMODATION (11.3)
actuate		adjust to
animate		compromise
assert oneself		conciliate
incite		concur
pertinacity		cooperate
etc.		tact
		etc.

+ ═══════════════════ × ═══════════════════ −

DISCREDITING		DISCREDITING
(c) AGGRESSION (11.111)		(d) ACQUIESCENCE (11.2)
assail		appease
disrupt		defer to
effrontery		surrender
intrude		yield
maraud		etc.
molest		
offend		
terrify		
etc.		−

We avoid this scheme for the present because it leaves no room to show the important detail of each of the main topics or the consecutive order from contention through ascendancy, submission, accommodation to covenance. We shall proceed now to study each of these, keeping in mind this alternative organization of the concepts (cf. 11.3, p. 244 ff).

11.1   CONFLICT

DISCREDITING CHARACTERISMS		DESCRIPTS
brawl	shindy	[altercation]
discord	spat	[commotion]
feud	squabble	[contend]
fracas	tiff	[contest]
fray	uproar	[dispute]
havoc	wrangle	[dissension]
hullabaloo		[quarrel]
imbroglio		[strife]
at [loggerheads		[struggle]
be at [odds with		[trouble]
riot		[tumult]
row		[upheaval]
ruction		[uprising]

For reasons that will be apparent, we have in the present and certain other vocabularies included a considerable number of terms which are generally descripts or perhaps only marginally characterizing in nature. It is not always easy to distinguish appraisives and descripts. I have followed the general rule that terms that count as appraisives are not self-applied in the first person present.

In 11.1 the terms that would most generally be used as descripts are in brackets at the right. No one involved in a confrontation with others could object to having the affair described in such terms. He would probably, however, be unwilling to hear that so far as his own part in it was concerned it was being characterized by the other terms. He would not be comfortable hearing it called a brawl. If, as is apparent, conflict is a normal part of life there must also be a neutral vocabulary in which to describe it. When an appraiser speaks of conflict in terms of the characterizing vocabulary he indicates he would not wish himself to be identified with it in those terms. The descripts (**altercation, commotion,** etc.) are grave and dignified, and not surprisingly, most of them derive from the Latin. Among the characterisms a slang origin is virtually certain for **spat, ruction, row, brawl,** and **tiff. Imbroglio** and **squabble** have equally humble origins.

The appraisives of contention show that although conflict may be pervasive or perpetual it is not in itself thought to be a virtue. While fortitude, combativeness (cf. the expressive **feisty** of American slang) and even the fury of combat may be praised, their virtue lies rather in their results.

We turn next to the modes of characterizing contention, that is, the person's particular way of entering into a conflict.

11.11   CONTENTION (largely discrediting) (Cf. 9.2, 11.2, 15.3)

11.111   INVASIVE CONTENTION*

ATTRIBUTIVE		DESCRIPTS
aggressive	impudent	[belligerent]
anti-social	inhuman	[defiant]
atrocious	inimical	[indomitable]
bellicose	insolent	[inimical]
bestial	litigious	[stubborn]
brash	malevolent	[uncompromising]
brutal	maleficent	[warlike]
censorious	malice,	
cold-blooded	malicious	
contentious	mean	
contumacious	meddlesome	
cruel	merciless	
disputatious	obdurate	
effrontery	obnoxious	
evil-minded	obstinate	
factious (fac-	obstreperous	
tion 13.6)	presumptuous	
ferocious	pugnacious	
fiendish	quarrelsome	
forward	rancor	
froward	recalcitrant	
impertinent	refractory	

* These lists must certainly call to mind the many British men-of-war that have borne the names not only of descripts or characterisms of fierce and tenacious resistance and counter-resistance in past centuries, but also of what are presented here as discrediting characterisms of invasive contention: not only the recent H.M.S. *Audacious, Dreadnought, Implacable, Indefatigable, Indomitable, Irresistible,* and *Obdurate* (1916), but also *Spiteful* (1794), *Termagant* (1781), and *Terrible* (1694). Obviously, *pour décourager les autres.*

It is interesting to observe the same inclination in the now mighty navy of the U.S.S.R. Ships named for attributes, as in the Royal Navy, number among many others the following with approximate equivalents: *Bditelnyi* (Vigilant), *Bessmertnyi* (Deathless), *Nastoychiviy* (Persistent), *Otchaianny* (Desperate). Some fifty destroyers are named in Jane's *Fighting Ships.* It is not readily evident to the non-Russian which of the attributes are discredits, but very likely: *Ozhestochonnyi* (Embittered).

The U.S. Navy names ocean and fleet minesweepers for attributes. Among them are the usual defiant vocabulary (USS *Dominant, Force,* and *Threat*) but also USS *Devastator.* Other navies have often followed the same conventions.

There is an obvious value for the *esprit de corps* of crews as well as patriots in such vocabularies. The discrediting titles will always be interpreted to mean that any aggressor will be visited with merciless, fearful revenge.

ruthless
scurrilous
spite, spiteful
sportsmanlike (cred.)
tendentious

truculent
uncompromising
ungovernable
vengeful
warlike

PROCESSIVE

abase
abuse (11.121)
aggrandize
aggress
annoy (2.22)
assail
assault
atrocity
badger
baffle
bluff v.
bother
chivy
coerce
conspire, conspiracy
daunt
debase
deface
defile
degrade
deprave v.t.
depredate
despoil
dishonor v.t.
show [disrespect
disrupt
disturb
duress
effrontery
encroach
flout
foment trouble
harass
harry
humiliate

iconoclasm
importune
act with [impunity
subject to [indignity
inflict harm
infringe upon
infuriate
injure
intimidate
intrude
irritate
(malinger)
maltreat
mar
maraud
(massacre)
maul
(mayhem)
meddle
molest
mortify
(murder)
mutilate
nag
obstruct
obtrude
offend
oppress
outrage v.t.
persecute
pester
plague v.
pollute
quid pro quo
rag v.

DESCRIPTS

[alienate]
[antagonize]
[challenge]
[defy]
[frustrate]
[outwit]
[rebuff]
[repel]
[repress]
[reprisal]
[repulse]
[retaliate]
[thwart]
[ultimatum]
[vie]

ravish (=violate)	torment
sabotage	torture
sadism	usurp
spoil v.t.	vendetta
stultify	vex
sully	waylay
tamper with	worry v.t.
tease	wrong v.t.
terrify	

SUBSTANTIVE

champion (cred.)	mob (13.6)
enfant terrible	paladin (cred.)
gadfly	upstart
interloper	vandal

Before we consider this vocabulary we may first glance at the bracketed processive descripts (**alienate, antagonize, challenge,** etc.). What cannot fail to surprise us is how few crediting appraisive or characterizing terms can be found under contention. One finds **champion, paladin, sportsmanlike,** and virtually no others. The vast number of discreditations would seem to show that the speakers of the language have had massive occasion to complain of the invasion of their goods or selves and far less opportunity to acclaim the defense or safety of these. There is another and more cogent reason. Whoever offends me by overreaching himself I visit with adverse *characterization*. But when I defend what I say I rightly possess, the plainest *descripts* of my action will be most effective. One never really sees himself as an aggressor but only as a defender and champion of what is right or good. As we have already had occasion to observe, self-applauding appraisals are somewhat absurd. As a result we need only the descriptive vocabulary to discourse about ourselves: *we* challenge, defy, frustrate, outwit, repel, repress, repulse, thwart, and vie with our adversaries; *they* coerce, defile, degrade, despoil, harass, infringe upon, molest, oppress, outrage, and torment. We are innocent and so a mere description of our deeds is a sufficient defense; we therefore avoid self-stultifying characterization. We may also choose to place our own effort in a somewhat better light by speaking of it in some part of the crediting tendentive vocabulary (9.0). The phenomenon of speaking of one's own effort in purely descriptive, of that of adversaries in discrediting appraisive terms, is not confined to contention.

The characterisms of 11.111 without doubt include the most powerful we shall encounter in our study. They reflect the seemingly limitless variety of man's inhumanity to man, particularly when we recall that the present vocabulary is but an inner core that is always being supplemented by other linguistic resources. In both language and action ever more effective devices of contention are sought as well as measures for responding to these. We are now concerned not only with contention, contest, competition, rivalry, ascendency, and power generally, but also with aggression, with active, outgoing offense which seeks the harm or destruction of others. It ranges from the merest playfulness of teasing, where harm may be nil, to the complete extinction of other persons.

Since the appraisives of contention appear in such overwhelming profusion, and are also highly repetitious, we may advance our inquiry by reducing the list to a comparative handful that may still show what is essential in it. Taking the most powerful group, the processives, some five subordinate groups may be distinguished, all of them forms of aggression. (All of the terms are understood as appraisives of actions taken *by* persons *toward* persons; the terms may also have uses in other contexts.)

(a) **aggress**
    offend

(b) **aggrandize**
    disrupt
    infringe upon
    intrude
    usurp

(c) **annoy**
    assail
    badger
    bother
    chivy
    daunt
    disturb
    flout
    foment [trouble
    harass
    harry
    importune
    nag
    pester
    rag
    tease

vex
worry v.t.

(d) **dishonor**
    disrespect
    effrontery
    humiliate
    intimidate
    maltreat
    molest
    mortify
    oppress
    outrage
    persecute
    plague
    subject (someone)
        to [indignity v.t.
    terrify
    torment
    waylay
    wrong

(e) **maraud**
    maul
    mutilate
    torture

As we proceed towards class (d) and (e), the moral overtones of these terms are more explicit; they are virtually moral discreditations. Their severity is such that they will not be self-applied in the present, and nothing illustrates their power better than situations where they have connections with the self. Confession and penitence, inherently looking to the past, may be couched in these forms. But in the present, while it is probably not logical nonsense, it is moral and certainly religious nonsense for a person serious in faith to pray, "Forgive me for the atrocity, murder, or torture I am about to inflict." One cannot both screw himself up to commit what in the very act he characterizes as torture and also be penitent for it in one and the same moment. But an officer can sign a death warrant or an order committing men into a battle which few of them will survive and also do so with genuine honor. In this case no one will properly speak of the officer in such a situation in any of the terms of 11.111.

In our abbreviated list, the first group (a) merely names the whole class, the second (b) refers to the invasion of personal time and freedom. Group (c) represents a series of charges of invasions of personal welfare from the mild to the rather more severe and annoying, but perhaps not always with untoward or even quite deliberate intent. It may be possible to fall into some of these through sheer bad habit. For the most part, the purport of the charges is that someone is accused of injuring feelings. The characterisms of (d) presume studied effort as to means and results and envisage a more or less serious degree of harm to an adversary that may in turn inspire moral recrimination. One may conceivably assail or annoy a person to induce him to mend his ways, but one torments, terrifies, and molests him to do him harm in a fairly unreserved sense. The final class (e) at the end represents the infliction of more or less irrevocable harm.

One could append to this class, and to 11.111 generally, even more serious charges: **malingering, mayhem, murder, massacre.** The first is aggression towards the fabric of the society that the agent-victim himself belongs to and, it is assumed, ought to be prepared to protect. The others (and perhaps even more heinous and insidious aggressions it is unnecessary to detail) represent deprivations where in fact there are obligations to loyalty. In the morals of war, as hitherto formulated, I have not *murdered* an enemy whose death I have effected, and the reason is simply that I have been thought to have virtually no obligation to him. I dare not, however, slash off his ear when I have him in my power as a prisoner: here obligations have reasserted themselves. In all such cases and indeed in many of the other aggressions detailed among the processives of 11.111 (as explained below and in the introduction to 14.0) we encounter acts subject not only to appraisal but also to moral judgment.

All of these terms have little standing in law, except for some of the more severe, such as **assault** or **murder**, but they are the common coin of moral characterization (cf. 14.01). All of them convey the severer of the two senses of **aggressive** identified earlier, that the measure undertaken, or the degree of it, exceeds in some degree, and perhaps exceeds as far as possible, the limits of permissible acts that may be committed on the body or mind of another person. Except for the usually playful **tease**, all are intended to discredit the subject.

The terms appear in their most powerful form passively in the present: "Stop nagging me!" "I'm humiliated!" "Why do you torment me?" For the time being, whatever virtues the subject (who is said to be nagging, humiliating, tormenting) may have are in these charges submerged in the characterism; if he oppresses or dishonors or terrifies, his virtues are practically nullified. One does not single out some *property* of a person for *description* when one speaks so. One seeks to render his whole being in one blazing word. One is trying to get at his inmost character. There are no rules and definitions for the application of the terms. It avails the subject little to try to repudiate the characterization, "You terrify me!" by a semantic discussion. Terror *is* the effect his conduct has had on the appraiser: only a new deed or a reversal of conduct can hope to modify the characterization.

Like all terms for the acts or states of persons, there are significant differences in power and effectiveness, depending upon the grammatical person of the sentences in which the terms appear. (What varies is not the meaning but the conditions under which one comes to learn the meaning.) It is in situations where someone, some here and present *you*, annoys me, and where emotions of some sort are precipitated in me, that I can best learn the depth and power of these terms. Yet my view is outward, not inward: there are no emotions named **torment, harry, chivy, badger, rag,** and **nag.** My principal intent is to characterize your action, not to report my emotions, although the terms are in some degree elicitive (cf. 15.1). My intent is to direct attention toward *you*, because if you are aggressing in the manner I indicate you will certainly not care a fig for *my* emotions or for the reproach that you have evoked them. Of course, it is all too evident that I am experiencing emotions or else I would not resort to this way of characterizing you, but it is *your* role in all this that is significant for me. I am producing the reason for a discommendation: you have aggressed against me.

In the second person, when I am moved to characterize A by saying, "You are aggressing against (some other person) B," or "annoying, ragging, nagging B," I do so because I virtually feel myself being annoyed, ragged, or nagged by A, or I am only one step from it. One does not need an elaborate theory of sympathy or empathy to understand this. Here again the direction is outward. What my own emotion is (probably one of indignation) may be shown, but it has not been asserted. I am discovering the best of reasons for a severe discommendation of A. This looms even larger than my feelings. Some of this applies also to my making a charge of aggression in the third person which may involve me more or less deeply.

This must serve as a mere sketch of the explanation of these terms which have usually seemed scarcely important enough for extended study, or in fact, any study at all.

From all this we see that a distinctly more serious and moral note has begun to appear in our series of genera of characterisms. Hitherto, from 6.0 through 10.0, the appraiser was in a position to survey the traits and qualities of subjects with some pretense to detachment because he himself could be assumed to be not under threat. The intelligence or judgment of the subject, his emotional makeup, his figure, movement and bodily responses, his address to action, even his sexual interests and practices (with the exception of aggressions such as rape) could be viewed with appreciation or disgust, yet they all concerned the subject principally as an individual and not as part of a social fabric embracing both himself and the appraiser. Increasingly from now to the end of Part Two we shall be dealing with actions and dispositions to action oriented toward other persons. In the social sphere (sociative, economic, communitive) we deal with subjects not only of appraisal or characterization but also of commitment and moral judgment; for example, deception (11.112), covenance (11.4), acquisition (12.22), and others. And since the usual objects, targets, or accusatives of moral judgment are just those actions whose characterizations are being analyzed in 11.0, 12.0, and 13.0, we can now begin to observe some aspects of moral judgment that lie outside the limits of our discussion of it in 5.0, that is, its relations to characterization and to action. The relation between judgment and characterization may first be considered briefly at this point.

As before, our classification of characterisms falls into the three classes: attributives, substantives, and processives. It is principally in the third that our evaluations fall under the purvey of moral judgment, that is, what we judge morally are the *actions* of persons. We do not, for example, punish persons for *traits* or *properties* they have even if these earn universal discredit and condemnation. Society for its own reasons undertakes certain commitments that govern actions. When these are thought to be violated, the processes of moral judgment are set in motion. Character is characterized and is commended or discommended, but only actions are subject to moral judgment, and then only when they appear to violate commitments.

Some qualifications or precautions are here in order. First, actions and traits are not always as easy to distinguish as the categories of language seem to presume. Then too, it is often possible to express processives as attributives, and vice versa, by a mere grammatical transformation. A circumspect moral judgment will seek to satisfy itself that it is dealing with an action and not, for example, with a mere disposition thereto.

Second, it will be mainly the discrediting processives that will be relevant in moral judgment. Few crediting actions appear to deserve not just commendation but the highest moral acclaim. As Kant observed, we do not deserve any particular praise merely for doing what in fact we ought to do.

Third, except for traits of the body itself, personal traits cannot be wholly separated from actions since, of course, nearly any manifestation of the life of a subject involves his exerting himself in some manner. But actions are not mere exertions. We shall leave to ethics the problem of defining the line between them.

With these qualifications in mind, we may now observe that actions are appraised *as well as* morally judged, and it is only because they are first appraised in certain terms that they may then appear also to deserve moral acclaim or blame. The arraignment and judgment of actions supervenes upon appraisal. If we enter into commitments to protect individuals from certain kinds of aggression, such actions must already have appeared to deserve characterization as dishonorings, intimidations, persecutions, torments, or atrocities. We do not characterize them so merely because they appear to violate our commitments. The characterizations have an original evidence in these cases whether or not they stir any thought of commitments that have been violated. Commitments are not in fact very vivid to the average mind, and it has difficulty reminding itself of them. But what such a mind beholds before its very eyes is decisive provided it commands a knowledge of the concepts of appraisal in one tongue or another. As we have urged, the center of all valuation lies here. It is, of course, obvious that in organized society both the processes of appraising and of judging are by now going on at once. It is, however, possible to see them as having the fairly distinct logical order that is pursued by our account.

We may say, then, that truly moral considerations begin to enter into the proceedings with the present section. The lines may be drawn about where we begin with vocabulary (d). In (c) it is still essentially only our sensibilities that have been violated. But to feel called upon to characterize a situation in the manner of (d) is inherently to involve oneself in the moral concerns of an aggressor and his victim. One may prefer to speak of some action as simply a warning thrust at someone to remember his duties rather than as a harassment; one may not wish to say that every punishment of a child is torment or maltreatment; and so forth. But *if* one feels constrained to declare actions of this general sort as harassments or humiliations, and not only that but torments or maltreatments, then moral considerations enter the picture, whether or not the formal apparatus of moral judgment is brought to bear. If, as suggested, we learn the meaning of vocabulary (c) by ourselves *being* annoyed or harried or nagged, we can doubtless best learn the meaning of (d), not to speak of (e), in the same manner. But there the similarity ends. No doubt one feels sympathy for the victim, under (c) above, who is pestered or whose emotional well-being has been disturbed, but has one any obligation not only to discommend, but also to interfere? We may find ourselves being characterized as meddlesome from the very victims who we think are being pestered. But the sequel of feeling compelled to characterize a situation in terms such as (d) has not just the melancholy result that we feel unhappy, or even sick as in (c). To witness what one characterizes as intimidation, disrespect, humiliation, oppression, maltreatment, and molestation of others is in a degree to *be* intimidated, humiliated, oppressed, and so forth if one fails to lend support to the victim. It is not reasonable or even "morally sane" merely to react to molestation and maltreatment with mere feelings of regret and unhappiness. I think no proper reading of the Christian gospel can draw that conclusion from "showing the other cheek." This is rather intended as a powerful device of *resistance*. He who truly sees an act as one of molestation and maltreatment resists it. But he must first convince himself that it warrants characterization as a molestation.

It is, of course, necessary to add that the fanatic and mad zealot may himself first need to be shown the alternatives to the characterizations he has urged. So the fanatic jingo is being asked by the pacifist to alter his characterization of war when he seeks to convince him that wars cannot right wrongs and that they breed other wrongs in their train.

It will be interesting to learn, by a comparison study, whether all languages have the means for making the distinction between (c) and (d) which can be observed in English. It is possible that other tongues and peoples may think of this difference in less emphatic terms or may even fail to find more than degrees of emotion to differentiate them. Only empirical study can determine this. We must not suppose that our own moral apparatus inheres in every tongue and culture.

What has been suggested here is the primacy of characterization to moral judgment. It is only because we are as confident as we are in the appropriateness of our characterizations that we may take additional steps to enact the pattern of choices which they indicate into durable commitments. Given these we may then proceed to moral judgment and to action, including in the latter such statutory legal processes as we see fit to devise. This is, of course, already explicit in the order of exposition from sections 3.0 through 5.0 above: appraisal, enactment, judgment.

When we add to this the fact that in all cases a certain cognitive assessment, a body of more or less explicit descripts may be prefixed to evaluation, we see that the classic problem of proceeding from 'is' to 'ought' is more complex than it has generally appeared to be. If this problem persists in the form it has usually been thought to have, the idea of "link" between the two "elements" can be comprehended only in terms of intervening connectives of characterization such as have been articulated here.

11.112 DECEPTIVE CONTENTION

PROCESSIVE

camouflage	distort	lure
chicanery	duplicity	malinger
con (=swindle)	entice	pose
cozen	foist	suborn
deceive	hocus pocus	trick, trickery
delude	inveigle	

SUBSTANTIVE

charlatan	poseur	sneak n.
impostor	quacksalver, quack	trickster
mountebank		

ATTRIBUTIVE

ACTION

devious	hypocrisy	stealth
disingenuous	shifty	surreptitious
furtive	sleight-of-hand	underhanded
guile	sly	

CONDITION

bogus	sham	spurious
fake	specious	trumpery
mock		

The deception we are interested in is the reprehensible deprivation of a person's power, property, or function. It is a form of contention or aggression though with the obvious distinction that it is contention under a false flag: at least one participant is unaware of the fact. We may ignore the mild or ironic forms which may be free exercises of imagination.

The most significant form of deception is the effort to gain ends by devices contrary to trust. We may coin for this the term *contrafidential*. Social living is permeated from top to bottom by a tissue of trust: you may be confident that the postman generally will not steal your mail; that the auto driver generally will not run you down as a piece of sport or sadism; that you will not be struck a blow by every passerby; that your hostess will not poison you;

that a woman generally will not be molested in a public gathering even if alone among a thousand men, and so on. Even if in all such cases there are laws, penalties and prosecutions that may hover in the background of public thought, or in the "super-ego," the real strength of custom lies in mutual trust, in the confidence that the laws will mostly be observed, and that there will be greater preference for civic order than for disorder. Yet it is only if trust of such sort generally permeates the fabric of society that contrafidential acts are possible. A competent and dedicated thief does not desire the destruction of society. His life is built on the fidential system. Trust is a condition for its own violation. This is a paradox all society must live with as best it can, reckoning that the rewards of widespread observance of law are greater than the risk of violations of social trust by a minority.

We must make a very large exclusion from our vocabulary of the characterization of deception. The whole list of deceptive acts, generally denominated criminal for reasons that may or may not derive from morals, is very much longer, including **burglary**, **larceny**, **fraud**, **robbery**, **embezzlement**, and so on. In all such cases there are precise definitions and rules of evidence laid down. There is little that moral judgment has to do *directly* with the matter. Someone, let us say, breaks and enters under such and such circumstances. In principle, this can be determined with complete objectivity. But for a court to decide that a first or second offender shall go free involves something other than objective evidence. The offender's character must now be scrutinized. We need a wise judge to follow and not merely a rule of thumb. We shall thus exclude from the characterisms of deception a vast list of what society or the law regards as crimes, misdemeanors, felonies, malfeasances, torts, and so forth, but what lies back of these in legislative and judicial thought and processes would, of course, have relevance for us. We may also exclude those forms of deception that are fully verifiable: **dupe, lie, misrepresent, prevaricate, false witness, malversation, perjury**. And, for that matter, lines need not be drawn so carefully but that a number of notions included in our list may not often find a place among these fully verifiable notions, for example, **deceive, delude, spurious, impostor, fake**, and probably others.

It may be thought that we are merely confining attention to the relatively vague aspects of deception that are of no concern to hard-headed lawyers. But the hard-headed aspects of the infraction of law which we have excluded are comparatively easy to establish, and they gain whatever appraisive or moral significance they have only in being referred to the matter of human character. Thus the witness says, I was there and there, saw that and that, said this and this – it can all be recorded precisely and perhaps even checked. But if there is no check, and if there are no corroborating witnesses, someone must first decide whether he is devious, perfidious, a charlatan, or not. Shall a confession be honored? Is the accused trembling from innocence or guilt? What are the chances of three independent corroborating witnesses being all mendacious even when their stories harmonize? This is not to say what is obvious, that we can at most reckon with high probabilities in all matters of fact, and alleged fact, but rather that judgment of fact, in such situations, is inexorably and inescapably grounded in the judgment of persons. What is admired in judges and barristers after years of service is not just their skill in the examination and summation of evidence – that we may take for granted. It is rather what we have called the power to characterize persons fairly. The skill in this lies not just in being able to produce characterizations that are always subsequently corroborated in the revealed actions of the subject. Nor is a characterism simply a "dispositional property" or a prediction, since of course it is not a property at all. Characterizing is something else. A shrewd power of characterizing a witness as devious, disingenuous or sly, as a charlatan, poseur, or quack, as being the sort of person that perpetrates or is the victim of schemes that are bogus or trumpery, or as the reverse of any or all of these is an indispensable condition for arriving at truths of fact. Without such power an attorney might not know where to begin to defend or prosecute. All the principal features of characterization are here displayed. There are no rules or definitions that can be followed, no sufficient and necessary conditions that demonstrate the correctness of the characterization.

All of the characterisms of this number are directly related to truth and falsity and thus to the appraisives of ponence in Appendix A 2.0. But now our concern is with truth telling rather than with truth itself, with communicating truth or falsehood rather than with the discovery of or demonstration of truth or falsity, with behavior and gesture and even with inanimate objects being made to appear to be something they are not rather than with the criteria of genuineness or correctness appropriate to such things. We wish to know how a person employs truths and falsities; even falsities of course have legitimate uses.

The moral relevance of the appraisives of deception derives from their use to characterize contrafidential speech, behavior, action or condition. When detected in deception, implicated persons are commonly subject to moral judgment as well as characterization; this is also often the case in other areas discussed in these latter sections of Part Two.

There are many more variations of this vocabulary in common speech. This is particularly true of the discreditings of the present section. Once again we are forced to note that man has had to expend much more verbal ingenuity on discredit than on credit. One is forced to repeat the commonplace that there are infinite ways to devise and utter falsehood and but only one way to tell the truth. The crediting terms will be found among the moral characterisms (14.01) and the general virtues.

No rigid line can be drawn between the characterisms of 6.312 (Veridiction) and those of the present number. The principal difference lies in the fact that in 6.312 we were concerned with truth-telling in a fairly general application. In the present number we are concerned with the employment of truth and particularly falsity as an instrument of contention.

11.12   CONTENTIONAL EXPRESSION

11.121   DENUNCIATORY

PROCESSIVE

abuse (11.111)	defame	obloquy
affront	[denounce]	philippic
asperse	show [disre-	rail at
backhanded	spect to	raillery
(compliment)	excoriate	revile
bait	execrate	slander
belittle	flay	slight v.
berate, rate	imprecate	slur
besmirch	innuendo	snipe at
calumniate	insinuate	stigmatize
carp	insult	taunt
castigate	invective,	threaten, threat
cavil	inveigh against	traduce
[condemn]	libel	vilify
contumely	malediction	vituperate
curse	malign v.	
[damn]	objurgate	

ATTRIBUTIVE

acerbic	insidious	sardonic
acrimony	invidious	scathing
asperity	mordacity	spitfire
backbite	mordant	virulent
billingsgate	opprobrious,	
foulmouthed,	opprobrium	
-tongued	rabid	

11.122   DERISIVE

butt (of ridicule)	jeer at	[ridicule]
chaff	lampoon	sarcasm
deride	laugh at	scoff at
poke [fun at	mock v.	snear at
gibe	rally v.t.	twit

The vocabulary of contentional expression is used to discredit speakers or their language or both. My enemies, I say, will speak in this manner. On the other hand, I may say of myself that I am condemning, damning, denouncing, and ridiculing certain persons, because these terms are descripts. I may, in effect, describe myself, but I shall never denounce or deride myself in normal circumstances using the vocabulary of characterisms. Old Bolsheviks may vilify themselves, but only after, not during, the fact.

As in the immediately preceding discussion of the processes of aggression, the evident depth of feeling that conditions the use of this vocabulary is best shown when it is used by the recipients or victims of aggressive expression about themselves. That is, the primary and most powerful form in which these characterisms appear is the present passive in the first person: "I am being defamed, maligned, vilified, traduced." It need scarcely be added that one does not characterize himself in these terms in the active present tense (I am defaming, maligning).

Considering first the denunciations, it should be noted that the corresponding descript **condemn** has already appeared at 5.22 as a moral outcome. Everyone sooner or later, possibly every day, will have need to condemn actions or persons or situations. But he may rightly resent having his condemnation characterized in most of the terms of the foregoing vocabulary. On the other hand, if a person is himself the target of condemnation, he may seek to diminish the force of it by trying to convince others that it is mere abuse, a libel, frenzied philippic, slander, or slur, that it is merely railing and invective and thus (to use an effective current characterism) seek to "defuse" the condemnation. All of the terms are powerful thrusts or counterthrusts. The emotion that lies back of them is one of the most potent of personal weapons, short of force. Nowhere, it is safe to say, are fact and reason so often and easily obscured and counterfeited as in the tactics of verbal aggression and counteraggression. Is the original condemnation fair? One may readily win sympathy with the countercharge that it is only defamation, or something similar in the rich vocabulary of 11.121, but then only with a certain kind of audience; another audience will readily fall back on a cliché such as "where there's smoke there's fire."

The processes of derisive expression introduce in a slightly twisted sense the dimension of humor and thus expand the range of expression. If anything, they are likely to be even more painful than the denunciatory modes. The reason that suggests itself is the degree of respect for the target that may linger in denunciation. Such expression at least takes the subject seriously, and may even honor him by recognizing his power or force, though it be condemned, whereas derisive expression reduces the subject to a cipher: he is regarded as having spoken or exerted himself for what amounts to nothing at all. Derision may succeed in finishing him off altogether. The characterisms of denunciation and derision are thus essentially cruel. They are manifestly devices of aggression.

For a proper understanding of contentional or aggressive expression, we must observe that the terms are all appraisives of appraisal, or appraisives of response, that is, higher order appraisives. We symbolize these as $A \times A$ (or A^2) or as AR. In such cases, M, let us say, is said by L to have aggressed verbally against N. L's opinion is expressed in terms of the characterisms of 11.121. Thus L appraises M's appraisal of N. In a particular case L may also be the particular person N. L will then be expressing his rejection of M's appraisal of himself.*

Is it possible for M to acknowledge the fairness of L's appraisal? If he did he would have to be looking back upon his past self whose expressions M has appraised, and he would now join L in characterizing them in the same terms. But M cannot endorse a *present* discreditation of himself whether it originates with others or himself. It may be a weakness of the human spirit that it cannot relish self-stultifying characterizations, or indeed, perhaps it is a strength, the self's conviction of its evident worth. Religions generally urge men to embrace just such characterizations of themselves. They urge them to be penitent, to acknowledge guilt. Of course, the characterizations must be such as have a proper origin. The prophets and pastors admonish as if they were voicing God's own appraisal of men. But even this is directed toward offenses already committed. Nothing, it seems, can induce us to discredit actions we are *now* undertaking.

---

* The situation may be spelled out in full detail as follows. We suppose that L says, "M's remarks about N were insulting, reviling, slanderous," in the terms of the vocabulary of aggressional expression considered in 11.12. We may call this remark q. What M has actually said and whether or not it is fair to N are of no interest to us. Suppose N is in fact L in a particular instance. In this case, L regards M's remarks as insulting him, L, but the results are otherwise parallel to the following:

(1) M has (at least) condemned N and since 'condemn' is simply a descriptive corresponding to the appraisives of 11.12, we assume M will readily acknowledge this.

(2) M's remarks about N are assumed to be either an appraisal of N, or a possibly emotive response to N (2.0).

(3) q is an appraisal of M's remarks and characterizes them as aggressive expression, as discrediting.

(4) Neither L nor M would utter q about himself in the present, though he might say this of his past action or speech.

(5) Thus M may now reject q as an unfair characterization, or, of course, penitently endorse L's characterization of his (past) action.

(6) Since the purpose of q is characterization, it may serve as a reason for discommendation of M. The content or meaning of q is not emotive even though it may arise in L while he is in a state of emotion.

(7) If q were a report of L's emotion, M might with propriety be indifferent to q and to L's state, but since it is a reason, it may claim the assent of M.

(8) An evidence of M's assent would be some mark or degree of penitence.

We have, then, a situation that resembles so many already considered. Here we say, "I condemn..." and the accusative may be variously 'you', 'him', and so on, but not 'myself' in the present. Abraham did not condemn himself when he bound Isaac to the altar on Mt. Moriah. And for different reasons no one convicts himself in present (wicked) acts, though he may be engaged in moral debate with himself. Nor will I presently appraise my condemnation of others in these terms: the use of **abuse** or **besmirch**, unlike the use of **condemn**, is confined in the first person to the passive voice ("I am abused," or "I am being abused"). They are true appraisives.

We may note again that while emotion is involved in using these terms they are not themselves emotive. When L complains that M has defamed or insulted or reviled him, his remarks will almost inevitably be accompanied by emotion. As in previous cases, the characterization serves to provide a unique kind of reason or justification for the emotion, but it is not in itself emotive. I hate you *because* you have defamed, insulted, or reviled me: the emotion of hatred and the reason for it are distinct. The characterization may *show* my emotion, but it cannot assert it: the term 'assert' would be meaningless here. Furthermore, although I may be feeling emotion when I resort to such terms, the state of my mind may leave you indifferent. What I now draw attention to is not myself but you and your discourse: my characterization aims to convey a *ground* for discrediting *you*.

The attributive form of characterization poses an interesting question which is particularly relevant here but could also have been observed in many of the foregoing sections. The subject of the processive and substantive characterisms is in general, if not invariably, the person. But the attributives are sometimes to be used of persons and sometimes of their actions, powers or physical aspects. Our subject is the appraisal of man, and we have excluded from it the assessment of such things as truth value for reasons discussed elsewhere (cf. Appendix A 2.0). The question is whether we are not in effect making attributions *to persons* when we use characterizing attributives *of their actions*, powers and the like. Must we or must we not do so? May we say that not Phipps but only his intellectual powers or the way he exercises them are superficial or trifling, only his judgments are arbitrary and prejudiced, only his physical appearance is dapper or unkempt, only his mood is jolly or morose, only his manner is contentious or truculent, and so on? In the present instance we hear *him* characterized as foul-tongued, sardonic, or sarcastic; we also hear *his speech* characterized as acrimonious, opprobrious or sneering. Surely the first kind of case involves the second: If Phipps is foul-tongued or sarcastic it is because of his speech. And does the converse also hold, so that if Phipps's speech was cruel then *he* must be? Can we not conjure up situations where we very much want to say, "Phipps reviled

Potts but he is really not a cruel person?" Or, in any event, do we not think it proper to make some kind of distinction, particularly in moral situations, between a person and his attributes, states, and actions? I am inclined to say that even if such a distinction can be made, we must not in general carry this to the point where we make excuses by saying, "It's not M, it's only his speech that is cruel." I am not, however, clear about how we draw lines here. A more searching examination of usage and much else is needed. Such questions arising from the attributive style of characterization, and many others, cannot be answered solely within the confines of a study of the evaluative vocabulary. These are questions to which ethics must address itself.

11.13   ISSUE OF CONFLICT

(a) ascendancy	(b) draw	(c) failure
conquest	impasse	frustration
mastery		loss, lose
success		miscarry,
supremacy		miscarriage
triumph		rout
trounce		shambles
victory		
win		

In general we expect conflict to issue in defeat, draw, or victory; usually not winning is defeat, and not losing is victory. Since these conditions are nearly always charged with feeling, it may be difficult to discriminate between descriptive and characterizing uses of terms in this vocabulary. Although one can rejoice in someone's defeat and deplore another's victory, there are no ready verbal devices to express this. Hence we have no fourfold organization of appraisives.

If it is necessary to single out descripts of winning, we may cite simply **win, victory, lose** and **defeat**. The strongest characterisms of victory, or the terms most pronouncedly characterizing, will be **conquest** and **triumph**, followed by **ascendancy, mastery** and **supremacy**. There is little to choose among the characterizations of defeat, unless there is an air of irrevocable loss, as in **rout**.

Quite obviously this vocabulary is scarcely to be exceeded in the depth of emotion it may reflect. This will not always be revealed in the simple terms themselves but in their context and other circumstances of use: the defeated will also have to pronounce the word 'victory' in conceding to the victor, but in another emotive strain. The fact of winning or losing will, in general, conform to rules and be conceded on both sides, but it is the characterization of the fact, not the fact itself, that is significant here, and for this no rules or definitions can be cited: how does one draw a line between a **triumph** and **trouncing** the opponent? Some of the primary traits of characterisms are manifested in the present vocabulary.

11.2 ASCENDANCY (Cf. 8.22, 9.3, 11.11)

POSITIVE CHARACTERISMS		+ NEGATIVE CHARACTERISMS
CREDITING		CREDITING
DOMINION		SUBMISSION
commanding	privilege	complacent
[command]	[prohibit]	deferent
condescend ($\pm$)	proud, pride($-$)	docile
dominating,	[require]	humility, humble
[dominate]	[restrain]	longanimity
heroic	vouchsafe	longsufferingness
imperious		lowly
lordly		mansuetude
masterful		meek
masterly		obeisance
magisterial		obey, obedient
[order v.]		resigned, resignation
outclass		retiring
pacify		subject n.
[predominate]		tractable
[prevail over		[yield]
(Cf. 11.3)]		[acquiesce]

SELF-AFFIRMATION		SELF-NEGATION
self-assurance	self-possession	abnegation
self-command	self-reliant	self-abnegation
self-control	self-respect	self-denying
self-esteem	self-sufficient	self-effacing

$+$ ════════════ $\times$ ════════════ $-$

DISCREDITING (Cf. 9.22)		DISCREDITING
ATTRIBUTIVE		ATTRIBUTIVE
DOMINION		SUBMISSION
arrogant	cheeky	bondage
authoritarian	cocky	craven
autocratic	cold-hearted	defeatism
brazen	harsh	dependent
callous	heartless	obsequious
chauvinism	ingratitude	plaintive

jingo,
jingoism
overbearing
peremptory

SELF-AFFIRMATION

conceit
egotism
self-centered
self-important
self-indulgent

presumptuous
thoughtless
unfeelingness

self-interested
self-love
self-seeking
selfish
swank

quietus
servile
submissive
subservient

SELF-NEGATION

self-abasement

SUBSTANTIVE

braggart
bully
egotist
ingrate
tyrant

SUBSTANTIVE

dupe
lackey
pawn
scapegoat
sycophant
toady
[victim]

PROCESSIVE

abash v.t.
arrogate
bluff v.
bluster
boast, -ful
brag
braggadocio
browbeat
bullyrag
cold-
    shoulder v.
[command]
cow v.
crow v.
deign

[dictate]
domineer
embarrass
[enjoy]
flaunt
hector
humiliate
mortify
nag
ostracize
overawe
prate
squelch
swagger
vaunt

PROCESSIVE

appease
fawn upon
grovel
quail v.
suffer
surrender
truckle

At the beginning of our discussion of 11.11 we detailed a number of processives of contention which were entirely descriptive in force. We then
proceeded to take up the characterisms that correspond, so to speak, to these
descripts. The same procedure may be employed here. Ascendancy and submission obviously manifest themselves in certain acts or inactions. Let us

look at these descripts briefly before we study the characterisms. We may detail the following list:

ASCENDANCY:		SUBMISSION
(a) [allow]	(b) [demand]	[defer]
[command]	[discipline]	[submit]
[dictate]	[dominate]	[yield]
[direct]	[enjoin]	
[grant]	[forbid]	
[manage]	[impose]	
[order v.]	[interdict]	
[pacify]	[prohibit]	
[permit]	[require]	
[vouchsafe]	[suffer (=permit)]	

These modes of ascendancy and submission are the ways in which, in general, persons or parties in the ascendant, or the reverse, act in maintaining their positions. Although the terms when taken by themselves are neutral, they can lose their descriptive character and take on the local color of the characterisms of 11.2 when they are associated with these: for example, one can dictate, bluster, and domineer, or can yield and appease. Inherently, then, there is neither virtue nor vice in these modes. There is a time for commanding and a time for deferring, there is also ill-timed command and deference. The preponderance of descripts of ascendancy may reflect that these modes are more commonly noted or acknowledged than those of submission. It is also possible that one could add further descripts of submission.

The characterisms themselves present quite a different picture from the descripts. They are plainly more likely to be accompanied by feelings, especially the discrediting characterisms. The crediting characterisms are sometimes ambivalent. It is fairly easy to employ some of them in a manner approaching discredit, for example, **lordly** and **imperious**. One could employ these in an admiring manner to characterize a successful military commander, or in contemning a conceited and arrogant person. In like manner, the proud man may be a person of deep self-respect but also arrogant.

Among the negative characterisms (**docile, humble,** etc.), many are associated in the Western mind with Christianity. Of course, Christians do not think of them in discrediting terms: meekness and humility are not to be confused with servility and obsequiousness. The intent of even the most pacific of the Beatitudes cannot be to praise what the discrediting characterisms of submission and self-negation discredit.

Numerically, the preponderance of terms lies among the discreditations.

One has occasion now and then to despise appeasement or surrender, or to be contemptuous of the pawn, toady, or sycophant, but if numbers of terms are significant we are more often likely to feel ourselves the victims of arrogance and bullying, or to be offended by the egotist and braggart.

The discreditations are typically unreserved: any thought of the subject's possible virtues are fully ignored or obscured when he is said to be a bully or a tyrant. The substantives are particularly potent as compared with the processives. A subject's actions may, on particular occasions, seem to deserve characterization as bragging, dictating, flaunting, or swaggering, but to declare a subject a bully, ingrate, tyrant, lackey, or toady is to appraise what appear to be ingrained or permanent habits. The attributives are rather closer to the substantives than to the processives in this respect.

The vocabulary suggests comparatively little that is actually subject to severe moral judgment, but it is particularly expressive of thought about character and personality. As with the appraisives of aggression, the modes of ascendancy are most poignantly learned from situations where one uses the present passive affirmative in the first person: I am being commanded and dominated, or being deferred to and obeyed; I am being appeased and fawned upon, or being browbeaten, blustered at, bullyragged, domineered, and overawed. One will once again refuse to use the characterisms of oneself in their active form. Strong feelings mark the use of the second person (you are bullying, nagging). The effectiveness of the terms in emotional circumstances derives from the images that lie behind them. These can easily be explored etymologically: coldness and hardness as of a metal (**brazen**), the chin or face thrust forward (**cheek**), masculine forwardness (**cocky**), lack of human warmth (**cold-hearted**), and so on through fairly evident derivations in **browbeat, dictate, domineer,** etc. The basic images are those of rising upwards and forwards and those of retreating and falling. Scarcely any other part of our vocabulary could be more interesting to compare with those of other languages in quantity, quality, and variety, as well as meaning.

11.3 ACCOMMODATION (CONCERN, SUASION)

PROCESSIVE (Largely Descriptive)
(a) PERSONAL CONCERN

[allay]

[alleviate]

[comfort v.]

[commiserate]

[be concerned about, over

[condole]

[console]

cotton v.

[reassure

[solace]

[solicitude]

[sympathize with]

(b) CONCURRENCE
   [accede to]
   [accommodate]
   [accord]
   [adjust to
   [arbitrate]
   [compromise]
   [conciliate]
   [concur]
   [cooperate]
   [placate]
   [rapprochement]
   [reconcile]
   [tolerate]
   [truce]
(c) SUASION
   [entreat]
   [persuade]
   [prevail upon]

(d) GRATIATION
   blandishment
   [cherish]
   [compliment]
   endear
   flatter
   [heed:]
      [caress]
      coddle
      cosset
      [fondle]
      pamper
      pet
   [ingratiate
   [oblige]
   [thank]

ATTRIBUTIVE
   affable
   altruism
   be [amenable to
   amiable
   amicable
   amity
   attentive
   benevolent
   boon a.
   brotherly, -iness
   charitable, charity
   circumspect
   compassion, -ate
   concord
   congenial
   considerate
   diplomatic

   friendly
   generous
   grateful
   gregarious
   hospitable
   humane, humanity
   irenic
   kind
   kindly
   merciful, mercy
   peace, peaceful, peaceable
   politic
   reciprocity
   tact
   thoughtful
   unselfish

SUBSTANTIVE (Both descriptive and characterizing)

accomplice	chap, chappie	colleague
ally	chum	companion
buddy	collaborator	compatriot

comrade	darling	pal
confidant	dear	partner
confrère	fellow	proselyte
crony	friend	protegé

At the beginning of 11.0 we posed a scheme alternative to the one we have followed for organizing the characterisms of sociation, but we set it aside as something of an oversimplification and in order to obtain a better opportunity to study the several modes in detail. We need now to remind ourselves of some aspects of this alternative scheme (numbered 11.01). The almost unmanageable complexity of this vast subject matter obviously admits of various plans of organization.

We may notice (in 11.01) first, that the contention vocabulary, which we have found to be largely confined to (c), Aggression, stands logically opposed to the vocabulary of (d), Acquiescence; the latter in turn has a corresponding crediting aspect of its own (b). At the same time Aggression stands over against the descripts of defensive contention (11.111) and against (a), Ascendancy.

With the present section still another pairing suggests itself. If aggression is in general likely to be met with defensive contention, there may be another alternative (at least from the standpoint of third parties) in the arts of negotiation and reconciliation. Our times are particularly plagued by bitter conflicts in which alternatives to contention are often as vainly as they are earnestly sought, but in which negotiation is often only a further form of contention. The language in which all this proceeds takes on a strangely involuted and paradoxical quality where, as in *1984*, war is peace and peace is war. But even a moment's calm reflection could remind even the most ardent militant that sooner or later there may be a genuine alternative to aggression, counteraggression, defensive contention, defamation, submission and ascendancy in genuine accommodation, or at least in covenance.

We see from 11.01 why most characterisms in 11.3 are crediting Some are also often used as descripts. There are scarcely more than a half dozen characterisms among the processives, and these are of only marginal significance. The majority (the descripts) may be classified under personal concern, concurrence, suasion, and gratiation. The tenor of the attributives and substantives inclines rather more to emotional accommodation than to other modes, such as intellectual or pragmatic agreement, but the apparent emotive emphasis can be misleading. We will not suppose that "real" accommodation will necessarily involve emotive harmony, although it is probably ingredient in any "ideal" harmony.

As noted, the processives are descripts. Except when we say someone has

offered or succumbed to blandishments or flattery or personal ingratiation
(**coddle, pamper,** etc.), the terms are used to describe ways in which minds
may be brought into some adjustment or readjustment to one another. The
terms range across intellectual, practical, and moral adjustment as well as
emotive. We might add **accede** to or **compromise** to the former and **allay**
(**fears,** etc.) to the latter, and doubtless there are also any number of other
phrases and idioms that might be appended.

We should notice the force of negation on these terms. The actions referred
to by the present processives are very "active:" outgoing effort is made. The
negation of the terms may, however, denote a kind of mere neutralism rather
than hostility (**not concerned about, not sympathizing, not cooperating,** etc.).

On the other hand, the negation of the attributives inclines more definitely
toward hostility. To be definitely not amicable, benevolent, charitable, considerate, friendly, hospitable, and so on may amount to actual aggression.

Further, some of the characterisms of negative ascendancy must also serve
as opposites to the present vocabulary of accommodation. The idea of accommodation as here conceived is one of coming to an arrangement between or
among equals or mutuals. An alternative to this may then evidently be self-
negation. For this the vocabulary of submission in 11.2 (**bondage, obsequious,
subservient, dupe, lackey, sycophant, toady, grovel, truckle,** and so on) must
be kept in mind.

Turning now to some of the more general questions raised by this vocabulary, we may first add something to our remarks on the reference of some of
the terms to emotion. Besides the earlier parts of 11.0, we should also recall
the vocabulary of the moral affects (5.1) that may accompany the moral
involvements (5.2). Certainly the pursuit of justice must frequently make use
of the vocabulary of accommodation and here as there both the affects and
the judgment may be brought into play. At the same time, many of the terms
will have more relevance to emotion than to judgment: there is far more im-
pulsion from the side of feeling toward the arts and ends of accommodation
than from that of concern for justice. It is because we cannot always count
upon mutual feeling to produce or preserve irenic or amiable states that we
resort to other measures, to the devices of covenance, legality and justice, to
achieve at least a desired minimum of order and respect. But the former is the
more basic. If it were not for our need for unions that may, in the end, be
traceable to an instinctive basis (a sociative or gregarious instinct?) and that
are frequently exposed to destruction, we would scarcely have thought it
necessary to resort to more formal institutions. Unions of men are natural,
but a constitution is necessary for a "*more* perfect union" – necessary that
is because we cannot expect the *most* perfect union of all, friendship, to be
realized in the body politic.

The range of the attributives, which are central here, is from those that reflect emotive concern (**amicable, charitable, compassionate, kind** and **kindly**) to fairly, though never wholly, impersonal concern (**benevolent, circumspect, diplomatic**, and **tactful**). Accommodation forms the intrinsic climax and goal of sociation. It alone can lend any significance to the processes of conflict and contention. Perhaps the natural state of man (happy myth!) is one of amity that is interrupted by dissension and restored by covenant to a state approaching minimal respect. We can legislate liberty and equality – but fraternity? Schiller and Beethoven think friendship the gift of fortune:

> Wem der grosse Wurf gelungen, eines Freundes Freund zu sein,
> ... mische seinen Jubel ein!

It is because society is not and will never be a sodality of friends that the processes of covenance must be seen as the practical though not the intrinsic culmination of sociation.

Lest we forget the realities, we must remind ourselves that we can only credit the process of accommodation, in adjustment, accord, and truce, by looking to the ends which are intended: the mutual accommodation of A and B *may* spell aggression against C.

We proceed now to covenance. As we have seen, the processes of accommodation have been thought of largely as a kind of development of like-mindedness or harmony without formality. For how can altruism, amity, brotherliness, compassion, comradeship, concord, or friendship be formalized without instantly becoming something else? Although 'diplomacy' names a profession, and indeed the most formal of all, one can scarcely imagine formal rules for being diplomatic or tactful.

11.4   COVENANCE

CREDITING CHARACTERISMS

ATTRIBUTIVE	DESCRIPTS
conscientious	[abjure]
dependable	[agree]
dutiful, duty (5.22)	[avow]
faithful	[bind oneself to]
fidelity	[commit]
loyal	[contract]
reliable	[covenant]
responsible	[discharge a duty]
trustworthy	[fiduciary]

[oblige oneself to]
[pledge]
[promise
[rely]
[renounce]
[repudiate, App. A. 2.0]
[responsibility for, or to]
[settle]
[trust, distrust]

DISCREDITING CHARACTERISMS

ATTRIBUTIVE	PROCESSIVE
dastardly	**apostasy**
disloyal	**betray**
SUBSTANTIVE	**break [faith,**
coward	**show bad [faith**
defecter	**defect** v.
poltroon	**jilt**
renegade	**perfidy, perfidious**
traitor	**renegue (renig, renege)**
	treachery
	welsh v.

The practical culmination of all the processes of sociation is covenance. It is akin, of course, to the development of commitments which we have explored earlier in connection with judgment. But we are not now concerned with the facts or acts of dedication to *ideals* or virtues (4.1) but rather with characterization of the ways in which persons maintain *social unions*. We have already seen several different kinds of union in the responses of persons to one another; for example, they may admire and adore one another (2.21), they may be united in fear and astonishment (2.31), in enthusiasm and rage (2.4). Persons are united in erotic or familial terms (9.0) and in modes of accommodation, ascendancy and submission, such as have been studied earlier in 11.0. Very often these are the firmest imaginable unions in which persons share their feelings and thoughts and join in common enterprises. But in the end this, alas, is not enough; it is necessary that formal unities be devised. These are the bonds of covenance.

I shall not discuss the nature of covenance itself; we are concerned rather with the characterization of persons in consequence of their covenanting. In 11.4 we have contrasted characterisms such as **renegade, defector, perfidious,** and **dastardly** with descripts of covenance such as **abjure** and **trust.** We are invited to occupy the appraiser's standpoint from which the subject has defected, or against which he has shown himself treacherous, perfidious or dastardly. When we characterize an enemy's act as dastardly we are not thinking him to have betrayed *our own* cause in the contest in which we are opposed, since by definition it is not *his own*, but yet to have betrayed some cause or connection we still share with him, for example, a code of military honor, or international laws of war, or the institution of the family, or "common decency," or something else on this order. In a more ordinary case where A and B have contracted together in some manner, A may find B breaking promises or showing bad faith and characterize him in appropriate terms. Accusations of this sort seem virtually to obliterate any thought of the other virtues a person may have – they are all-or-none, as we have observed of other characterizations.

We readily use or affirm the descripts of covenance in the first person but not the characterisms, whether crediting or discrediting. Most persons are likely to think of themselves in crediting terms – they would like to *hear* themselves so characterized – but *speaking* is another matter. We say, "You are (or he is) a conscientious, dependable, reliable sort of person," but we would hesitate to ask, "Are you a conscientious (dependable, dutiful, reliable, trustworthy) sort of person?" since the answer could have no authority. Speaking of oneself in these terms is something we feel may "come better from some other source" than oneself. This is not a matter of modesty or social propriety. To characterize in these terms is to set a certain stamp or imprint that reflects the personality and standpoint of the appraiser; for A to issue a "certificate" of A's own loyalty or trustworthiness is an absurdity, even if not a logical one. (Of course, such a term as **faithful** has also a descriptive use in reference to personal relations.) In speaking of myself, I may well say, "I keep my promises," since I am speaking in descriptive terms, but saying that I am trustworthy is scarcely worth the utterance. Of course, although I do not use the first person in crediting terms in the present ("I am trustworthy"), I shall nevertheless controvert negative or discrediting appraisals of myself in the first person present ("I am not disloyal, perfidious, dastardly, a coward") unless I see myself as an ironist, comedian, anti-hero, or possibly, a penitent.

Earlier in 11.0, we found **compel, contend, defy, repel, obstruct,** and **coerce** among the descripts of contention. These are actions good or wicked men may equally well feel called upon to pursue. This may seem to reflect only typical western morality, but this is not so. The nonviolent actions of Gandhi were accurately described by any of these terms. It is just conceivable, however, that there may be moralities which oppose *every* possible form of contention. Similarly, in our study of ascendancy and submission in 11.2 we listed a number of descripts on which characterisms were based: **command, direct, discipline, forbid, pacify, defer, submit,** and **yield.** There were also descripts of accommodation such as **accord, adjust to, concur,** and **tolerate.**

All of these terms being descriptive may be meaningfully employed of oneself in the first person. Only when the actions are those of other persons do we speak of them, using the vocabulary of characterization, as being variously praiseworthy or nefarious. Similarly in covenance, we may ourselves avow, pledge, or promise, we may disavow, renounce, or repudiate, and we may *describe* others as having done so. Again, we *characterize* persons, and their habits and practices in covenanting, in the vocabulary of 11.4: they betray, break faith, and defect. Particular acts that are appraised with the processives may also come under the eye of moral judgment. The attributives and substantives are all terms of particular potency.

These characterisms raise no novel problems about appraising, but it may be well to append to this account a consideration of the difference between the appraisal of covenants and the appraisal of covenanting persons.

According to Austin, when we utter certain words or phrases in the first person under appropriate circumstances, we perform but do not describe acts. In the other grammatical persons, an act or performance like this may be described but it is not performed. Our business is really not with the nature of covenance itself but with the characterization of the person or of the condition or state that may be presumed to be brought into being by covenanting. Whether we agree with Austin's view of performatives or not we may quite readily agree that we should find some way to speak of the manner in which we covenant and the appraisal of the success or failure of the act itself. This is one thing. It is another to characterize the condition that is brought into being by covenanting. Certainly Austin's account of the first of these is important. (He does not consider the second.) We may here recall briefly some of what he says.

In his William James Lectures, Austin detailed some half dozen of what we may call evaluative terms that may be applied to acts which include those we have here called acts of covenance. Failures in covenanting he referred to as infelicities. These appear in several forms:

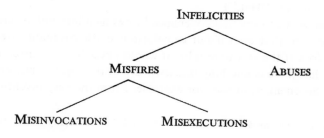

There were further refinements of these into such acts as misapplications, flaws, hitches, and insincerities.*

Now these are certainly appraisive terms, in our sense, and as such are relevant to what we are doing. They are not, however, part of the appraisal of man which is the subject of Part Two. They might, therefore, deserve a place on a par with topics such as ponence and inference which we have taken up in the Appendices. What *is*, however, relevant to the appraisal of persons in Austin's classification is the personal *habit* or *pattern* of thought, behavior, or character that may issue in misinvocations, misexecutions, abuses, insincerities, and so on. What shall we think of, how shall we appraise and characterize a person who is *given to* insincerity, abuse and other "infelicities" of covenanting? To this I think the answer or part of it has already been given in the appraisives of deceptive contention (11.112) and other sections of Part Two, or in the appraisives of covenance which we now have under consideration in 11.4, particularly those that may arise from habits of producing hollow professions, insincerities, vitiated acts, and the like.

We have therefore "bracketed out" the question of the nature of and the evaluation of acts of covenance themselves just as we have bracketed out the study of truth, meaning inference, aesthetic value and much else since we are here confining ourselves to the characterization of man.

A final topic for consideration before we complete our study of sociation is this. Since, as we have urged, the process of sociation may be thought to proceed toward and to culminate in those social unions which are thinkable only on the basis of covenance (we shall come to the larger notion of community in 13.0), the question arises whether somehow covenance, as a unique capacity of minds, possesses some kind of value in itself. We may obviously covenant just as we can concur and tolerate for nefarious ends. So indeed we may misuse all our other powers: intelligence, judgment, expression, tendence and the rest. And yet we may ask whether covenance is not a unique functional power that in some measure helps to define man, certainly man as we have known him in history. In order to test this, we need only search our minds about a very commonplace phenomenon, covenanting among those who have been morally cast out of society: honor-among-thieves. (For brevity, let us call this the "Hat.")

The Hat seems to say that covenance brings men into unions greater than themselves and that even if put to nefarious ends, covenants are crediting *in themselves*. If the Hat were false, it would never have occurred to anyone to think that there is anything praiseworthy in the loyalty, bravery, or solidarity of his enemies, in war, for example. From the very invention of war,

---

* J. L. Austin, *How to do Things with Words*, Harvard University Press, 1955, p. 12ff.

generals have devised means to demoralize their enemies. Nevertheless, they never fail to admire an adversary who cannot be demoralized, or to despise one who falls into shreds at the first skirmish. The reason is that covenance is thought to be an inherently crediting process.

The descripts of covenance, including **abjure** and **renounce**, show us man submitting himself to the rule of law. Law is a creation of man with the aid of which he undertakes to free himself from momentary caprice: the human scene is subjected to a measure of prediction and control. Being but man and not God, he may on occasion seek to have the best of both worlds: a law to protect him from others while he himself exploits others. But he cannot wish also to legislate this, and could scarcely even utter the wish. He merely gives in occasionally to the temptations of cheating and dishonesty that are made possible by being part of a fidential system.

We must observe the Hat and its consequences cautiously. It does not show that we do not need to distinguish characterisms from descripts nor that every agreement or commitment is noble. But it does tend to show that the safety of concerns that transcend individuals and the good of a plurality of persons are possible only with covenance, even if the conception of them is misguided. *The fact that* man has devised techniques of agreement and commitment is inherently crediting. His covenants, binding his future actions to general law and not to the whim or inclination that may then animate him, are a credit to him in the sense that he has enlarged his view of himself as a being that perdures in time. Once such covenants are entered into, the larger concerns of a community are possible, and only then.

We may compare the issue about the inherent crediting character of covenance to certain other problems that have been stirring in recent years. The homosexual has argued his "case" in many ways, as have the supporters of other departures from the received code of the Christian tradition, such as premarital and extramarital sexuality. But only recently has one heard (particularly from liberal theologians) that while these departures cannot be commended, they nevertheless can or may all be forms of essential and deep concern and love. Thus, proceeds the argument, the objects of these loves may be mis-taken, misguided, illtimed and also lead to deeper personal harm, but they may also nevertheless be manifestations of a profound human value. For all concern, if it is truly selfless and generous, is a thing of value. Is it not conceivable that many "illicit" loves are of this sort? Even homosexual love? And so forth, and so on.

The parallel is obvious. The force of the one argument or the other, the Hat or the argument about sexuality rests on the same foundation: that the phenomenon itself, whether it be covenanting or lowing, is to be characterized creditably even apart from the end to which it is put.

I do not, however, wish to leave this subject without raising some further doubts. In general, I would think it surprising to hear a judge take much note of the Hat, or to be inclined to mitigate sentence because of selfless behavior among a band of gangsters. Thus the point of our argument is that the Hat shows *in general* the value of law and law abidingness, yet characterization of *individual* persons, looking toward their moral appraisal and judgment is something else and cannot stop here. It is not enough to know that there may be genuine honor among thieves. The question is, what is the overriding supreme characterization of these persons in particular? Is the responsibility they manifest to their fellows that of thieves or is it in honor of law? If they can honor fellow men who happen to be fellow thieves, why not all men? If a person is truly responsible and trustworthy (looking to the present vocabulary in 11.4), he is not merely someone who can be trusted by the gang boss to share the loot with his accomplices but he will also honor all those that make up the fidential system of the community.

The Hat represents either the merest rudiment of an ethic that is struggling to be born, like the fierce relationships of the hierarchy of feudalism (many a noble lord or laird was nothing better than a gangster), or it is the faint reflection of an ethic that may be in process of dissolution. Either way the ethic shows itself worthy of the respect paid it in the terms of this vocabulary.

12.0 ECONOMIC CHARACTERIZATION

If we are thinking of man and his character, should we concern ourselves with economic matters at all? What have these external things to do with him essentially? On some externals of course, such as air, food, and water, his very physical existence depends, and we must define or delineate him in part in terms of them. But he also makes himself utterly dependent on inessential physical commodities and on types and varieties of goods, which he then fancies he cannot do without. This would be of little interest to us but for the fact of the scarcity of desired goods, with a consequent scheme of competition for them. Various traits of character are evoked in him when his *wants* in relation to goods and services go far beyond what might be regarded as his *needs*. Dependency on material goods or services, whether it be real or fancied, is the basis for considering economic characterisms in the framework of the appraisal of man.

Possession is the first notion around which economic characterizations are built, particularly when this is accompanied by the complementary notion of deprivation, or the threat of deprivation, of a particular commodity or service. What is deemed essential or not obviously varies. Pure air is only now recognized as an economic necessity; water in certain places often has inspired competition because of scarcity; food is always in some degree scarce somewhere. The principal economic themes are always scarcity and affluence. Scarcity can depend on a low volume of available goods or on high and desirable quality with a consequent heavy demand. In general, a world with an unlimited supply of all goods would be one in which it would not occur to us to employ our present vocabulary of economic characterization. One of the basic themes of all such discourse must therefore be possession.

There is an amazing tissue of trust, fiction, and verbiage of all sorts that seems necessary to establish possession. A complex machinery seems to be needed so that men may bind objects to themselves and make them their own. The impulses toward acquisition and possession are powerful. When we think of the scarcity of many desired objects we see that some men must succeed and others fail and that they will be bound to appraise one another in terms reflecting the fact. They are bound to compete with one another. The brief vocabulary in 12.21 reflects the manner in which persons characterize one another's participation in the process of acquisition through exchange.

An economic community is possible only if agreement or at least custom is established in regard to the medium of exchange and the exchange itself. In each of these fraud is possible and is viewed as serious in every society. Some of its modes are the execution or pretension to execute an agreement which proves to be fraudulent, the offer of falsely valued media of exchange (in barter the violation of the agreement, in monetary exchange the offer of false coin), or the violation of the terms of the act of exchange itself. The essential parts of the process are the agreement and the execution of it. It is an agreement that binds persons to one another in the manner already mentioned in 11.4. With the violation of such bonds, persons fall back into a state of contention where at least one of them will prove to have committed an aggression. If not only the economic contract and sociative covenant are violated but also implied commitments (5.0), the matter is one for moral judgment and thus takes a step beyond characterization.

It is a melancholy fact that all economic relations are always in danger of falling into fraud. The extremest possible statements have been made on this subject: "*la propriété, c'est le vol*," said Proudhon: all property is theft. Other more moderate maxims of the order of *caveat emptor* remind us of the fraudulent potentialities of economic exchange. It is not surprising, therefore, that appraisals and characterizations in this domain mostly touch on fraud and the possibility and likelihood of fraud.

We turn first to the consideration of economic value and then of economic conduct. The second has by far the larger vocabulary extending over the areas of acquisition (by exchange or simply by depriving others of goods) or possession, and of provision or distribution.

12.1   ECONOMIC VALUE

(a) **bargain** n.	(b) **costly**	(c) **waste**	(d) **lucrative**
brummagem	**dear**	**tawdry**	
cheap	**expensive**		
shoddy	**luxury**		

We now consider briefly the economic values of 12.1. The descripts corresponding to these would merely show that prices of commodities, their relations in terms of the system of exchange, vary up and down, also from place to place, and time to time. But none of this would say what is said in 12.1. The mere fact that a commodity had attached to it a higher price number at one time as compared with another might not at all indicate that it was now more expensive, for obvious reasons.

The characterisms **brummagem** (the term is derived from characterizing goods of inferior quality originating in Birmingham), **cheap**, and **shoddy** are somewhat more than economic in nature, and are rather unlike the remainder of 12.1. They can mean that goods are deficient in quality, not just inferior at the price quoted, but at almost any price. In this sense, they come close to the rejectives in Part Three, signifying detritus or rubbish. More than economic considerations are involved, ranging over a wide area, aesthetic, technical, even cognitive.

Again, one may note in the use of these terms an effort to keep an eye on both economic (exchange, demand) considerations and on such as are aesthetic, technical, or other and to keep them in direct relation of variance with one another. But the difficulty of this is notorious. It is possible for objects of high aesthetic value, for example, to be in low demand, or objects of no such value to be in great demand, for other than aesthetic reasons. The present condition of the market for all kinds of aesthetic objects and objets d'art, where demand is great and far outruns the supply of truly valuable goods, affords an instructive example of uncoordinated values.

The characterisms of the second column are fairly strictly economic in nature. As we have indicated, **expensive**, **dear**, and **costly** may have little to do with price. They are used principally to effect comparisons among a number of kinds of goods valued. That is, to have money is obviously to have a certain degree of freedom. Money is in itself not wealth but access to wealth. Hence to speak of goods in any of the terms of 12.1 is to be making comparisons among goods and our access to or possession of them. To say a jewel is expensive is to say that buying it might limit one's access to other goods, perhaps even necessities, to a painful degree. To speak of it as a luxury would be to declare it a commodity most persons would be likely to dispense with, at least in most circumstances. To speak of wasting a commodity is to declare that an act has been committed which in effect deprives someone of something useful, necessary or agreeable. The housewife complains that bread and clothing are dear because their present price means that purchase will deprive her of other needed or wanted goods.

It is apparent that one will generally not apply these terms to objects or services with which one identifies or associates himself closely. I will not readily admit that I am now wasting something valuable, or that what I sell is cheap and shoddy, or that what I am buying is expensive, if this means I am depriving my child of food, and so on. Clearly the principal use of these terms is to characterize the behavior of others, not ourselves, since they do not, in general, reflect credit. One tends to see something of another person's character in actions of his that involve luxury or waste, or in buying things that are expensive if it endangers other values, or in selling shoddy goods, and so on.

The term **lucrative**, on the face of it innocent, has a faint aroma of disapprobation about it. The history of the term shows some foundation for this. Though the Latin *lucrum* means merely gain or advantage, earlier sources indicate an association that yields also **loot**, as well as **lucre**. Sometimes the term may be used to characterize a person in the sense that it praises his luck and cleverness as well as his success in economic enterprise. On the whole the term, as already said, is not heavily discrediting, even if not neutral. There can be no doubt of its belonging among the characterisms.

12.2 ECONOMIC CONDUCT

12.21 EXCHANGE

(a) **bargain** v.	(b) **mercenary**	(c) **beg**	(d) **peculate**
chaffer	**prostitute** v.	**cadge**	**usury**
haggle	**venal**	**wheedle**	
palter			

The basic form or descript of this process is that of bargaining, that is, the effort to induce exchange by offering and receiving what is deemed to be the value of the objects or the services in the transaction. But such processes offer difficulties and problems so familiar it is scarcely necessary to translate them into abstractions except for the purposes of theory. **Haggling, paltering** and **chaffering** are not charges of crime nor of moral offense. They are simply ways in which a party to a process of bargaining or a third party may characterize the process. He will observe in it the effort of one person to elevate the price, or of the other to disparage the product. There may be fraud lurking in the shadows of it, but actually fraud is no more nor less a definitive part of it than of any other effort to complete an economic transaction. The present set of terms reflects little honor on the economic process, but there are also more respectable ways in which bargains are struck. The vocabulary for these is not distinctive: vice rather than virtue stirs interest.

The characterisms in the second column are discrediting in most uses. Particularly in its verb form, to speak of a person as prostituting himself is to say that something is offered for *mere* money which is beyond price. Sometimes this takes the form of altering something in itself priceless in order to obtain a quick or easy or certain economic gain from the sale of it. So much of prostitution can be defined. We have already said that a charge of prostitution for sexual purposes is not one of characterizing: it is to use the name of an outright occupation, and the substantive *prostitute* is a descript. Other uses of the term are subtler. What will really constitute alteration of, let us say, a literary work to serve a political purpose? And is this always prostitution, or may it not, as in certain countries, be called "enlisting artists in the struggle for socialism?'' What may count as reward, besides money? And so on. Such discriminations are not easily made. In general, the charge of prostitution is used to discredit a person because of the context in which a service is rendered; the charge of being mercenary is based on the purpose which actions serve. They cannot be defined merely in terms of the acceptance of monetary reward: both respected wives and soldiers may be rewarded.

In contrast to the foregoing terms, which are used for the characterization of distribution for the sake of gain, **begging** and **cadging** are for characterizations of acquisition without recompense but also without deception. Neither of them is deemed to be a moral offense or crime, although they are deviant ways of adjusting oneself to the economic process. They are generally not self-applicative.

These few terms give us examples of ways in which the sheer exchange of goods or valuables may be characterized.

12.22   ACQUISITION

CREDITING CHARACTERISMS

honest	**incorruptible**

DISCREDITING CHARACTERISMS

ATTRIBUTIVE

avaricious	**fraudulent**
covetous	**furacious**
cupidity	**greed**
dishonest	**rapacious**
envy	**unscrupulous**

PROCESSIVE

abscond	**[fraud]**
bamboozle	**hoodwink**
[bribe]	**loot**
[cheat]	**malversation**
[con =swindle]	**[nepotism]**
[confiscate]	**palm off**
[defalcation]	**pillage**
[default]	**[plagiarism]**
[defraud]	**plunder**
extort, extortion	**purloin**
fake	**rapine**
filch	**reave**
foist	**swindle**
[forge]	**[theft]**

SUBSTANTIVE
bandit   **deadbeat**
crook   **thief**

The way in which goods or services may be obtained are these: one may acquire them by fair exchange, entering into and consummating covenants or contracts, by gift from a present owner, or simply by stealth or force. Acquisition by exchange is comprehensible from what has just been said and from previous consideration of covenance. Characterization of fraud will be taken up in the present section. We shall then consider the remainder of the characterisms under economic conduct, those of possession and provision.

We see at a glance that the characterisms of 12.22 are largely discrediting: many of them tantamount to crimes. They reflect one of the things deemed criminal in our society in high degree, that is, interference with the ownership of goods or a discrediting manner of obtaining them. Since there are fairly clear conventions regarding these, the processive and substantive classes of the present number will be largely composed of descripts that are to be applied to subjects in a fairly objective fashion: like the terms for deception in 11.112 they have a recognized standing in the law. A few terms are somewhat vaguer, looser or more figurative in application, e.g., **bamboozle, filch, foist, hoodwink, palm off**, and **plunder**. The actions described or characterized must also be thought of as aggressions and thus more determinate or more overt devices of contention such as were discussed in 11.1.

To get at the foundation of these discredits we may ask a question which may at first sight appear either naive or mischievous, or even worse, namely, why are deprivations of property thought to be vicious, criminal, or in any event discrediting? To answer this we must first ask why possession and acquisition are thought to be virtues. The answer to this cannot lie merely in the praiseworthiness of thrift, industriousness, self-reliance or other such shining Puritan virtues, virtuous as these may indeed be. Nor can we interpret discrediting acquisition as merely vicious by convention, so that if we abolished the convention of property we would also at one stroke abolish all crimes against property as well.

I believe the answer to the question lies in the connection between property and life. The right to property is only incidentally a command over things distinct from the person. What is basic to it is the right to *privacy*, the right to the self, to oneself. If this is invaded by every other person, the self itself disappears. Property is simply an extension of the self. To possess it is to draw a line at some fixed distance from the naked physical self and to include all that falls within it in the person. We will not undertake to define a minimum to which to confine the right to property. We have seen in our time that the expectations of well-being are relative to the economic level that a society has attained. We turn aside from this issue but only because the language of value has no decisive bearing upon it. It is sufficient that a given minimum or average is deemed a legitimate expectation in virtually every society. (The question of excesses, of maxima and minima is to some degree touched upon in the characterization of possession and provision, 12.23 and 12.24.)

The basic reason why we must regard possession and acquisition in some certain degree as virtues is then that if I have a right to life (as said by Locke and Jefferson, to mention no others) I have a right to what sustains life, for life unsustained is simply death. Therefore, I must be allowed to draw a circle at just that distance from my physical self that will include within it the means of sustaining life. Only if something is proper-to-me can the term 'property' have any meaning for me.

If there is to be property and privacy, it must obviously be respected. So much I think will be granted by everyone. But where the line is to be drawn and at what remove from the physical self – that is the question. Socialism has always insisted that at least the means of production must be socialized and thus removed from privacy. Usually, in practice it has not challenged possession of most articles of personal use. We shall not try to examine the appropriateness of the line drawn by socialism between public and private. We merely wish to affirm that the social orders so far devised have always recognized property in some form. No order so far has managed to conform to the Marquis de Sade's program of utmost liberty of everyone over everyone else, for this is no order at all.

The foregoing is meant to express the conviction that the characterisms of 12.22 have an authority that extends beyond the mere system of conventions of English-speaking of of European peoples. In all societies, I believe, there will be some such recognition of property and privacy as will give meaning to these characterisms, though in some more and in others less. If they now appear to be too weakly designated when we speak of them as characterisms, this is because of the greater degree of possessiveness in some societies as against others, or the greater degree of offensiveness of acting stealthily or using force. In all cases, degree of discredit is reflected and the force of the discreditation is the greater because the individual may be certain that his impression is shared by virtually every other member of society. This unanimity forms a strong basis for the characterization of such acts by society as moral offenses or crimes or both. The reason for this has, I think, already been laid down. Everyone at some point will draw a line about himself which he regards it offensive to have violated by others. It does not require the least

appeal to *sympathy* to see that most of the acts characterized in 12.22 are
invasions of this sort, provided, of course, that there is evidence of deprivation, that it was deliberate, and that it was undertaken by stealth, or force,
or both. This is an instance where the abstract is as potent as the particular –
if one hears that someone has been defrauded one takes offense whether one
is a witness to the event or not, just so long as it appears it might have happened to oneself. Of course, our habits of self-exculpation are deeprooted;
we can always see distinctions that will appear to relieve us of obligation to
see ourselves as threatened or "involved."

As already noted a distinguishing trait of the processive discrediting modes
of acquisition is the possibility of providing them with definitions or objective descriptions. This is true of all such actions as have fallen under the
purvey of the law, for here great effort has been put forth to make precise
what will constitute a particular kind of offense. When this has been done
one moves away from characterization – courts of law do not exist for the
purpose of characterization but for the maintenance of what society has
decreed as law.

In other respects the modes of 12.212 conform fairly obviously to the
traits of characterization in general.

12.23 POSSESSION

POSITIVE CHARACTERISMS	+	NEGATIVE CHARACTERISMS
CREDITING		CREDITING
(a) **affluent**		(c) **mendicant**
opulent		
rich		
wealthy		
+ ══════════════════	×	══════════════════ −
DISCREDITING		DISCREDITING
(b) **moneybags**		(d) **deprivation**
nabob		**destitute**
plutocrat		**indigent**
		mendicant (+)
		mendicity
		needy
		pauper
		pittance
		poor
		ragamuffin
		want n.
	−	

Since provision must depend upon possession, we may begin with the latter. We turn first to the positive crediting characterisms of possession. In a sense we must say of them what we said of **dear** and **cheap**. **Rich** and **poor** resemble these, except that they are commonly attributed to persons rather than to commodities. **Rich** and **poor**, as descripts, merely indicate quantitative directions of the accumulation of or access to wealth. But they are also commonly used as characterisms. We must, for the time, take them apart from moral considerations, which in any event vary with the reigning economic and social ideology. The communist does not deplore wealth or affluence, but only its unequal distribution or what he thinks is its misuse in noncommunist societies. In general, wealth, or access to it, seems to be prized as at least *one*, if not the only good, in most societies. We should of course recall that certain schools of Christianity provide exceptions to this. We will let it stand, however, as a term that is a crediting characterism in the most typical contexts. The banker J. Pierpont Morgan pointed out that the Biblical maxim did not read, "Money is the root of all evil," but rather, "The love of money is the root of all evil." It is difficult, in general, to resist the satisfying impression made by a well-supplied household or economy. To feel forced to add, "but only if there are no others that are in misery, woe, or want," is, I think only to underline the strength of the attraction, not to cast doubt upon it. Quite other is the thought behind genuine policies of renunciation followed by certain religious orders. It is significant however that no crediting negative characterism (c) readily comes to mind except possibly **mendicant**. We are at liberty, of course, to praise and to embrace vows of poverty, but our language has virtually no ready-made resource for speaking of it as a virtue.

In contrast, we may observe the larger number of discrediting negative characterisms found in 12.23 (d). Some exhibit a certain pity or compassion, but they do not imply that deprivation is, in itself, anything to be sought for. The term 'discredit' is here somewhat inaccurate in that in most instances the person himself who is being characterized as a pauper or ragamuffin is not, in parts of our society, held to have done or to be doing something discrediting. Rather his *condition* is thought to be discrediting but possibly to someone other than himself. This is the most compassionate view to take. But who has not heard persons of affluence speak as if the poor *in general* had no one but themselves to blame for their condition? Such an attitude is very likely to prevail only in societies like our own which set great store by the capacity to acquire goods. Perhaps it was better described as the acquisitive society, by R. H. Tawney, than as merely the affluent society, by J. K. Galbraith.

The terms **mendicity** and especially **mendicancy**, could well occupy a place intermediate between, or neutral as to, credit and discredit. The mendicant orders or friars of the middle ages were reputable folk who made their way in the world by begging. It is, of course, a pretty question whether all these attitudes can genuinely coexist: reputability, discredit, compassion. Yet such seems to have been the case with these orders. They sought to share the life of the outcast and discredited. At the same time one gave them a crust or a farthing out of compassion, because to leave anyone to starve would be discrediting. Despite his condition, the mendicant was a person to be respected, like no common or lazy beggar, because he was following what was thought to be an injunction of the Gospel. All this has, however, virtually lapsed, and it is significant that now scarcely a single term of credit (c) exists for a state of deprivation.

Rich men have ever drawn discredit upon themselves, if only as shown in the envy of others. But we must not read into history too much of our own thoughts, so deeply infused with democratic and socialistic ideology at nearly all levels. Kings often were invested with pomp, wealth, and splendor quite willingly and generously by their subjects because they were in some sense identical with the state, which was itself therefore being honored. The mistake of Louis XIV was merely to have uttered (if he did) *l'état c'est moi* so late in the day. We cannot attribute our own use of the discreditations in (b) only to envy, if only because this is too simple an explanation. The moneybags or miser is despised because of what he does or fails to do with his wealth. Our discreditation of him will rest on something other than envy if we are convinced he has acquired his wealth by the exploitation of others. The plutocrat, if the term is used literally, is despised because of the faulty basis which mere financial considerations provide in deciding the destiny of a nation or community.

It is apparent here, as with all characterisms, that the basis of credit and discredit arises from the impression created in the appraiser by the subject. They therefore do not serve to describe objective traits. The other principal features of characterisms are likewise evident. Particularly the characterisms under (b) are meant to make declarations about character. The characteristic referred to occupies nearly the appraiser's entire view, or overview, of the subject. If we think of the subject as rich or needy or penniless or indigent, we are not thinking of his distinguishable traits but thinking of the whole subject *in terms of* a certain characteristic. It is obvious that we cannot formulate exact specifications for the use of the terms. And characterizations in these terms are not yet the same as passing moral judgment on subjects.

12.24 PROVISION

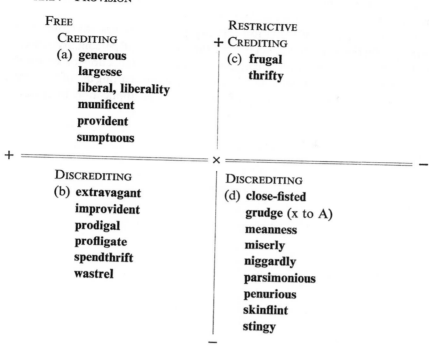

FREE
   CREDITING

(a) **generous**
     largesse
     liberal, liberality
     munificent
     provident
     sumptuous

RESTRICTIVE
+ CREDITING

(c) **frugal**
     thrifty

DISCREDITING

(b) **extravagant**
     improvident
     prodigal
     profligate
     spendthrift
     wastrel

DISCREDITING

(d) **close-fisted**
     grudge (x to A)
     meanness
     miserly
     niggardly
     parsimonious
     penurious
     skinflint
     stingy

When we turn to the characterisms of *provision*, a clearer picture emerges. The fourfold division is filled at each corner, and the terms are in convincing relation to one another. (The titles 'free' and 'restrictive' are merely a somewhat more specific way of listing the positive and the negative characterisms.) The terms have force because they present the subject in a very definite light. If we think him generous or extravagant, thrifty or miserly, the thought looms large before us: we are thinking of the whole man in these terms, or of the man wholly in these terms. Even so, the terms have not yet, by themselves, the quality of moral judgments on him.

The characterisms exhibit the manner in which we are affected by the subject. In each case, it is the appraiser who is deciding where to set the limits between munificence and extravagance, between thrift and parsimony. He is thus revealing something of himself in drawing just this line and just this characterization. He reveals not only what his degree of affluence is, but what he thinks it is. And he may reveal even more of himself. So, for example, a person may defend what is obvious miserliness by appealing to the fact that human affairs are hazardous and unpredictable, that wars and disasters can quickly wipe out fortunes if they are not carefully safeguarded, and so on.

What is revealed hereby is the determination to "survive" at any cost: the pursuit of the illusion of individual "sovereignty."

The characterisms of provision are thus particularly apt examples of the principal features of all characterisms: the overview of personality reflected and underlined in each characterization, the clear reflection of or on the character of the subject, the fourfold crediting or discrediting use of the terms, and the essential unspecifiability of exact terms of application to subjects.

13.0 COMMUNITIVE CHARACTERIZATION

With 13.0 we come to the end of the appraisives that concern specifically the character of man. In this survey, we may sometimes appear to go beyond what may be thought the limits of character: it is possible to suppose that intelligence, behavior, and social status and comportment lie outside the field. It is not necessary to draw lines too strictly. We ask whether in a given area there are prominent virtues and vices that are thought to characterize man at his best and his worst either in respect of what is narrowly called his character or of his principal powers. In this respect, a glance at the roster of virtues in 14.0 will show that the characterisms of behavior and intelligence certainly qualify to be placed here.

Our next question concerns the appraisives and moral concepts in the communitive sphere. The communitive area extends from the seeming or comparative trivialities of social comportment and status to the social virtue of law abidingness and to social vices such as treachery and anarchy. The terminating position of the communitive is not meant to suggest that it is inherently the "highest" of values. Although anarchy is without doubt thought to be a vice in our world, it is by no means obvious that conformity is a virtue. The communitive virtues and vices are therefore to say the least on their mettle, if not on the fire.

13.1 SOCIAL COMPORTMENT (Cf. 8.24, 8.25)

CREDITING CHARACTERISMS

(a) ATTRIBUTIVE
chivalrous
civil (8.24)
complaisant
convivial
cordial
courteous
gregarious

(b) PROCESSIVE
behave
comport (oneself)
jaunty
polite (8.24)
presentable
sociable
well-mannered,
manners

DISCREDITING CHARACTERISMS

(a) ATTRIBUTIVE

bumptious
naughty
rowdy
rude
stuffy (8.25)
uncouth
unsavory

(b) PROCESSIVE

misbehave
misconduct
miscreant, miscreancy
misdeed
peccadillo
scandal

(c) SUBSTANTIVE

blighter	jackanapes
boor	lout
bounder	lubber
brat	oaf
busybody	offscouring
cad	ogre
chuff	parasite
churl	pest
clod	prig
codger	rascal
coxcomb	rotter
curmudgeon	scum
gadabout	slattern
hag	yahoo
hooligan	

The characterisms in the early parts of 13.0 have little or none of the life-or-death quality of many of the terms in the later sections: **anarchy, outlaw, traitor, treason,** and the like. The latter are comparatively rare in occurrence, since few societies are in a *perpetual* state of convulsion. But the characterisms of 13.1 to 13.5 are often accompanied by feelings just as deep as those that may accompany the characterizations of social conformity. Whether it is a matter of moment or not, we must recognize that everyone sooner or later is gratified by evidences of courtesy, refinement, or civility in persons and disconcerted by rascals, rowdies, or stuffed shirts, and may sense all this deeply.

We have sought to sort out these modes of social characterization into several fairly cohesive classes, mindful of the fact that other schemes of classification may be equally meritorious. One may also wish to hark back to the diathetic characterisms of 8.0, for example those touching on air, bearing, or manner, since decisive classifications are sometimes difficult to make. Thus, **polite** may as easily fall under Presence in 8.24, reflecting a more inner disposition than the characterisms in 13.1. But although the creditings and discreditings of this vocabulary touch primarily on the externals of behavior, they have an inner tone as well.

It is evident that if we were to take sufficient trouble we could introduce our fourfold classification into the present analysis, but it does not seem particularly rewarding. For example, we could think of our habit of regarding

the comportment of persons in terms of "roughness" and "smoothness."
So one could have:

POSITIVE CHARACTERISMS		NEGATIVE CHARACTERISMS	
CREDITING	suave	diamond in the rough	
	diplomatic	rugged	
DISCREDITING	dandy n.	oaf	
		clod	
		uncouth	

But more than a brief suggestion of this seems a rather jejune exercise. It is
sufficient to place the terms among creditings and discreditings. Something
close to the foregoing has already appeared in 8.24.

When the terms are placed according to credit and discredit we begin to
see subtleties of difference. To begin with the credits, we notice that **behave**
and **behavior** are unique in that they are often used, especially toward children
in eminent degree. That is, "Behave yourself!" means you must exhibit good
or approved behavior, not just manifest behavior in the psychologist's sense.
(Sooner or later, some precocious child will respond to this command by
trying to divert attention from the eminent sense to the general psychological
one where it is sufficient to breathe to behave. "I *am* behaving!")

The phrase "knowing how to comport oneself" exhibits the same eminent
sense (and this is the sense which leads us to number it among the present
credits), as against asking, "How did he comport himself? Well or ill?"
Sociable and **civil**, comparing their present with other uses, also exhibit
something of this character. **Presentable** is obviously a somewhat question-
begging term; it is made usable only by the speaker's being able to presume
that the listener knows what in particular he has in mind. This leaves us with
the near synonyms **courteous** and **polite**, and with **chivalrous**, which moves
more explicitly in the same direction. **Cordial** is obviously close to the diathetic characterisms but is properly placed here to show a contrast to the
numerous forms of uncordiality shown among the discredits.

Earlier we have remarked on the "inner disposition" of diathetic terms.
This remains an important difference from the present class. It is evident
that here as there we presume a feeling and responsive being behind the
comportment, but in the present instance we are interested particularly in
the façade of the personality. Were the person to suppress the exterior manifestations we might still suspect him of caddish, cloddish, priggish thoughts
and feelings but our appraisal would have to be more subtly oriented toward
the diathetic, toward his inner state.

A characteristic common to all members of each of these classes is that the subjects (in the appraiser's view) all earn praise or blame for their manner of comporting themselves through their own exertions. The actions or behavior on which the characterisms are based are thought to be within the control of the individual. In this sense, particularly, the discredits distinguish themselves from those under 13.2 (Social Status), although a true snob would think no one could of his own effort cure himself of these defects by an effort of will. In the latter event, bad comportment is closely associated with status. On the other hand, the same snob would, of course, excuse discrediting (caddish, cloddish, loutish, oafish, rude, unsavory) behavior in those he regards as having an exalted status by right of birth or origin. Such are the vagaries of social esteem from a rapid and superficial survey in our society. Comparison of habits of characterization in these respects in other social orders and other linguistic communities should prove particularly instructive. Are the same distinctions present and observed in Red China, Albania, Botswana, West Irian, Kamchatka and other exotic communities? Questions of this kind may appropriately be raised regarding the next section as well as this one.

13.2 SOCIAL STATUS AND IMAGE

CREDITING CHARACTERISMS

ATTRIBUTIVE

breeding	polished
cultivated	pomp
decorous, decorum	refined
fashionable	status
genteel, gentility	stylish, style
modish	well-bred

SUBSTANTIVE

brahmin	mandarin
gentleman	patrician
lady	

DISCREDITING CHARACTERISMS

ATTRIBUTIVE

backwater	demi-rep
common	faux pas
conventional	gauche
déclassé	ill-bred
demean	parochial
demi-monde	pretentious (8.23)

provincial	ragtag-bobtail
punctilio	riff-raff
rabble	ruck
raffish	snub

SUBSTANTIVE

dandy n.	plebeian
factotum	snob
flunkey	tramp
fop	vagabond
outcast	vagrant
outsider	waif
pariah	

As just indicated, the characterisms of 13.1 are thought to be deserved through the exertions and shortcomings of the subjects. Those of 13.2 tend to be deserved, it is thought, through existent conditions, such as birth, rather than effort. Persons thought to deserve the creditings in 13.2 of course, might, and in general, would exert themselves; but even so, status (notice that this term is also employable in the eminent degree) would seem to be deserved because of an existent condition: A is cultivated not only because he exerts himself in self-cultivation but he *is* in a condition or situation to be able to do so. The terms **refined** and **polished** are similar in their workings.

Similarly, among the discreditings, it will be thought by those who take such characterizations seriously, that persons literally *are* all of these dreadful things. How or why? The only answer that appears to be accepted is, by being what they are.

In general, this is the tendency that runs through the use of all of the terms in 13.2. It is doubtful that the terms will survive efforts to improve their "image," yet such efforts seem constantly to have been made in recent centuries as democratic levelling proceeded. That is, one wanted to improve and "spiritualize" (I will offer the source of the quotation in a moment) such terms: that is, **cultivated, gentleman, refined** and many others were to be employed not of those of fortunate birth but of *true* merit and distinction. The same thing happens with any number of other characterisms which originate in actual exemplifications, and thus teach us a valuable lesson in the mutations of significance of characterisms. The process is described simply and accurately by C. S. Lewis in the preface to his *Mere Christianity*:

The word *gentleman* originally meant something recognisable; one who had a coat of arms and some landed property. When you called someone "a gentleman" you were not paying him a compliment, but merely stating a fact. If you said he was not "a gentleman" you were not insulting him, but giving information. There was no contradiction in saying that John was a liar and a gentleman; any more than there now is in saying that James is a fool and an M.A. But then there came people who said – so rightly, charitably, spiritually, sensitively, so anything but usefully – "Ah, but surely the important thing about a gentleman is not the coat of arms and the land, but the behavior? Surely he is the true gentleman who behaves as a gentleman should? Surely in that sense Edward is far more truly a gentleman than John?" They meant well. To be honourable and courteous and brave is of course a far better thing than to have a coat of arms. But it is not the same thing. Worse still, it is not a thing everyone will agree about. To call a man "a gentleman" in this new, refined sense, becomes, in fact, not a way of giving information about him, but a way of praising him: to deny that he is "a gentleman" becomes simply a way of insulting him. When a word ceases to be a term of description and becomes merely a term of praise, it no longer tells you facts about the object: it only tells you about the speaker's attitude to that object. (A "nice" meal only means a meal the speaker likes.) A *gentleman*, once it has been spiritualized and refined out of its old coarse, objective sense, means hardly more than a man whom the speaker likes. As a result, *gentleman* is now a useless word. We had lots of terms of approval already, so it was not needed for that use; on the other hand if anyone (say, in a historical work) wants to use it in its old sense, he cannot do so without explanations. It has been spoiled for that purpose.

Now if once we allow people to start spiritualizing and refining, or as they might say "deepening," the sense of the word *Christian*, it too will speedily become a useless word.

Doubtless, it is too late in nearly every case to make the protest that Lewis makes, even admitting its appropriateness. The reason, of course, is that the terms *have* been "spiritualized" as he says. We may put it in broader terms by saying that the terms have been both generalized and specificated. They have been specificated by selecting some set of properties that appears central to the Christian or the gentleman (ignoring Christians like Henry VIII, Torquemada, and Senator Joseph McCarthy, and gentlemen like the Marquis de Sade and the Prussian Junkers) and generalized by application to all those who have the properties. This is a common device for the development of characterizing terms. Even individuals (as well as groups such as Christians or gentlemen) may serve the purpose. Names such as those of Napoleon, Sade, Sacher-Masoch, Stalin and numberless others have undergone this process. (Cf. discussion of 6.1, end.)

The generalization process is plainly responsible for the characterizing use of such terms in our list as **backwater, gauche, plebeian, provincial, parochial, ragamuffin, rabble, tramp, vagabond**, and **vagrant**, and of course **brahmin, genteel, gentleman, gentility, lady, mandarin**, and **patrician**. Since the ranking of individuals is an occupation mankind finds so difficult to resist, we may of course expect it to leave interesting effects in all languages, not excepting those spoken by groups most committed to democracy and egalitarianism.

Perhaps **snob** and **snub** deserve distinct mention. **Snob** in particular has had a variety of uses which we shall not attempt to review. For our purposes, its most interesting trait is that it is a complex or higher order appraisive. If A says B is a snob, he appraises B adversely, particularly in respect to the appraisals, judgments, or characterizations that B offers of, let us say, C. We have noticed a number of other appraisals of this sort, some of which are detailed in Appendix H.

13.3 SOCIAL REPUTE AND REPROACH

CREDITING CHARACTERISMS

a [character*	notable
credentials	noted
credit	personage
distinguished	popular
eminent	prestige
estimable	prominent
famous	reputable, repute,
illustrious	reputation
luminary	respectable
noble, nobility (14.01, 14.4)	lion, lionize ($\pm$)

DISCREDITING CHARACTERISMS

discredit	infamy
disgrace	notorious
ignoble	odium
ignominy	shame (G. Schande)

The present number presents very general characterizations. It is indeed somewhat problematic whether this body of concepts belongs here or in Part Three. 'Generality' as applied to them means that they could occur as predicates of subjects other than persons. Yet careful reflection on them should show that they first appear meaningfully in relation to persons.

Among themselves they show quite significant differences. Among the creditings some three record merely the fact that the subject enjoys applause of one kind or another on a significant and public plane: **famous, noted**, and **popular**. The attribution itself adds a little further luminescence to whatever the subject itself already enjoys. A second group records the additional fact that the subject is not only in the public eye, but that he does so by reason of a kind of figure-ground principle; as a figure he has a kind of luminescence, either from within or from reflection, as compared with others in his immediate surroundings. These terms are **distinguished, eminent, illustrious, luminary, prominent**, and **obscure**. The reason of such eminence remains, of course, to be supplied. The subject gains slightly more luminescence than he already enjoys simply by being spoken of in these terms.

* Two quite different senses of the term are relevant here: (1) testimony as to character (in the moral sense) or ability; (2) a personage or an odd or idiosyncratic person.

A further set of terms is characterized by a circularity which we have already observed in previous cases. Those among the creditings are **estimable, notable, reputable**, and **respectable**. None of exactly this sort is to be found among the discreditings. Rather, we find here the record of the fact that the subject undergoes a negative response: **disgrace, ignominy, infamy, notorious, odium**, and **shame**. It is evident that the attribution of these adds heavily to the subject's existing discreditation. President Franklin D. Roosevelt's characterization of Pearl Harbor day as a day "that will live in infamy" did not merely take note of its existing discreditation in the eyes of most of the world, but indeed added further discredit to it simply in the utterance. Each of these terms (**disgrace... shame**) similarly adds its own measure of discredit in the utterance. But what exactly the discredit is, is left void! Your deeds, I say, are disgraceful, ignominious, infamous, notorious, odious, and shameful. Even if I am not echoing some other person's charge, I have, at most, said that they hereby enjoy discredit in my eyes. If we ask why the subject deserves discredit the answer can only be sought in a recursion to other characterizations. This is dictated by the generality of those terms, which may as easily be placed among the general appraisives of Part Three as here. The discreditings particularly may be thought of in connection with the vices considered in 15.0, since whatever ranks as vicious will also deserve ignominy, odium, shame, etc.

13.4   INTERCLASS AND FACTIONAL APPRAISIVES

aristocrat	**patriotism**
authoritarian	**progressive**
bourgeois	**rabble**
conservative	**reactionary**
demagogue	**servitude**
democratic (as appraisive)	**tory** (as appraisive)
despot	**totalitarian**
downtrodden	**tyrant**
figurehead	**utopian**
menial	

The list represents but a small sampling of the expressions which classes or individuals representing class standpoints may employ in reference to one another. In general, these reflect economic or political directions of thought or action. One might also have a selection of terms used by occupations of one another, or by occupations of themselves. We would thus gradually work toward numerous slangs, argots, and jargons which, of course, are appraisive in large part. Our century, which has exhibited so many hatreds and interclass or interracial conflicts, is surfeited with such appraisives and characterisms, of every sort and of every degree of strength and violence.

The terms of 13.4 are characterizing in every respect. They present an overview of the subject that is almost invariably holistic and uncompromising. So for example **bourgeois**: the middle class character is oversimplified. With **demagogue, despot, figurehead, jingo, rabble,** and **tyrant** one salient feature seems to express every other trait of the subject. In such characterizations the very soul or character has appeared to stand revealed, usually in all its grim essence. The mere word serves not only to draw attention to the subject but to loose currents of passion against it. There is nothing of which the hot-headed rebel is so certain as that this is what the subject truly *is* – the very verb 'to be,' ordinarily so colorless and catalytic, acquires force and color.

What is most unmistakable as a mark of the process of characterization is the thread that binds the appraisal or characterism to the speaker. "A is bourgeois!" He speaks of others but reveals himself. "B is a demagogue." We can readily draw some fairly reliable conclusions about the speaker. "C is a patriot." Unless he is ironic we feel the speaker's admiration. "What a rabble!" "*Odi profanum vulgus.*" The remarks are fully intelligible only when we know who is speaking. We are in the very center of the area where we must respect *ad hominem* considerations as relevant.

It is true that such terms are rarely used (I do not mean reported) without emotion, but they are far from being merely emotive in the sense of the shallow theory that draws our attention to this obvious fact. It is not the case that **bourgeois** is merely a noise or a bludgeon. The fact is it is packed with great significance, and the mere utterance of the term in the right circumstances, to the right audience, at once calls up effective images of what are said to be the perpetrators of endless grief and woe. He who flays "the tyrant" knows that the term will conjure up a hundred thoughts and connotations that release as many feelings. No body of terms has ever effected so much with so comparatively little effort as the appraisives spoken by the Lenins, Hitlers and Maos of this century. The foregoing vocabulary represents the type of these powerful instruments of change.

13.5   CULTURAL LEVEL OR ORDER

CREDITING CHARACTERISMS
civilized
cosmopolitan

DISCREDITING CHARACTERISMS
(a) archaic   quaint
    backward   savage
    barbarian
    barbarous, barbaric   (b) gentile
    clannish   heathen
    decadent   pagan
    fin de siècle
    primitive
    provincial

This class of characterisms, compared with those that immediately follow, have an air of smug academic contentment. Some of the terms are on occasion also employable in fairly descriptive senses, but they rarely lose all of their characterizing aroma. "A is archaic, barbarian, primitive." Who has said so? Obviously someone who deems himself and his kind to be far advanced in civilization and cultivation. "B is quaint." Who is speaking? Evidently someone "*too* long in city pent." "C is clannish." The speaker has long since reached an independent position, detached from the herd. "D is cosmopolitan." The speaker may be an awed admirer of the racy life of the big city. And yet again, he may be hurling a charge from the Kremlin against the foes of the Revolution, the international bankers, Jews, Zionists, aesthetic formalists, etc. In each instance, the term leaves a trace, like a snail's, and it can be traced back at last to the man, *ad hominem*, like all true characterisms.

But we must treat this class of appraisives with the utmost seriousness. Although issues of political character may appear to be more significant than those of the present number, the choices that now confront mankind may well be more momentously those between civilization and barbarism, than between the political ideology of East and West. We can here do little more than identify the problem as seen from the standpoint of appraisive language. We must recognize that the concepts are unavoidably evaluative and appraisive and that they are absolutely indispensable to the characterization of man. The discredits are nowadays reluctantly assigned. We are inclined to suppose that we no longer have the problems of rising toward civilization from barbarism simply because no one any longer consents to be called barbarous and all pretend to civilization. This has little to do with so-called primitive or recently primitive peoples who now earnestly aspire to a place in the sun: the Atlantic world has barbarism of its own.

Instead of undertaking a study of the concepts themselves I may content myself with pointing out the necessity of such an inquiry. It must be an inquiry from examples whether or not the examples consent to be cited. A most untoward result would be to allow these concepts to slip into disuse. For if we are correct, it is of the very essence of appraisal that the appraisive "phenomenon" owes its existence to the concepts, the exact reverse of the situation with descriptive concepts. What is needed is not only *analysis* and discussion of civilization and barbarism but also active *use* of these concepts in application to present phenomena.

In the early parts of 13.0 we have taken the community somewhat for granted. Society at this level organizes itself, to be sure, but no durable political substance needs to be presupposed. Social status and comportment are most often built against the background of formal political structure, but this is not definitive of them. For our purposes, it will suffice if we place the informal communitive structure near or alongside the formal one. The formal structure and the appraisive ideas it harbors are then the next topic to be considered.

Should characterization necessarily extend also to the political life of man? Using a guide we mentioned previously, we may ask what virtues of character emerge from the body of appraisives in this sphere. We know that in certain ancient societies the political fabric was moral through and through, that the truly moral man there was *homo politicus*, that his character was not to be distinguished from his public being. For a member to withdraw from such a society would appear to be not only a defection but an actual betrayal of it. To go beyond the bounds of all society or to advocate this would seem even more wicked. Moral character was evidently connected with conformity to law if not defined by it.

It is fairly evident that our notion of personal morality repudiates such an equation. On the other hand, if we look toward the "socialist republics" it is virtually impossible to distinguish one side from the other. Both of them are absorbed in a higher substance called ideology. The public confessions of apostates to these regimes cannot be analyzed into distinct moral and political components.

The question, therefore, is vital in our time how one can keep law-abidingness from degenerating into conformity, in its current derogatory sense, freedom into anarchy, and deviation or dissent into treachery. Questions of this sort can probably only be answered by a thorough study of both ethics and political obligation, which cannot be undertaken here. We shall pursue it to such a length only as seems necessary to establish the framework of appraisive language.

The numerous and varied sociative characterisms of 11.0 together with the economic and communitive make up the field of the social appraisives. (The sex-related appraisives fall now to the social, now to the constitutional appraisives, that are comprised of the behavioral, diathetic, and tendentive.) How do we draw the line between the sociative and the communitive? We shall first offer a brief answer to this question.

If we look back over 11.0 we see that the emphasis there is entirely on the individual. It is he who associates (or "sociates") himself to others in such ways as contending with, aggressing against, accommodating himself to, submitting to, covenanting with other individuals like himself. In the last instance, covenanting, we are, of course, on the verge or already in the midst of a kind of new phenomenon: a kind of community has arisen. At least a condition, the covenant, for the establishment of a community has taken shape. It is not, however, a necessary condition of it. Economic community (using the term somewhat loosely) presupposes some kind of covenanting to facilitate orderly economic processes. But there is here as yet no imperious necessity for those bonds that unify men in communities or societies and are the condition for more elaborate orders, such as cities and nations.

In the present number the emphasis has shifted away from the association of *individuals* to the social fabric itself or to the individual in reference to this fabric. In whatever way the social bonds may arise, the individual is now to be thought of as being subject to them. It is convenient to hark back to a classical distinction of the sociologists between *Gesellschaft* and *Gemeinschaft*. Two or more individuals do not merely associate themselves with one another (*gesellen sich zu einander*) but have something in common (*haben etwas mit einander gemein*), and that which is common unites them. It is a problem for political philosophy whether this "something" is a literal reality or only a manner of speaking. It is sufficient for us to recognize the idiom, even if we do not analyze it in detail. We can identify and clarify the appraisive vocabulary independently of the analysis.

13.6   THE COMMUNITY

assembly	crowd	mass, masses
bee	coterie	meeting
cabal	crowd	mob
caucus	faction	polity
clique	federation	press
coalition	fellowship	rally n.
conclave	gang	rendezvous
confederation	group	team
congregation	horde	throng
convention	host	union

The foregoing list will provide the reader the opportunity to make precisely the kind of discriminations the author has risked making throughout on every subject matter. The list contains both the descripts and the characterisms that are devoted to the subject of the community in English. The question now is; which of the foregoing are truly one and which the other? Before reading further one may wish, therefore, to pause to make such a selection.

Before indicating our own selection of the explicit characterisms we may make another observation about the foregoing terms. Some of them illustrate particularly well a phenomenon which one can discern in other lists that mingle descripts and characterisms and which is readily exhibited in virtually all terms that are purely descriptive. The phenomenon in question comes to light in slightly ironic questions that have roughly the form, "Do you call that a...?" In such questions a descript can be instantly turned into a characterism, or may appear, at least, to do so, for purposes of jest or irony. "Do you call that a dog?" "Do you call that an automobile?... a shoe, a knife, a hat? etc., etc." Perhaps names of articles of manufacture are most likely to appear seriously in such contexts since their constitution *is* subject to manufacture, whereas an animal is either a dog or it is not. (Of course the manipulations of breeders take on some of the traits of manufacturing.)

Here, then, the "pure descripts" of our list simply designate the *fact* of some sort of social organizing. But each of them lends itself readily to use for the purpose of characterization. So one may come away from what is or appears to be a fraudulently conducted public assemblage (a meeting of aldermen, or legislators, or teammates, or a committee) and be prepared to denounce it "for what it is:" "I don't call that a caucus, a convention, a congregation, a polity, a federation, a team, I call it fraud, anarchy, a kangaroo court, star chamber, tyranny, etc." In short, the descripts have so definite a character that we see the lack of some definitive trait as a defect of character in it. Certainly a large part of Platonic, or at least platonizing analysis, proceeds in this way. One asks after the "nature of man" seeing this as "what nature intended man should be," "what is proper to him," "what he is as such," and so forth. So also we may have very definite ideas as to what a team or a legislative body is or ought to be. Thenceforth terms such as convention, polity, congregation, federation, committee, team, and numerous others may serve the purposes of characterizing and not just of description: they are being used in the *eminent* degree or sense.

I would suggest, therefore, that many, if not all, of the foregoing can serve as characterisms in the manner described. At the same time there are a number which are rather unmistakably used *only* as characterisms. I would set up the following division:

(a) [assembly]   [convention]   [meeting]
    [bee]   [convocation]   [polity]
    [caucus]   [crowd]   [press]
    [coalition]   [federation]   [rally]
    [conclave]   [horde]   [team]
    [confederation]   [host]   [throng]
    [congregation]   [mass, masses]   [union]

(b) cabal   faction   gang
    clique   fellowship   mob
    coterie

    I should now suggest that all of the terms in (b) are characterisms. Of these, all are discrediting, except **fellowship**. The terms in (a) as we have just seen will serve a characterizing function when the user is seriously offended by the behavior of a particular assemblage and thus sees such a lapse as a discreditation; occasionally he may also characterize what he deems a "well-conducted" assemblage by the positive use of the terms in the eminent sense: a "real federation," a "real polity," and so on. This use of 'real' we have also remarked on elsewhere. 'Mere' serves an analogous purpose with substantives as a mild discreditation. (See Normatives below, 15.4.) The analysis of all these concepts as usually undertaken by political theorists or sociologists construes them, I think, largely if not altogether as descripts. Even in its early beginnings sociology raised the question of the *nature* of the crowd or mob, and thus, I think, thought of the term '*mob*' as a descript. What we wish to draw attention to is the characterizing use of both classes, (a) and (b). We may also ask whether the (b)'s are ever descripts and can be given analyses as if they were.

    The terms in (b) have all the principal traits of characterisms that have been repeatedly identified earlier, First, to characterize any assemblage as a cabal, coterie, clique, gang, or mob is to think of it as having a more or less depraved character through and through. We are thinking of it as a whole, and not of a specific mob property or gang property some assemblage has. Being a mob is not a property of anything as is having so many members, or having such and such purposes. We take in the assemblage by an *overview* as with all characterisms, and it is its *character* that we appraise; or, to put it another way, we appraise it as having a certain character.

    Second, we are here characterizing something, not judging it, though our characterization subsequently may enter into the judgment of it. A group can be characterized as a mob, but only individuals may be judged in our order of things. Here the question is, *who* is guilty or responsible? It is altogether obvious that persons do not behave in crowds as they do outside such a context. They frequently may be appalled at their own complicity: "I wasn't myself." The mob acts, but only individuals can be blamed – blamed for what they have done in mob actions, and only for what *they* have done, and no more. Guilt is either specific and personal or the charge degenerates into rhetoric, abuse, and aggression.

Third, the charge that something is mob action is an expression of an appraiser's response and of his holding it to someone's discredit. But no decisive criteria can be followed here. The ascription is extern; it is never self-applied as of now. One always has more generous ways of characterizing what one is oneself doing than this. But obviously, here as elsewhere a trait cannot be a true descript if it is limited in this way and is in principle impossible to be discriminated by *all* observers. What is said of **mob** is in essence true also of the other discrediting characterisms. **Fellowship,** a term sometimes weak or slightly sentimental in connotation, is roughly similar to previous crediting characterisms.

13.7   SOCIAL CONFORMITY, CONFORMITY TO LAW

(a) **free, freedom**   **legitimate**
    law-abiding   **liberty**
    lawful   **rightful**
    legal   **rights**

(b) **anarchy**   **misdemeanor**
    caitiff   **misprision**
    crime, criminal   **outlaw**
    culprit   **pirate, piracy**
    de jure   **rebel**
    defeasance   **renegade**
    desert v.   **revolt, revolution**
    desperado   **foment [revolution**
    felon, felony   **scofflaw**
    illegal   **sedition**
    illegitimate   **subvert**
    illicit   **traitor**
    infringe   **treason**
    lawless   **turncoat**
    licentious,   **usurp**
      licence   **violate**
    malefactor   **wrongful**
    malpractice

The characterisms of this section at first glance appear to be drawn from legal phraseology and thus would seem to raise the question why only these from among the huge arsenal of legal terms are quoted. The answer essentially is that they are not necessarily legal terms, though in particular instances many of them *also* have a legal use, for example, **crime, defeasance, felon, illicit, misdemeanor** and certain others. But what we are drawing attention to in this body of terms as a whole is something that lies back of or underlies the law, something without which the law would be unthinkable or inoperative. We must first ask what makes the law obligatory, what puts it into effect?

The law, we shall be saying, cannot be self-effectuating on pain of involvement in a vicious circle; the law may enjoin or forbid certain actions, but it cannot make it unlawful to defy the law. For such an act (making it unlawful to defy the law) either merely repeats the terms of the specific law or ordinance itself, in which case the act is superfluous, or it does not repeat it. If it does not repeat it, the act, thought, movement, or disposition of mind that commands obedience to the law is trans-legal. If such an act or thought must be presupposed, it falls outside the domain of the law. The law is not self-effectuating but must derive its authority from another source.

I do not suggest that this problem is unknown to jurists. The fact is, the age-old dispute over natural law is essentially a dispute over the limits of the law and the transcendence of the law: it is essentially a philosophical dispute, even when it has been carried on by lawyers, legislators, as well as jurists.

We must take up this question of the foundation of the law in some detail. In order to do so, I shall consider one of the notions in our list which, in principle, challenges this foundation, the idea of anarchy.

The kind of anarchist I have in mind is entitled to the name although he may have a minimum in common with the actual advocates of this position who are heard at the present time. He insists upon the dissolution of all bonds of social and political union; he envisages a world where a certain amiable character pervades human relationships, and where tolerance is in principle as well as in fact the practice and habit of all persons. As to the question what is *likely* to happen in an anarchic society if it evolves out of one similar to the present one, the eighth book of Plato's *Republic* may still be our best guide. I am rather more concerned with the political or moral foundations of such a society.

I shall come immediately to the point. The question is, can the anarchic state fail to punish and discourage intolerance and other violations of anarchy? The social anarchist cannot merely join hands with the moral anarchist who tries to ban evaluation, judgment, morality, 'good', and 'bad'. He is, we assume, sincere and deeply committed to the prevailing of a certain kind of social order. He regards it as his first duty to combat intolerance and he must be ever alert to this vice, which will inevitably threaten to invade from without or to spring up from within. It is evident that he will have as formidable a task to prevent the clash of interests in the anarchic society as anyone has had to harmonize discordant interests in the classical state. But if the anarchist is serious, he will have to bring into being, or carry over from the old society into the new, some apparatus to effect this end. What is virtually certain not to happen is that interests, either in the long or the short run, will of themselves be harmonized or harmlessly segregated. In plain terms the anarchist has to enforce his program. One cannot imagine an anarchist program without moral fervor, but what is fervor without force? We seem compelled to identify morality with the resort to force. There are two considerations here. One is the likelihood that the anarchist society can be maintained only if it enforces its laws. The other is the need to recognize the essentially moral origin of this state, as of any other. The first of these will of course be an unwelcome development for the political anarchist, the second will be distasteful to the moral anarchist who wants to banish all thought of morality. In order to convince either of these of the error into which they have fallen we must consider the foundations of this and other societies.

Anarchists enjoin or forbid certain things because, or insofar as, they regard themselves as a community. But what constitutes them a community? It is of course nothing other than an act of trust and commitment by each and every member that enters into it. When the anarchist prescribes tolerance and forbids conflict these are particular laws which every member must observe. These laws, however, can obtain only if the individual honors his commitment establishing the community. This commitment can also be made to sound as if it were a law like other laws: a law that says that the laws must be obeyed.

But what has happened to the anarchist's "law-less" state. In the first place, he has to treat intolerance and conflict as vices and punish them. But more than that, there appears to be an even more general law which seems to pervade his society and to command that the laws be obeyed. We have then, even in anarchy, a society permeated by law. The point now is to see the difference between the two kinds of law which characterize not only this society but every other.

The commitment establishing a society is simply a way of ordaining that the observance of such and such ordinances shall characterize all members of this society, without exception. If they are members of this society they acknowledge this commitment and undertake to observe these ordinances. Eschewing intolerance and avoiding conflict, in just such and such ways, happen to be the ordinances of the anarchistic society. (We have here called them ordinances so that they will not be confused with the "law" that commands the citizen to obey the law.) Other societies will have other ordinances, but all societies will have as a necessary aspect the characteristic that all members are obliged to obey the ordinances.

What now is this law that commands us to obey the law? It is not a law at all, but an obligation that has been embraced by the citizen when he enters into membership in society. The act of undertaking this obligation is nothing other than a moral act. The act comes to light, for example, when the anarchist citizen asks why he must obey the ordinances of his society. The only answer is that he is obliged to obey them *in virtue of his being a citizen.* But this is also the only answer that can be given to the citizen of any other community except of course a prison. What anarchy reduces to is merely the maximization of internal tolerance in a society. But this is fully compatible, in principle, with any existing form of self-governing society.

There is therefore no way for man to live beyond the scope of morality except to live beyond the scope of society itself. This area of commitment and its complementary idea of trust is the domain of moral values. The first manifestation of moral values is readiness to obey the laws of the community and this is its moral fabric. A true community is therefore a moral community and it is inherently self-governing. That is to say, it lives according to a law whether it is under surveillance or not. A member of such a society is one who by definition can be *trusted* to obey the law.

We may now examine the character of the basic commitment somewhat more closely. Such a commitment is essentially unwritten and unwritable. That is, it cannot be written in the same sense as legal codes or ordinances are written. Societies that have explicit religious systems understand this perfectly well. The participant in the social body dedicates himself, he literally delivers himself up to the sway of the moral system together with the command to observe the community's explicit written laws. But the dedicatory act and the written laws which depend upon the act are entirely distinct. Only regimes that are unstable and uncertain of their survival try to make the dedicatory act (we may think of a "loyalty oath") a part of the written law. This is, however, obviously foolish, for we can always ask whether the regime can trust the taker's oath. If it cannot, it is no better off for his having taken it, although it may now complacently imprison him as if he were a common law breaker. He is certainly not that. He is an extraordinary lawbreaker, since he breaks no ordinary law.

This can perhaps be illustrated by the oaths of office taken by presidents or other officers of self-governing communities. The oath of office of a president is part of an act some certain citizen takes, which makes him president. It is not the act of a president, since a man cannot both take the oath while president and become president by the same act. He does not merely agree to abide by the laws. He undertakes to govern by the laws in situations that are, when he takes the oath, impossible to foresee. He is expected to exercise judgment, to be guided by a strict code of behavior, not merely to obey the law, as any ordinary citizen must. It is for these reasons that such oath takings are lifted out of the ordinary and surrounded with all the pomp and solemnity the community deems fitting. Such oaths are moral acts.

There is also a logical absurdity in ignoring the difference between moral and legal acts. Suppose the demand is heard (again we think of American "loyalty oaths") that we reduce everything to explicit written law. We have then the body of explicit law; call this L_1. We now enact a law which enjoins the observance of L_1; call this L_2. But this is obviously insufficient. We have stiffnecked citizens who refuse to observe L_2 or whose loyalty to L_2 is in doubt. We therefore enact another law which commands the observance of L_2 and prescribes punishment for failure to do so: call this L_3. And so forth, and so on, ad infinitum. The error lies in trying to reduce L_2 to the level of L_1 in the first place, that is, in failing to see that laws are one thing and moral commitments are another. There are but two alternatives. If the whole series of laws L_1, L_2, L_3 ----- L_n are but laws as L_1 is a law, then they are nothing more than the spilling of infinite barrels of ink, repeating the same law, L_1, ceaselessly. But if L_n is thought to differ from L_{n-1}, then it should be seen at once as a different kind of act, not covered by L_1 or any law like it. In that event the procedures for ordinary laws and their violation are altogether beside the point. The person who will not commit himself to a community does not violate its laws: he steps outside it. Laws are enacted for members of a community who are morally obligated and have morally obligated themselves to obey them. If the community fails to obey them, and insofar as it fails to obey them, it already ceases to live as a community. Of course the death struggle may be long and drawn out.

For reasons thus stated at length, our body of appraisives includes a class of concepts concerning conformity to law. This, I believe, is all that needs to be mentioned from the vast area of statute law in a study of appraisive concepts. Concepts such as **crime, culprit, scofflaw** and the like must first appear in the area of moral ideas. If they enjoy no respect as moral ideas the whole body of statute law is either a tissue of air, or what is worse, an instrument of sheer aggression.

With the foregoing exposition in mind, we may now examine somewhat more closely the other concepts of the present section. We have been concerned to show that society and social institutions presume a certain commitment or conformity to law. I think we are in no danger of subscribing to the existence of mythical entities if we say that such an act is in some sense presupposed. Our obligation to submit to law must be distinguished from the commands of the law itself. We therefore distinguish between two kinds of conformity: first, conformity to such laws or ordinances as our social order has devised for all its members; second, commitment to this order as against any other, or as against no order at all. The first I call *ordinative conformity*, the second *commissive conformity*. Each of these is susceptible to violation, disconformity, or crime, and we must distinguish accordingly between ordinative crime and commissive crime, which are utterly different from one another. Discrediting or crediting affirmations toward persons will take the form of the following expressions of appraisal or characterization.

13.71 APPRAISIVES OF ORDINATIVE CONFORMITY	13.72 APPRAISIVES OF COMMISSIVE CONFORMITY
CREDITING	CREDITING
(a) **free, freedom**	(aa) **law-abiding**
lawful, law-abiding	
legal	
legitimate	
rightful, rights	
DISCREDITING	DISCREDITING
(b) **caitiff**	(bb) **anarchy**
crime	**desert** v.
culprit	**desperado**
defeasance	**lawless**
felon	**licence, licentious**
illegal	**outlaw**
illegitimate	**pirate, piracy**
illicit	**rebel**
infringe	**renegade**
malefactor	**revolt, revolution**
malpractice	**foment [revolution**
misdemeanor	**scofflaw**
misprision	**sedition**
violate	**subvert**
wrongful	**traitor**
	treason
	turncoat
	usurp

Presuming an act or other token of commissive conformity, we may see fit to characterize certain persons, A, B, C, or their actions, in terms such as those of 13.71. It is not only the culprit's or felon's act that is presupposed, but, of course, our own, that is, the act of person who in speaking of others uses the terms **culprit** or **felon**. (Speaking may mean either *using* the term or *reporting* it. Only the *use* of the term involves the presupposition.) So when B says of A that A is a felon, B and A may be inferred to be subject to the same system of commissive conformity. Similarly, the other terms of 13.71 presume a common conformity. The most essential feature of acts of characterizing (the reference back to the characterizer) is exemplified in the use of (b).

We could extend these remarks even to canon law and to systems of religious belief or dogma. **Heresy** is a term on all fours with **felon**. If I charge A with being a heretic, I presume that he and I are committed to the same system of belief. Only on that condition does the characterization have any significance other than a mere report. Clearly **heresy** is a characterism.

A further feature of characterization that is confirmed is the reluctance to apply the terms to oneself here and now. However, if a subject countenances such an application he will seek to weaken its implications or to dismiss it as a mere *report*: "I'm what *you* call a criminal or felon." He may go so far as to renounce a previous conformity by saying, "I'm not (or no longer) bound by *your* laws." No one willingly applies the terms to himself now unless he can accompany them with some sort of claim to self-extenuation: "I can't help myself... I'm getting even... I'm doing it for D," and so forth.

The principal deviation from other characterisms among the present set is that we seem to have very precise definitions for them. In fact, however, the terms of (b) are exceedingly general, and precision among them is somewhat illusory. For example, the law may not be precise as to the difference between a felony and a misdemeanor, and where in the past precision has appeared to prevail, closer attention reveals that the terms may be entirely circular in definition. Thus a felon was defined as one who committed an act for which he forfeited his possessions; and a felony was defined in terms of the kind or degree of punishment meted out for it. But since forfeiture and punishment are subsequent to the crime, any act might conceivably count as a felony if it was severely enough punished. Of course, no one is accused of a crime called 'felony' but of a very specific act such as murder, which presumably can receive a precise definition. No one, however, is presuming that **murder** is a characterism. We may say, therefore, that these terms are of the same degree of indeterminacy we have attributed to other characterisms.

We consider finally the appraisives in 13.72. We are now even more plainly in the region of characterisms: assuming commissive conformity, offenders under (b) sooner or later may be brought to the conviction that they have indeed broken the law, or if not, they may say that there was a miscarriage of justice. In both cases, their commitment to the social substance can stand unimpaired. If, however, they are charged in the offensive terms of (bb) they may readily accept the characterization if they are prepared to make their way outside this or perhaps even any other social order or alliance, If, in the previous cases, we had a parallel in **heretic**, here we find it in **infidel**. We may ask, what crime has the infidel committed? The answer is, in terms of ordinative conformity, none: we have reached beyond the limit of crime in this common sense. Hence, the *compassionate* churchman in all times has sought either to persuade the infidel or to establish a *modus vivendi* with him, a condition that prevailed in the Middle Ages intermittently vis à vis the Arab and the Jew.

How, then, can we deal with the political infidel? I should think in exactly the same way. Wherever possible, he should be "bracketed out." But the problem is really not how to deal with those who wish to opt out, or to drop out, but with those who will not, those who wish to set only their own terms for remaining attached to the substance. This, however, cannot be permitted: the whole point of a social order is its transcendence of the individual.

The characterism **law-abiding** in (aa) lends itself to misunderstanding. The scope of the term 'law' here may well be the laws referred to in 13.71, that is under ordinative conformity. But the act of agreeing to abide by these laws is not itself an ordinary enactment of such laws: it is itself an act of commissive conformity. Thus **law-abiding** is first of all a characterism under 13.71, and this will generally comprise **law-abiding** (aa) as well.

The appraisives or characterisms of (bb) bristle with the anger of a social order that cannot come to terms with its heretics and so tends to push them over the line towards the infidels. Or one can also state the reverse: finding infidels in its midst, the social order seeks to treat them as heretics in order to punish them. The fact that the terms are imbued with such passion shows how bitter the struggle may be across the invisible line that is crossed and re-crossed when persons enter or leave a given social order, or any and all social orders. The entire vocabulary is presented from the standpoint of those who remain in the order and condemn those who depart. But the key word here is 'depart.' If there had truly been a departure, perhaps the passions would never rise to such a pitch. The fact appears to be, the departees have both departed and not departed: they have waged a kind of ceaseless rear guard action, or attacked the old order from within. The subtle variations on these themes are all reflected in the varied vocabulary of (bb).

This clearly is not a vocabulary of description. Neither is it a vocabulary reflecting readily adjudicable matters. If there *were* a law to appeal to, such bellicose situations would not arise. But this is inherently impossible. The

law arises in acts of commissive conformity. But if no such act has transpired
there is no recognition of law. Most societies seek as far as possible to
assimilate these "crimes" to the side of heresies, where they can be punished
within the bosom of the social order. The true rebel, desperado, pirate,
renegade, scofflaw, or above all the revolutionary, however, is not taken in
by this. He declines to undertake the act of commission or commitment or
refuses to honor it. As Locke saw, there is only one appeal, "to Heaven,"
and in the end, this is to say, to force. It is natural to expect a violent reply to
the violent characterisms of (bb). There is no general solution to this situation,
or perhaps the solution is, in one word, history, that is to say, the leapfrog
motion of one system of conformity replacing another in the process of time.

Yet in all these convulsions, one fact remains. The succession of convulsions does not show that acts of commissive conformity are superfluous, but
rather that they are necessary and virtually eternal. They are, after all, a
succession of – conformities! Anarchy is not so much absurd as in the end
impossible and inhuman.

To review this somewhat complex matter, we may observe again that we
have two orders of conformity. First, the laws or ordinances themselves
command assent. If we abide by the laws we engage in acts that are lawful
or legitimate, that accord with our rights and those of others. If we do not we
are subject to the characterizations of (b) as malefactors or felons, as guilty
of malpractices or misdemeanors, and the like. Second, if we not only fail
to observe ordinative conformity, but renounce all obligation whatever, we
defy the commissive conformity our particular social order has exacted of
us. We are now characterized in the much severer terms of (bb). It should
be repeated, however, that the vocabulary (bb) bears the impress of a social
order that *demands* this conformity although it is impossible to demand it of
right. In truth, such an order may at most *remind* us of a freely taken obligation. If we now convince ourselves that we must renounce the obligation, the
vocabulary of (bb) will appear to us to presume more than it dares. Ordinarily
many of the crimes designated in (bb) are punished as transgressions against
ordinative conformity. I may, of course, agree to be tried and to be punished
under this conformity. But a person who has renounced all obligation will,
if he is in a position to do so, refuse even to recognize the charge against him,
if it is expressed in terms such as (bb). Thus only heretics can rightly be
punished, but not infidels. Everything depends upon whether we agree to
be charged as heretics or not. The true infidel will refuse even to make a
denial of the charges, since a denial implies recognition of jurisdiction.

It is safe to say that the subtleties and complexities of these characterisms
exceed those of any others we have studied, and also that, for the individual
and his society, no others are of greater moment.

We have now surveyed the several areas of the material characterization of man. Man is of course not the only accusative of appraisal. In the appendices we consider a number of others. We turn now to the general moral characterization of man and to the summation of his character in the doctrine of virtue and vice.

14.0 VIRTUE AND VICE: INTRODUCTION

The appraisal of man's character culminates in the language of virtue and vice. Before proceeding to the exposition of this language in some detail, we may pause to trace some of the connections between moral judgment, as outlined in 5.0, and appraisal in the foregoing sections of Part Two. The theory of virtue and vice provides a link between the two.

We often speak of such and such a person being a good or a poor judge of character. In fact, however, it is not precisely character that we judge. As we have viewed the matter, to judge is to consider an *action* in the light of certain commitments and to be prepared to undertake certain actions in turn, for example, punishment or reward. In general it is not character that is punished or rewarded, at least not in a morally circumspect society. Punishment is itself action, and action such as this should only be elicited by other actions. We must then distinguish *judging actions*, which may lead immediately to return actions, and *judging character*, which may issue either in no action at all, or perhaps action only in the sense in which we act if we avoid contact with a person whose character we have judged adversely.

We need a clear distinction between appraising (judging character) and moral judgment (judging actions) because we are only a part of the time concerned, in evaluation, with questions of right and justice, which are the narrow concern of moral judgment. It is appraisals that we are more often concerned with, and these may have little to do with the weighty matters of the right or the just. In general, the accusative of appraising is the good, although this term serves only the purpose of linking appraisals together and is itself without material content (15.0).

At the same time, it is important to emphasize the close connections of appraising and judging. Although we do not, in our sense, judge character or institute return actions because of our appraisals of the character of persons, we do quite plainly regard their characters as bearing upon the quality of their actions. The judgment of the action must, in general, be corroborated by the appraisal of character. Favorable appraisal of character often wins mitigation or pardon for acts which, in other circumstances, are reprehensible. Extremes of punishment will be avoided unless the actions of the person appear to issue from a character irretrievably corrupt, defective, or deformed.

But the reverse is not the case. Unfavorable appraisals may or may not be corroborated by actions that are themselves reprehensible: they run the gamut from "hunches" and "intuitions" that may be sound, but may also on the surface be scarcely distinguishable from superstitions, to well-founded insights into dispositional properties regarding probable or possible actions and habits. To be sure, we should always remind ourselves to be alert to "evidence" for appraisals, although this is not the evidence we demand for the truth of assertions. We should take the trouble to learn the skill of appraising as we do other skills. But the point is that skilled appraising cannot always point to palpable actions or to regularities or patterns of actions. What it is that is here called for has now been set forth, I hope, in the exposition of the vocabularies of appraisal in the foregoing sections of Part Two.

The distinction between judgment and appraisal becomes clear when we see that the ultimate issue of appraisal is the virtues and vices. The outcome of judgment is, in the extreme case, the doom of an individual, whereas the outcome of appraisal is a summation of the person's character in terms of his virtues and vices. These are in turn appraisives themselves, or certain of them that are singled out for emphasis. Since, however, virtues and vices do not bear these respective labels explicitly, the screed of them set forth here may appear somewhat arbitrary. For while the appraisives are all "there" in the language waiting to be identified, the particular emphasis that elevates some of them to the "pantheon" of the virtues and vices must needs reflect the author's ear for what is most highly and emphatically appraised.

Finally, an important source of connection between judgment and appraisal should be mentioned. Throughout the preceding sections we have made use of the division of appraisives into attributives, substantives, and processives. This distinction is not always critically significant because what is expressed now in one form can often by grammatical transformation reappear in either of the other two. The numerous forms that may thus variously appear are generally too obvious to deserve specific mention. But there is also a significant difference among these three classes, particularly the processive in distinction to the others. Quite commonly what is being appraised by the processives is acts or actions, the very subject of moral judgment. As a result, characterization by means of processives may often have a seriousness by comparison with which characterization in attributive or substantive terms may appear aloof and detached. Such processive characterization may, in fact, amount to moral judgment. Here we not only allow ourselves the "luxury" of making up our minds about a person's character but also prepare to act, for example to reward or punish him.

Processive appraisives, since they are directed toward personal actions, thus play a role both in judgment and in appraisal. In judging we will always want to satisfy ourselves *both* about the person's character and his explicit actions, as we have already observed.

The presence of the processive form and the fact of the increasing emphasis upon man as a social being as we proceed to the tendentive, sex-related, sociative, and communitive spheres of appraisal thus add additional connecting bridges between moral judgment and appraisal to those already afforded by the virtues and vices.

A term will be taken to be a processive here (independent of possible transformation to other parts of speech) when in fact it is used appraisively in verb form. Usually the strongest processive appraisives will be those in which the verb form is grammatically the fundamental. (Thus **fool** appears in etymologically fundamental and strongest form as a noun, **deceive** as a verb, although other speech forms are readily available.)

14.0 VIRTUE AND VICE

The final section in Part Two concerns the virtues and vices, both those especially derived from the foregoing areas of characterization and those that are more general and ultimate. Before we take up these topics we consider briefly a vocabulary of characterization in 14.01 lying between the previous areas and the virtues and vices themselves. As the previous areas bear upon particular types of virtue and vice in 14.0 so the area of moral characterization is of particular relevance to the general and ultimate virtues and vices considered at the end in 14.4.

A foremost purpose of these terms is to serve to characterize the habit and pattern of behavior and conduct of persons who have either been involved in or are exempt or exonerated from the moral involvements in 5.0. It will be observed that most of the discrediting terms characterize various degrees of human delinquency, whereas the crediting terms often affirm the negation of such delinquency (e.g. **impeccable, innocent**).

14.01 MORAL CHARACTERIZATION

CREDITING

ATTRIBUTIVE
blameless
creditable
decent
ethical
(**good** 15.6)
guiltless
honorable
impeccable
incorruptible
innocent
(**just** 5.32)
loathsome (15.2, 5.1)
meritorious (v. Deserv. 15.2)
moral
noble

praiseworthy (v. Deserv. 15.2)
reputable
righteous
upright
virtuous
wholesome
worthy a. and n.
PROCESSIVE
behave (eminent sense)
forbear

DISCREDITING

ATTRIBUTIVE	PROCESSIVE	SUBSTANTIVE
abandoned	misbehave	blackguard
amoral	misdemean	knave
arrant	offend	reprobate n.
atrocious	seduce	rogue
corrupt	sin v. and n.	ruffian
debased	transgress	scamp
delinquent	violate	scapegrace
depraved	wrong v.	scoundrel
disreputable		sinner
dissolute		villain
evil		
flagitious		
foible		
heinous		
ignoble		
immoral		
incorrigible		
infamous		
iniquitous, iniquity		
malevolent		
monstrous		
nefarious		
outrageous		
peccable (=liable to sin)		
perverse		
pravity		
profligate		
sinister		
scurrilous		
sordid		
squalid		
unethical		
vicious		
vile		
villainous		
wicked		
(wrong a. 15.6)		

The creditings and discreditings of persons take on an increased tone of seriousness as we proceed from the characterization of the intellect in 6.0 to that of the community in 13.0. It is not surprising, therefore, to find a class of general characterizations of persons that, at least when discrediting, have a quality of finality about them. But, as may be expected with such general and ultimate terms, of which we shall have much more to say in Part Three, they say little or nothing of a material character. The appraiser simply sets a final stamp or seal on the appraisee, as if to say that he knows what to expect henceforth from him morally (5.0) and otherwise (6.0 to 13.0).

The counterpart of the moral characterizations of 14.01 is to be found in the general and ultimate appraisives of 15.0. In 15.0 the range of application of the appraisives is unlimited; they may be applied in aesthetic appraisals and even in cognitive and logical contexts; they are not narrowly moral in significance, although this may be one of their uses. In 14.01 we confine ourselves to appraisives which are virtually confined in application to persons. It is only persons who can be blameless, blameworthy, innocent, depraved, infamous, wicked, and so on. The exact classification one way or the other, however, may be left to the reader's judgment: it will generally not be difficult to find occasional applications of moral characterisms to subjects other than persons. It goes without saying that, being general, the terms of 15.0 also readily find application to persons.

To the extent that the characterisms are the culmination of the foregoing body of material characterisms (6.0 to 13.0) they present a much less awesome face than they do when we confine our attention wholly to general commendatives such as **good**. For now, by the device of referral or recursion back to the body of material characterisms, we have a clue to their significance.

We shall be brief in our treatment of these terms. What is really weighty in them will be taken up under the discussion of the virtues and vices particularly in the final section on general and ultimate virtues and vices, 14.4, since the substance of these is based upon the moral characterisms of the present section.

The vocabulary of 14.01 could be expanded or contracted at will: the list is full of near synonyms. There is not much to choose, for practical purposes, among the several crediting attributives except emphasis: **decent, good, wholesome, worthy, honorable, just** and **upright**, like all the others, are significant only if we are referred to more material characterizations already considered. Some terms are scarcely to be distinguished from the general deservatives (see 15.2), e.g., **reputable. Righteous** is now thought to be obsolescent, except in phrases such as 'righteous indignation'. **Ethical** and **moral** have seemed to gain currency as moral characterizations in their own right, although properly they might well have been excluded from such use (if anyone really had anything to say in such a matter) and confined to the definitions 'pertaining to ethics or ethical matters' and 'pertaining to morals and moral matters' respectively.

A few terms are clearly only negations of vices, e.g., **blameless, guiltless, innocent, sinless, impeccable**, and **incorruptible**. As usual, the discredits do not praise the contrary of what the virtues or creditings praise: they say virtually the same thing, for they condemn that which deviates from positive values. The vocabulary is to be explained by reference to concepts already considered. Where the terms are virtually commendatives the burden of assigning significance to them is on the user thereof.

As noted, a principal source of the commendatives in 14.01 is observation of the moral involvements of persons set forth in 5.0 or their degree of innocence of reprehensible involvement. We have postponed consideration of them since they fall so essentially and climactically under the characterization of man of Part Two. Many of the descrediting terms are employed to characterize either ingrained habits or passing episodes of actions subject to moral judgment, particularly in their outcome (5.22).

We must also turn back to the material characterizations of Part Two if we are to support moral characterizations. Little perhaps can be said of a man's *character* if we consider only his *intelligence*, although the knowledge he has, to a high degree determined by his use of his intelligence, certainly bears on the outcome of all his moral deliberation. We move forward, then, to *judgment*, which can play a more decisive role both in determining the person's ability to make practical and utilitarian decisions as well as in the areas of counsel, discrimination, and arbitrament. Yet even here, we will make allowances for moral errors if there is demonstrable incapacity of judgment. In the third area, *behavior*, we begin to see rudiments of moral thought. We expect a certain level of seemliness even though local variances in this respect are enormous. The fourth area, the *tendentive*, at least in our society, is of unmistakable moral importance. Effort and enterprise are necessary to the conduct of life, and the terms, *effort* and *enterprise*, are themselves readily recruited as appraisives. This area is largely defined in terms of the individual person's effort, and would thus *prima facie* appear to have a maximum of moral relevance. (Who should care if *I* do nothing whatever to care for myself but give myself up to voluntary neglect and starvation, if I am not a parasite on others? But if there is a *we* of which I am a part, my lack of resoluteness in face of danger rightly earns me the sobriquet of *coward*.) Next, the area of *sexuality* has always provided a ground for moral credit and discredit, as has already been noted at length. As we turn to the final areas of the *social* and *economic* it is evident we are at the very heart of what has moral relevance.

Taking discredit as more forceful than credit, if we now ask, what wickedness, what evil is, we can only answer that if we wish to make accusations of this sort we must be ready with apt characterizations of the person's failures in relation to his community and indeed to the very idea of community, his aggressions against others, his self-assertiveness in sexuality and ambition, his misuse of his intellect in the pursuit of any of these ends, and so on, or literally hold our peace.

We may now proceed to the doctrine of the vices and virtues in order to show what may be salvaged from it for present day purposes. This will place the substance of concepts of the present section in a larger framework and complete this part of the theory of appraisal.

(A) *The Scheme of Characterization.* We have surveyed the appraisal and characterization of man in his several aspects, as follows:

Intellectual	6.0
Intelligence	
Judgment	
Communication	
Constitutional	
Behavioral (Figure, Motion, Body Response)	7.0
Diathetic (Temperament, Mien, etc.)	8.0
Tendentive (Volitivity, Enterprise, etc.)	9.0
Social	
Sex-related	10.0
Sociative (Ascendancy, Submission, Accommodation, etc.)	11.0
Economic	12.0
Communitive	13.0
Moral	14.01

Each of these has appeared to stand more or less apart, but in fact each aspect of man has but a relative independence and must be thought in relation to all the others. All of the characterisms under these headings taken together afford only a partial picture of the range of appraisal. They cannot by themselves fully evoke the realities of actual appraising, which resorts also to numerous other means of expression.

We began this inquiry by an intuitive choice of the vocabulary of appraisal, a choice made as far ranging as possible. The divisions are those that have appeared, in the course of our scrutiny, to be those most appropriate to this vocabulary. Of course there may be more worlds and more dimensions to man than this. There is, for example, a notable absence of all concern with history in this scheme. The reason is that there appears to be no explicit vocabulary for the appraisal of man as an historical being of any extensive sort. There are, no doubt, certain *general* appraisives that figure heavily in history: **significance, importance, greatness, influence, prematurity** and numerous others. But they are not exclusively historical appraisives.

Historians may reject the very thought of anything's professing to be history that is couched in the language of value judgment, explicit or implicit. But history is first of all concerned with the affairs of human beings. It is hard to see how one can speak of such affairs without characterizing the events that men participate in and that can scarcely even be thought of without them. To speak of men, the interpersonal processes they are involved in, and the causality and responsibility pertaining to their actions is unavoidably to characterize them. Given the clues to what constitutes characterization in the vocabulary assembled here it is easily demonstrable that the history of human beings is never written without appraisal of their actions. Nor is it a matter of argument since one can show it simply by reading virtually any page of reputable historians. Elaboration of this theme cannot, however, be taken up here.

We have undertaken two serious tasks (among others even more important): identification and choice of value terms, and classification and articulation of them under a general scheme. Every science has the same kind of decisions to make. Even the identification of what is physical and the subject of the physical sciences is by no means obvious to the naked eye – choices and distinctions must be made. Every science must hammer out such divisions as seem appropriate, the divisions are not always clear-cut, logical, exhaustive, and made according to a single principle of division.

(B) *The Relevance of Virtue and Vice.* The first question we consider about the virtues and vices is why and how we encounter them in this discussion. We must see what is peculiar about these terms.

One might say that what we have been concerned with all along is virtue and vice in man. In our age the terms 'virtue' and 'vice' have an old-fashioned air. Are they, then, necessary to introduce or to perpetuate in a discussion of value at the present time?

The first thing we must notice is that nothing essentially new is introduced with the mention of virtues and vices. The terms given in the subsections of 14.0 have all actually made their initial appearances before, in sections 5.0 to 13.0. What we are now doing is singling out certain of the characterisms of these sections for emphasis and labelling them virtues and vices in accordance with long tradition. Thus wisdom, fortitude, temperance, and justice (or better, σοφός, ἀνδρεῖος, σώφρων, δίκαιος, or the same notions in substantive form) are the classic, cardinal, or natural virtues, and faith, hope, and charity are the theological or Christian virtues. This makes a pat scheme of seven, always a lucky number. But what we need are not lucky numbers, but an understanding of what we are doing in appraising and what emphases are necessary in the vast throng of terms we employ. We must not make of these concepts little demigods of language that are altogether useless except to be installed in a series of stained glass windows. The class of virtues, if we are to continue to use the term, must embrace a much larger store, and we must appeal to something other than worshipful tradition to justify their being accorded any kind of eminence.

I believe subsequent considerations will justify our perpetuation of the notions of the virtues and vices. When we look back over the characterisms of 6.0 to 13.0 we see that they are already divided into crediting and discrediting types. In principle, and by definition, every characterism is devised, so to speak, in order to reflect credit or discredit on a subject. Some characterisms, of course, are somewhat ambiguous, and some of them can shift their allegiance from the side of credit to that of discredit, or the reverse; we have no space to examine the concepts in greater semantic detail than is necessary to help us understand the processes of appraisal, characterization, judgment, and the rest. With this in mind, we may say that in general all the credits are virtues, and the discredits vices. Since no new terms are being introduced, if we now single out any terms as pre-eminently virtues and vices, these can only serve the purpose of a necessary emphasis.

The elevation of the virtues to prominence has also a more momentous result, namely that it contributes to the analysis of the general and ultimate appraisives of Part Three, which we shall presently undertake. We hope to correct the habit of moral philosophers of confining their attention to the most general and ultimate of our appraisives, and to draw attention again to the centre of all moral philosophy, the theory of characterization and of virtue and vice. The concepts of Part Three, taken apart from Part Two, to say nothing of Part One, are trunks and branches without roots and without earth to stand upon. The tree of value must first be seen as a seed that sprouts in the earth before it reaches out in every direction in space. There must first of all be a study of virtue and vice.

(C) *Meaning of Terms.* We must now take up the explication of the terms 'virtue' and 'vice.' We notice that rather different things are often brought to mind by the use of the singular and of the plural forms of these terms. If we speak of the virtue*s* and vice*s*, first of all a body of terms such as we have in the natural or theological virtues seems to be meant. The virtues are set forth as supreme ends or ideals of conduct which with suitable effort we may realize in life. Similarly the vices are identified as an underworld of horrors that beset or are perpetrated by weak and wicked human beings.

The singulars of these terms are also somewhat varied, depending upon whether we speak of virtue, or a virtue, of vice or of a vice. *A* virtue or *a* vice, we may presume, is but an instance of the foregoing, the virtue*s* or the vice*s*. This leaves us, then, with virtue *tout court*, and vice. We must first glance at the history of these terms.

Popularly, the term virtue has hovered somewhere between a characterism and a descript in the category of sexuality. In a journalistic sense, we are led to believe that what remains of virtue is a vanishing attribute of the single girl. Curiously, the very virtue that has been exacted of the female is named by a term that is manliness itself; *vir-tus*, derived, of course, from L. *vir*, man or male. (This sense of actual force or power is preserved much more strongly in Spanish *virtud* and French *vertu*, than in our *virtue*.) In Greek, ἀρετή derives from the name of the god symbolic of all male power, Ares, or Mars. What was evidently intended by the application of the masculine term to the female was, therefore, the identification of a property that was as central to a female's maintaining her proper and indispensable position in the human society as was the corresponding property in the male to his own. Only by a woman's purity and fidelity could the male be certain he was siring his own offspring. Therefore, he valued these properties in her as highly as the power to beget in himself and even designated them by the same name. Female virtue is thus directly linked with the oldest uses of the term, but it is itself a late and Christian, evidently not an ancient Roman or Greek, use of the term. Ancient peoples also, of course, valued this property but under other names, such as L. *castus*.

The foregoing has led us informally into the central significance of the term 'virtue' from which its implications for value theory are derivable. When we go back to ἀρετή, or to *virtus*, we have the idea of "active quality, power, strength, efficacy," and of the "capacity to effect a definite, specific result," to paraphrase Webster and Wyld. Everything has, in other words, a function. From this Plato proceeds to the idea of a thing's purpose or good; ἀρετή is the link between what a thing is and its value. Each thing in its kind has a form underlying it and embodies a unique power or potency. If it is allowed to act in accord with this, it acts by nature, acts as nature intended it should act. Otherwise it is a thing weak, distorted, or monstrous.

These two senses of 'virtue', as *function* and as *good* persist into modern speech. For in addition to the first sense, active quality, power to effect a result, we also have virtue as the conformity to morality, as excellence or worth or value, and indeed this is now its foremost sense. (We even have in English and French the usage that is so evident in Plato: "in virtue of.") I shall provisionally distinguish these two uses of the term respectively as the *functional sense* and the *appraisive sense*. If under *virtue* we think of the efficacy or power, the faculty or capacity inherent in a thing, that is virtue in the functional sense. If we inquire after the value or worth of it or its conformity to right or excellence, that is the appraisive sense of the term. As we proceed we shall offer a view of the relationship between these two.

(D) *Virtue and Vice: Functional and Appraisive.* We shall now develop an application of the distinction. If we turn to the virtues which we have identified (the responsibility for the choice, of course, is our own; there has never been any systematic method of establishing virtues as virtues), we see in 14.0 a number of terms which differ from their previous appearance in Part Two in most cases only in form. In all cases in Part Two we have cited terms in that one of their parts of speech which is basic and original and from which their other forms are derivative. (For example, **obstinate** appears instead of **obstinacy**; **boor** instead of **boorishness**.) Now we must observe that custom has decreed that the virtues and vices shall be named by abstract nouns. A, a subject, is acute or creative; the virtues are identified as acumen or acuity, and creativity or creativeness. The same pattern is to be observed in all of 14.0.

We ask something very different when we ask whether A is acute and when we ask what acumen is. (We cannot merely follow the advice of a dictionary. We would be much richer in linguistic creativity, though not in resource, if there were no dictionaries to stand as sources of eternal dogma. Dictionaries are but makeshifts to correct the wretchedness of our education and memory.) Though we may have no hesitation in saying A is acute, we shall ordinarily pause somewhat longer before we venture to say what acumen is. The problem acquires a kind of "metaphysical" character from the Platonizing capacity of European languages all of which have devices for turning every adjective (if not indeed every other part of speech) into a noun. Once this is done, the word sits in remote and splendid isolation as if it harbored some great mystery within itself. And while the capacity to nominalize (or "substantize"?) is not what Platonism as a system of argument rests on in the end, it certainly contributes to its power.

Must we take these terms so seriously and with all this solemnity? We may be inclined to detonate such monoliths. Is there not difficulty enough with explaining the use or behavior of, say, **acute, wise,** and **seemly** without adding the unnecessary difficulties of a "metaphysics of language" involved in such "beings" as have been made of **acumen, wisdom,** and **seemliness**? The feeling men have professed to have about the virtues is akin to ancient reverence for the gods, and indeed some of the virtues and vices enjoyed a status such that the name of one was virtually that of one of the others. If we can now divest ourselves of such superstition about these forms, what purpose do they or may they yet serve?

To answer this question, we turn to our distinction. Although all our credits have some claim to being virtues, and our discredits to vices, we can identify fairly easily some of them as especially deserving of these titles of nobility by asking what it is that we most esteem under intellect, judgment, and the rest of the categories. When we ask what we esteem under intellect, we ask what work it does, what its power is, its capacity to effect a result: we are asking what the function of the intellect is. We are told perhaps that its function is to understand. To understand is an accomplishment, an achievement, a successful outcome. What then do we need in order to understand? The answer is reliably given in the virtues listed: acumen, creativity, imagination, and the rest. We ask in short after the *function* of the understanding or intellect, and we see it made precise in these appraisives or characterisms of the intellect.

But we have also another sense of virtue, the *appraisive*. We may illustrate this by reference to another area of characterization. When we turn to 14.31 we see the behavioral and sex-related vices and virtues apparently stated only in highly moralistic, that is, appraisive terms. What has happened to the virtue of sexuality, certainly an indefeasible aspect of man's nature, in purely functional terms? This does not seem to have appeared at all. We shall examine the reasons for this below. For the present, we are merely pointing to examples differentiating the appraisive and the functional sense of the term virtue, here displayed in strikingly different examples.

The virtues and vices derive from that which we most esteem or deplore about a person's intellect, judgment, and other powers, and from the most significant and abiding traits of the person. Such traits generally have been thought to constitute a person's *character*, whether estimable or deplorable. We shall give some further consideration to this notion at the end of Part Two. In dignifying anything with the name of a virtue or a vice, we must think of it in reference to the relatively stable and continuant properties of the person. If something is a vice, this is more than a mere lapse or shortcoming. If it is a virtue, it is more than just a passing episode of success or accomplishment. We always mean that the χαρακτήρ is deeply graven.

We shall divide the virtues and vices among three large classes, the intellectual, the constitutional, and the social, as follows:

Intellectual Virtues and Vices	14.1
Intelligence	14.11
Judgment	14.12
Communication	14.13
Constitutional Virtues and Vices	14.2
Behavioral	14.21
Diathetic	14.22
Tendentive	14.23

14.1   INTELLECTUAL VIRTUES AND VICES

The virtues and vices of intellect form a fairly distinct family comprising intelligence, judgment, and communication. It is evident that intelligence and judgment are almost unthinkable for us apart from communication. The threefold division is not intended to ignore this fact. Its aptness on other grounds is obvious: communication must, of course, be presupposed in other areas, particularly those touching the social order.

14.11   VIRTUES AND VICES OF INTELLIGENCE

acumen	**eccentricity**
imagination	**obscurity**
originality	**obtuseness**
profundity	**shallowness**
subtlety	**stupidity**
wit	

Considering now the intellect more closely, we ask first about the possible addition of further terms from 6.1. In all cases we should refer back to the appropriate characterizing vocabulary: the present choice of virtues and vices from among the earlier vocabularies may sometimes be rather idiosyncratically my own. (In this and most succeeding subsections, virtues are listed at left and vices at the right).

It is evident that we will seek the virtues largely if not wholly under the *attributive* terms of 6.1. A few of the *substantives* may, however, suggest further intellectual virtues or vices, for example, **genius, foolishness**, and **pedantry**. There is no reason to exclude these if we think them central to intelligence. **Genius** as a personal substantive might also be placed among the general virtues (14.8). It is a term of immense breadth but it is shallow, a circumstance that does not, however, diminish its power in what might be called the learned vernacular. **Pedantry** is indeed a kind of vice, but since it conjures up mainly the thought of special professions such as the legal and academic, it scarcely deserves to be considered among the vices of the intellect as such. Of fools there are so many sorts that the meaning must be left to the context. This is not to deny that intellectual foolishness may not be a fairly readily identifiable vice of a rather broad sort. In general the other substantives seem roughly provided for by the terms of 14.1.

If other concepts from among 6.1 were to be added to 14.1, I would first suggest **fatuity** since it adds a high-flown note not sounded by **stupidity**. **Ingeniousness** may seem to fall as much or as often to judgment as to intellect. What it says may be inadequately covered by the present panel of virtues and it may therefore deserve special mention. Among the rest, I should be mildly inclined to dignify **inscrutableness, nebulousness** and **triviality** with the name of vices.

The terms for the virtues and vices of the intellect help us to set forth the nature of it in what we have called the *functional* sense. We are thinking of the intellect as theoretical intelligence, the capacity to understand, to devise explanations, whether this be a capacity exercised by the professional or the layman. All men must grasp explanations, even if they are weak at devising them. We set forth these outstanding traits (virtues) as intellect in the functional sense, that is, as delimiting what we expect of an intellect that *works*, that accomplishes what it sets out to do. If we ask what *it* is, if we ask by what right we carve out this phase of our thought as if it were some kind of self-contained unity, the answer can only be indirect: that we do discern the kinship of all these appraisives and characterisms. If they do not say what intellect is, nothing else does or can do so.

It is also evident that this body of terms as generally used also answers the *appraisive* question about the intellect. Insofar as the intellect can be taken apart from all other areas of appraisal, the virtues, or credits, serve to provide the only possible answer to what one *ought* to do with the intellect, and the vices, or discredits, what one ought not to do with it. If this now is met with, "And *why* would we use intellect in such a manner as to receive these plaudits?" the answer has to be flat and uncompromising: You are pretending to be satisfied only with hardheaded answers, when in fact what you are asking shows that you either don't know or are feigning not to know what the term *intelligence* means. The question is irrelevant and incompetent. To say someone has intelligence *is* to attribute a virtue to him *pro tanto*. To say, "'tis a pity he's intelligent," is absurd except if said in relation to some other enterprise the subject is engaged in.

We shall assume here, as elsewhere, that the negations of the virtues generally count as vices: **lack of creativity, acumen, subtlety** and the rest. Certainly these do not redound to the credit of the subject. On the other hand, negations of vices may yet be far from outright virtues: *not eccentric* and *not stupid* may not be significant commendations, hardly even faint praise.

Intellect is thus a term that is by no means a neutral descript, nor is it a mere substantive or class name like 'ship, or 'elephant' or 'carpentry.' To speak of an intellect is necessarily already to speak in normative terms. Nothing functions as an intellect except properly or improperly, and what this means is set forth schematically in the virtues and vices of the intellect.

14.12 JUDGMENTAL VIRTUES AND VICES

astuteness	captiousness
consistency	credulity
discretion	folly
liberality	prejudice
objectivity	
reasonableness	
sagacity	
sensibility (sensitivity)	
wisdom	

It will not be difficult to select from among the characterisms of 6.2 those that have at one time or another served as virtues or vices. The craft terms in 6.21 name traits that are unambiguously virtues of the judgment, but they are rather easily employed in selfish concerns. From among **astuteness, canniness, cunning, discretion** (the better part of valor, we recall), and **shrewdness**, we have limited our choice to **astuteness** as most commonly capable of serving as a virtue among these.

Some of what we have said of intellect allows itself to be readily reformulated in application to judgment inasmuch as the line between these two is not always easy to draw. Where the intellect is devoted to general explanations seeking ever broader, more powerful hypotheses, judgment concerns decisions in reference to particular cases: procedures to be followed, diagnoses, classifications, discriminations, decisions, applications, choices of courses of action, and the like. To be endowed with judgment is to have good judgment and poor judgment is simply want of judgment. The nature of judgment in the functional sense (which is more fully shown in 6.2) is schematized in the virtues, as here detailed. For the same reason as in the case of intellect, the appraisive and the functional expositions are again one and the same.

If we can segregate judgment from all other faculties, and to the degree that we can, the possession of it is in itself an asset of character. But this must always assume that other things are equal, and makes assumptions about the kind of issue brought before the bar of judgment. As we saw in 6.2, some judgments essentially show concern for the self. But a general asset of character should show no such limitation. For this reason, *astuteness*, with its strong self-inclining implications is a virtue only in a qualified sense. The others, however, have the most general import, and would thus be full assets of character. In the same way the vices of **credulity** or **gullibility** would mainly tend to harm the individual, whereas the vice of **prejudice** might have the most untoward results for others. It would therefore constitute a much more serious vice.

What we call judgment is an accomplishment or an achievement just as the intellect is. Hence to say what it is, what its function is is to say how it is conducted at its best. Its function and the appraisal of the function are one and the same. This identification will not prove to hold in all areas where virtues are celebrated, as we shall see.

14.13   COMMUNICATIONAL VIRTUES AND VICES

conciseness	**mendacity**
eloquence	**nonsense**
sense	**obscurantism**
truthfulness	**prolixity**
	sententiousness

We confine attention to these few virtues and vices. Because we seem to be able to set communication at some further remove from the person than we are intellect or judgment, we judge the person and the product apart from one another. We often think we or others are capable of some kind of thought which however resists getting itself clearly expressed. Usually the matter is merely left hanging so. One cannot quite say that "language" is to blame – language is always *somebody's* language and is as clear or obscure as it is made. On the other hand, how the person can be clear without showing evidence of it is also a mystery. In the end we shall have to acknowledge both the person and his discourse as characterized by these virtues and vices – this at least is how we speak. But it is the person that is in the end decisive.

Conciseness can be a virtue of discourse and **prolixity** a vice, in the functional sense distinguished above, only to the extent that concise discourse does and prolix discourse does not communicate. But this is evidently not a strong sense. Somewhat the same must be said of **eloquence** and **sententiousness,** or perhaps the case is slightly stronger. It is often urged that the simplest modes of expression are the most effective, that is, communicate most or best. And it is often quite obvious that simple language is also the most eloquent. The speeches of Lincoln are often cited. Pretentious, sententious and overblown language likewise may be said to communicate little. But in none of these cases is the matter so flatly put as in the opposition between **sense** and

nonsense. Clearly these traits most squarely identify a virtue and a vice of both the person and the medium of expression. The case is very strong.

We should consider, however, that sense and nonsense apply largely and perhaps exclusively to discourse that seeks to convey knowledge or information. Communication, we are therefore assuming, is essentially confined to this in the present context. Some will object to this, of course, insisting on other avenues of communication besides those mentioned: artistic, poetic, perhaps even mystical modes of expression. These may of course be quite properly called modes of communication. All that we must observe now and rather insist upon is that there is no vocabulary for successful and unsuccessful expression in these domains of expression that compares with the two powerful appraisives we use for the success or failure of *discursive* communication.

In this instance, then, I would say that **sense** and **nonsense** quite evidently set forth the virtues and vices of communication in the *functional* sense; they state their very essence. But it is equally evident that they do so also in an *appraisive* sense. Nonsense by its very nature must be avoided, if one is pretending to communicate. Of course a comedian has other uses for it, and if he communicates, it is on another plane.

This, I think makes matters as plain as they can be made about communication as discourse. But since our ultimate subject is man, we must ask also whether these are virtues and vices of man, whether they touch his character. To put it strongly, is the habitual utterance of nonsense, for example, a defect of character? (I can only say that my own fondness for the commodity prevents me from being consistent about it.) The vices of communication *can* become vices of character if they are conjoined with other vices, for example vices of aggression and deception. Congressional filibusters might serve as examples.

14.2 CONSTITUTIONAL VIRTUES AND VICES

As the name indicates these virtues and vices pertain to the response of the person to his environment with feeling, purpose, and effort as determined by deepseated or even innate endowments and powers. The areas comprised are the behavioral, diathetic, and tendentive.

14.21 BEHAVIORAL VIRTUES AND VICES

seemliness	unseemliness
propriety	impropriety
becomingness	carelessness

We may first remark on the slight awkwardness of the term 'behavioral' for some of the characterisms and consequent virtues and vices in this class. Clearly, behaving is a *doing* of something, even if it is what is called doing nothing, whereas this class of terms must embrace not only processives but also some physical attributives (such as **hardy, rugged, robust, puny**) and attributives relating to dress or appearance (such as **frowsty, unkempt**). All the others are, however, appraisives of acts. The name of the class serves more of a designating than a descriptive function. It may also be remarked that 'behavior' may often embrace much more than what is being characterized by these terms.

If we ask, what are the behavioral virtues and vices in the functional sense, the readiest answer that will be suggested is that they have no such sense. In the preceding section, we could say that (in the appropriate sense of 'communication') if p made no sense it simply did not communicate. Making sense constitutes communication; it is its very function, and in that sense its virtue. (Different kinds of sentences may of course, make sense in quite different ways.) Is there any such thing to be said about behavior as constituting its essence? If there is, it may have little to do with the characterisms of 7.0 or the virtues of the present number.

We do, however, definitely accept and reject certain forms of behavior, and the characterisms of 7.0 are the first evidence of this. We find that we have definite opinions on the shape of human bodies (**rugged, plump, puny**), their attitude or motion (**loiter, loll, lounge**), their appearance (**neat, unkempt**) and so on through agitation, facial comportment, and ingesting.

But although we have definite opinions on these matters and express ourselves vigorously, the important question about behavior is whether the *processives* (particularly) are saying that the body or the person is functioning well or ill when credited or discredited. What we *intend* to say by these terms is that certain kinds of behavior do and others do not exhibit what may *properly be expected of* the body engaged in fundamental tasks and operations. One may readily agree that it is strange that mankind should come to such conflicting conclusions as to *what* is proper. But there cannot be very much doubt that the convictions enshrined in our vocabulary that some kinds are proper and some are not are widely shared. (How widely is a matter for empirical investigation.)

The processives of 7.11 (as applied to the body) seem clearly intended to discredit a pace that falls below some norm for speed of motion. Motion as slow as *that*, they seem to say, will hardly count as an effort toward carrying out some purposeful end agreed to be desirable. In 7.21 a movement that appears agile or nimble appears as one uniquely suited to a certain kind of body, no doubt a young one. Awkward, clumsy, fussy, poky, and restless movements, given certain ends, fall short of advancing the body in achieving such ends. In 7.23, motion that is boisterous, berserk, or frenzied is discredited because there is thought to be no good reason or excuse for it in its context. (We may of course attach such purposive conditions since the only behavior we are concerned with is guided by purposes.)

But certain of these characterisms do not at all lend themselves to functional interpretation. The alternative we recall is to regard them as "purely appraisive." In this case I think we must attribute to them something very close to an aesthetic function. The attributives of the body and its appearance (7.11 and 7.12), and certain others that are fairly easy to identify are of this sort. These are concepts that are remote from any bearing upon the character of their subjects. It is inevitable that the external form of man should be subject to appraisal from several points of view.

The point now is that, if the concepts we have proposed under the behavioral virtues and vices are properly chosen, the range of meanings for the characterisms will afford us a key to the application of these concepts to behavior. The virtues of behavior, we suggest, are propriety, seemliness and becomingness. (The same terms could also reappear elsewhere, e.g. among the diathetic virtues.) I believe these concepts do sum up what we are meaning to convey in most cases in the characterisms of 7.0. Those that are more doubtfully subsumed under them are the various "aesthetic" appraisives and those that are closest to being descripts rather than appraisives, for example, most of the attributives for physical figure (7.11), and for movement and locomotion. (Shape and size of the body *can* be functional.)

Of course one could easily extend the list of behavioral virtues and vices by mentioning those characterisms that are simply very prominent in certain times and places, for example, **cleanliness** (next to godliness), and **abstemiousness, voracity,** and **dissipatedness.** But this is scarcely significant.

We can see how adequately **propriety, seemliness,** and **becomingness** set forth the appraisive force of terms in 7.0 if we limit attention to those which are least descriptive and are most plainly appraisive and characterizing: **dally, dawdle, loiter, slouch; frowsty, sloppy, unkempt; boisterous, bedlam, pother; gawk, ogle, maunder, screech, whine, smirk, snicker, snivel, leer; bolt, gobble, guzzle, glutton, dissipated.** With these to guide us, we may see whether the others fall nearer the appraisive or the descriptive side. These may also serve to test to what degree behavioral vices (and virtues) are susceptible of a functional interpretation.

The behavioral characterisms and their corresponding virtues are obviously not as simple as they appear. We have perhaps succeeded in hinting at a number of problems they raise.

As we have noted, the behavioral virtues and vices are partly coextensive with the diathetic. We shall now undertake consideration of these.

14.22   DIATHETIC VIRTUES AND VICES

(a) **good temper**	(a) **ill temper**
equanimity	**irascibility**
cheerfulness	**misanthropy**
(b) **vivacity**	(b) **sloth**
(c) **self-confidence**	(c) **diffidence**
(d) **frankness**	(d) **affectation**
simplicity	**deviousness**
sincerity	
(e) **graciousness**	(e) **vulgarity**
(f) **dignity**	(f) **stodginess**
	frivolity
(g) **humility**	(g) **pride**
	vanity

Before we endeavor to identify the most prominent virtues in 8.0 we may again cast a rapid glance over this section. Not all the concepts in 8.0 seem altogether characterizing. Especially 8.11 (Moods and Tempers) has many terms by means of which we would rather seem to *describe* the apparent present state of the subject. If we think his mood is anywhere outside a certain norm or average, one way or the other, we may say he is either cheerful (or some alternative) or morose (or some alternative). What we naturally or normally expect is some fairly colorless "normal" condition. The positive terms (**cheerful, exuberant, merry,** etc.) seem to take note of a buoyancy of spirit but without giving any strong sign of crediting (cheerfulness may irritate), and the negatives behave in corresponding fashion. Some of the negative terms are virtually discrediting, such as **mope, maudlin,** and **mawkish,** but they may be a little closer to actual behavior terms than moodwords. No actual virtues or vices emerge here.

The terms for *temper* on the other hand are definitely crediting and discrediting. That is, we not only take note of the subject's temper but think of it as good or ill temper; and we characterize the subject in terms of equanimity and irascibility, leaving no doubt that the conditions characterized are crediting or are not.

This gives us reason to number the most prominent of the concepts under temper as virtues and vices, while at the same time no vices or virtues emerge from the preceding moods. We have thus the virtues of **good temper** and **equanimity** and the vices of **ill temper, irascibility** and **misanthropy**. (It is not necessary to offer a defense of just these as virtues and vices, for our purposes; they are obviously representative of the group of characterisms from which they are drawn.) Moods are of course passing episodes, sunshine and shadow, but tempers are a lasting, if not indeed, as popular thought makes them, permanent and indelible dispositions to act, behave, and respond emotionally. This is consistent with the virtues and vices characterizing character.

With *la condition humaine* (8.12) we are again dealing with concepts that do not directly lead to virtues and vices. They are of course the most deeply human of all the concepts we consider, being all of them built on compassion and concern for human well-being or misery. They are, as it were, the end product of the person's commerce with his world, determined by the larger world of which he is a part and by the unique response he has made to it. The appraiser's role here is quite different from the customary one of appraising. He sees himself to a degree sharing the subject's place and situation. The place of the terms is therefore rather special. It is a matter of opinion whether one wants to put **malcontent** and **misanthrope** here or among the tempers, although we have placed **misanthropy** among the vices since it may also appear as a moodword.

The *temperaments* (8.13) again present a picture different from the foregoing classes even if we discount altogether the medieval psychology and biochemistry in which they originate. The line between temper and temperament need not be carefully defined. Perhaps one may say that while temper is an *emotive* disposition to behave, temperament is a disposition that reaches beyond the emotive to the *tendentive* and other ways of reacting to the environment. As we pointed out in 8.13 the predicates other than the humoral (**choleric**, **phlegmatic** and **sanguine**) are more definitely characterizing, and so might, if anything depended on it, be thought of as virtues or vices, most likely the latter.

We turn now to a larger source of virtues and vices, the characterisms of air, bearing, mien and manner. These fell into five classes; and the virtues and vices among them might include the following:

Vivacity-Placidity
   vivacity   ‖ **sloth**

Confidence-Diffidence
   self-confidence   ‖ **diffidence**
   humility   ‖ **conceit**   **pomposity**
                                    ‖ **haughtiness**   **pride**
                                    ‖ **impudence**   **vanity**

Sincerity-Pretension
   frankness   ‖ **deviousness**

simplicity	**affectation**
sincerity	**pretentiousness**
Presence	
graciousness	**vulgarity**
Gravity-Levity	
dignity	**frivolity**
	stodginess

I shall again not seek to be too precise in trying to identify virtues and vices. Let us take the five classes separately.

Although in the title **vivacity** is opposed to **placidity**, if we are seeking a vice corresponding to vivacity it is not difficult to find, for it is one of the seven deadly sins, *sloth*. This is the concept among the discreditings which appears to have most to do with character. While other virtues or vices may also be suggested here, I think these will suffice for our purpose. Perhaps **spiritedness** (Plato's θυμός) might be preferred to vivacity.

We must immediately observe that although we have here, as in the other four classes, made room for a fourfold division of characterisms, **vivacity** (or **spiritedness**) and **sloth** represent only the positive-credit and negative-discredit classes. These are the most numerous classes. The negative-credit class, represented by **quietude**, and the positive-discredit class, represented by **flamboyant**, and **tenseness** scarcely do more than round out the logical possibilities. Their having only a representative or two suggests that the weight of tradition is squarely behind the approval of **vivacity** and the disapproval of **placidity** and its kin terms – a most significant feature of our system of values, confirming at least superficially our Occidental attitudes toward action and inaction. We shall have occasion to remark in much the same vein on the distinction of other virtues and vices in this large class.

In the next division, **confidence**, or perhaps **self-confidence**, naturally opposes itself as a virtue against **diffidence**. The two remaining classes are also well represented by characterisms. First, we see that a considerable array of gently crediting terms is represented among the negatives: **modesty, reticence, meekness, humility,** all of them receiving the approval of Christianity and also other faiths. Second, the positive side comes in for some share of discredit: **impudence, haughtiness, pomposity, conceit,** and **vanity**. Certainly no screed of the received vices could afford to omit **vanity**, and perhaps this vice may serve to represent the whole class.

We notice that a tempering force in the form of the negative-credits has been at work to tame the sanguinity of **self-confidence**, which might easily extend itself wildly. And it is worthy of note that the official morality of te

Christian world ("blessed are the meek") though always assailed *in fact*, throughout history, received little explicit intellectual challenge before the nineteenth century. It is obvious that a basic division, schism, or antinomy has prevailed in our moral thought. Even if this may not mean that two moralities have asserted themselves they often represent extremes in each other's eyes. The diagram represents their cross currents:

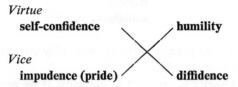

Virtue
  self-confidence   **humility**

Vice
  impudence (pride)   **diffidence**

Assuming **diffidence** to be a vice (the vice may also be phrased in stronger terms), the diagram shows plainly that virtues are always compatible with, are simply the inverse way of expressing the corresponding vice, standing diagonally opposite. To praise **self-confidence** is to scorn **diffidence**; to praise **humility** is to scorn **impudence**. The real moral struggle lies in the will to maintain confidence without impudence, and humility without diffidence, or worse. This struggle has been felt throughout the Christian ages. Only in the past century has the gospel of self-confidence, even of impudence, sought to assert its exclusive moral "right." "According to what standard is objective value measured?" asks Nietzsche, and answers, "According to the quantity of increasing and more organized power alone." (*Will to Power*, § 674.) And he repeated the same theme a hundred times over. But if this in some ways makes a virtue of impudence, in our time a counter current has set in motion, not indeed enough to stem the tide of "power" but to assert a full alternative to it. This is the gospel that makes diffidence a virtue. Both of these repudiate the classic Christian view that the way to virtue lies in tempering self-assertion and yet in asserting oneself in the world and doing its work, taking care lest the assertion issue in pride and the tempering in weakness.

   The kinship of all this with the tendentive needs only to be remarked. It is not easy to draw the line, but in principle it turns on the question of how internalized these modes of response are thought to be. Here we are thinking of them as having always an inward seat. In the tendentive we think more of the public role of the individual and less of his expression of himself and his feelings.

   This exposition of pride and humility may enable us to be briefer with the remaining virtues and vices. **Sincerity** and **pretension** involve the idea of the congruence of the outer and inner person. Some of the source of this would of course have to be sought elsewhere, ultimately in the logical idea of truth and falsity. It is, however, fairly plain from the very fact that two corners of the fourfold alternative (8.23) are unfilled or nearly so, that there is little doubt of the necessity of those values. Frankness, simplicity and sincerity are always appreciated, although as we learn from Thrasymachus' view of the virtuous man, he may be thought a fool or simple-minded. All that this shows is that there is a streak of cynicism that may be more widespread than we suppose. In the same way, everyone may think it wise to suspect every other person of deviousness and pretense, but he simply cannot think of these in crediting terms no matter how much he may in secret admire "cleverness."

Much the same may be said of the virtues and vices of presence. One is occasionally forced to look through the externals of crudity and vulgarity to the genuine and honest diamond in the rough beneath. But this is commonly less in actual admiration of a crude exterior, which may remain offensive, than it is of a detected virtue of insight, intelligence, effort, or forthrightness of communication. This removes the matter to another sphere. Turning to the other side, the simplest of intelligences is generally able to recognize genuine grace and charm though often deceived by mere exterior suavity and pretense. No one, however, is likely to praise the vices, except ironically and cynically. As in the foregoing case, sincerity if indeed sincerity, cannot but evoke admiration, and its full contrary contempt.

Finally gravity-levity evoke a similar approach. Real dignity is praised and frivolity condemned. But we have learned from innumerable sources (including the psychoanalytic) of the vices of false dignity and of the grim determinants that often lie behind stern and unbending attitudes.

The question that finally emerges is what picture of man from the constitutional side arises from the virtues and vices so stressed and on what its authority rests or appears to rest. We see the definite emotional profile or character of a person emerging from the pattern of the emphatic virtues and vices. Such a person maintains himself as a distinct entity with a "place" that is unassailably his own only through self-confidence and lively alertness and responsiveness to his environment. He must always remain in command of himself, must not let events take command of him, and evidence of the latter will be shown in his failure to cope with his situation. This will readily reveal itself to others in what they see as ill temper, irascibility, or sloth. Moreover, "putting himself through" (*sich durchsetzen, durchhalten*) will predictably come to an end through diffidence or frivolity. Vanity and affectation will be evidence of weakness. A person in command of himself, on the other hand, has nothing to fear from others and can reveal himself and frankly and sincerely. Regardless of adversity he cannot but earn the applause of others for his internal equanimity and confidence and for his dignity. We have, in short, the ideal of the confident and happy man. When such an ideal falters it has been for want of opportunity to realize it. Whether it will not only fail of realization but lose its magnetism as an ideal only the future can tell. The hopeless and helpless person in an urban, mechanized environment has problems unlike those of his ancestors.

14.23   TENDENTIVE VIRTUES AND VICES

(a) **pluck** **resoluteness** **spontaneity**	(a) **foolhardiness** **recklessness**
(b) **caution** **circumspectness**	(b) **fickleness** **truancy** **vacillation**
(c) **audacity** **constancy** **perseverance**	(c) **fanaticism** **pigheadedness**
(d) **fortitude** **courage**	(d) **pusillanimity**
(e) **industry** **patience**	(e) **sloth**
(f) **competence** **prudence** **resourcefulness** **temperance**	(f) **ineptness** **intemperance**

We turn now to the area of the will of man, to his energy and drive and power to assert himself. In some sense it is life itself and therefore cannot surprise us in turning up as a major area of characterization. The full alternative to it is nothing other than death. But between life and death we cross so vast a continent that it is the relative directions rather than the termini themselves that are definitive of difference, the directions namely of turning toward inaction or ataraxy, or toward motion and growth.

We are told that the will is evil by Schopenhauer. It springs from need and thus from suffering. Only in rest is there well being. The subject of the will is bound on Ixion's wheel, or he is forever struggling like Tantalus with no end to his effort in sight. The will cannot cease its urge any more than time can come to an end. And if we can overcome it, the outcome is annihilation, nothing. The closing sections of Schopenhauer's *World as Will* turn towards mysticism and towards the religion and philosophy of the East. In our time discontent with "Western Civilization" has led many to turn in the same direction or to seek still other ways of "dropping out."

Virtually none of this is reflected in *our* language. The function and thus one of the virtues of man is seen in effort. The young poet may say,

> Ach, ich bin des Treibens müde!
> Was soll all der Schmerz und Lust?
> Süsser Friede,
> Komm, ach komm in meine Brust!

But the author of *Faust* finally says,

> Wer immer strebend sich bemüht,
> Den können wir erlösen.

Individually, we occasionally may be weary of effort, exertion, *Treiben*, but the pace is set by those with energy, drive, *Streben*. This is western man's or one can say, echoing Spengler, Faustian man's version of one of the cardinal virtues, the functions of man. Is it and must it be definitive of him? This question should prompt us to appraise once again the multitude of patterns of living, some energetic and some virtually somnolent, from the energetic syndrome of European civilization now felt at the ends of the earth to the passivity and pacificity associated with the Orient and Polynesia. Must it not, in the end, be a relative matter? There cannot fail to be effort everywhere in some degree, but its intensity varies greatly.

Variance of effort seems a safe enough generalization. But western man has only begun to divine the ominous changes in store for him if he should ever learn how to harness fully the energy of mechanical and electronic slaves and to put them at the service of an automated economy. But just as, hitherto, sexuality has been linked only with reproduction, so the tendentive has been wholly associated with the assurance of survival. Suppose for a moment that work and effort are made obsolete by the machine. How will human energy be expended? We have seen one remedy for this eventuality evolve in the past century and a half. Its name is sport: sexuality and tendence threaten to remain only in athletic form! Since both are immense reservoirs of energy, their survival is scarcely in doubt, but their form is still in an evolving state. The paradigm of a soul that has lost its occupation, its reason for effort, in a word, its proper work, is an engine such as the "exercycle," a treadmill infinitely more degrading than the stoop labor of the peon. The lesson is, if there is nothing tendentive, it is necessary to invent it. It is fortunate that witnessing sports spectacles, with their immense displays of power and effort, inspires empathy and uses up the interested grandstand observer's energy in what appears to be almost the same degree as the players'. What is obvious is that society must make provision for the tendentive when its traditional channels begin to vanish, and the development of sport in this century and in the closing decades of the last indicate the kind of provision that has already been made.

It is said that the golden age of leisure is but a mirage and that the supply of food and other necessities is not superabundant but actually is falling behind need and demand. This may indeed be true. There is no proof that such an age must come. But the fact is it can come and the phenomena that attend its advent, that is, the substitution of sport for work as an outlet for effort, do not wait for the perfection or full realization of the age of automation. What is fairly certain is that for the foreseeable future the substitute phenomena will increase to a vast degree. This is sufficient to show what needs no proof, at least in this society, that effort is creditable, other things being equal.

We turn now to the particular qualities that appear to have been most celebrated in this respect and that appear functionally as virtues. As before, the clue to the virtues of this side of man is to be sought among the characterisms. What are singled out as virtues differ from the characterisms as such in that these seek to characterize individuals, individual actions, and states and episodes of individuals, whereas virtues are inherently generic in intent. Man, and man at his best, it is thought, will exhibit such and such virtues. The "best" here is simply the fulfillment of function: the appraisal and approval expressed is inherent in such fulfillment. To identify the virtues we therefore turn to those characterisms that are applied to the more than passing states of this or that individual. But no hard and fast line can be drawn here between two vocabularies. A person's specific actions or behavior may be characterized as resolute, fickle, or timid (perhaps even excused in the latter two cases), but we also single out **resoluteness** as a virtue and **fickleness** as a vice. When we do so we are singling out traits of character that are seen as particularly in accordance with or incompatible with the tendentive *function*.

What we now encounter more or less for the first time in our series of areas of characterization, is not just traits of character, or even manifestations of these in behavior but the *actions* of persons. Since, as we have seen, these are what we find ourselves committed for or against, tendentive characterization, when negative, can virtually become an accusation and thus bring in its train the procedures of moral judgment.

We cannot suppose, as have emotive theorists from Hume onwards, that such accusations are mere name-callings, that they merely show that the speaker has suffered a feeling of offense. When one reflects on the matter, is not Hume's emphatic pronouncement on the nature of vice altogether incredible!

When you pronounce any character or action to be vicious, you mean nothing, but that from the constitution of your nature you have a feeling or sentiment of blame from the contemplation of it.*

* Hume, *A Treatise of Human Nature*, Book III, Part I, Section I.

No one will honestly admit that he regards another's behavior as discrediting merely because he himself has felt offended or has had his sensibilities or sensitivities wounded. Something else must be or appear to be offended. So indecent exposure, emphatically treated as a source of offense in Western society in, say, 1900, if not thought quite so serious now, was thought an offense against the office and function of sexuality in a civilized community, a distortion and perversion of it. Even more so, no one can really think that dastardly acts are merely acts which disappoint *our* feelings, wishes, and wants. What we wish to say is that such acts are offenses against reponsibilities and commitments. So the dastardly or cowardly act is an offense against a whole tissue of circumstances in which trust and reliance have first been evoked and then frustrated or destroyed.

To have a purpose is self-evidently to be determined to bring it to fruition. To maintain this determination *is* to show courage and resoluteness, to be patient of adverse circumstances, and to falter in this determination *is* to be variously fickle, foolhardy, timid, indolent, cowardly, dastardly. Once these are expressed as substantives (**courage, timidity, fickleness**, etc.) their power seems curiously enhanced. They have assumed the status of deep-graven characters, or stigmata. The archaic psychology inherent in this must not be viewed as reducing the whole vocabulary of virtue and vice to nonsense. Rather it compels us to seek other explanations and explications, as for example, the present one of treating virtues as ways of expressing convictions about man's unique essential functions.

The distinctness of functions and thus of families of characterisms and of virtues often leads to familiar human tragedies. What, we may ask, is courage and patience without intelligence? The possibility of exercising all the tendentive functions without intelligence and good judgment is as tragic as the contrary possibility, impotent and irresolute intelligence and judgment. There are characterisms that tend toward a union of these functions. We see these among the characterisms of Capability (9.31) and Management (9.32). We have there enclosed in brackets a number of these that have first appeared under judgment (6.2): **astute, canny, cunning, shrewd, wily, befuddled, bemused**, and perhaps also **adroit, aplomb** and **prudent**. Judgment here appears to be heavily in service to volitivity and purpose. However, this is not surprising. We remarked of judgment earlier that it is in general concerned with action and arises out of the necessity to act. We must still think of it as having its place alongside of intelligence and as arising from the necessity of appealing ultimately to intelligence, to the understanding (ultimately theoretical) of the nature of the situations before us in our enterprises. But if judgment has or needs intelligence at its back, it is equally evident that its face is turned toward the necessity to act.

It should be remarked that divorce between volitivity and intelligence is as fertile a source of comedy as of tragedy. Intelligent irresolution, and resolute stupidity are sources for both, for each of these characterizes but a half or a fraction of a man. In this "honest or well intended halfness" Emerson saw the essence of the comic.* But deficiencies also characterize the indubitably wicked men of history. Examples are too numerous to mention.

The keynote of the whole class is purpose and the several virtues and vices reflect the postures that may be taken in accordance with or in some way contrary to purpose. The term purpose here is preferable to will although purpose is certainly the area in which what is called the will is exercised. Inasmuch as life virtually *is* will or purpose there is no need to argue the essentially functional nature of what we have credited as virtue.

We may also observe that what is considered here is essentially personal purposes. Social, sociative, and communitive purposes are scarcely possible or thinkable without presupposing these. Of course, even the social virtues must in the end be personal, but their reference to others or to the community is not directly involved in the tendentive. This may best be illustrated by considering the vices **cowardice** and **dastardliness** which do not appear here although **courage** and **cowardice** are familiarly coupled as virtue and vice. If we reflect on the matter we see that cowardice presupposes a community which one belongs to. One may display a weakness of ardor for or dedication to his own cause or purpose, but it is an error to speak of this as cowardice: a cowardly or dastardly deed is first of all a betrayal not of *my* cause but of *our* cause. If *I* am not part of a *we*, I do not deserve to be declared coward or dastard if I fail to further its interest.

Such vices, and corresponding virtues, may also be genuinely and sincerely applied to enemies. When they are, they charge a betrayal of ideals which can somehow be shared even with enemies, which transcend communitive and national lines: codes of chivalry, military honor, gentlemanliness, good sportsmanship or the sporting chance, *bushido*. The very appeal to such virtues amply demonstrates the awareness of a *Gemeinschaft*.

We may review briefly the emergence of the tendentive virtues and vices from the characterisms. Classes (a) and (b), both the virtues and the vices, are cut from the same fourfold piece of cloth that has appeared as Address. Obviously praising resoluteness and pluck is virtually doing the same thing, in the same or another context, as condemning vacillation; and caution and circumspectness and similarly related to foolhardiness and recklessness. The virtues in (c), **ardor, constancy, courage**, and the like, are closely related to those in (a). As already noted their corresponding vices are not **cowardice**

---

* Emerson, R. W., "The Comic."

and the like, but rather miscarriages of ardor such as **pigheadedness** or fanatic conduct. Thus these vices should be carefully distinguished from those in (a), such as **foolhardiness**.

Sloth, which has already appeared as a diathetic personal vice, reappears now as an even more deepseated aspect of character: a failure of nerve, of the sinews of purpose. The remaining negative characterisms suggest only the most pallid of diversions.

As we have remarked, man frequently faces tragedy through discoordination of intellect and purpose. The virtues of enterprise, particularly **competence** and **resourcefulness**, come as near as any terms we have to expressing their effective coordination, and **ineptness** the contrary. **Prudence** may be thought of in close connection with such virtues. This brings us finally to **temperance**, which deserves somewhat more extended consideration.

Temperance, a celebrated Classical and Christian virtue, was sometimes thought to be peculiarly a virtue of appetite. Without examining this in detail we must yet think it extraordinary that the virtue of appetite is the restraint and thus in a degree the negation of appetite. But if the virtues are expressive of the proper functioning of capacities, why must one suppose that appetite must inherently deserve negation? As we saw with sexuality, our system of morals has failed to accord a unique virtue to the exercise of this instinct, with far-reaching and often deplorable results. But the matter is not improved by suppressing the instinct, or piously and didactically propounding a negative virtue as proper to it, or again by abolishing all caution or restraint on the instinct.

Temperance has been placed in an ambiguous position: it is to be the virtue of appetite yet unlike the other virtues it is not to signify the advancement of the capacity it is used to characterize. Thus it finds itself in the position of being a policeman while posing as a patron, a phenomenon not unfamiliar in our world. Temperance can only be freed from this plight by recognizing a larger sphere of authority for it: not narrowly the satisfaction or negation of appetite but the conduct and management of life in which appetite is but one large ingredient. It is the virtue characterizing the manner in which decisions are taken in the conduct of life, portioning out the person's energies in various directions. The unlimited indulgence of appetition or emotion is a characteristic intemperance but so also is the limitless extension of intellectuality and ambition in persons and peoples. Thus the temperate person is a balanced person.

This exposition of temperance as a virtue of will and decision is closer to Plato's than to the Christian view. There is no thought of an ascetic suppression of appetite in Plato: medieval practices of this sort would have horrified him. Plato thought that σωφροσύνη, or what we call temperance should be exercised by all persons not just those in whom bodily appetites are strongest. Temperance is the virtue characterizing governance: it is self-control. Every citizen must be master of himself or he can be of no consequence in the true state.

What we have in mind as temperance – it may often be closer to prudence or even wisdom – is a virtue that presupposes the centrality and authority of purpose as an indefeasible part of man's being. It will be interesting to see whether the philosophy of man that may underlie cultures markedly different from the Occidental truly affirm a less tense and purposive way of life, or whether they merely direct effort just as sedulously in other directions.

14.3   SOCIAL VIRTUES AND VICES

The tendentive and sex-related areas are easily interchanged in this series: some of the tendentive presupposes the social fabric, and it takes no extensive argument or doctrinaire adherence to Freudianism to show that sexuality is essential and constitutional. The order of the larger divisions is thus not to be treated as inflexible.

14.31   SEX-RELATED VIRTUES AND VICES

purity	**concupiscence**
chastity	**lecherousness**

The brevity of the roster of the sex-related virtues and vices should not be thought of in a manner to underestimate their power. No characterisms have had greater force, unless possibly those relating to aggression, presently to be considered.

The astonishing thing about sex-related characterisms and vice and virtue is, as we have seen, that there is not one word, that is, no single word in English that flatly endorses the phenomenon. There is nothing to suggest that it can culminate in a definitive maximum of physical satisfaction. There is no suggestion enshrined in a concept that such satisfaction is fairly universally sought after. The virtues traditionally characterizing the phenomenon seem anything but functional: there is no suggestion that the sexual phenomenon may be an achievement in the sense we have been employing here, or even a suggestion that the occurrence of the phenomenon and the maximization of its occurrence may, in some society, be thought to be a good. If such thoughts have been thought, and obviously they have, they have never in our culture been thought to name virtues, nor the want of them vices, so far as the official enshrinements of language are concerned. But in the popular thought and pornography of the post-Victorian, mid-Freudian era in which we live voices have been heard that praise the phenomenon itself. No doubt there are new characterisms and virtues and vices in the making. I am not judging this want of positive evaluation of sexuality in Christian culture adversely. There is no point here in our taking a stance regarding this, one way or the other. It is the *facts* of evaluation that we are concerned with; not the evaluation of our evaluations.

There is one area, however, in which sexuality has received, in general, positive and crediting appraisal, namely in that one of its effects which is the production of offspring. The Old Testament injunction to be fruitful and multiply is, of course, an indirect endorsement of acts necessary to this fruitfulness. When we turn, as we now in this century so easily can, to the art and culture of so-called primitive peoples and observe the vast effort expended by nearly all such peoples on the insurance of fertility, we can see how much closer the springs of our tradition are to the general custom of mankind than we ourselves are. Fertility until this century has been thought good nearly everywhere and always. To that extent sexuality has also been declared good. Yet the Christian centuries have for the most part said no, or said so only reluctantly, if at all, or *sotto voce*. In general the virtue that has been allowed to sexuality is like the negation, temperance, which is sometimes regarded as the *virtue* of the *appetites*. Thus the functional sense of virtue is entirely set aside. Sexuality is no virtue or function of man as man; only intelligent, end-controlled, restrained, and somehow unerotic sexuality is to be praised, if at all, and it is intelligence and prudence that are the virtues.

I believe that this is, however, not as strange as it sounds. On the face of it, only the negation of sexuality is virtuous. But another interpretation is probably more proper. The Christian tradition for its own reasons (none of them to be traced to the four Gospels) insisted on ignoring the hedonic factor of sexuality. It was a contingent, concomitant fact, to be sure, but so was the fact that there were two sexes and not three or more, or that the phenomenon seemed to flourish only in certain parts of the life span and not in others. Hence sexuality simply received a more confined definition: to be fruitful and to promote maximum fructuation were the goods of the phenomenon, but to enjoy it was perverse. Suppose killing animals was a particular pleasure for the human species. Institutions might still deplore this pleasure while praising the production of meat for food. The sexual phenomenon in time came to be surrounded with numerous institutions and responsibilities (marriage, the family, the age of consent, avoidance of incest) and it was in terms of these that virtues came to be defined. Thus **concupiscence** and **lechery** could be vices, and **purity** or **continence** virtues even when **fertility** might itself enjoy very considerable credit.

What has happened to challenge this is that whereas formerly the hedonic factor was incidental to fertility, now fertility tends to become incidental to the hedonic. As it becomes even more incidental and finally eliminable at will, the phenomenon is even more identified with all the tradition thought corrupt and lascivious. In this manner sexuality quite literally returns to its equivalent in German, *Lust*, that is, pleasure. It cannot then be any longer spoken of as the *lust* of standard English, for this is, or was, a vice.

It is all too easy, in unison with the journalistic "Freudianism" of many current periodicals, to join the incessant flaying of the dead horse of Victorian mores and with it the way in which two thousand years of Europeans came to terms with the phenomenon of sexuality. Seen from the standpoint of the breadth or narrowness of the definition of the phenomenon, the traditional Christian virtues obviously make full sense. The fact is that man now has a different phenomenon to live with, made different by the techniques of physiological control of fertility and also, more importantly, an urgent need to control fertility. It is as yet too early to say what new virtues and vices will now evolve. Sexuality, including especially, its hedonic aspect, never seemed to appear in the form of a *function* the realization of which was a way of man's achieving an integral part of his humanity. What was functional was rather fertility within certain social bounds and within the framework of a certain definition of man. It is not surprising that this should appear restrictive from the standpoint of the new sexual phenomenon. From this standpoint the traditional sex-related virtues and vices are never geared to the *functional*, they are always only narrowly appraisive and invariably negative. As we have said, a new sexuality will breed new virtues and vices. It is also easy to overestimate the magnitude of the so-called sexual revolution.

It is important to notice that the virtues and vices under the diathetic could conceivably preserve their validity under any sexual regime once it developed its own institutions. We should again recall the moral regime in *Brave New World*.

Wherever we are identifying virtue and vice we are entering the domain of functions that are absolutely necessary to man and that individually and collectively we can scarcely think of man as lacking. We cannot think of him as only an intellectual or a cognitive being, or a physically and emotionally responsive being, or a sexual being. Each of these taken by itself and without the presupposition of the presence of the others (and of those not yet explored as domains of virtue and vice) will turn out to be a caricature of a man. Though mankind owes immense debts to virtuosos of thought and of feeling, for example, it may nonetheless think them somewhat absurd, unless the virtuosity is truly awesome and unless it fully obscures wants in other directions. Each virtue then, as we have said, is an integral function of man, and to approach a proper perfection of such function is to deserve the most positive and crediting appraisal. We have shown that the successful exercise of intelligence is the fulfillment of human function in this important respect. The emotional life of man, on the other hand, is a thing of such profuse variety that it is more difficult to spell out what an emotional norm for man must be. As we look over the credits and discredits of behavior and the emotive constitution, we see that the trend of appraisal in English favors an equanimous temper, is compassionate of human affliction, and encourages a lively, confident and straightforward manner.

In the instance of sexuality we seemed at first to find no proper recognition of the necessary place of the phenomenon in the life of man. But once we see that it is our age that has increasingly identified the hedonic element in the phenomenon as its essence, whereas previous ages have summed it up in very different terms, we see that the vocabulary of virtue here as much as elsewhere has sought to draw attention to the essential and the functional and that of vice to exhibit what is malfunctioning. If sexuality is conceived of in broad terms so that the phenomenon is not just sexual acts but includes the entire cycle of conception, gestation and nurture and the institution of the family, then the sex-related characterisms reflect accurately what western man has regarded as the virtue, in the sense of a *function*, of sexuality. The repudiation of these virtues, or functions, by the newer attitudes of a freer sexuality is in part owing to the separation of sexual acts from their causal consequences in birth. From this standpoint, pushed to its extreme, the virtue, in the sense of a proper functioning of sexuality, would be the maximization of its sensual satisfactions both in quantity and in variety. If one goes as far as proposed moralities, the connection of birth and fertility with sexuality is fully severed. In this outcome the virtue, the function of sexuality can be nothing but maximized satisfaction. Obviously no such an outcome, even if ever realized, will supplant older institutions overnight.

14.32   Economic Virtues and Vices

affluence	**avarice**
generosity	**covetousness**
honesty	**deprivation**
incorruptibility	**dishonesty**
liberality	**envy**
thrift	**extravagance**
	greed
	miserliness
	rapacity
	unscrupulousness
	venality

"Happiness," says Aristotle, "needs external goods [among other things], for it is impossible, or not easy, to do noble acts without the proper means."* We think now of goods and possessions in the broadest sense: air and space as well as food, water, clothing, shelter, and so on. Man is a physical being and to deprive him of a rightful share of participation in the universe of physical goods so far as he desires it, is in degree to reduce his participation in the life of the world he is born into, and perhaps to deprive him of life. Therefore, there can be no question that transaction with physical goods is a defining or functional feature of man and that possession of them is the source of a family of virtues.

All societies have had to reckon with the fact of relative scarcity of goods. We are as yet unable to say that this state of affairs will, or will not, continue indefinitely. It is, however, likely to remain. It follows that schemes for the allocation, distribution, acquisition, and possession of goods are always and everywhere necessary. Frequently, and most commonly, such distribution of goods has not been a mere mathematical division of goods but has been tied to other virtues: to distinction of birth, to service in the community, to industriousness and enterprise, and so on. The socialisms of the past century have sought to break down these marriages of convenience between economic wealth and other virtues, or alleged virtues. They have argued that wealth is good, and good for all without distinction, except when the individual voluntarily withdraws, if he can, from the whole proceeding, refusing both to produce and to consume. One of the appeals of socialism has been its resolute confrontation with the fact that if relative scarcity of goods is inevitable or endemic, unequal distribution can only aggravate the sum of suffering in society. Equality of distribution has appeared, therefore, to be the preferable alternative so long as scarcity prevails. Conceivably this may be unnecessary if the volume of goods is increased to a truly "affluent minimum," and beyond.

It is evident, then, that affluence or wealth is the prime economic virtue. To achieve it, individuals or their society must, as is the case with all virtues, exercise self-discipline, and this is true whether the society elects egalitarianism or ties access to wealth to the practice of other virtues or habits. In any event, affluence must be defined in something less than, and probably far less than, unlimited terms. Yet, of course, this is compatible with the maximization of virtue: one simply defines it in terms of the maximum available, which may vary from one community to another. But whether one elects socialism or not, it is evident that, given a confining scarcity in any degree, deprivation cannot even be coped with if one permits unlimited maximization of wealth at the personal level.

* Aristotle, *Nicomachean Ethics*, 1, 8: 1099ᵃ 15. See also *ibid*. X, 8: 1178ᵇ 30 ff.

It is evident that these are not merely narrow economic issues. They concern a prior identification and election of values, or as we are saying, a comprehension of the definitive and necessary functions of man that constitute his virtues. I believe this can be formulated in broad enough terms so as not to confuse wealth with the grasp for status and power. Western society, especially since it has set itself to perfecting the arts of production, inevitably breeds and sets up for emulation a type of person who can never find or define himself within the subcutaneous limits of his naked body but only in terms of what he eats and wears, his domestic environment, his manner of transporting himself, and so on. It should be emphasized that needful as shelter and food may be there is no reason to define wealth or affluence in mere physical terms which are in the end so often, if not inevitably, stupefying and brutalizing. In our society no one needs to be reminded of the virtue of wealth, but everyone needs to be enlightened as to the quality of alternative forms of it. Without shedding hypocritical tears, we may yet say that none deserve greater pity than those who can only define their function and virtue in terms of physical affluence. Man lives by bread, but not by bread alone.

There are three families of economic virtues established in our society as they are now reflected in English: **affluence, thrift**, and **generosity**. I leave **honesty** for a somewhat separate treatment at the end. Thrift is a necessity and not just a Puritan aberration. It follows from accepting affluence or wealth as a value together with recognizing the apparent impossibility of a limitless augmentation of personal wealth. The deprivation of others must accompany scarcity if one seeks to maximize wealth at the individual rather than at the collective level. It should be noted that thrift and its contrary, waste, may be no easier to practice or avoid at the collective than at the personal level. Yet progressively more and more of the economic processes in question are taken out of personal hands so that thrift *must* be practiced at the collective level if the community is to survive.

Of course, the virtues may change their quality somewhat in being shifted to a higher level and concern may rightly be expressed whether they at all survive *as virtues*. This is particularly true of generosity. It may be difficult to see how this virtue can even survive in collective practice if it is not learned at a personal level. Thus most societies which in the past effected a tiny redistribution of wealth through alms giving and "charity" have shifted to a redistribution through one or another form of taxation. But to pay taxes and to give alms are utterly different. This leads some to deplore the demise of the compassion evinced in generosity, and others to regard generosity as only a salve to guilty economic conscience. But it is probably premature to mourn the passing of occasions for generosity, compassion, or charity, that is, the virtue itself, *caritas*. It is overwhelmingly likely that despite a possible grow-ing revulsion at the accumulation of physical goods, affluence will in one form or another be a primary goal for persons and communities, and depri-vation a vice; that despite the paternalism of modern governments thrift will remain a personal as well as a social function and virtue, and waste and extravagance vices; and that despite the same collective procedures, gener-osity and liberality will remain as necessities of conduct, and avarice and miserliness remain vices. In fact the growth of collectivity can only expand the necessity of such virtues: the increasing complexity of production, the necessity of participation in the economic process, and the interdependence of persons make the cry of "let others take care of themselves" of simpler and more individualistic ages less fitting and more and more callous. But these virtues and vices may assume different forms in a new context.

We turn now to the core economic vices: **envy, covetousness, cupidity, rapacity,** and **venality.** The question is how these may be interpreted as a malfunctioning of economic process, or of participation in it, since of course we regard all vices as malfunctions. The first four (and there are, of course, other related terms) would seem to arise in differing ways in different societies. As we have said, in earlier ages access to wealth was restricted, rightly or wrongly, by convictions about other values or virtues such as distinction of birth. Here in some sense, an unequal distribution of wealth was either agreed to or acquiesced in. But even in such societies limits were recognized. If reliance on almsgiving to readjust inequities of wealth seems to us shabby, guilt-ridden, and stingy, it nevertheless springs from a recognition of such limits. For the rich to overstep *this* limit was then rightly characterized as covetousness, cupidity, and rapacity. Each person in such a society had by virtue of his being and birth a fixed place with an assigned right to wealth in a degree that had been assigned him on the basis of his function in the society (artisan, peasant, man-at-arms, nobleman, cleric, etc.). It is obvious that the vices just listed can by definition infect only the haves in society; these stand accused of having failed in the performance of the function assigned them. All such societies have problems about "fair shares," as indeed must all societies that are not programmatically and, one might almost say, fiercely egalitarian.

Modern industrial capitalist societies controlled by economic oligarchies, show even a little less imagination than the medieval state: allocation of wealth is made (by the "unseen hand") on the basis of giving the greatest share to those who, by and large, already have the greatest share. Unless measures are taken in good time, the vices in question, which can only grow ever fiercer, are inherent in such societies. It is not surprising that Marxists see these as inherent contradictions which by nature's dialectic lead to their own destruction. But of course numerous palliatives, applied in due time, appear to be able to outwit the dialectic almost indefinitely.

The logic of the egalitarian or welfare state (are there any pure examples?) seeks to structure a situation that makes these vices impossible. For if all persons possess equal access to wealth, none of them in particular deserves envy, greed or covetousness. Of course, if there turns out to be a Politbureau or Party which stands to benefit, ways and means of exploitation inevitably will be found and practiced. With this the old cycle begins again. These and the other vices here considered are diseases of social organisms. Public virtue is as difficult as private, since there are never wanting occasions that make the social body forget or misconstrue its function.

Finally, **venality** deserves special mention. It is, of course, of the same origin as the previous vices; an inordinate impulse to share in or to aggrandize one's share of a society's wealth is at the back of it. But its form is special. The individual is often guilty of a breach of trust in allowing that to enter into the market place which he has promised to maintain intact, far from such concerns. It is an economic disease unique to those who have received a particular trust: the judge, the doctor, the teacher, the public servant, the cleric. What is entrusted to their possession for specific disinterested purposes is turned into a commercial commodity. Thus the venal sets the limit of what may properly enter into the economic domain. The cynical "every man has his price" challenges the view that there is such a limit.

There remains the question of virtues or vices governing the transactions of exchange and ablation. In the narrowest sense economic exchange processes exist for the purpose of facilitating the access of persons or groups of them to available wealth subject to a more or less strict rule of reciprocity, which is defined in financial or monetary terms we need not describe here. It is evident that this access is subverted by departures from the rule of reciprocity. Any intentional departure is characterized as dishonest. Actually honesty and dishonesty have already been encountered at the beginning of this discussion in the more fundamental class of terms, **avarice, envy, covetousness, rapacity.** It is these that are the real vices here. That the value of X is not identical to that of Y for which it is exchanged is scarcely significant by itself, nor is the verbal form of honesty and dishonesty, apart from an intention to acquire a benefit and to deprive someone else of the same. We therefore regard dishonesty as a vice to the extent that it implies avarice and rapacity. For it is not a mere discrepancy but deprivation and the subversion of the system of access to wealth that condemns dishonesty. Beyond this, it may also be interpreted as a subversion of covenance and as a form of aggression.

The economic system is certainly the most "artificial" of the areas of appraisal we have covered. But it deserves to rank as partially definitive of man's being since it has long since, some thousands of years, become the formalized system by which man sustains his physical life. Even recorded European history is replete with examples of modes of acquisition that are pre-economic, where human life is cheap and acquisition is effected by simple plunder, pillage, rape, and theft of neighbors and their goods. We must observe that this is the terminology not of such ages themselves, but of the nascent economic age shaking off these habits and developing the economic dimension of human life. The tenuousness of the hold of this system is shown by the ease with which individuals and communities slide back into pre-economic habits. It is evident that the present screed of vices might not even be intelligible to earlier people. It is strictly devised to designate departure and deviance from the present system of economic exchange.

14.33   COMMUNITIVE VIRTUES AND VICES

In the subject matter of the sociative (11.0) and communitive (13.0) characterisms we reach what have always appeared to be the summit of the virtues identified and celebrated by Christian civilization (Judaeo-Christian would be more accurate) and reflected in the appraisives of English and probably all Western languages and still others. The institutions of government and social life owe a great deal to civilizations still more ancient than the Christian, in Egypt, Babylonia, and of course Greece. With Socrates, Plato, and Aristotle we reach a clear conviction that life in the community, the city, the state in large part defines man and thus prescribes his functions or virtues. If we speak of a distinctly Judaeo-Christian culture we do so because these two components have left even deeper marks: the moral awareness and the indignation of the Prophets, the warm compassion of Hillel, of Jesus and his followers. The assertion of "politicality" as man's differentia in the genus animal in Aristotle's definition of man is replaced in the Christian scheme of virtue by the assertion of the necessity for men to identify themselves with one another not only on the generic but on the personal level. Only in this way, says the Christian, has man finally achieved full humanity. Certainly, in this very term, the Roman *humanitas*, many of the conditions of the Christian ideal are already met, but *caritas* is something yet more, a love or concern for one's neighbor *as oneself*. Our version of the (very unfixed) list of the virtues, especially the social virtues, must certainly include and culminate in the virtues of compassion. These not only continue to hold their power in our time but assert themselves even more strongly in a world that must live with deadly threats and counterthreats, deterrents, and counterdeterrents: it is astonishing that more moving appeals to compassion are made in an age in which formal Christianity has declined than were ever heard in the centuries of its institutional dominance.

To see what must enter into our selection of the virtues we may first glance over the numerous classes of sociative and communitive characterisms in 11.0 and 13.0. As between these two classes the greater number of virtues is to be found in 11.0. In 13.0, only in the section on social comportment is there much to be found that touches the virtues very closely. The reason lies in the essential difference of 11.0 and 13.0. As we pointed out at the beginning of 13.0, 11.0 comprises the relation of individuals to one another and 13.0 the social fabric itself. But when one speaks of virtue and vice one must speak of individuals. To be sure, this may also be extended to the relation of individuals to the community, but virtue and vice, merit and guilt can ultimately rest only on the shoulders of individual persons. The virtues of communities, or the want of them, reside only in the persons of their members.

In 11.1, conflict is characterized but without *direct* reference to the individuals participating in it. 11.111 clearly involves the individual and indeed many, if not all, of the terms in substantive form (**impertinence, brashness, disputatiousness,** etc.) frequently serve to attribute vices to persons. Only pugnacity perhaps will sometimes serve as a virtue: the French army prided itself on *audace*, on *cran, élan, furor Gallicae, offensive à outrance*. One hesitates, however, to say that persons other than pugilists and those who follow the profession of arms would agree that there is much to be said for any of the other terms in 11.111 as the source of virtues. Indeed, in most cases it would be a simple self-contradiction to assert this. Only **sportsmanlike** offers a real model of a virtue. One ought not confuse the characterisms of contention and aggression with those of the class of tendentives. What we praise in acts of and in inclinations toward unreserved commitment and dedication to enterprise is already sufficiently set forth in 14.5 (Tendentive Virtue and Vice). The praise of conflict, contention, and aggression can only go beyond this to signify that the appraiser does not shrink from the wilful infliction of pain and even death in order to achieve his objective. It is interesting to note that the only way this can be done is to take the names of outright vices, and cynically rebaptize them as virtues. Men are such that after they have heard for a long time that they *must* condemn vice and follow virtue, they will eventually attend to contrary gospels extolling cruelty, fury, and frightfulness and condemning enfeebling herd– and slave-moralities (such as Christianity is said to be). But this can never succeed in the end: either it always remains a paradox as audacious as the praise of cruelty itself, in which case everyone knows fundamentally there is something essentially discrediting, not crediting, and shameful in it, or it takes a respectable place among the tendentive appraisives as sanctioning the use of such force as necessary, and no more, to gain compliance with what on other counts is thought just and needful. The use of paradox is widespread in all appraisal particularly in contentious times.

But of one thing we may be certain; paradox succeeds only so long as original usage, and so long as fundamental feeling in favor of the phenomenon survives. It testifies to the vitality of the phenomenon that is the target, not its impotence. We therefore take as a guideline for our thought that the use of nearly all terms in 11.1 as a whole to designate virtues is either paradoxical or it is an exaggerated effort to state the tendentive virtues (14.5).

COMMUNITIVE VIRTUES AND VICES

benevolence	aggressiveness
brotherliness	arrogance
charity	bestiality
compassion	brutality
concord	callousness
conscientiousness	cold-bloodedness
faithfulness	contentiousness
fidelity	contumacy
freedom	cowardice
humaneness, humanity	cruelty
humility	deceitfulness
kindness	derisiveness
long-sufferingness	evil-mindedness
loyalty	ferocity
mercy	fiendishness
pride	hypocrisy
self-effacement	malevolence
self-possession	malice
self-respect	meanness
trustworthiness	mercilessness
unselfishness	perfidy
	ruthlessness
	scurrility
	self-righteousness
	selfishness
	servility
	spitefulness
	tendentiousness
	unfeelingness
	vengefulness

It may be noted first that none of these is drawn directly from the characterisms of 13.0 but from 11.111, 11.3, and 11.4, Contention, Accommodation and Covenance. A careful survey of 13.0 will reveal very little that is promising so far as the virtues are concerned. Vice and virtue, we must repeat are personal and not the attributes of a *Gemeinschaft* or social substance, except perhaps in the case of **freedom**. Commonly, we do not wish to speak of anything as either a virtue or a vice unless it is somehow deep-seated. That is why the figure of the deeply graven mark has preserved itself in the term 'character', in numerous languages. Though we may agree with Aristotle that man is a political animal, a little reflection will show us that there is as much or more to be said for amending this to "social animal." For unless law-abidingness, for example, is a trait of character, we will be hard put to name virtues that arise solely out of the communitive-political area. On the other hand, terms for both virtue and vice abound in the sociative area. This is not difficult to explain. Only by long training and conditioning can men define themselves in terms of their political or legal allegiance or rank. What matters to persons is persons. This is no doubt disputed in all forms of Marxism, which tends to shift the locus of all virtue into the social-political area and would also tend to view the foregoing vices not as traits that stand on their own feet but as the consequence of political or class causes. I am content to say that the shape of vice and virtue as reflected in non-Marxist cultures is substantially as it is presented here. Man can and does define himself and his function in terms of his relations with other men, but not in terms of his invented political institutions.

As we survey the communitive virtues I believe we must make an important distinction between the Christian and the Roman virtues, as follows:

ROMAN VIRTUES	CHRISTIAN VIRTUES
benevolence	benevolence
concord	brotherliness
conscientiousness	charity
faithfulness	compassion
fidelity	humility
loyalty	kindness
pride	long-sufferingness
trustworthiness	mercy

There are noteworthy differences between these two sets which I would venture to state as follows. There is certainly a sufficiency of terms in Latin to show that the Romans held one another in esteem, that they were capable of and practiced warm personal kindness, that they were benevolent and capable of magnanimity and mercy, that they celebrated friendship. The terms charity and compassion, of course, are themselves of Latin origin. But when we look more closely we see that the several terms that lie in this direction have a considerably different quality from the Christian vocabulary. *Caritas*, though it is the origin of **charity**, is nearer to high **regard**, **esteem**, or **respect** than it is to **love**. **Kindness** is rendered in Latin approximately by *benignitas*, *comitas, benevolentia, humanitas*. No one may deny that Romans were individually capable of warmth of affection toward children or wives or friends. Nevertheless, qualities of this sort were not celebrated as traits of strong character, and there is no tendency to "universalize" them, as responses deserving to be taken toward all men regardless of state or station or relationship.

Love and concern, generalized and particularized, are the note introduced by Christianity. Where there has been concern before, it has been at most a concern for those that concern one, and beyond that at most a general benignity and benevolence. It is now a concern which is love itself for all men solely because they are fellow men. What is more, it is not just a laudable attribute, it is an imperative: "This *commandment* I give unto you, that ye love one another." It therefore takes a large step beyond the Roman *humanitas*, which is a gentle and civilized response toward others, even strangers, but not necessarily including a concern for them *as for oneself*.

While the differences are palpable they must not be allowed to obscure the connections between the two schemata. **Benevolence** deserves to be thought a common ground between them.

Each of these sets of terms represents a reflection on human nature, a view of what is essential in our nature. Benevolence and concord are the values that the civilized Roman thought a community should rise to. The poet of I Corinthians 13, however, says unless there is also charity, ἀγάπη, it will profit us nothing. This is a new view of man, or the view of a new man, not just a new set of goals for men. The pride of the Roman is from this standpoint merely pompous and vain self-assertion: men have more to be humble about than proud, says the Christian.

At the same time, if the two sets of virtues, the two views of the function of man, did not in fact work in antagonism it was because they could in many ways supplement one another. There was nothing that entailed *ceaseless* subversion of society and its bad habits by Christianity. It was not, in principle, a Maoist Cultural Revolution which needed to be more or less continually re-enacted. It could, therefore, look forward to a society united, so far as it was a secular state, in concord and benevolence; the other Roman virtues were to be maintained intact. From time to time, however, the retreat of monks and mystics from the active scene, and the appearance in Christendom of radical pietists, Methodists and primitive Christians has reminded the Christian world that pride and humility are incompatible and that true compassion may need to subvert the superficial accord and concord in society.

Nothing, however, challenges conscientiousness, fidelity, loyalty and trust, virtues which Christianity did not invent and might not have succeeded in sustaining had they not been already the cornerstones of the ancient Jewish and Roman communities.

The claim of each of these sets of concepts to be virtues in the functional sense depends on the possibility of construing them as ways in which man most nearly realizes himself as man in observing them. If indeed men cannot live apart from one another, then the absolute condition of their living with one another is to observe trust, the basis of the stern Roman virtues. Each deed, and each one is as exemplary as any other, helps to make or break the community. Christianity, the first gospel that was addressed to an urban civilization, spells out even more radical necessities. Not only must citizens not betray trust and loyalty and observe the remainder of the essentially negative and prohibitive virtues: they must also manifest a positive concern for one another, for they cannot escape one another.

We return now to the vices listed above. The vices other than **cowardice, evil-mindedness, malevolence, meanness, vengefulness, spitefulness,** and **scurrility** are most often adverbial in force, signifying an excess in the pursuit of some goal that is utterly destructive of it, even if the pursuit is successful, and even if the goal had some original merit. Everyone expects a soldier to employ force according to command, nor ought anyone to be surprised if he exercises it, lawfully. The manner and degree of the resort to force are, however, not without limits. The semantic imagination now gropes for expressive devices to characterize observance or transgression of limits. The eating habits of carnivores which, to be sure, are not pleasant to behold, but are as innocent as anything else in nature, are drawn upon to characterize falsely the inhumanities of human aggression: truly an insult to the animal kingdom. Thus we have **swinishness, brutality, bestiality, cold-bloodedness,** and **ferocity,** although no one can say what pigs or other beasts do that is comparable to the wanton murder, torture, or mutilation men have inflicted on one another. In fiendishness man reaches toward the transcendental.

The purpose of all of these is to speak of violations of what one may expect in a response that is natural or suited to the occasion. **Inhumanity** states this purely formally and represents the general type of all these others. The want of such restraint as is thought natural to demand is expressed in **callousness, mercilessness, ruthlessness,** and **unfeelingness.** The concepts, therefore, express essentially a normative appraisal, the limits of applicability being left, of course, to the appraiser.

We are left with terms that seem to express a positive will-to-evil: **scurrility, malevolence,** etc. These terms should be used with more than a little caution. We should ask what it is we are discrediting in a person we call malevolent other than his alleged will-to-destroy-*us*, and what else we are saying of him other than that he is *our* adversary? We cannot suppose that he wishes universal destruction, for this is either romantic to the last possible degree or sheer lunacy, and not to be respected in either case. The terms are essentially blanks which say nothing until their empty form is filled with something palpable. Compared with an accusation of cruelty, callousness, or ferocity, a charge that someone is malevolent tells us virtually nothing. Perhaps **vengefulness** and **spitefulness** tell us slightly more.

We may remark finally that one should exclude from the virtues and vices terms used only to characterize particular events and actions (for example, the processives under 11.111). Vice and virtue are especially concerned with traits of character or dispositions to respond.

These, then, are the considerable resource of terms to attribute communitive and, especially, sociative virtue and vice. As in previous cases, we can discern their functional character and from these easily see why they also have appraisive force. The rather formal character of the group just considered provides a transition to the most general attributions of virtue and vice, to which we now turn.

14.4   GENERAL AND ULTIMATE VIRTUES AND VICES

VIRTUE

(a) **innocence**	(b) **honor**	(c) **rectitude**
integrity	**humanity**	**righteousness**
magnanimity	**nobility**	**uprightness**

VICE

(a) **delinquency**	(c) **corruptness**
knavery	**depravity**
perversity	**inhumanity**
unprincipledness	**miscreancy**
(b) **dishonor**	**turpitude**
disreputableness	(d) **evil**
infamy	**iniquity**
	vileness
	wickedness

(A) *Generality and Ultimacy.* Our language and, one may surmise, every other presents us finally with a body of appraisives that are applicable essentially and probably exclusively to man, unless there are higher orders of beings. We have encountered these in 14.01 under Moral Characterization. That vocabulary is for direct application to persons. As we saw, moral characterization is essentially general and formal; its content is only to be found in characterizations expressed in the concepts found in 5.0 and the later sections of Part Two. We now encounter the moral characterisms again, this time in the form of virtues and vices. These are the moral, or as we shall say, the ultimate and general virtues and vices. With these we complete our survey of the characterization of man.

The virtues and vices we now consider have a scope and a degree of ultimacy and finality that are nowhere to be seen in what has gone before, and perhaps even an air of doom in the most original sense of this magnificent word; judgment has been pronounced and fate has been sealed. If they are placed into some kind of classification, as above, we can see in their more emphatic degrees, (b) under virtue, and (d) under vice, the content of such commendation or condemnation. We must now relate them briefly to areas already traversed.

We have before us in our language the graven image of the sense of value of at least a thousand years and beyond this in parent languages, of yet more thousands. But we must ask whether this vocabulary represents archaic responses or whether it is indispensable to our appraisive thought. It is not enough to ask whether it merely has some interest for us. Rather, is it needful to us? Would moral thought be meaningless without such ideas?

I believe the present concepts are indispensable to us if they can be shown to serve two important purposes: first, they should be *general* and serve the purpose of uniting man's efforts at appraising into a *whole*; and second, appraisals in these terms should be *ultimate*, presenting a *final* judgment of character. Such concepts as these are necessary if we are to hold together the vast body of appraisives and characterisms relating to man. Moreover, we must hold them together. The story of the virtues, if we exclude the last set, suggests that man, each man, is a kind of corporation with many different branches and divisions, each largely self-sufficient. This impression, though misleading, has been unavoidable up to now. The appraisives simply do fall into reasonably distinct families. To do them justice we must isolate and study them in company with others that have a comparable character and function. Only so can we really discern the unique function of each appraisive. But this is not the end of the story.

It is obvious that each and every man is under *all* of these jurisdictions, and that he functions in each of them, unless he is detached by some fate or accident. His tendentive activity involves his intelligence, his capacity to communicate, his involvement with others personally and socially, and virtually all of the rest. His social or sexual self-assertion involves communication, volitivity, judgment, emotivity, physical presence and exertion, and perhaps all of the others. Possibly only intelligence can operate in high independence of most of the others, but we must add, not for long. We are always *whole* beings involved in all of these functions, and all of them are reciprocally influential. The whole person acquires a unique quality from the way the elements mix in him. We have, then, a total person to survey and a total person to make the survey.

Where, now, are the characterisms for such a total quality if not in the general and ultimate virtues now under consideration? Their purpose is to transcend the local nature of the other appraisives. Particularly the vices seem to storm the heavens (or the gates of Hell) and speak as only, one supposes, God might be permitted to speak; individual men are judged and on balance declared to be creatures of good, or of evil, iniquity, and wickedness. While a benevolent and permissive age tends to shrink from such flat condemnations, the traditional vices and virtues will nevertheless very likely be able to preserve themselves.

We must observe further that just as the several families of characterisms already treated represent the right-functioning of man in his several capacities, or the contrary, so the ultimate virtues should set forth what an older ethic was willing to call "the whole duty of man." Of course, contemporary existential thought is hostile to any effort to excogitate such ends and duties: it is said there can be no defining man's essence in such an *a priori* manner. We cannot pause to deal with such criticisms except to say that our own interest here is largely descriptive to see what *in fact* has been called upon as the final court of appeal. The received virtues and vices are our best clues to this.

As we glance over, especially, the vices we have a sense of finality already remarked on. Contemporary man is increasingly reluctant to make such irrevocable pronouncements. He can no longer so readily as formerly acquiesce in the condemnation of persons to death, and he is reluctant to declare men irredeemably wicked, evil, and iniquitous. It is *not* certain or obvious that this is not just a failure of nerve, and for all one knows, it may be, as the gloomiest prophets foretell, the telltale mark of moral disintegration, rather than the harbinger of an era of love and peace. Our present task is not to make or refute such prognostications. It is rather to ask what function these appraisives now serve. It is apparent that their broadest purpose is to declare that a man deserves unreserved condemnation or that he deserves virtually unqualified trust.

We may remark that some of the terms are more ultimate than general; thus in the condemnation **wicked** there is little reference to the early part of our list. It is heavily weighted with relevance toward the middle and end of the series. If we say a man is wicked we are most concerned about the corruption of his volition. He is likely to be thought a malefactor in the sociative,

economic, communitive and possibly the sex-related areas of conduct, but
there is no reference to corruption of intelligence, judgment, or expression,
except possibly in the contemptible ends these have been made to serve; if
he is a person of poisonous temperament or other such diathetic vices this
may confirm us in our view of his wickedness but cannot lead to such a
charge of itself. This is equally true of the virtues, both (a) and (b): they also
take account mainly of that which a person does in his concourse with persons, not with intellectual, aesthetic, or expressive matters.

(B) *The Virtues and Functions.* We shall now take up the principal question regarding these terms namely in what sense the virtues reflect the *function* that may be ascribed to man, or the vices departures from such function?
We shall consider them both in themselves and in relation to those others
that have already been taken up.

The first group of virtues (a) contains two that are negative in character,
innocence and **integrity**. To these we might add **irreproachableness**. He who
is, as the Latin has it, *integer* is untouched, unbroken, whole. He is complete
and sound. But in English, **integrity** has little reference to negation. It is used
to attribute strength to a personality because the subject's capacity and intention are sound and have been realized in action. **Magnanimity** adds breadth
to strength.

Rectitude, righteousness and **uprightness** have reference as much to the
character of the person's moral judgment (5.0) as to his actions. These virtues
have a somewhat Biblical and archaic ring. But if indeed archaic they afford
us an interesting historical perspective. Mention may also be made of the
Biblical **just,** that is often so close in meaning to **righteous** and **upright**. One
recalls the Psalms in this connection. These terms or meanings are not likely
to be restored to wide usage in the foreseeable future. The reason is probably
that they have too "moral" an air for our time, and this in the sense that they
are rather too prescriptive for a permissive age – one that is just conceivably
willing to be pulled but is unwilling to be pushed into anything like the
"paths of righteousness."

Honor and **nobility** are in origin devised only for the purpose of enunciating
the fact that someone is known to possess certain virtues, which then must
be otherwise specified. **Honor** in this usage is without content of its own.
Noble likewise simply connotes fame or renown, being derived from L. *(g)no-
scere,* to know. Even in such contexts as that of the code of honor or the
code duello and in the use of the term to signify female virtue or chastity it is
the *repute* of persons, how they are known by others they respect, that is
decisive. It is not, of course, as if the person were concerned *only* about his
name, and as if the substance (or want of it) behind this were of no account.
It is assumed that the repute and the reality are or ought to be one and the

same. Only by an effort is it possible to make the two coincide, but certainly not just the effort to put as good a face on matters as possible, by false devices if the truth fails. To ascribe honor to a person is thus to say that one believes the favoring account published of him. To *be* honorable is to deserve such repute, the reasons being specified elsewhere. **Noble**, similarly, begins as a term applied to a tribe or clan that is *known for* virtues and deeds that are praiseworthy on their own account. In time, of course, the term ossifies into the notion of a hereditary line which may or may not be represented by paragons of virtue and chivalry. These two terms offer little that is positive in the roster of virtues. They begin by signifying repute and only by repeated use in such a connection do they appear finally to signify virtues themselves. But if they do so, it is only in a vague and derivative sense. It is useless, I suggest, to try to excogitate in them much in the way of a positive designation for virtue.

We are left, then, with the term **humanity** as the principal ultimate and also general term for virtue. As the broadest possible term **humanity** evokes considerable feeling and may be the most significant term of all the appraisives that have come before us. Instead of measuring man on a divine scale (and the vices are in danger of assimilating man to the fallen angels) the term straightforwardly connotes the conscious identification of the subject with the rest of his species, thinking what they think, suffering in their suffering, rejoicing in their joy. **Humanity** as a virtue is in the best sense, being all things to all men. And in this sense it is what we regard as eternally praiseworthy in the men we think great. This is to say that the concept is meant to comprise in itself all of the positive right-functionings that have already been set forth as the virtues of intellect, behavior, tendence, sociation, and the rest. It is the ideal that is most congenial to man insofar as the still pursues the goals he prescribed for himself in the Renaissance, the Enlightenment, and the liberal revolutions of the last two centuries.

Turning to the vices, we find that they are all essentially deformities. As we have already remarked, it is principally to the areas other than the intellectual and behavioral that the general virtues apply. The vices are even more closely relevant to these remaining fields than are the virtues. We have first those that are defined in somewhat negative fashion (a); some of these are aggressions. They rise by degrees through (a) and (c) and proclaim not just the appraiser's rejection of the subject but more significantly his charge that the subject departs from an original wholeness or health, which is presupposed. We see this most plainly in **corruptness, depravity, miscreancy**, and of course **inhumanity**.

The accusations in (b) operate in a manner similar to **honor** and **nobility** among the virtues, since they state no particular charge. Their use is a way of subscribing to the published want of repute of the subject. In origin **turpitude** may have similar significance. It is now closer to (d) but perhaps not quite so severe or irredeemable.

This leaves the ultimates in (d). All of them are concerned in one way or another with a presupposed standard which has been utterly and irrevocably subverted and defied. **Iniquity** and **vile** are more severe than their originals in Latin. **Vile** derives from *vilis* signifying the lowest order on a scale, for example, of economic status. **Iniquity** is plainly concerned with exceeding or with failure to reach a standard. **Wickedness** is cognate to **weak** (and thus to G. *weich*, soft, and *weichen*, to depart from). Thus the wicked man is feeble, unhealthy. **Evil**, finally, seems related to *up* and to *over* and thus connotes even more than the others a *trans*gression, an excess. Possibly **depravity** is even more drastic than any of (d).

In all instances an implied norm has been violated until finally the subject is declared virtually irredeemable. As already remarked, the areas succeeding the intellectual and behavioral are principally in question. If we then demand to hear what has finally led to such a sentence of doom the case must rest upon the preceding vices. A charge of wickedness or depravity can never stand alone. To support it one can only speak in terms of vices already discriminated. All of these terms are unmistakably interpretable in terms of regarding vice as the malfunction of the person. The ultimate vices signify the ultimate breakdown of the person. But it is a breakdown the extent and reason of which is hidden from the subject. Could he apply these concepts to himself he would be taking at least the first step toward his rehabilitation.

I reject the shallow claim that these vices are moralizings which mankind must overcome. We may learn to pronounce the terms with more compassion, but there can be no healing until disease is diagnosed. For our age the health and disease of the spirit of the total person, his wholeness and deformity, seem best expressed in his humanity and inhumanity. These concepts appear to comprise all the others and also to form a fitting climax to them.

PART THREE

GENERAL AND ULTIMATE APPRAISAL

15.0 COMMENDATION

We have now finally arrived at the appraisive vocabulary that has so often been considered in independence of the whole preceding body of character-isms: in the last sub-sections of 15.0 we come to the vocabulary **good-ex-cellent-valuable** (and their negations). These are *ultimate* and also *general* appraisives, a distinction which will be clarified as we proceed. It is sufficient for the moment to say that all terms here are general, including the ultimates, that is the general vocabularies "govern" or "range over" all of the preceding terms in the characterization of man and a considerable vocabulary besides. The term **good**, to take the prime term of the class, is employed not only to commend men, their works, and all other human concerns, but also to com-mend other things. What this further field may comprise is suggested in the Appendices: A (objects of the intellect), B (transcendental and religious appraisives), C (aesthetic appraisives), (D humorous appraisives), E (physical appraisives), and F (general or metaphysical appraisives).

This may suffice to introduce the general and ultimate appraisives. I shall postpone consideration of the many other theoretical problems surrounding these until we come to the ultimate commendatives in 15.6. The preceding topics in 15.0 can largely be treated apart from these matters.

15.1 ELICITIVES

CREDITING

(a) **awesome, awe-inspiring** ($\pm$)
    gladsome
    winsome
(b) **impressive**
(c) **felicitous**
    marvellous
    salubrious
    stupendous
    wondrous
(d) **alluring**
    astonishing
    astounding
    charming

edifying
engrossing
gratifying
ingratiating (Obsol. as v.t.)
inspiring
interesting
moving (App. C 3.1)
overwhelming
pleasing
prepossessing
reassuring
stimulating
tempting

thrilling	(f) agreeable
titillating	delectable (App. E 3.0)
uplifting	lovely
(e) delightful	pleasant, pleasing
restful	pleasurable
wonderful	(g) poignant ($-$)

DISCREDITING

(a) boresome	odious	revolting
bothersome	pitiful	shocking
burdensome	tedious	sickening
fearsome	woeful	sobering
gruesome	(d) aggravating	startling
irksome	annoying	stultifying
quarrelsome	appalling	stupefying
tiresome	confusing	tantalizing
toilsome	debilitating	terrifying
troublesome	depressing	upsetting
wearisome	disconcerting	vexing, vexatious
worrisome	discouraging	worrisome
(b) disgusting	disheartening	(e) creepy
offensive	distracting	dreary (Cf. G. **traurig**)
oppressive	disturbing	ghastly
provocative	enervating	grisly
repulsive	exasperating	hideous
(c) awful	forbidding	horrible
distasteful	harrowing	onerous
dreadful	horrifying	pathetic
fearful	infuriating	rankle
frightful	irritating	repugnant
mournful	jarring	terrible
nauseous	provoking	

Once we develop the notion of the elicitive appraisive term, the class is easy to identify and possesses a significant "naturalness." Many of the terms are employable in art-critical contexts and therefore many of them would re-appear among the aesthetic appraisives which we are here leaving out of account, except in Appendix C. But each of them also has a considerably wider use. The terms may be used of persons, places, scenes, acts, procedures in great variety, and this breadth of reference places them among the general appraisives. We must remember that this generality concerns only the variety of subjects they are applied to, and that they are not vague in being general. On the contrary they are most often powerful and specific in the particular feelings or responses that are uniquely referred to in their meanings.

The subclassification of the terms by their inflections (-ing, -some, etc.) is at first sight pedantic and mechanical. But such ways of classification do bring out certain important traits. (In order to satisfy oneself regarding the extent of these classes one may consult a rhyming dictionary. One must, however, survey long stretches of terms before turning up genuine elicitives.) Thus the -ings in general all signify effects on persons of the objects appraised. The -fuls raise questions about the pathetic fallacy. We shall also point out other possible classifications besides the inflectional.

The first thing to be observed of this body of terms and also the deservatives in 15.2 is that many are based on verbs that are themselves characterizing terms in the processive mode. These verbs have already made their appearance in our list. It would be a tedious task to show exactly what relation the participial or gerundive form in 15.1 bears to the verb forms that have already appeared. (The index will readily show where the parent verbs occur elsewhere in our list.) As meanings, elicitives are relatively independent of the parent verbs: they are thought of as appraisives that may appear in independent predicative or attributive form as adjectives. It is only for reasons of reference back to the parent verb that they are to be thought of as participial or gerundive in form: we may call them quasi-participials.

One result of this is that the terms must *qua elicitives* not be heard as participles: "He is stimulating" must not be thought to say that he is now actually stimulating anyone. Actually "is stimulating" would only rarely be used with the sense of the transitive verb *to stimulate*, perhaps only in a rare and awkward exchange, such as: "Is he stimulating the freshman class?" "He is stimulating."

We thus invite the reader to hear "A is stimulating" as meaning simply that A tends to stimulate auditors or observers in suitable circumstances. We are permitted to infer that the person asserting this has found himself to be stimulated by A at some time or other. We are then speaking of events principally in recollection or in anticipation, not as a present process. The same is true in all of the crediting -ings, except possibly **alluring** and **ingratiating**.

The terms all have a twofold function: as adjectival to their subjects they say what the subject's power is; they also say that the power has elicited or will elicit an effect in an observer. It is hard to say which of these is more prominent, but in intent it is the first. Our attention is being focussed *on the subject*, and we are saying something about its causal or dispositional properties, whether or not they are *now* being exercised.

While the foregoing considerations are most evident in the -ing appraisives, they are equally applicable to the others. Perhaps they are, if anything, even more evident with the -ives (**impressive, oppressive, offensive, provocative, repulsive**).

We turn now to another aspect of this class of terms. It is often remarked of these and other terms, especially superlatives (**splendid, marvellous, magnificent**, and the like) that they now mean virtually nothing and that they have been used for so long to bludgeon people for the purposes of advertising and other forms of propaganda that they are reduced to mere hurrahs. It is certainly true that in most instances one is better advised to avoid these in the present juncture, but this has nothing whatever to do with the core of meaning of these terms. It is conceivable that all of the appraisives we have been considering in this study will eventually suffer complete corruption, but if so the society that speaks such a language will itself either have been completely corrupted or demoralized or if not, it will have somehow hammered out a new vocabulary of appraisal with the vitality which an earlier English once had. All this is possible. The point, however, is that in a very real sense nothing has really changed very much. A respite from the overworked vocabularies (**splendid, stupendous, colossal**) for a more or less extended time can restore the original force of the terms. Overwrought uses of language testify far more to maladies of persons than to breakdowns in languages. We may assume that, for the foreseeable future, our language in all its original and accumulated richness, subtlety, and suppleness is there to be spoken even if we are for the moment so mad or distraught as not to speak it. It is not a question of what is "good English" but rather of availing oneself of the resources we have. Hence we consider all these terms, even the "shopworn" superlatives, as possessing all their original force.

We may now consider this vocabulary in somewhat further detail. I believe the observations just made about some examples from the -ings apply to virtually all of this subclass. This if A says, x is tempting, where x may be drawn from a large variety of substantives, then either A is tempted by x, or believes others will be or generally have been tempted by x or believes that x tends to tempt persons. This will apply to all -ing appraisives provided the verbs can occur in transitive form. In at least one case this form is missing: **ingratiate** in transitive form is obsolete; hence we can only with impropriety or difficulty say that "x is ingratiating" comes down to saying that x ingratiates someone, or tends to. (This does not apply to the reflexive form.) **Prepossessing** is slightly awkward for similar reasons.

Repugnant, having the Latin form of participle rather than the English is assimilated to the elicitives in -ing. **Grisly** and **ghastly** are also best placed with these terms, insofar as they are used to mean causing terror, horror, or fright, or tending to.

As we have said, the -ives behave virtually similarly to the -ings. Among the -somes, we may assimilate to the preceding analysis all except a few doubtful ones. In the usual cases, we may say that if A says x is -some, if A is, for example, bothersome, burdensome, etc., then A is bothered by, burdened by (encumbered by, feared by, irked by, tired by, troubled by, or awed by) x, or tends to be. **Gladsome** differs from the others in that it is not derived from a verb; yet it belongs among the elicitives, since its primary meaning is *productive of gladness,* and this, of course, could be assumed to be gladness in the speaker. **Gruesome** differs still further in that **grue** is now altogether absent. Yet etymologically it is like G. **grausam**, which would be 'tending to produce *Grauen*', that is horror or fear. **Winsome** is even more obscure, but is likewise fully elicitive. Of course, it has nothing to do with winning (not even winning favor) but derives from *win* in the obsolete sense of joy or pleasure. (Its origin is similar to that of G. *Wunsch*, or wish.) What is winsome therefore pleases or tends to produce pleasure in itself. Of course, there are numerous other appraisives in -some which are not elicitives, for example, **fulsome, venturesome, mettlesome, handsome** and others. These we take up elsewhere. **Toilsome** and **quarrelsome** are more like terms in -ous and -ful. **Noisome** seems now an altogether direct and positive appraisive and therefore is placed with the estimatives (15.5).

It should be made clear that virtually none of the terms in 15.1 is "moral" in nature. They refer solely to what is intuitively felt as (approximately) agreeable or disagreeable to feeling. I think we can see what the difference is in a term like **loathsome** (14.01). This term seems to me to be essentially moral in nature. One ought to withhold it, therefore, from application to persons except for their most reprehensible actions. Therefore, I place **loathe** among the moral affects of 5.1. **Loathsome** could also be placed among the deservatives of 15.2.

Turning next to the elicitives in -ous, we notice that if an occasion, or a choice of words or other means is declared felicitous we are to understand that it evokes in us a feeling of felicity or good fortune. A salubrious climate tends to promote health. We are similarly thought or said to be plunged into a stupor or struck senseless when something is declared stupendous – or so it seems! We may enjoy comparable states of wonder when we say something is wondrous or, via the Latin *mirabilis*, marvellous. So also, feelings of nausea, odium, and tedium are said to be precipitated when we speak of the nauseous, odious, and tedious. **Hideous**, though it is closely associated with these, is not an elicitive. These terms like the previous refer us back to our *feelings* or to our *responses toward* what the terms are predicated of as much as to the objects of the response. Wonder, felicity, what seems to appear as stupor here, nausea, odium, and tedium are all powerful and exclusive emotions that during onset occupy every last corner of one's being. They appear to be good or evil incarnate. They preoccupy and prepossess the soul. **Wonderful**, unlike the rarer, more "poetic" and stilted **wondrous**, is so pale one may as well abandon it as an elicitive. Only its lingering origin qualifies it to be numbered here.

Pitiful and **pathetic** deserve somewhat special mention. If A is declared to be in a pitiful or pathetic state, it is not merely said that he does inspire pity but, I think, that he should. I have accordingly placed them both here and in 15.2, with the Deservatives.

The root verbs of some of the elicitives appear to fall somewhat more explicitly in the area of the emotions, particularly the terms in -ful and -ous. One might also include **agreeable, pleasurable, terrible, horrible, pleasant**, and perhaps others among these if they had not degenerated into mere vapid commendatives or the contrary.

This subclass should be distinguished also for another reason: in their common use when they are predicated of objects or scenes they appear to raise the spectre of the pathetic fallacy. The terms in -ing are rather explicitly free of this, since when taken literally they appear to say only that objects can elicit such and such a response or even an emotion in us, but not at all that the object somehow harbors any emotion or other mental condition. The terms in -ous, and -ful on the other hand *appear* to do so. There is also a larger problem about empathy and expressiveness that arises from our using such phrases as 'sad music'. The question then is whether words like **mournful**, when applied to such subjects as music, are only elicitives or whether beyond that they also attribute a trait to them which we otherwise attribute only to persons or minds. Are we willy-nilly making such an attribution in any use of 'mournful music' and comparable phrases with **delightful, fearful, felicitous, marvellous, nauseous, stupendous, tedious, wondrous**, and **wonderful**? I believe these terms, if we think carefully of what we are saying, whatever objectivation of feelings they may in origin have implied, are by now only either rather pallid general crediting terms, which like all other terms of this class need to be supported by more material characterizations to have any force, or they are in fact only elicitives like the other terms in 15.1, possibly somewhat more emphatic. Or we may ask ourselves, where, if anywhere, the nausea, tedium, fear and so on *are* if not in ourselves, or imputed to others, when we use the terms.

The most that needs to be remarked is that **mournful**, like **sad**, in 'sad music' may indeed be a term involved in the empathy problem and thus possibly in the pathetic fallacy. If so, the term is being used less as an appraisive term than as the name of a rather unusual datum which deserves analytical study by aesthetics.

The appraisive or commendative force of the elicitives as a whole is in general dependent upon whatever appraisal we believe suits the many feelings and responses that the terms cover. Any theory of value, I think, grants that pain and distress, other things being equal, do not deserve to be desired, and that pleasure or felicity do. Issue arises only over the view of naturalists that all commendations are in the end nothing more than more or less explicit appeals to, or elicitations or imputations of such feelings.* The thesis is, in short, that the present class of terms may comprise the explicit elicitives, but that in the end *all* commendatives are nothing but elicitives.

I believe we have given ample reason beginning with the discussion of the difference between response and appraisal in 2.0 and 3.0 for rejecting such a view of appraisive and commendative terms. Elicitive terms have a definite, lesser, role to play in commendation. They have in essence a unique kind of honesty or caution about them. They say little or nothing of the subjects they are applied to but simply confine themselves to recording reactions or possible reactions to them. If we are thrilled by S, we may wish to draw a distinction between this and an outright commendation of S by saying what feelings it stirs and letting it go at that. Elicitives thus deserve a place as a kind of bridge between the characterisms of Part Two and the stronger commendations later in Part Three (which will necessitate a heavier degree of support by recursion). "Is S really good, excellent, meritorious, first rate?" "I'm not sure, but it (or he) is impressive (thrilling, ingratiating, stimulating)." If ultimate commendatives are only elicitives at best, this familiar conversation embodies only a fairly vapid redundancy.

One final question about elicitives is whether in saying that S is stimulating or thrilling we are not attributing this result to some causal agent in S which is left indeterminate and a bit mysterious. I think in fact we may but I do not think we must make a mystery of it. "S is thrilling" confines itself to a causal result, real or possible, but it invites question about the ground of it: the question is really one that is to be answered by a material characterization of S. "What was so thrilling about the Horowitz concert?" We are being asked to characterize the playing or the selections on the program, and so on. If we are patient enough to think about this, some answer can generally be found.

15.2 DESERVATIVES

CREDITING: Bracketings [ ] to Discredit

| acceptable [un-] | admissible [in-] | advisable [in-] |
| admirable | adorable | well-[advised |

---

* Hume, *Treatise*, Book III, Part I, Section II.

allowable	inviolable	presentable [un-]
commendable	laudable	reputable [dis-]
creditable	lovable [un-]	respectable
defensible [in-]	memorable	satisfactory [un-]
dependable	notable	supportable [in-]
deserving [un-]	pardonable [un-]	tolerable [in-]
desirable [un-]	passable	valuable [in-]
enviable [un-]	permissible [im-]	venerable
excusable [in-]	praiseworthy [un-]	warrantable
honorable [dis-]	preferable	worshipful

DISCREDITING: Bracketings [   ] to Credit

abominable	lamentable
assailable [un-]	laughable
blameable	loathsome (5.1) (14.01)
blameworthy	ludicrous
censurable	objectionable [un-]
contemptible	pathetic
culpable [in-]	pitiful, piteous, pitiable
damnable	questionable [un-]
deplorable	redoubtable
despicable	reprehensible
detestable	reproachable [ir-]
discreditable	ridiculous
execrable	risible
inexpiable	suspicious (=deserving suspicion)
insupportable	

Deservatives are, first of all, general appraisives and unlike characterisms they have little or no content of their own. Their parent verbs indicate in what mode the appraisal is to proceed: laughing, despising, lamenting, tolerating, and so on. Though imperative or hortatory in form, they are in content little more than summary or final assessments whose appropriateness depends on the reasons that may be made available elsewhere in the form of supporting characterisms. Though essentially general in scope, it is obvious that they will in many cases (mostly the discreditings) be used in the appraisal of man and his works and effects. They often appear on their own feet as highest condemnations and commendations (adorable! despicable!) The tone with which they are uttered may obscure the fact that they say nothing of a material character. Nevertheless, as summarizings, they serve an important purpose.

Although, like the elicitives just considered, these terms derive from parent verbs (*accept, admire, abominate, assail*, etc.), they must first be allowed to have a full adjectival sense. We may call this the primary sense. The subject is *in sum* credited or discredited. In a secondary sense the force of the verb is taken into account: we *may* be inspired to engage in an actual lament for a subject declared lamentable. The primary sense is probably not to be separated wholly from the secondary. The latter is far more expressive but it is recessive and may be in process of disappearing. In scarcely any term that is here listed, however, is the disappearance complete. The secondary lives if it is kept alive, that is, if the speaker truly thinks of what he is saying. If he declares things despicable, he may be evincing his own despisal and also saying that in fact they are and deserve to be despised. Here all the verbs, except perhaps *redoubt* are alive. (*Contemn* also is becoming rare in American prose.) To utter the deservatives in this fully "meaningful" sense one need not be an etymologist.

Therefore, while we insist on the primacy of the adjectival use, we assert that the power of the terms comes from their more extended structure deriving from the parent verbs. We may first observe the source of their significance somewhat more closely. We ask what it is that we really are saying with these deservatives.

Fowler observes that a class of terms in -able which is, I think, identical with this vocabulary is a class of gerundives. "The English adjectives in -*ble* from verbs, like lovable, might well enough be called gerundives from their similarity to the Latin gerundive," although, as he goes on to say, the term gerundive is not in fact used in English grammar.* Latin, in fact, has available not only the true gerundive (which, of course, is a participle) to express that which is thought to be deserved, or necessitated, or obligated (as with the present class) but also a number of terms in -*abilis* (usually it is -*a*-) that are all deservatives. Hence, the formal precedent for our class of deservatives is Latin itself. The following are virtual synonyms of their present cognates and all are deservatives:

acceptabilis	*culpabilis*
admirabilis	*damnabilis*
adorabilis	*despicabilis* (late L.)
commendabilis	*detestabilis*
laudabilis	*execrabilis*
memorabilis	*lamentabilis*
notabilis	*reprehensibilis*
venerabilis	

* Fowler, H. W., *A Dictionary of Modern English Usage*, Oxford, 1937, p. 214.

The deservative and gerundive force of a term like *tremendous*, in Latin, *tremendus* (to be trembled at), is concealed in English although etymologically it contributes to our use of it as a superlative. It is heard in Latin as a deservative and not as a mere superlative (cf. the stanza beginning *rex tremendae majestatis* in the *Dies Irae*).

It scarcely needs mention that the vast majority of terms in -ble in English are of no concern to us. They are what one might call capabilitives and are not appraisive in nature. (One may think of *handleable, audible, bridgeable, walkable*, and so on.) I believe the present list of deservatives of true gerundive character in -ble is virtually complete. It is also noteworthy that almost our whole list is either drawn from Latin directly or built on Latin verbs. Love and laugh are rare exceptions. *Per contra* -bles built on northern verbs are almost without exception capabilitives and not deservatives.

What, now, do these terms say? In all cases, insofar as they are not just used as vapid credits and discredits, they say (in predicative use) that the subject *deserves* to be served as the cognate verb indicates, and they are all passives. That is, A deserves *to be* accepted, admired, adored, abominated, assailed, blamed, and so forth. Or A is fit to be, ought to be, can only be, must be, is worthy of being, can and in fact should be, accepted, admired, etc. They have the power, moreover, of doing what they say deserves to be done. If someone says in suitable circumstances that B is acceptable, commendable, defensible, damnable, questionable, and so on, we may presume that he then and there accepts, commends, defends, damns, or questions B. It is not merely to say that B *could be* accepted, commended, and so on. The terms *do* what they *say*, and thus they are performatives, but probably not in Austin's sense. Thus these verbs indicate the speaker's support and involve also the person to whom they are addressed. The person addressed is not left in the neutral or passive state of a mere listener: he is involved in the concern of the speaker. If I say to you, A is acceptable, I not only accept A but I ask you to accept him. Of course this is, in degree, inherent in all appraisive language. The request for the support of others is equally significant with the speaker's support. Such terms play a most important part in the maintenance of the moral community.

We may now consider what these appraisals request if they are addressed to us. For this we must turn to the original occurrence of each of the verbs in question.

A large and representative sample of the deservatives may be referred back to the earlier occurrence of the parent verbs in 2.0, 3.0, 4.0, and 5.0. They request appropriate responses, appraisals, enactments, and judgments as follows:

RESPONSES (2.0)

admire	abominate
adore	contemn
desire	deplore
love	despise
	detest
	redoubt

APPRAISALS (3.0)

accept	assail
praise	eschew
prefer	execrate
tolerate	[laugh at] (11.122)
value	ridicule

ENACTMENTS (4.0)

honor v.

venerate

JUDGMENTS (5.0)

advise	blame	question
pardon	censure	reprehend
warrant	damn	reproach
	object	

Under the responses, in declaring B to be abominable, deplorable, and the like, I not only hope that my auditors will join me in abominating or deploring B, but I say B deserves it, and I seek to invoke support of my appraisal. But *can* I request anyone to love, adore, abominate, or despise B? Certainly I can, though I cannot oblige him. "An *obligation* to enjoyment is a manifest absurdity," Kant says, and so it is.* In the very act of addressing whoever hears me in the vein of these deservatives it is true I may request him to join me in admiring, adoring, abominating the subject. Perhaps only in an over-anxious state will I appear to be saying he ought to feel, or ought to feel obliged to feel something: to admire, adore, desire, love, prefer. We must consider carefully the basis of our enlisting the support of others.

To the degree that the parent verbs are really active in the sense of these terms, or in other words, to the degree that they are not mere straightforward commendatives (the primary sense mentioned earlier), the palpable effect of such verbs is to be seen by going back to sections 2.0 to 5.0 to see what function the verbs perform. This will have a most important bearing on the current significance of the deservatives.

* Kant, *Critique of Judgment*, § 4 (footnote).

(1) Responses (2.0) provide the most difficult problem. Let us say that I am saying A is desirable, lovable, or detestable. In the end responses arise from *causes* fairly remote from our control, although deliberately formed habits can modify them. They may also be impervious to *reasons*. Since I can scarcely or only with difficulty, if at all, determine or fully control my own desire, love, and detestation (though I assume we can control our *behavior*), what is it I am asking of you when I say A deserves love, desire, or contempt? I think I am saying to you that if you are the kind of person I am, if you meet my expectations, you *will* feel a certain way. I will not merely be disappointed in your failure to do so as I may be in your performance at chess or water polo: I will be disappointed in *you*. I can only feel my own feelings and therefore I cannot but regard them as the standards which feelings should conform to. On the other hand, I can very well understand, and be expected to understand, what other people's appraisals and judgments are: I am not at liberty to be my own standard in such matters. When I now say A is lovable or contemptible I am, as shown earlier, here and now manifesting my love or contempt in speaking so, and I am saying that A conforms to the only standard of love and contempt, *sheerly as love and contempt*, that I can be expected to know, namely *my own*. If you do not now love or detest A, I cannot but regard you as deviant in your emotional make-up.

There is, however, one more thing that must be said here. We ought to choose our words carefully and not simply utter any commendative that comes to mind. Love and hate are brutally final. We should therefore search our minds as to whether we really mean to rest matters on this incorrigible basis or whether we may not be better advised to say that A is preferable (preferring is the *outcome*, 3.13, of an appraisal and subject to modification in a manner suitable to appraisals), or reprehensible (reprehending is a mode of *moral involvement*, 5.2, and thus leads us into the area of the deliberating judgment).

This may serve to elucidate the terms traceable to parent verbs particularly in 2.0. When we turn to the parent verbs in other parts of Part One we find the following.

(2) The deservatives from 3.0 are derived from the outcomes or sequels of appraisal: **accept, prefer, tolerate; assail, eschew, execrate.** Hence when I say A is acceptable, preferable, and so on, I am saying A deserves to be accepted, preferred, and so on. I imply (if I choose my words carefully and properly) that I have appraised A and that my appraisal has issued in acceptance, tolerance, and so on. I now ask you to accept the result of this appraisal. It is perfectly proper for me to do so. Appraisal is not emotive response. When I appraise, my appraisal either holds for everyone or it has been misconducted. Hence I demand your assent to my appraisal, or at least

I assure you that a properly conducted appraisal will issue as mine has.

(3) The deservatives from 4.0 (**honorable, venerable**) will be a good deal less easy to support on grounds analogous to those from 3.0. Here we enter the realm of ultimate commitments. These are certainly subject to modification (so indeed are feeling responses in 2.0) but there is no known or acceptable criterion of choice among them. They must hence stand wherever they stand. Of course, we are relating **honorable** and **venerable** to 4.0 quite deliberately with rather more strictness than is absolutely necessary. We can always regard them as having their primary sense and defend their application to A by recursion to characterization.

(4) The deservatives from 5.0 will in turn signify the demand for approval of my processes of moral judgment. Since my judgments have presumably been arrived at by deliberation, I can invite and demand assent, and this can properly be withheld if the process of judgment has been demonstrably misconducted.

Of the terms cited here, there remain two, **laughable** and **ridiculous**, whose parent verbs have actually occurred under aggression (in 11.0). (The first is merely a descript.) It is, however, not always easy to draw the line between the oblocutives of 3.0 and the derisive characterisms in 11.122. **Ridicule** is, I think, not generally an oblocutive (a sequel to appraisal), but we can certainly say "I find that ridiculous" in a context of appraisal and not just in a derisive manner. Thus it can safely be classified under 3.0.

Finally, we may reiterate what was said earlier about the performative or one might say, dicastic, power of these terms. They have in a peculiar sense a stronger effect than what they seem to have it in them to say, because the mere utterance of them in appropriate circumstances *does* something, as if giving vent to a response even when no response is actually felt. To say something is despicable is to despise in a sense even more potent then evincing the gestures of despising. Something has been, as it were, recorded and made "official." The more restrained or measured the tone, as of a judge instructing a jury, the more effective the pronouncement. These, it appears to me, rather than those that are generally accompanied by 'hereby' singled out by Austin (i.e., formal contractual enactments) are the true performatives, for here something *is* literally being done with words. To say, "It's commendable," *is* to commend no matter what else is said or done.

Despite their power and effectiveness, terms in this vocabulary have nevertheless no content of their own. They derive their force from the parent verbs, asserting that the subject deserves a certain response. But the reasons must be sought elsewhere. If these are not forthcoming the terms will still *do* what their parent verbs imply, but their doing is only formal. If negative, they are virtual aggressions against the subject. We see from this why there must be a recursion of all terms to characterizations that have some content.

We must turn to Part Two if the deservatives are challenged in any way. They are, as it were, "sentences," summations, contentless declarations of desert or guilt. They embody no "evidence" any more than the jury's verdict embodies evidence: for here we wish at last to be detached from the evidence; we ask for something like the enunciation of an inferred statement. We should, however, guard against endowing them with that touch of superstition which latterly has crept into the view of performative terms. The terms lack any content of their own beyond informing us of the response they are to evoke. If we seek or need content we must look toward characterization.

15.3   FAVORITIVES AND ADVERSATIVES

FAVORITIVES

ATTRIBUTIVE

advantage	dependable	reliable
auspicious	favorable	safe
benign	halcyon	salutary
boon n.	propitious	secure

PROCESSIVE

advance v.t.	ennoble	meliorate, a-
batten	enhance	nurture
benefit	enrich	promote
better v.t.	forward v.	propagate
cultivate	foster	refine
develop	further v.	support
emend	improve	

ADVERSATIVES

SUBSTANTIVE

fiend

incubus

ATTRIBUTIVE

(a) adverse	drastic
baleful	grave
danger	jeopardy
deleterious	pejorative
dire	peril
disadvantage	plight
dismal (L. *dies mali*) (App. E 2.0)	ticklish
disservice	

(b) bane   nasty
    calamity   nefarious
    catastrophe   noisome
    disaster   noxious
    emergency   nuisance
    grievous   obnoxious
    hazardous   ominous, omen
    liability   perdition
    maleficent   pernicious
    malignant   precarious
    menace   sinister
    minacious   stigma
    minatory   taboo
    mischief   untoward

PROCESSIVE (Cf. 11.111 PROCESSIVE)

    afflict   exacerbate
    blight   harm
    damage   hurt
    decay   impair
    decline v.t.   obtrude, obtrusive
    desolate v.   obstruct, obstructive
    devastate   ravage
    disturb   ruin
    encroach   tragedy, tragic

The present vocabulary shows important differences as between the processives and the attributives. The processives are the more basic and simple. The attributives raise all the questions that commonly arise with dispositional terms. We may consider the processives first.

To speak in such terms as **betterment, benefit, nurture, depravity, impairment** and the like is to speak of deeds or trains of deeds being undertaken. An alteration is being realized, and we may ask, what kind? There is, in a sense, only a formal answer to this question: there is a presupposition that some state is being brought closer or is being thrust farther away, and what is being said of this state is that it is in some way normal or desired. A depredation or mutilation is a serious and possibly irreparable departure from a norm; enhancement and refinement presuppose that the state left behind is less than conformable to such a norm or desired condition. Beyond this the terms say nothing of a material nature, and it is idle to seek more significance from them beyond displaying an arrow from or toward a norm.

The terms have no material significance apart from modification of directivity toward norms, and this is to say an alteration in character. The processives of this vocabulary are, as it were, mere blanks. The assertions in which they appear gain significance in the degree to which it is possible in the course of development (to benefit or to impair) to replace one characterization of a subject by another. For these we must turn to the only truly material terms of value that are available, the resources of Part Two, for example, if one is talking of persons and personal concerns. (Of course, one also can use the terms in numerous connections other than those of human beings: animal husbandry, for example, or manufacturing, or various natural processes such as healing or corrosion.) To speak in terms of depredation is to speak as if one were prepared to characterize the subject *thus*, before an untoward event, and *so*, after the event. If one is not really prepared to fill in the blanks, the terms are used in a vacuous or in what one may call a *semantically dishonest* manner – where one may as easily be deceiving oneself as others. So A may exclaim that B has ruined his (A's) reputation, or his fortunes, or his property, or his person. But this is a void unless we are told how A was previously characterized or appraised and how he is now, or is now likely to be, characterized. Often, of course, convention and context usually leave no doubt as to the characterisms that are at issue. But to say "matters are improved" or "have deteriorated" with no such clues is literally to say nothing; it is semantically, though perhaps not morally dishonest. It was perfectly well understood, in an older manner of speaking, that a woman ruined was to be henceforth characterized as a strumpet or tart or whore and no longer characterized in such terms as innocence or chastity. In every case the processives of this vocabulary are significant, not in themselves, but only if one can supply characterisms that support them.

This affords a clue to the nature of all general appraisives. To speak of them as "general" is not to say that they are vague, but rather that they are indeterminate. As a class they are most aptly termed, somewhat pretentiously, *appraisive syncategorematics*: to determine their significance the way must always be open to supporting characterizations. We may now give a preliminary account of this process of referral back to characterizations. (When we come to the ultimate commendatives we shall give an ampler and more precise account of this.)

If we use the vocabularies of 15.0 the way must always be open for clarification, since without it the terms are only formal and indeed empty. So, a student submits a musical composition or a poem and is given to understand that certain changes are necessary; the work needs some kind of "improvement." A competent instructor may know how to evoke or elicit these "improvements" by characterizing the work: it is "jerky," "self-conscious," "too sophisticated for the subject matter," "dead and dry," "unrhythmic," "verbose," "vapid," and so on. (I am not saying that this is always what is appropriate as criticism; what is needed may be something much more technical and formal; considerations of that sort are less involved in what is here referred to as characterization.) Merely to say that it needs improvement is literally empty talk unless it can be referred back to a characterization. Appraisives of this sort are like promissory notes, without value unless supported by proper collateral. There is no firm termination to this process. It can continue until the characterization produces conviction, in one direction or another.

We are, of course, supposing that these terms are being used with an *appraisive intention*. Sometimes they are not. It is apparent when one speaks of advancing a cause, cultivating the soil, enriching the diet, fostering research, furthering one's interests, nurturing crocuses, propagating the species, or of injuring the ligaments, debasing the coinage, demolishing fortifications, devastating the forests, tampering with the jury, and polluting the rivers, that these uses are almost or altogether fully condition-determined and not appraisive. In these cases the characterizations that lie back of these processes and support them are all agreed upon. A polluted river kills fish and contributes to disease. The characterization of such water as deleterious and of water free of such traits as salubrious is no longer a matter of appraisive deliberation.

In the appraisive use of these terms, if some measure or process tends to enhance, nurture, refine, or support A or to devastate, pollute, or debase A, we are led to believe that the promise of supporting characterization will be made good. Thus we say, the Moslem alterations of Ste. Sophia in Istanbul debased it, meaning that formerly it was, let us say, "radiant with the splendor of its mosaics" and later "deadened by pretentious, oversize Arabic calligraphy." When we speak of the desolation left by hurricanes, earthquakes, or other natural processes, or of the enhancement of the landscape by the processes of nature unaided, the supporting characterizations are too obvious to need specification.

The concepts of the present number are all causative in a fairly straightforward sense. The attributive terms are dispositional in nature; so also the few substantives. The processives are used to indicate that changes are afoot. We have explained how we are to "read" these changes. In general, the favoritives commend and the adversatives discommend or condemn implied mutations. Specification of these must be "made good" by reference to characterizations. Here the speaker would be called upon to characterize the subject before, after, and perhaps during some causal or other change.

Since the attributive terms are dispositional, they are somewhat more complex than the processives. We may consider briefly their essential features.

The favoritives may be classified in further detail as follows:

(a) **auspicious**   (c) **advantage**   (e) **fortunate**
    favorable   **useful**   **lucky**
    salutary   (d) **benign**   **propitious**
(b) **safe**   **halcyon**   **timely**
    secure   **mild**   **windfall**

In predicating an (a) of an event we say that the apparently ensuing event is to be characterized in crediting terms drawn from various sources of appraisives that are yet to be specified. One may also apply the terms to completely extra-human subject matters though even here the characterization may in the end, reflect human interests. (The vocabulary of 15.3 forms the substance of the efforts of astrologers and casters of horoscopes!)

In predicating (b) we are saying that a given subject will be characterized in some foreseeable future in no less crediting terms than it enjoys now. To say a subject is useful (c) is to say that some other subject causally related in some way to it will be characterized or be characterizable in some crediting manner. To possess an advantage is to be able to show or to deserve a certain crediting characterization at some given time, particularly in the future. **Benign** (d), if it is placed here rather than among terms for mien or air (8.2), is close to the terms in (a), though perhaps with a stronger reference to present characterization as well as the immediate future. Both **halcyon** and **mild** (the terms themselves are neither weak nor mild) also strongly characterize the present in crediting terms while necessarily reflecting a reference to a characterization of at least the immediate future. Context often suggests that this may not extend explicitly to the remoter future. Halcyon days are sometimes ominously brief. (Who does not know the enchanting origin of **halcyon** should hasten to the **NED**). The terms in (e) say that crediting characterizations are in order under just some particular causal conjunction of occurrences and no other or others presently of interest.

Pursuing the same distinctions, the adversative dispositionals largely represent the contrary of the foregoing terms, but there are a few of a rather different nature. We may note the following which are not precise counterparts of the previous: **calamity, catastrophe**, and **disaster. (Mischance, misfortune** and **mishap**, though close to these are rather to be thought of as counterparts of (e) above.) These three seem to be present in their significance, but a moment's reflection shows that it is actually the reference to the future that gives them their overwhelming force. A calamity is not just "for now" but refers us to future options that have been destroyed. All of the terms imply a certain irrevocability. What has been characterizable creditingly *thus* previously, is now irremediably (perhaps) characterizable discreditingly *so* henceforth.

Stigma offers a somewhat different representation of irremediable discredit. It borders on the transcendental (v. Appendix B). Equally near to the transcendental are **fiend, imp,** and **incubus.** These are strictly substantives, rather than attributives and may be segregated in a distinct class. A fiend deserving the name is a being whose foreseeable acts, in fact the totality of whose acts, deserve the extreme of discredit. The extremity is often pressed to the level of the transcendental.

Finally, some of the present terms may appear in a clearer light if we contrast the adversative appraisives with the terms for affects of causal involvement (2.31). A sample of these affects may be recalled:

be [anxious to	**fear**
be [apprehensive that	**foreboding**
confidence	**hope**
presentiment	**panic**
scare	**trepidation**
dread	**worry**

We see once again that response and appraisal (or characterization or commendation) are fundamentally different. While one or more of these affects may be felt when we appraise a situation in adversative terms, the one is not the other. We must therefore resist the temptation to suppose that to say A is malignant, menacing, or sinister is simply to say someone dreads, fears, or worries at the thought of A: he may feel so and again he may not. There is no way in which any kind of analytical legerdemain can "reduce" these adversatives, which are appraisive terms, to emotive responses. It is nonsense to suppose that they somehow contain or embody or even express these responses, for reasons already considered.

A most significant step has been taken in the present section for the analysis of value terms. With terms such as **better** (the verb), **benefit,** and **meliorate** we see we are near the last stage of our inquiry, the problem of commendation itself.

15.4 CONFORMATIVES

CREDITING
ATTRIBUTIVE

adequate	**appropriate**	**aright**
apposite	**apt**	**authentic**

authoritative genuine **real** (aux.)
basic meet a. (also metaphysical
choice natural use, v. App. F.)
condign normal regular
due order, orderly sound
essential ordinary $(-)$ stable
exemplary outright $(-)$ suitable
fit a. perfect unmixed
  proper

PROCESSIVE
conform
do v.
rehabilitate

DISCREDITING
ATTRIBUTIVE

aberrant deviant immoderate
abnormal egregious imperfect
amiss exotic $\pm$ irregular
bizarre $\pm$ extravagant odd
blemish extreme routine
chaos faulty, fault shortcoming
conformism flagrant unmitigated
conventional flaw wayward
defect, defective humdrum wild
detriment, -al

PROCESSIVE

abase v. pervert v.
detract (from) transgress
err (App. A. 2.5) trespass
lapse

15.41 NORMATIVES

basic essential
canonical (normal)
definitive

Like the other terms in 15.0, the conformatives are also syncategorematic. The terms are powerful in use, often employed to sweep aside opposition to given appraisals, and also semantically dangerous. They may communicate absolutely nothing while pretending to make the most momentous assertions. A conformative is significant only if the implicit or presupposed norm is evident, but since it is not supplied by the term itself (being purely formal), the context must supply it. If this is wanting, the term may continue to be emotively effective so long as the fraud is not discovered or so long as no one cares whether anything is being communicated or not.

Now such terms as these are absolutely indispensable, notwithstanding the perpetual temptation to misuse them. We say. "That's abnormal!" "That's perfect!" but a clue must be given as to what normality or perfection is for this category. What is requisite is that the norm be forthcoming and distinct from the present use, that it be defined independently of it. We would notice the mistake in saying that someone consumed an immoderate quantity of food when, it turns out, 'immoderate' was defined only in terms of just the quantity of food consumed, but without any provision or warning that the present use was intended as definitional and stipulative. In one way or another we must be able to determine from the context what norm is presupposed. There are different norms appropriate to Christmas dinners, to survivors of a shipwreck adrift on the high seas, or to a jockey who has to ride this very afternoon.

The foregoing applies to conformatives where a distinct norm is being appealed to. We must distinguish these from presentations of norms themselves. We must, that is, distinguish (a) those which imply the congruence of a presented instance to a norm, from (b) those which assert some set of properties as being the norm to which conformity is required. The first is the *conformative* use; the second is the *normative* use. In (a) the norm must, of course, be sought elsewhere. If in fact no norm is forthcoming the terms are used vacuously, except for their accumulated *emotive momentum*, which, of course, may be enormous.

Consideration of some examples will help to clarify the distinction between the conformatives and normatives.

"That's no way to treat a child." We cannot suppose that this is being said for the purpose of offering a kind of definition of child nurture. (A definition of this sort certainly should not be negative.) Usually in such instances, the listener will know that the critic means by "proper child nurture" nurture that is not cruel, or vindictive, or unreasonable, or permissive, and will also know how to make appropriate application of these terms. This is a conformative statement.

"It's abnormal weather we've been having." "I don't think it's sound business practice." "It was a perfectly natural thing to do." "That dress will do for the occasion." It should be evident in all these examples that the speaker must, in principle, be prepared to expound the abnormalities and proprieties he is appealing to (normal weather for this time of the year, principles of sound business practice, etc.). All of these are conformatives, as is the next example.

"Why buy a Blowhard V–8 when you can afford to buy a real car?" **Real** is a favorite conformative, constantly appealed to. With its aid one can transform virtually any class name into a conformative.

"Keeping files is an essential part of your job." This is a plain example of the normative: the job in question is being defined, or a part of its definition is being given. Innumerable other examples are readily constructible.

The vocabularies of 15.4 and 15.41 are not always fully distinct. We must, therefore, observe that the following usages will all occur. (a) *Conformative implying a norm:* all but the last of the foregoing examples. When it is said that a norm is implied it must not be supposed that somehow the norm is "contained in" the term, but rather that the speaker is in effect inviting a demand to produce a definition of it. The terms in both classes are, as has been said repeatedly, purely formal. (b) *Conformative used as a norm.* This is fraudulent if the present case is made to appear to conform to an independent norm but is actually an *ad hoc* definition. It is, of course, not fraudulent if the particular case is present as the paradigm case, the definitive case. "Napoleon had all the qualities of a great general." (c) *Normative established by definition.* Ordinary speech is almost always too informal to afford many examples of this. It will, therefore, occur mostly in what is deliberately official. (d) *Normative established by exemplification.* What is essential to (d) is that the purpose or the center of interest is the general rule or definition not the particular case. It is otherwise the same as a nonfraudulent case of (b). One suspects self-deception or worse in the use of the Napoleon example by an historian who in effect first reads off Napoleon's abilities, then makes them definitive of a great general, then finds "Napoleon had all, etc." Of course this must be done subtly. "What is needed is a young Josiah Royce," escapes this in the mid-twentieth century since in fact he is dead. But who has not heard of commendations for appointment being tailored for particular appointees, live and appointable?

The distinction between the normative and conformative is not altogether coincident with the segregation of terms themselves as presented here. The essential distinction, therefore, is between presenting or setting up of a norm and asserting the conformity or disconformity of the instance in relation to it. Each case must therefore be considered clearly in and for itself.

It should be noticed that, if the present classification is correct, **normal** and **abnormal**, especially the latter, are to be considered as conformatives, not normatives. (Of course there would scarcely be any point to a "negative normative:" a negation here, including **abnormal**, states that the example does not conform.) **Normally** attached to a sentence seems to have the force of converting it into a normative: "The members of the cabinet are normally of the same political party as the president." It is, of course, possible to use **normal** as a normative. Only an empirical study would be decisive about the use of all of these terms.

We may reiterate that this entire vocabulary is formal only. The terms point in some direction where we must seek the shape of the norm that is presupposed. There we expect a definition or description of the norm to be forthcoming, or possibly a characterization. So if we are told that A is inappropriate, we may receive as an answer to the question. "Why?" the characterizing replies that A is too sophisticated, or too uncompromising, or too squeamish or too splenetic, or what not. Or we may be answered with a set of virtues that are requisites; these we have considered in detail. (We are not here dealing with formalized norms that cease to be appraisive, for example "choice" beef *must be marbled with fat,* heavyweight boxers *must weigh 175 pounds or more,* fish taken from a stream *must be at least six inches in length,* and so forth.) To speak in terms of conformatives without reference to some kind of norm is at least semantically fraudulent. On the other hand, deliberately and carefully constructed norms are not readily found. How far poetic idealization can transcend ordinary efforts of this sort can be seen in Job's glorious lines about the battle steed:

> He paweth in the valley,
> and rejoiceth in his strength;
> He goeth on to meet the armed men...
> He saith among the trumpets, Ha, ha;
> and he smelleth the battle from afar off,
> the thunder of the captains,
> and the shouting.*

An alternative arrangement for 15.4 is suggested in the following sketch of a fourfold ordering of terms. It is evident that conformity is and has been variously appraised in different communities or civilizations. Plato's state and ancient China laid great stress on the virtues of conformity and stability and held change, progress, and novelty suspect. Our own times have seen bitter confrontations between radicals and conservatives. Conformity is thought of only with strong disapprobation in one quarter but is held in esteem elsewhere. **Conformity** as an appraisive has become largely the property of the dissenters. A small sampling from the terms of 15.4 exhibits the opposing standpoints and explains itself. The vocabularies could easily be expanded from current journalism.

---

* Job 39:21–25.

CONFORMATIVES   +

POSITIVE CHARACTERISMS	NEGATIVE CHARACTERISMS
CREDITING	CREDITING
authentic	exotic
exemplary	fresh
genuine	original
normal	unconventional
etc.	etc.

+ ═══════════════════ × ═══════════════════ −

DISCREDITING	DISCREDITING
conformism	amiss
conventional	blemish
humdrum	defective
routine	deviant
etc.	etc.

−

From this we see plainly how both conforming and non-conforming can each have a crediting and a discrediting orientation. Each of these will be needed on appropriate occasions for the presentation of our thought.

15.42   MATURATIVES, APPRAISIVES OF DEVELOPMENT

ATTRIBUTIVE		PROCESSIVE
CREDITING		CREDITING
durable		culminate
fresh		flourish
mellow		endure
mature a.		mature v.
precocious		prosper
		thrive

DISCREDITING		DISCREDITING
(a) anile	(b) childish	decay
decrepit	immature	deteriorate
dotage	inchoate	disintegrate
moribund	premature	regress
obsolete,	puerile	stagnate
obsolescent	underdone	
senile	juvenile (−) or	
stagnant	[juvenile]	
stale		

What is characteristic of the maturatives as a kind of special case of the conformatives is the factor of growth, of alteration in time, but also something more, as we shall presently see. The terms are useful both in their original literal sense, referring to the life cycle of organic beings, and their metaphorical sense, applied to innumerable entities that may be construed as having careers. The maturative vocabulary spells out the several stages of the cycle.

We could regard every stage of organic cycles as equally normal. We learn again that, "to every thing there is a season, and a time to every purpose under the heaven." We could also declare every deviant condition as normal if we thought a suitable causal explanation for it was forthcoming. But what is involved in the idea of maturing as an appraisive is something more than that of conforming to a norm. There must be the further thought of a unique optimum condition prevailing at some time during the cycle, otherwise infancy and anility would not be regarded as deficiencies. Both of these are, of course, normal since they are causally inevitable. The maturative vocabulary does not express itself as to when such a special time, a culmination or apogee is reached. It merely makes available to us expressions for it. The exemplifications of maturity must be regarded as variable. It is frequently thought that the imaginative poetic capacity flourishes best in childhood and youth; Freudians have developed theories of the artist's regression to such a period. From this standpoint all other periods are ones of immaturity or senility, so that poetic senility may set in at twenty. At this age, however, athletic maturity is only being fully reached and continues for some years. Again, at that age intellectual capacities are usually nowhere as powerful as they are some years thereafter and may often increase continuously during a lifetime.

The maturative vocabulary is therefore built around the ideas of (1) growth, (2) normality of development, and (3) culmination. (We exclude neither "cancers flourish," nor "anything causally explainable is generally thought to be normal or unanomalous"). Only if we look at growth and normality from the standpoint of culmination can we speak of maturing: if we can regard the body as reaching a unique summit of physical development at, let us say, age 20–24, then we have a way of interpreting growth and development on either side of this period.

I think we can also say that growth apart from culmination is no value, since it cannot very well be thought desirable if it runs to limitless lengths. Since the economic and industrial revolution, and especially in our own times, economic growth has appeared to be an inherent value with no thought given to whether this can really be projected into the infinite future. For obviously if no other factors are allowed, an earth covered a hundred feet deep with manufactured products, even just six-penny nails, is as desirable as what we have now. Pragmatism, so far as I can see, offered nothing more than *growth* as a human ideal, perhaps another consequence of the "Protestant ethic." Its weakness as compared with other ideologies as various as Platonism, Roman Catholic Christianity, and Marxism was in offering no genuine apogee for growth. The complete leveling inherent in existentialism offers even less substantial goals than this.

We must be careful not to read too much or too little into the fact that we have this particular scheme of appraisives. The fact that we have such notions of maturation and culmination does not entail our having suitable exemplifications of them firmly in mind, either in personal consciousness or in the body politic. But, equally, the fact that we have such notions is some indication that we have all along felt the necessity of organizing processes that perdure through time along the lines of development, fruition and satisfaction. In this sense no appraisive concepts can be more significant than those of the present number.

15.5   ESTIMATIVES

CREDITING

(a) champion
    classic
    consummate a.
    glorious
    fabulous
    foremost
    formidable
    immortal
    inestimable
    invaluable
    lofty
    matchless
    paragon
    paramount
    peerless
    prime
    stellar
    superb
    superior
    supernacular

    supreme
    surpassing
    topnotch
    unequalled
(b) conspicuous
    distinctive
    extraordinary
    noteworthy
    outstanding
    peculiar
    phenomenal
    pre-eminent
    salient
    sensational
    unexampled
    unique
(c) important
    momentous
    weighty (G. wichtig)

DISCREDITING

(d)	commonplace	(f)	debris
	bagatelle		derelict
	banal		detritus
	fair		dross
	feeble		flagrant
	hackneyed		jetsam
	innocuous		leavings
	mediocre		refuse n.
	mere (aux.)		rubbish
	middling		rummage
	ordinary		shambles
	so-so		trash
	typical		useless
(e)	base	(g)	abject
	nugatory		abysmal
	nonentity		flagrant
	null		outright
	petty		rank a.
	rank a.		unconscionable
	trifle, trifling		unmitigated
	trivial		unspeakable

With the estimatives we have still another class of *appraisive syncategorematics*. Although they are comparatively numerous, they are in large measure repetitive in meaning. Like the preceding several classes, they have only a syntactive or formal function so far as their significance is concerned. With no content of their own, we are being referred back to other ways of appraisal. If we are dealing with human subject matters, the characterisms of Part Two must furnish the needed reference. They differ from the conformatives in not implicating a norm. They simply indicate that the characterizations that may be implicated are of a certain degree: the creditings or discreditings may be unreserved, or qualified in some degree.

Among the crediting estimatives, we may discern some three groups, each based on a somewhat different image. The crediting group (a) uses the figure of a *summit*. By definition, a summit is a single point and distinguished from all its surroundings. This image is so inevitable it would be surprising if it did not occur in virtually every language. In (b) we have before us the closely similar idea of a *figure arising out of a ground*, a familiar visual (and also auditory) phenomenon, whereby a member of a group gains eminence simply by the way in which it contrasts with other members. So also may individuals be deemed by those who appraise them. A third image (c) exploits the idea of *gravity*. A member is distinguished by its sheer ponderousness. To cope with it there is no alternative to walking around it. Or it may serve as the support of weaker members, or its impact may be greater than that of any others. Perhaps still further distinctions may be made.

It is evident that these images are selected because their potency is likely to match the strength of feelings that may concomitantly be had toward subjects. What more enthusiastic approbation can be offered than to see the subject as a lofty summit, or a brilliant, arresting and inescapable patch of color. But for that very reason, it is easy to be carried away and to enjoy not only the brilliant quality of the subject, but even perhaps to respond to the strength of one's response. It is obvious that audiences often enjoy not only the singer's performance but are carried away by their own applause to it. There is escalation and feedback in this. It is the enjoyment of the enjoyment that is being enjoyed!

For this very reason, the impression is likely to take hold that something significant and material has been uttered in the mere speaking of these terms. But we must repeat, the terms are but syntactive; in and of themselves they convey nothing relative to the subject; it is only what they point toward and promise that has any significance. They are like the final numerical score of a football game or tennis match. A gambler may be likely to have *only* an interest in the score, since this is the only aspect of the match that has any significance for his business or livelihood. But any true *amateur* will want to know much more than this. How were the points made? What brilliant plays, what errors of judgment were made? This is like asking, "What do you mean?" or, "Why do you say so?" to someone who has expressed himself in terms of the estimatives of 15.5, and indeed of any of the commendatives in 15.0.

It is evident that the discrediting terms in (d) (**mediocre**, etc.), despite appearances are not at an intermediate degree between the outright rejectives of (e), (f), (g) and the crediting terms just considered. Such terms are used to reject subjects however adequately these may serve in certain respects. The figures of the summit and of the figure on its ground are rather less evident than that of a void in the discreditings in (e). The discrediting vocabulary in (f) is but a trifling fraction of a whole range which the P, M, and S appraisive tongues ceaselessly augment.

A familiar complaint is heard about the vacuity of superlative terms. But it is apparent from what has been said that it is an idle misapprehension of their function to look for content in them. If they are significant, they are so only in terms of concrete, significant characterisms, such as we have set forth in Part Two.

15.6 ULTIMATE COMMENDATIVES

CREDITING	DISCREDITING
asset	bad (worse, worst)
credit	demerit
excellent	foul
good (better, best)	worthless
great	
merit	
precious	
valuable, value	
welfare	
well adv.	
worthy	

(A) *The Recursion of Commendation.* With the large overview of valuing situations and processes afforded by the foregoing investigations, we may proceed with some confidence toward the examination of ultimate appraisives such as **good** and **bad**. This brings us nearly to the end of our study, but considering the place that the good has always occupied in the thought of moral philosophers it is inevitably one of the most important topics of all. We maintain, however, that the role of the good in value inquiry has been exaggerated, at the expense of topics of far greater practical importance, those namely that we have already considered in detail. We here accord it a place of significance but without permitting an overstatement of its role in valuation. There are no doubt numerous weighty issues about the good which have here been left out of account. At the same time a somewhat different frame of interpretation may have been afforded.

The good, or **good**, as we see it, is an ultimate and somewhat abstract notion. It is ultimate in the sense that it may presuppose for its clarification or support any and all of the whole previous train of appraisive concepts. It is without significance except in reference to them, and so far as evidence is concerned they are all independent of it. Its generality rests on the fact that it is the only notion that may be involved in *all* of the foregoing. This is not true of special commendatives. If one asks what all of the numerous crediting terms have in common, if anything, one may perhaps say, the good: they all affirm something good of the subject, the discreditings something bad. But such a common feature is necessarily very dilute since it is involved in so many hundreds of different contexts. We shall consider this question further below.

Good and commendations in general are significant only in terms of a reference back to a body of characterizing concepts. If we are thinking of man this means reference to the appraisives and characterisms of Part Two. We call this *recursion*. The underlying principle Z is:

> In all uses of 'good,' recursion to material characterims and appraisives must be assured either as explication or evidence.

We may always demand an explication of the term, and this must be forth-coming in terms of some part of the appraisive vocabulary. We must expect, "A is good," to be met with, "Why do you say so?" The response to this may be to offer characterizations or judgments (each in appropriate cases) either as reasons or as analyses or explications.

When **good** is used without available recursion to possible supporting characterizations, it will still retain its capacity to commend and what appears to be its emotive power or momentum. It is like a cheque on a bank: its significance depends upon the funds back of it – these are like the character-isms that support **good**. The sight of a cheque is also a source of pleasure to the payee who receives it – this is like the emotive power associated with **good**. Even a worthless cheque, so long as its fraudulence or insufficiency is not known, will for a time produce pleasure; and so long as we have not yet discovered that there are no characterisms for it to recur to, **good** may still exert its emotive power. But once its pretense and want of support is exposed, it will cease to be significant, and its power to arouse any feelings should likewise vanish.

The support for a commendation can also come, for a time at least, from another quarter, a frankly *ad hominem* kind of source. I respect a commenda-tion because so and so has issued it. This has even more similarity to the receipt of certain cheques: I accept so and so's cheques and even his mere IOU's because they are always good: I accept so and so's commendation because they are always made good by supporting characterizations on demand. What no one will expect me to respect is the mere outer form of negotiable instruments without the facts, convictions, and conventions that lie back of them.

(B) "*Emotive Meaning*." The theory of emotive meaning expects some-thing very similar to that. **Good** as possessing emotive meaning hopes, as it were, to gain favor, to produce emotive euphoria, simply from itself alone; it is apparently thought to "embody" and "convey" euphoric emotion. It receives no support from what the speaker may properly be expected to *say* in rational support or explication of it: since nothing is being asserted, no evidence can be brought forward to support it. Moreover, all crediting terms, including characterisms, have only this kind of significance – characterisms do not serve to support commendations. Commendations embody and con-vey not thought but emotion.

Our investigation has led to diametrically different conclusions. The idea that words can *convey emotion* is utterly void of significance. Furthermore, the idea that emotive language is somehow determined by or "embodies" emotive responses is simply a *hysteron proteron*. We are invited to think that our emotions are essentially blind and that they are originating and ultimate springs of action. Just the reverse is true. Why do I hate B? I hate him when I come to *see him as* a fool who has acquired a position of power and responsibility, or as a peevish, irascible pedant, or as a reckless fanatic in whose hands an enterprise will decline or come to ruin, and so on. The emotivist alternative is to suppose that I think up terms like 'peevish' to "express" my hatred and as a kind of epiphenomenon of my hatred. On the contrary, characterization should be looked upon as the wisdom of the emotions. The education of the emotions begins with learning how to characterize, and only from this can we proceed to commendations and discommendations. We must therefore recognize the proper function of characterization and its relation both to life, which it can serve to rationalize, and to expressions of commendation and condemnation, for which it provides the foundation.

The purpose of characterization is to rationalize the emotions, and it can do so either in the best or the worst sense of the term. Emotion is conveyed not by the sentence that charges someone with being a crackpot, sycophant, jackass, or pedant – it is a mere manner of expression to say so – but *by the fact that* the subject was appraised in this manner. When we express ourselves in that manner we probably also feel a notable degree of emotion, and when we hear someone appraised in this manner we may grasp both what is being said and the fact that whoever has said it has felt a strong degree of emotion.

There is far less emotion in these situations than the notion of emotive meaning suggests. But even assuming emotion to be literally felt in them, it is meaningless to suppose that it is conveyed by some form of words. What is necessary to "convey the emotion" is for the speaker to characterize a subject by the verbal instruments which the listener also uses to characterize comparable subjects: if the emotion accompanies the use in the first case it may do so also in the second. In short, characterizing and commending terms seek to signify in the same manner as the rest of language. They seek to convey our *thought* when our emotions are stirred. If we do not wish to express such thought there is scarcely any alternative but to bare one's fangs. But behaving in such an overt manner should not be called an *expression of* the emotion – it *is* or *is a part of* the emotion, quite a different thing. It is, however, the only thing one might reasonable mean by the phrase, "emotive meaning". Who can really believe that commendation (and its contrary) and characterization are processes as crude as this?

To see in so-called "judgments" using 'good' the mere expression of emotion is thus to reduce appraisal to an exercise of force. Probably all interchange among persons, even reporting the time of day, intrinsically involves or is accompanied by emotions in their many degrees and kinds, named and nameless. All human response involves an expenditure of energy. But to see *only* this in appraisal is to make a monstrous distortion of this aspect of human life. It is refuted by the massive fact of the enormous resources, inexhaustible in power and subtlety, of appraisive language itself. So rich is our creativity in this regard that we are never content to speak only the A-vocabulary (many are virtually ignorant of most of its resources), but we have resort also to the limitless resources of M, S, and P vocabularies. Words rarely fail even the most cloddish person determined to utter an appraisal. If he hates, the chances are very near certainty that he knows *why* he hates. He knows what it is to feel mere "blind" hatred and how to recognize this. If you tell him that his reasons here, now, and always (for this is what the emotive theory demands) merely put a verbal gloss on what he feels (and all feelings may as well be thought blind according to the theory) your charge will offend his understanding of his involvement. Moreover, as we have insisted, telling him that he is merely "translating" or "embodying" his feelings into words is a mere facile phrase. In short, he knows that bringing down invective on an enemy in an effective manner is using a weapon that differs not only in degree but in kind from spitting in his face.

The whole emotivist program is misconceived because it resorts to the crudest reductivist procedures, generates a fictitious category of meaning, and offers little more than literary metaphors when it talks of the role of emotion in valuation. It is not easy to see why it has been thought to be a potent explanatory device.

Thus we can neither confine the analysis of appraisal and appraisive sentences in the narrow bounds connoted by such phrases as 'emotive meaning,' nor restrict ourselves in such an analysis to the study of good. Some theories of value of this sort seem to begin where we end, but in fact unless one goes back to where we have begun, the beginning *is* the end. *After* the good there is little more to be said; to hover endlessly on it alone is vacuous; the only alternative is to examine the whole appraisive process. These then are the reasons we have left the good for the end of our study. In fact, of course, it can commence or complete it, so long as it is not treated as if it stood alone.

(C) *Commendation.* The good and bad, have in effect, been under study here wherever we have considered crediting and discrediting vocabularies, that is to say, from the very beginning of the vocabulary of characterization. These and other commendative terms have numerous dimensions of meaning which have been revealed by the division of the areas of characterization. By referring to these we are able to give a more detailed and systematic account than is usually afforded by dictionaries, although of course that is far from being our principal end in view.

If we follow St. Thomas Aquinas, we find the idea of the good divided among the honorable, the delightful, and the useful.* If we turn to Wyld or the NED, the result is not very different: the principal areas of use are said to be these:

I Morally excellent, kind, pious;

II Agreeable, amusing, salutary;

III Useful, efficient for a function;

IV Adequate, valid, effectual ("in good faith," "give a good account of oneself," "take good care to").

All of these are preceded in the NED by the general description, "A term of general or indefinite commendation." This is corroborated by what has been said here provided we seek also the means that are available to render the commendation in **good** definite. This is to be undertaken through the process of recursion as prescribed by principle Z. So far as application to persons is concerned, our body of characterisms affords detailed means for this. Man is no doubt the most important subject of appraisal for us but there are means also for other recursions, for example the appraisives of arguments, ponents, aesthetic data, and so on, presented in their essentials in the Appendices. As we are using the term, an actual recursion is undertaken when the user of a commendative or discommendative is pressed either to say what he means by it, or to give his reasons for it. Hence what we shall attempt here is not itself recursion but a clarification of just how the previous sections afford the means of recursion. There are commendations, such as some in class III which are, of course, of no interest here: we are not concerned with good knives and bad apples.

To set forth what may enter into the recursion of **good**, we proceed first to the general and ultimate virtues (14.4). If we speak of persons, human institutions, human relationships, and human actions as good or bad it may suffice to recur to such terms as those of 14.4. We have there set forth how we employ concepts such as **integrity, honor,** and **humanity** to characterize persons. It will be remembered that it was only in deference to our linguistic and evaluative customs that we set forth the virtues and vices in their distinctive style, which is traditionally substantive as to grammatical form and separated from other characterisms. In fact, however, they are merely more eminent and significant characterisms.

The general virtues in turn inherently recur to the more specific virtues

---

* St. Thomas Aquinas, *Philosophical Texts*, ed. Thomas Gilby, Oxford, 1956, § 215.

and vices which precede them, that is, to the specific virtues from 14.1 through 14.3 the behavioral, diathetic, tendentive, sex-related, economic, and social. Less often the general virtues recur to the intellectual, judgmental and communicational virtues and characterizations. A rich variety of different ideas and ideals comes to mind when one reviews substantives of highest commendation of persons in various languages: the upright or righteous man of Biblical tradition, the *bonhomme*, the *prud'homme*, the *honnête homme*, the *schöne Seele* of German literature, the Confucian *jên*, the Greek ideal of κᾱλοκᾱγαθία, the *optimates* of Roman politics, the ἄριστοι of idealized Greek society, and yet others.* (Perhaps the colorless phrase, 'an able man,' would commonly recur to the intellectual and associated virtues in 14.1, 14.2, and 14.3.) The recursion of these would take us not only into verbal analysis but involve search into the literary, social, and religious sources of ideals.

The recursion to 14.0 is only one step in the process. The next step is to recur further to the characterisms of 7.0 to 13.0: behavior, tendence, sex-relatedness, sociation, economic process, and community. This opens up wider possibilities of interpretation. The appraiser, then, who has told us that A is good with some kind of "moral emphasis" and has been requested to specify his meaning or to explain his reasons, must seek and find them among characterisms applying to persons, actions, situations, institutions, or relationships expressible in the appraisive vocabulary, or among other appraisals which will be considered below.

(D) *Recursion to Determinate Conditions.* Is this as far as the recursion can be carried? In the next sections we shall explore recursion to Part One. But before we do so we may ask whether the recursion of commendations must or can be carried over to descripts and descriptions. Our reply is that characterizations are irreducible quantities, as ultimate as the molecules of a chemical compound, qua compound. This needs some further defense, to which we may turn immediately.

Let us take **dignity** or **pretentious** and reflect on how we learn these terms. For **dignity**, one may point to the stance, the bearing, the degree of inflexibility, the slowness of motion of the subject: no precise stance or motion is to be discriminated, but these are the kinds of traits, or sets of traits, that are particularly to be observed and themselves perhaps characterized. One may also speak in terms of other supporting or parallel characterisms until the unique character **dignity** is finally discriminated. With **pretentious** one may be invited to observe relative size, distinctness of color, amount of ornamental detail, discrepancy between the apparent claims of the structure and the result it delivers, and so on. Recourse may be had to other characterisms,

---

* Not to mention, "You're a good man, Charlie Brown!"

also, drawn from the vocabulary for air, bearing, mien, and manner.

What these examples show us is not that the characterisms somehow "contain" this descriptive reference as part of their meaning but show rather the precise "objective" aspects that are being discriminated in the characterization. The instruction in learning such a term as **dignity** is not to see that someone is x feet tall, or has y stance, but rather, to observe his height, his stance, and to characterize *them*. To learn the use of a characterism is not to be told "what it means" in "descriptive" terms, but to be told what precisely we are being invited to characterize. If there is circularity in this, there is no remedy for it.

If we are asked for a recursion of **good** where capacities of intelligence are particularly under consideration, we shall first be referred to a certain constellation of characterisms from 6.0. There is no standard choice of these to be specified in advance; immediate context is obviously decisive as well. If A commends B as good or competent in this sense, he is likely to speak of B's breadth of intelligence, his capacities of discrimination, counsel, and arbitrament in judgment, his capacities for expressing himself. If evidence about intelligence or judgment in "objective terms" is demanded, we can do no more than point in a certain direction and show what in fact is being appraised. To support a commendation of intelligence means being able to ask or answer relevant questions: "How is B at figures and mastering statistics?" or "How does he arrive at decisions?" The answers will cite and appraise factual matter.

The question of supporting commendations is therefore something entirely different from supporting descriptions – a not unexpected result. We cannot derive or deduce commendations or characterizations from descriptions of the appretiands. If we could, commendations would be descriptions. We have, however, ample reasons for denying that they are. When we ask for determinate conditions we are asking less for logical support for the characterization than for a more detailed or ample account of what is being characterized. If this is supplied, and if we command even a rudimentary understanding of the language of characterization, we can decide whether we can endorse the characterization.

It is such processes of exploration of each other's minds, as it were, and not efforts to "resolve disagreement in attitude" directly that may be considered as the relevant approach to the resolution of differences in evaluation. No one readily or knowingly submits to having his "attitudes" revised and reorganized by others. He has, however, no reason to resent a request for further and more detailed, or ampler and more comprehensive characterization.

At the present time policemen are the subject of often limitless condemnation. If, however, one could produce a climate of calm consideration, a common ground could be found. Law is inherently meant to have the force of a legislating community behind it. One may therefore expect its force sometimes to be palpably felt. At the same time, such a force is no abstraction. It is *this* person in uniform laying hands on *this* suspect in *this* way. We cannot excuse his every act simply because the law must be enforced. Neither can we expect the law to refrain from resorting to force. The characterization of the policeman's act must consider the policeman neither as a mere abstraction ("the law") nor as only a particular personality in the narrowest personal context. The only alternative to seeking fair characterizations in this manner is the sanguinary clash of two blind "attitudes."

If we listen carefully to our evaluations, our characterizations and commendations we learn that we seek to support commendations by offering reasons. We need not apologize for using the word 'reason' here; it is not the exclusive property of our fact-finding and theory-building capacities. The reasons we offer are our more detailed characterizations of the subjects of commendation. Emotions commonly accompany our commendations without being identical with them. We may thus not only discommend someone but indicate we hate him. But what we are seeking reasons for is not so much our hatred as our discommendation. We are perfectly capable of distinguishing between an irrational response whose resort to characterization merely "rationalizes" the particular hatred or love in question, and a hatred or love which is fully and amply supported by structures of characterization. The emotive theory supposes no one can make such a distinction. The only remedy is to have a better ear for what is being said. This is not the first occasion on which philosophers have put words into our mouths because they have been turning a deaf ear to what we have said. It is in fact one of the pathologies of the profession.

What we can hope to find for our commendations in recurring to determinate conditions in the subject of appraisal is not demonstrative proof for them, for no conceivable amassment of such description can have such an outcome but rather an ampler account of what we believe ourselves to be characterizing and commending. Assuming that there is a *lingua franca* of characterization – a very searching condition – a resolution of our problem is always possible, and that is, a commendation mutually acceptable to ourselves and others, subject to the limitations of all appraising.

The problem of finding reasons for commendation is not one of undertaking the hopeless task of finding support for an *ought* in an *is*, to adopt the favored philosophical idiom: since commendations and their supporting characterizations are already of the same "genus" this celebrated "issue" does not arise.

(E) *Recursion to Acts and Processes of Response.* The characterisms of Part Two begin with the conduct of intelligence and then expand toward conduct in socially oriented actions. All of these bear directly on the commendation of persons. We turn next to the acts, powers, and procedures of Part One. These may express themselves in characterization and eventually in commendation. Here the questions that must be raised are: What is the pattern of A's responses (appetitions, sympathies, antipathies), how does he conduct his appraisals, how does he arrive at or observe his commitments, how does he conduct himself in his moral involvements and moral judgment? Answers to these questions are obviously relevant to the commendation of persons.

The general question we must consider is how various acts or procedures are to be evaluated. In and of themselves they are all of them neither to be praised nor dispraised: everyone at one time or another quite properly craves, wants, hankers after, admires, abhors, mistrusts, approves, depreciates, commits himself, censures, repents (to make a selection at random among the verbs in Part One). The relevance of these acts or procedures to commendation is not, therefore, that they occur or do not occur, but must rather be that they are directed toward proper accusatives or are misdirected, that they are or are not properly conducted.

We begin with fruitions or satisfactions and responses. In an important sense we cannot misconduct satisfactions and responses since they are not conducted at all. Yet although they are not conducted, whether properly or improperly, still, they are permitted to occur. They are indulged and the subject frequently earns blame from this, or of course commendation.

Indulgence, then, or permitting responses to occur, must be evaluated and is one source to which commendation must recur. When we now ask how we are to appraise such indulgence we find that actually we have already considered the matter in the diathetic, tendentive, sex-related, and sociative characterisms. Thus, admirations, affections, likings (and their dyspathic contraries) prove to have been characterized under mood, human conditions, engagement, amatory concern, and various sociations. The responsional characterizations in 2.4 (also classified under 8.3) show particularly well what is available here to recur to in our commendations. When we compare these characterizations, for example, with the noncharacterizing terms for the direct pathic responses in 2.2 (sympathic and dyspathic) we see that the responses are often found to be overreactions, excessive, more than the occasion warrants: fuming at, bearing grudges, being enraged at, flying into a temper, etc. Or the subject's composure is adversely spoken of, he is thought to have given way to emotions when he might have controlled them, and so on.

We should emphasize that it is not the passing response that is generally under consideration in the commendation of persons, but rather the habits of response of the person. Characterization always seeks to get at the permanent possibilities, likelihoods, and even (pretended) certainties of conduct.

(F) *Recursion to Appraisal and Characterization.* The test of a commendation is its recursion to characterisms and to the various acts and procedures involved in valuation. We turn next to recursion to the processes of appraisal and the question whether the pattern of appraisals meets a certain standard. We therefore envisage the appraisal of appraisal itself. There are several ways in which characterizations might themselves be appraised. For example, they might be found more or less witty, or more or less poetic. But for the ultimate commendation of a person these traits would not be thought to be very significant. The desiderata here will be whether the appraisals have been conducted in a manner to seek their own correction, whether they have shown effort to appraise what they purport to appraise, and whether they show a command of the available instruments of the concepts of appraisal. These requisites are all inherent in the notion of appraisal itself, and they of themselves prescribe its proper conduct.

It is questionable whether we can compress these requisites into a simple evaluative term comparable, let us say, to **truth**, but perhaps the term **fair** will be most characteristically employed in this connection. We must, of course, be careful to distinguish it from **just**, since this term is to be reserved for moral judgment where we have prescripts or commitments to conform to. This is not altogether easy to do: we should be reminded of the fact that one term must serve for both **just** and **fair** in Spanish, Italian, French, and there is no full congruent in German. The phrases 'fair characterization' and 'fair appraisal' have, however, a certain standing in English and may be appealed to so long as we do not suppose that appraisals, when fair, may be "derived" from principles of some sort.

(G) *Recursion to Moral Judgment and Enactment.* It needs little argument to carry the recursion of **good** to moral judgment and to the enactment on which it rests. As we saw in 5.32 the process of judging finally faces an appraisal in terms of **right, wrong, judicious, injudicious, justice, injustice, partial, impartial.** Such appraisives are not characterisms. They are based on the procedural principle I have formulated as T in discussing 5.32:

> **Right** and **just** are concepts without essential content serving a
> purely formal and adverbial purpose in assessing the derivation
> of present decisions from supervenient obligations.

The complex process of moral judgment issues finally in a decision taken either in accordance with, in defiance of, in ignorance of, or with indifference toward supervenient obligations. If these are not at hand, it is needless to speak of moral judgment at all.

The question about the recursion of good to the present areas comes down, then, to how the person plays his role in all phases of moral judgment. Does he grieve or protest at what is incompatible with commitments, feel indignation at, accuse, and hold culpable those who violate them, admonish or rebuke where this has a likelihood of mending affairs, intercede or supplicate for those wrongly accused or unjustly punished (one must here refer to T), recant or repent his own errors, absolve from guilt those who have shed its burdens justly, and so on through the outcomes and sequels of the processes of justice, formal or informal as outlined in 5.0? A code of immense and searching demands is set up, honored as often in the breach as in the observance, but ceaselessly appealed to, particularly if one himself suffers injustice in violation of T.

If we have been correct in urging the necessity for supposing that men must have entered upon certain commitments for the procedures of moral judgment to have significance, then this likewise must enter into any recursion of the idea of good to the habits and practices of moral judgment. It is not necessary, of course, that one and the same use of the term **good** should involve or entail all of the areas in which recursion has been explored, but clearly we will *sometimes* commend persons in such a way as to lead us to recur beyond all the virtues of 14.0 through all the areas of characterization from 7.0 to 13.0 to moral judgment (5.0) and enactment (4.0). I shall not enter into the question of what the substance of commitment should be in order for the recursion of commendation to be carried out successfully: that is, what commitments are compatible with the good. But at least some indication may be given of the direction which commitment is likely to take if it is brought to the agent's attention. Briefly it is as follows.

First of all, we need respect only persons who have basic moral intelligence. This is to be defined as an intelligence that employs a full gamut of characterisms. These, we have said, are the originals of all valuing. All other value concepts take their rise in a significant body of characterizing terms.

From this core there then develop the virtues and the ultimate commendatives. This body of terms certainly can be conceived to depart quite considerably, for some persons or societies, from the body here assembled. One can envisage a fairly broad negation of the sexual, tendentive, and economic ethic adumbrated by the present body of characterisms. But even radical schemes which readily come to mind make only what prove to be very partial adjustments. We may take economic characterisms as an example. Both a conceivable economy of limitless plenty and the present economy of scarcity and thrift are entirely expressible in the present vocabulary. (Would the discrediting concept **waste** be likely to fall entirely into desuetude?) For example, the acquisition vocabulary (12.22), in effect says, *if* there is property that is private then these are the modes of theft, but nothing is said of property which is not private or goods lying outside the domain of property. Hence, if there is no property at all, it is safe to assume that there can be no cases of theft. But no conceivable society can make *what we call theft* a virtue. Or again, do we wish to condemn wealth rather than praise it? We already have the means at hand in 12.2: **nabob, moneybags, plutocrat**. Do we wish to praise non-engagement instead of engagement? The means are readily available in 9.22. And so on.

At the same time, what appear to be some radical departures from the present scheme are readily conceivable for which new characterisms would have to be found. Under economic possession (12.23) we find no characterisms crediting poverty: this is easily conceived and was occasionally in the past praised and practiced as a virtue. No crediting of pure sexuality comes to mind in 10.3: this is an accident of our history that might have been different. Again, certain societies in the past celebrated homosexuality as virtuous and sanctified the occupation of the female prostitute. Such practices change significantly in different societies; it is too late in the historic day to condemn them as satanic institutions even if they do not regain crediting.

On the whole we may say that the English vocabulary evinces a greater flexibility among the peoples that speak the language than we are likely to expect. Even a considerable convulsion in practice is unlikely to turn the moral system fully upside down. At the same time the core vocabulary we have studied does reflect an ethic with a definite structure and character.

The results may be summarized by saying that the body of characterisms in English shows a considerable latitude of moral custom except in certain significant details; that moral intelligence is first of all the possession of and the capacity to employ a significant range of characterisms such as these; that the categories or systems of characterisms in actual use beyond those here represented are probably broadly congruent, although their differences from the standpoint of the present study would be for us far more significant; and that the existence of systems of characterisms *in use* entails the fact of allegiance to commitments. The last point deserves further elaboration.

The person who would say, "I believe in the advancement of evil, wrong, wickedness," clearly wouldn't be using these terms in any received sense; what in practice his commitments would be is indeterminate. He might be saying something paradoxical merely for the "effect" he creates, thus not actually departing from a more orthodox scheme of value. He might simply be expressing a taste for practices this society condemns and expecting to evoke shock in so doing. But most societies can absorb quite severe convulsions. In any event, these terms ('evil,' 'wicked') are not to be defined in terms of some actual list of deeds and practices. The satanist will have to go to much greater lengths either to place himself outside *this* domain of values or outside *every* domain, if that is his aim.

In general, sharing and using an appraisive vocabulary is virtually conclusive evidence of sharing a set of values. We may advert once more to Hume's profound remark in "The Standard of Taste," quoted in the introduction.* To use value terms is to acknowledge the sway of precepts, be practice what it may. It would be an empirical matter similar to our own investigation to determine actual use. Having determined this, we can with some effort determine the character of moral codes. This fairly readily yields consequences as to what counts as a good man in such a code. It is really quite difficult to escape the jurisdiction of such codes, as our discussion of the Hat and of anarchy earlier will have shown.

But for one further consideration, the role of satisfaction (1.0), this completes our discussion of the recursion of good. Our purpose in pursuing this matter into all the corners of Part Two and Part One has been to show how we can and must meet the demand that implicitly confronts every use of the ultimate commendatives either for reasons for commendation or for an elucidation of commendation. To be significant, each use of **good** or any other commendative or discommendative must find its recursion in these earlier modes of characterizing, appraising and judging. For the "moral" use of good (class I) set forth so pre-eminently by all lexicographers we must recur first to the virtues, thence to the areas of characterization, particularly 10.0, 11.0, 12.0, and 13.0 (parts of 8.0 and 9.0 also may be relevant), and then to the procedures of 3.0, 4.0, and 5.0. If we must seek the recursion in other areas (class III and IV) we may need to turn to 6.0 (intelligence), or 9.0 (tendence). For class II (agreeable, salutary) we particularly need to turn to 7.0, and 2.0 (response) but also to the body of aesthetic appraisives sketched in Appendix C.

In these recursions we have focussed attention particularly on the commendation of the "good man," merely as an example. Recursions for uses of 'good' to commend entities other than persons are not of course covered by the characterisms from 6.0 to 13.0 and the virtues of 14.0 since Part Two confines itself to the characterization of man. We must therefore recur to other vocabularies, some of which are given in the Appendices.

---

* Hume, "Of the Standard of Taste," quoted above p. 22.

16.0 ABSOLUTE VALENTS

avail (Cf. L. *valere*, to be strong)
count, v. intrans. (= be effective) (Cf. G. *gelten*)
deserve (5.22)
do, v. intrans. (= suffice)
merit v.
rank v. intrans.
suffice
be of [value, be [valuable (Cf. F. *valoir*)
be [worth..., **be [worthy of**

As we had occasion to observe regarding satisfaction (1.0), the beginning and end of our study are intimately allied. Both are concerned with *having value*. In 1.0 we studied the person's possession of value. We could call this an *act* of possessing, if possessing were an act. Here the individual possesses the value *x*, or the value of *x*, by enjoying *x*. Without this unique and unanalyzable experience there would be no vocabulary of value, even if there were other vocabularies. Life, and life at other "levels" than man's, is scarcely thinkable without the energy and impetus provided by constant or repeated satisfaction of need and want, and the ceaseless alternation of want and satisfaction.

Enjoyment, satisfaction, gratification, fruition all approximate to the idea that must stand as the anchor of the whole process of appraisal. It is not to be taken in a narrow sense, where it merely designates the satisfaction of immediate physical need or want. But this *is* the link to other "levels" of organic beings, and what the concept of enjoyment connotes is that man is among those beings that are not indifferent to their environment: all of them can and do, as seems fit to them, resist certain forces in the rest of nature that are arrayed against them and acquiesce in others. Selection and choice are obviously endemic to such beings.

The class of beings capable of making selection, must be regarded as including, in degree, all of the higher animal beings and not just human beings. In this interpretation we must not be deterred by charges of anthropomorphism but rather try to see how we may extend the idea of selection to ever broader areas. We must use behaviorism as a weapon against itself: if we assimilate man to the animals, we assimilate animals to man. Otherwise, the behaviorist repudiation of the two levels thesis about animals and men was a sham to begin with. Selection is a reality on both levels, and the more complex articulation of human choices signified in the several areas of characterization results from the greater complexity of man's grasp of the environment: grasp of time, space, objectivity, kinship with kind leading to sexual, sociative, communitive, and other relationships. The grasp of an objective world in space and time is one of the decisive determinants in the development of man's concept of value. In order to arrive at such a concept, an animate being must first of all distinguish an object, something distinct from him, ob-jected to him. How close to or far from this man's fellow animals are can only be surmised. Predatory animals seem to have something of a sense of it over a limited range of action: the world appears as having a career stretching beyond the here and the now. Man is able to gain a clear recognition of the limits and context of his habitancy of space and time. It is not only present havings that are enjoyed but also that which is to be had at some other place or moment, that which may be counted upon to offer satisfaction when it is encountered, that which can be recognized in its recurrence as what has previously afforded satisfaction, and so on.

If these modes presuppose a steady and objective order, they involve no less the thought of the self as distinct from, yet participant in that order. This brings a step closer the possibility that the value sought after is likewise independent, is *there* to be had, and that *it*, not only the quest for it, and not only the consuming, enjoying and having of it, are valuable.

Decisive as the grasp of objectivity (and of course also the recognition of kinds and classes) is for the consciousness of things valued, there rises above the plane of fellow animals an even more potent determinant, the consciousness of kind. It is inappropriate to suppose such an awareness in the orders below man. To be sure, the individual horse, tame or wild, no doubt recognizes horses as a kind of class when he encounters and associates himself with them, but he probably has no awareness of himself as a member of this class or of all of them, himself among them, as "we" or "us" or "ourselves." He is instinctively drawn toward a mare and not a cow, but he has no awareness that, let us say, fat pastures are "the kind of thing *we* want." When and only when an animate being recognizes who *we* are, recognizes that we want it and that we are many, does he begin to understand that a value is not only *his own* enjoyment of something. He learns from "us" that certain things are *to be* enjoyed, something to be prized. When he then finds it interesting that prizings differ he has begun to ask, has this *object* a value that has escaped *me*? All of this can occur only in a community.

We move from one pole in having value to another. We begin with satisfaction or fruition, the self's enjoyment, and arrive in the end at the idea that something is *there* to be enjoyed by beings like ourselves and enjoyed with them in a community. What we often wish to call the objectivity of value is simply a community of recognition and a "genuine" value enjoys such a recognition. We acknowledge this in the language of the absolute valents.

This, then, is the terminus of our study, the concept of *being valuable* or *having value* which in French is so inimitably and justly put in the single word *valoir*, originally, 'to be strong'. It brings us finally also to value theory proper for which we have provided but a chart, a prolegomenon. Such a study must explore in deeper fashion the role of the concept of value on all phases of human life. Indeed it has in several hands in the past already received searching examination. I have hoped to extend and advance this examination with a study of the language of value.

To return to the first and last topics which have engaged our attention, we may say that so long as man knows how to enjoy so long will he also evaluate everything that he enjoys and everything that is a condition of enjoyment. As long as he does so the future is bright for his values even if they are threatened from other directions. It would be beclouded only if he ceased to compare them and to seek that which he thinks has in it the requisites of affording satisfaction. It is not the complexity or frustration of modern life that threatens this pursuit as much as the numbing of vital response. Enjoyment and deprivation are the very school of value, and the history of man shows that the course is an arduous one.

CONCLUSION OF PART THREE

In concluding our inquiry into fundamental value theory, the means and ends of its procedures may bear still one more iteration. The basic presumption and method of this inquiry is that one must clearly identify the reals or *realia* that are to be explained before one proceeds to explanations and theories. The realia of value are the actual judgments, appraisals, and characterizations, and thus necessarily the value terms and concepts involved in them. These must first be identified. This task is one that demands the drawing of lines which at the borders are not always perfectly clear. But there is no question that there is a heartland of terms and expressions that exist, that have in some sense been devised, for the purpose of making appraisals. We have confined ourselves to one of the several vocabularies. In the introduction we identified the A, S, P, and M vocabularies, and even these may not exhaust the field.

The point of identifying and insisting upon these as the realia, the explicanda, of the situation is to reject what so-called naturalistic moral philosophers, from Hume to Stevenson, have always thought were the bedrock of the valuing "process," the feelings or thoughts or attitudes of the appraiser. The less said about the Stygian darkness of "attitudes" the better. We should not introduce such notions as explanatory devices: they are only new explicanda, obstacles which we have interposed between ourselves and the solution to our problem. As to feelings and mental states and objectives, these are not ready-made quantities to be taken for granted: we have yet to identify that to which our appraisive language alone can afford the clue.

It is necessary first to get a large view of the explicanda, the reals, in such an inquiry, what might perhaps be called value facts, if this is not misleading. I do not wish to include under such facts such things as what have been called mores or moral customs. Much information about this has been gathered since the late nineteenth century. But the data that have been gathered would be far more significant if the researchers had been more keenly aware that it was their own moral or evaluative judgment that inevitably guided the choice of the facts they thought relevant, and that they ought in consequence always to have accompanied their inquiries with reportage on the value vocabularies of the peoples in question. What they often reported was often completely suffused by their own moral evaluations of primitive or exotic tribes and their behavior. Only reportage on the evaluative discourse of these peoples themselves could *enlarge* our knowledge of value facts.

There is therefore no substitute for a direct survey of each language group of its own body of value explicanda. The task we have undertaken sets forth a form which such surveys or inquiries may choose to follow. It would be an error to suppose that value explicanda or realia will prove to be identical everywhere with what we have set forth here either in form or substance, and thus that English appraisives exhaust the subject.

Our procedure therefore has been to remain as close as possible to actual valuations, or at least to paradigms of valuation. But in centering our attention upon the hard facts of the terms used in appraisive utterances, rather than upon the far softer soil of feelings, attitudes, and inclinations, or upon acts of preference, approval, and their contraries, I am conscious that even so we are not yet near enough to even harder facts of evaluation, the sentential utterances themselves. For who cannot see in an instant the difference between any of the terms here studied, all of them untimely ripped from their contexts, and the simplest evaluative utterance set in its time and place. We may study at length the appraisives we employ, for example, of things, or animals, or persons, or places, but what can match an earnest appraisal whose delivery is set in its occasion?

We have had to proceed like young doctors who must first dissect cadavers and analyze typical cases and who must then learn to treat something quite different, the *whole* man, woman, or child. Such whole beings may interact with the physician in subtle and pervasive ways, and he may rarely encounter again the paradigms of his student days. We cannot define those who achieve the peak of the profession as the ones who are icily "objective" in diagnosis and therapy. For we must also write into the necessities of the profession the capacity for interaction that mixes sympathy for and distance from the personality of the client in an indefinable ratio.

So too the study of appraising presupposes one's recognizing the phenomenon to be studied and the capacity to be both moved and unmoved by it. It demands also a knowledge of the paradigmatic types that are afforded by the appraisive vocabulary we have here examined.

In the end the decisive reason why we cannot stop at the level reached by what may be called psychological naturalism is that there are not just sets of appraisive feelings, attitudes, and inclinations waiting to be bottled into appropriate appraisive language. If we identify the inchoate feelings we have not or have not yet articulated into words with a definite class of appraisive feelings and attitudes, what light, even a faint and feeble one, has been thrown thereby on the explanation of the processes of appraisal? The fact is, there are no appraisings until we have found words for them.

APPENDICES

In introducing Part Two and in the consideration of intellect in 6.0 we have adverted to the fact that the appraisives of man are but one species (or perhaps genus) of appraisives. There are also other subjects of appraisal besides man. In all of these man takes an interest: but for his interest they scarcely exist, though we may safely sidestep this metaphysical issue. We have been concerned less with the subjects man himself appraises, than with man as the subject of appraisal. We may illustrate this by a glance at two areas that we have not considered, the aesthetic and the religious.

Perhaps only man has genuine aesthetic capacities. Hence his aesthetic capacity should be one of the subjects in the characterization of man just as intellectual capacities are considered in 6.0. But just as 6.0 contains no consideration of such values as significance, truth, falsity, or validity, Part Two contains no inquiry into beauty, ugliness, or other forms of aesthetic value. The same may be said of religion. Certainly capacity to devise religions, to engage in religious observances, and to have religious experiences is an important aspect of man. All of these should appear in the study of the characterization of man. But the holy, for example, whether we think this stands for anything real or not, is a value that deserves independent consideration.

The first Appendices now undertake to give a brief review of matters that either do not fall into the domain of the characterization of man (**true, beautiful, significant, valid, sacred**) or were omitted from Part Two simply because they were of a complexity that could not be considered without undue lengthening of the text (aesthetic capacity, religious response). We may also note that in the case of economics, we have considered economic value in the text in 12.1, although by parity with aesthetics it ought to have been omitted. We included it nevertheless because for our purposes it could be run through briefly.

Various topics for which we could not afford to digress in the text are taken up in the later Appendices.

APPENDIX A – OBJECTS OF THE INTELLECT

A1.0 SIGNIFICANCE (SIGNIFICATION)

A1.1 ABSOLUTE SIGNIFICANT
have [meaning
make [sense
mean

A1.2 UNDERSTANDING

A1.3 INTERPRETANCE

construe	**gloss**
distinguish	**hermeneutics**
elucidate	**interpret**
exegesis	**render**
explain	**translate**
explicate	

A1.4 SIGNIFIC ENACTMENT
define
specify
stipulate

A1.5 SIGNIFIC CHARACTER

abstruse	**nonsense**
clear	**obfuscate**
confused	**perspicuous**
distinct	**precise**
intelligible	**senseless**
lucid	**significant**
manifest	**unfathomable**
meaningful, -less	**vague**
nebulous	

A2.0 PONENCE

A2.1 ABSOLUTE PONENT

be	**hold**
be [so (G. Sosein)	**obtain**
be the [case that	**prevail**
be the [fact that	

A2.2 COGNITIONS

ascertain	find
assent	know
confirm	verify

A2.3 ASSESSIVE PROCESS (Correctible)

assay	doubt
assess	estimate
con (= examine)	examine
consider that	judge
deem	question v.

A2.4 ASSESSIVE ENACTMENT

agree (to)	gainsay
assert	maintain
assure	object v.
concur	presume
contend (= maintain)	repudiate (11.4)
deny	

A2.5 COGNITIVE APPRAISIVES

accurate	mistake
apocryphal	obvious
authentic	plausible
authoritative	questionable
believable	straightforward
correct a.	tell-tale
credible	tenable
credentials	true, truth
dubious	unfounded
error, erroneous, err (15.4)	ungrounded
exact	verisimilitude
exaggerate	veritable
false	verity
illusory	well-grounded
imaginary	

A3.0 INFERENCE

A3.1 ABSOLUTE INFERENT
entail
imply
it [follows that

A3.2 LOGICAL INSIGHT

A3.3   RATIOCINATIVE PROCESS (Correctible)

argue	**derive**
conclude	**determine**
contest v.	**dissident**
controvert	**illation**
debate	**infer**
deduce	**reason** v.

A3.4   CONCLUSIVES

confute
prove
refute
solve

A3.5   LOGICAL APPRAISIVES

(a) COMPATIBILITY

anomaly	**conclusive**
antinomy	**consecutive**
coherent	**fallacious, fallacy**
compatible	**logical**
consistent	**quibble**
contradict	**rigor**
contrary	**sophistry**
extraneous	**unfounded**
incongruous	**ungrounded**
obvious	**valid**
paradox	**well-grounded**
truism	(c) GENERAL
(b) CONSEQUENCE	**eristic**
absurd	**logic-chopping**
	logomachy

In order to survey the immense fields of significance, ponence, and inference without being altogether superficial, we point out first that, as in the main text, our interest is centered only upon the concepts or the vocabulary of the subject. Accordingly, we have condensed it and sought to bring out the parallelism in it so that it can be understood, if not at a glance, then at least without demanding undue effort. We may consider the subject by studying the parallelism in the table that immediately follows.

The strictest parallelism here obtains among the corresponding members of the N.1 (absolute significant, etc.) line and N.5 (signific character, etc.). For example, in the sphere of significance there is a value present in the form of

	Significance	Ponence	Inference
N.1	Absolute Significant	Absolute Ponent	Absolute Inferent
N.2	Understanding	Cognition	Logical Insight
N.3	Interpretance	Assessive Process	Ratiocinative Process
N.4	Signific Enactment	Assessive Enactment	Conclusives
N.5	Signific Character	Cognitive Appraisives	Logical Appraisives

meaning, having meaning, making sense, and perhaps other kindred concepts. It is absolute, because for the work of the intellect to be conducted at all, a linguistic or symbolistic expression must either be significant or not, or one must be able to say in what manner it departs from this. Similarly, with ponents (propositions), we must be able finally to assert the proposition (other terms may be employed here) or not, must be able at some point to say something holds, obtains, is so, is the case, is the fact, etc. Again in inference, the connections usually called syntactic or logical either hold or do not, something follows or it does not.

The function of the N.2, N.3, N.4 terms is to express an appropriate appraisal or process of appraising of the subject matter: terms (words, expressions, symbols, formulae), sentences (propositions, ponents, constatives), arguments (proofs, inferences). Various degrees of the values are now allowed for and in all cases not only may absolutes be expressed (p holds, or simply, p), but also in many cases we must content ourselves with indicating in some way to what lesser degree our intellectual faculties are satisfied in the present case. Thus if we cannot say simply S is significant, we may be able to say that it is confusing, unintelligible, abstruse, etc.; if we cannot simply assert p, we may be able to say it is tenable, barely plausible, groundless, incredible, etc.; in the third case we will need a much larger vocabulary than merely 'it follows' and 'it does not follow' in order to make appropriate logical appraisals.

The vocabularies resemble more than a little the general vocabulary of value of the main text. We have not only the possession of value in the sense of 1.0, Satisfaction, and 16.0, Absolute Valents, but also a vast appraisive vocabulary in Part Two by means of which we arrive in one degree or another at the conviction that we have acquired, embraced, or possessed a value on a variety of subjects. 1.0 and 16.0 are thus parallel to absolute significants, ponents, and inferents, (N.1); the appraisive terms in the three areas parallel the huge body of appraisives in Part Two of the subject matter, man, and in some measure the general and ultimate appraisives of Part Three, (N.5).

We must be careful to allow for the uniqueness of each of the fields of significance, ponence and inference and avoid over-simplification and artificial parallelisms. Under ponence we must distinguish the vocabulary of that which I call 'cognition', but which might better be called 'cognizing', or 'grasping the truth of' something. Its various forms are ascertain, confirm, find, know, verify; of course the negations of these and other such processes are assumed without course.

There is a parallel of this family of terms for significance and inference. Thus we would have something like 'understand' for the first and something like 'grasp the fact that one thing follows from some other' for the second. The latter can also be called logical insight. Certainly both of these "acts" are necessary for conducting the signific and inferent enterprises. They may therefore be assumed. (N.2)

In each of the three areas we now find that the human mind, and generally any rational mind, must also engage in a process of probing and weighing of matters. Significance and truth do not lie upon the hand, as the Germans say. So we must engage in processes of interpreting what purports to be significant (construing, elucidating, explaining, interpreting, translating – these terms are also used in other connections of course); of assessing what is asserted, or at least uttered, (considering, judging, assessing, doubting, questioning); of ratiocinating, of weighing logical value (deriving, determining, inferring, reasoning, probing, proving, arguing, and so on). Here we take these as efforts to determine value. We have said that these processes are "correctible". The terms 'correcting' and 'probative' would also be appropriate in all three areas. (N.3)

Finally in each area a real intellectual *act* occurs. These are the enactments, signific, assessive, conclusive: we define, assert, and prove (solve, refute). (N.4)

These in outline provide the principal vocabularies which are necessary in one way or another for the appraisal of the subject matters in question. We can see a fairly clear parallelism with the main body of our text with its concentration upon the appraisal of man. The classes N.2, N.3, and N.4 are paralleled somewhat as follows. Interpretance, assessive process, and ratio-

cinative process, that is, the (c) group, have their analogues in 3.11 (Probations). The N.4 group, signific and assessive enactment, and the conclusives
have their analogues in 3.13 (Verdictions) and possibly some of 3.2 (Appraisive Sequels). The closest analogue to the N.3 group is possibly 3.12
(Appraisive Registry).

There are also aspects of 4.0, Enactment, and 5.0, Moral Judgment, that
may suggest comparisons with various aspects of all three areas.

Even more interesting perhaps is the fact that we must make a considerable
effort to see a connection between 3.0 Response and any aspect of the three
intellectual areas. There are in fact no analogues as matters stand now with
the division into the five subordinate areas. But there cannot fail to be such
analogues. For man's cognitive and logical activities though they may appear
to soar far above the mere psychological and physiological functioning of
the physical person are surely rooted in this – unless we can without question
accept the platonizing view that intellect in itself transcends the body and
all physical facts and functions. There is, I am saying, on the contrary, a
psychology relevant to signifying, cognizing, and inferring. It is, however, as
yet in a thoroughly backward state: the logicians and semanticists have other
fish to fry, and the psychologists have no conception of the issue. We may,
however, hazard the prediction that in due time this too will come under
investigation. If so, we shall then have a parallel also for our Response (2.0
in main text) in the sphere of the intellectual appraisals.

Since we have merely intended to suggest the main lines of parallelism,
the foregoing may suffice for the present topic.

APPENDIX B – TRANSCENDENTIVES

B1.0   RELIGIOUS APPRAISIVES

B1.1   DEVOTION (Cf. 4.3)

CREDITING CHARACTERISMS	DISCREDITING CHARACTERISMS
PROCESSIVE	
bless	blaspheme
benediction	desecrate
consecrate	idolatry, idolatrous
dedicate	sacrilege
hallow	sin
penance	
rite, ritual	
sacrament	
sacrifice	
sanctify	
solemnize	
unction	
venerate (4.3)	
worship	
ATTRIBUTIVE	
(a) divine	(c) profane
holy	ungodly
sacred	(d) impiety
sacrosanct	irreligious
saintly	sinful
sinless	peccable
(b) devout	(e) unctuous
pious, piety	sanctimonious
reverent	
votive	

B1.2   DEVOTIONARY PLACES AND PERSONS

sanctuary	Paradise	saint	satan, satanic
shrine	Heaven	savior	Hell

Religions, theistic, non-theistic, or atheistic, are all concerned in a most eminent way with values. So important a place has religion occupied in human life that no one can afford to ignore its relevance. If we accord it scarcely more than a footnote of space this is but the consequence of the fact that we are interested only in the *concepts* of our subject matter, and the range of purely religious concepts bearing upon value seems to be surprisingly brief. Their potency, however, far outweighs their brevity. I shall be forced to appear somewhat dogmatic by my choice of what appear to me to be the essentials.

What *is* religion? Or indeed is the sprawling phenomenon that stretches far and wide in every corner of man's time and space any one thing? Is it not foolish to presume to say anything on its essence in a few words? I shall not hesitate to do so since the alternative is to say nothing.

I shall be so bold as to say what, in a word or two, religion is. It is, I believe, devotion or dedication of the self, an unreserved giving, surrender, *Hingabe* of it, to powers unseen, rarely to powers seen. Whatever else it may be it is always this, whether this be regarded as its essence, or only an invariable accident or property of it, to borrow familar traditional terms.

Religion reaches into every moment and act of life and aims to transform everything by its presence. The first requisite is for the person to perform acts of dedication and devotion following a prescribed convention or symbolism. It is not at all necessary that he have a clear idea or even any idea of who is to receive this gift of himself.

The vocabulary of dedication (B1.1) is exclusively Latin, except for **hallow** consisting of various ways of saying dedication but also introducing a second characterizing feature. This appears (B1.2) in the terms **hallow** and **sanctify**. Anything that has been given to the unseen powers is now set apart; it is transformed; it is no longer what it was or what it seems. Such a thing, or person, or act, or place is said to be holy, sacred, divine, or imbued with the power of the unseen. Of course it deserves special care. A special place, a sanctuary or shrine will be prepared where the devotee can renew his devotion or devotement (B1.4). What is now delivered up must not be desecrated. To speak of it in an inappropriate manner may be blasphemous (B1.3).

The devotionary act is to be thought of as standing in a necessary relation to an inner (B1.5) devotionary state of mind or attitude. Which of these now comes first, the attitude or the act? All religions appear to move between these two poles. What is surprising is that there is so little universal conviction that the proper attitude, or state of the soul must come first. The mystics, protestants, and pietists all say so. But in general, religion, if it be sufficiently public and appropriately spectacular, can renew and affirm itself simply by emphasizing and glorifying the devotionary act. Perform the act, it says, and the attitude or state of the soul will take care of itself. As an institution, religion is always the work of the Thyrsus-bearers, not of the Mystics. The priesthood, the pharisees, theologians, cohens, and levites know that the mystic has really sounded the inner and life-giving chord, but they are also aware that religion will disintegrate if the cult is given over to them. Religion is unthinkable without institutions.

But this has given only one side of the phenomenon of religion. The picture we have drawn emphasizes that aspect of it where the devotee is brought into contact with a substance apart from this world, that transcends it, lies over, around, and under it and may finally be reached in an after life. This is the occult aspect of it. If this were all, it would be nothing more than an escape from reality. In fact, however, the substance apart makes itself felt everywhere in this world. Its potency extends to the pagan and impious as well as to the devout. It is well therefore to be in communion with it, to guide one's steps by it, to hearken to its commands.

It is evident that such a system of thought and habit will be determinant of the moral climate wherever it holds sway. It provides answers for moral questions, solutions for moral problems. Men *may* eventually find such answers and solutions without reference to a transcendent substance. Since the Enlightenment they have been assured this was possible and inevitable – time was said to be on its side. Our time may witness a crescendo of doubt that may eventually overwhelm these confident assurances.

B2.0   TRANSCENDENTAL INTENSIVES

(a)	(b)
afflatus	**demon**
charismatic	**devil**
cosmic	**diabolic**
deathless	**fateful**
deify	**ghostly**
ecstasy	**indescribable**
esoteric	**ineffable**
immortal	**infernal**
miraculous	**macabre**
providential	**occult**
transcendent,	**uncanny**
transcendental	**unfathomable**
transfigured	**weird**
undying	
unearthly	
wizard	

It is difficult to say whether belief in the supernatural decreases, holds its own, or actually increases at the present time. The relative decline of religion is no measure of it. It is safe to say that, whatever the outcome, the foregoing vocabulary is likely to maintain itself although the actual or original significance of the terms may be somewhat obscured. Even if the decline should become even more palpable, the terms could maintain an indefinite vitality by increasing their adverbial use as their attributive and substantive use diminishes. That is, whether belief in literal immortality, a genuine Providence, Paradise, devils, and occult or infernal events maintains itself or not, the terms will be likely to maintain their use as ways of intensifying the significance of almost any even quite ordinary attribution. There is always a need for superlatives and what intenser superlative is thinkable than one that reaches beyond the edge of the world known to us? So we may doubt or disbelieve that there are occult or supernatural qualities, events, persons, places, or objects and yet wish to intensify our attributions or descriptions by looking toward unknown dimensions of being. And where belief is deeply and genuinely felt, as indeed it still is, the power of the terms is felt to be almost literally infinite. Such a person shudders at hearing an emphatic "God damn ..." in a manner that the faithless cannot begin to understand.

APPENDIX C. AESTHETIC APPRAISIVES

C1.0 AESTHETIC POWERS

PROCESSIVE	SUBSTANTIVE	ATTRIBUTIVE
fancy	aesthete	fastidious
taste	connoisseur	
imagination	dilettante	

C2.0 AESTHETIC CHARACTERIZATION

C2.1 CHARACTERIZATION OF AESTHETIC ORDERS

C2.11 ELEMENTAL CHARACTERISMS
SOUND

CREDITING	DISCREDITING
euphonious	brassy
mellifluous	doleful
melodious	drone
	jangle
	leaden
	noisy
	raucous
	screech
	strepitous, strepitant
	wail

SIGHT: LIGHT AND COLOR

CREDITING	DISCREDITING
brilliant	drab
limpid	dull
lucid	flashy
luminous	garish
refulgent	gaudy
vivid	lurid

SIGHT: MASS AND MOTION

CREDITING	DISCREDITING
dainty	awkward
deft	clumsy
delicate	dumpy
fragile	gross
graceful	hulking
lambent	ungainly
lank	unshapely
lissom	
lithe	
wan	

C2.12   FORMAL OR CONTEXTUAL CHARACTERISMS

ORDER

PROCESSIVE

CREDITING	DISCREDITING
order	deface
organize	defeature
unify	defigure
	disarrange
	disarray v. and n.
	disfigure
	disorganize
	distort
	garble
	mutilate

ATTRIBUTIVE

CREDITING	DISCREDITING
balanced	amorphous
coherent	askew
concent	awry
figured, figure	chaos
harmonious	clutter
luxuriant	confusion
orderly, ordered	congested
organic	conglomeration
rapport	contort, contorted
	cramped

deformed
discord, discordant
disintegrate
disordered
disorganized
distorted
encumbered
imbalance
inchoate
incoherent
incongruous
jarring
medley
misshapen
stunted
tortuous
void

EMPHASIS

CREDITING	±	DISCREDITING
accent	conspicuous	anticlimax
acme	distinctive	lopsided
apogee	emphasis	monotonous
climax		

C2.2   CHARACTERIZATION OF ARTWORKS

C2.21   STYLE, TOTAL EFFECT

VIVACITY

POSITIVE CHARACTERISMS	NEGATIVE CHARACTERISMS
CREDITING	
exotic	calm
exuberant	mild
euphoric	[quiet]
fanciful	tranquil
fantastic	
lifelike	
racy	
vivacity	

(±) bauble
flamboyant
showy

DISCREDITING

din	frigid
grotesque	pompous
outlandish	prim
pandemonium	staid
phantasmagoria	
racket	
topsy-turvy	dead
turgid	lifeless
wild	

CONCINNITY

CREDITING	DISCREDITING
[clean]	[dirty]
concinnity	filthy
impeccable	fusty
neat	litter
spick and span	mess
chic	dingy
natty	dowdy
nice	draggled, bedraggled
refined	frowst
smart	frowzy
stylish	rickety
suave	scrubby
	sloppy
	slovenly
	tatterdemalion
	tattered
	tawdry
	uncouth
	decrepit
	dilapidated
	disarray
	dishevelled
	slapdash
	slipshod
	unkempt
	untidy

SPLENDOR

    PROCESSIVE

        CREDITING

        adorn

        decorate

        embellish

        enhancement

        titivate

    ATTRIBUTIVE

CREDITING	DISCREDITING
decor	**banal**
elegant	**banausic**
glamor	**grotesque**
gorgeous	**vapid**
grandeur, grandiose (−)	
lavish	**affected**
magnificent	**arty**
magniloquent	**mannered, mannerism**
majesty	**pretentious**
opulent	
palatial	
pomp (not **pompous**)	
resplendent	
rich	
spacious	
splendid, splendor	
stately	
sumptuous	

C2.22   INFORMAL TYPES

    burlesque

    caricature

    conceit (literary sense)

    doggerel

    elegiac

    extravaganza

    irony

    jeremiad

    lampoon

    paean

    panegyric

parody
philippic
romance
satire

C3.0 GENERAL AESTHETIC APPRAISIVES

C3.1 ELICITIVES

CREDITING	DISCREDITING
affecting	**eyesore**
delectable	**lachrymose**
enchanting	**soporific**
entertaining	
expressive	
imposing	
ravishing	
titillate, titillating	
toothsome	
touching, touch	
(= **affecting**)	
soporific	

C3.2 ULTIMATE APPRAISIVES

CREDITING	DISCREDITING
attractive	**hideous**
beautiful, beauteous	**slight** a.
chef d'oeuvre	**tasteless**
comely	**ugly**
excellent	**uncomely**
exquisite	**unsightly**
extraordinary	
fair	
good	
great	
handsome	
lovely	
masterpiece	
perfect	
pretty	
sightly	

spectacular
sublime
supernal
tasteful
virtu

The area of aesthetic appraisal is of great extent. Many of the things that have been said in the main text about evaluative terms in general, or moral appraisives in particular, are of equal force here. I shall confine myself to presenting the foregoing excerpt from a vocabulary of aesthetic concepts and explaining it in the briefest terms. No study of this vocabulary could ever aspire to completeness since criticism of the arts constantly expands its terminology by devices such as metaphor, nonce words, reinterpretations of old terms, and so on.

We have shown how the horizon of the appraisive vocabulary must be extended far beyond the handful of terms that have generally received concentrated study. In a similar manner, the habit of confining aesthetic inquiry to the study of a handful or even a pair of terms (i.e., **beauty, ugliness**) is so obviously absurd that one has difficulty in explaining how it could have developed. **Beauty** and **ugliness** have played two roles: (i) they often serve as the most ultimate or most general appraisives in the field, and when they do, they must of course be supported by characterizations drawn (it is here suggested) from the elemental and formal aspects of the subject matter; (ii) where they have served to name a particular aesthetic value distinct, for example, from the sublime, and other values, beauty appears to have a number of more or less definite criteria: unity, variety, appeal in whole and part, and so on. Where (i) prevails, **beauty** is a general appraisive among others and in itself formal and empty; it is fulfilled only in reference to more material aesthetic characterisms. These are suggested here in C2.0.

Thinking of aesthetics as the "analysis of beauty" continues usually in the hands of amateurish philosophizers (including not a few professionals) who are often ignorant of the history of the subject and unable to assess its significance. Or it is carried on by those who are utterly deaf and blind to what is occurring in the world of art and criticism in their own century.

The study of critical language is only a part of what may be called aesthetics. It is an important part but must be undertaken in conjunction with a larger theory of the subject matter. Aesthetic criticism is talk about the arts (and more than the arts), but art is itself a doing and not a talking. It is quite proper to confine the philosophy of science to the study of the language of science because science necessarily issues in a linguistic product (including of course mathematics). But art is not in this sense a linguistic product (not even in literature). One must therefore accord criticism a rather subordinate although admittedly a very important place. To suppose that aesthetics is exhausted in the study of critical language is to remain on its periphery.

The categories of analysis here are not arrived at solely by the study of aesthetic critical language, but by a study of the character of artworks in all the media that are practiced. Proceeding in this manner, by regarding the artwork or aesthetic object (object found to have aesthetic import) as a complex of elements in a kind of vital relation to one another, we are provided with a clue for the study of the language of aesthetic response and criticism. I shall now briefly explain the classification of terms.

In C1.0, as in Part One of the main text, we present a mere handful of terms (hardly even that) which designate aesthetic powers or acts, processes, or procedures. English is singularly barren in terminology here and is accordingly compelled to speak about aesthetic response and creativity in terms other than any specifically invented for the purpose. There is for example, no really suitable term for the lover, amateur, devotee of art or aesthetic objects generally. **Aesthete** is uttered only with apologies. **Dilettante** is inevitably redolent of superficiality. **Connoisseur** suggests not a passionate concern with the aesthetic substance but rather a professional and possibly overrefined concourse with it. The explanation of much of this is to be sought in the sociology of art. These shortcomings may sometimes have hindered the flourishing of aesthetic consciousness and concern, but language is not an insuperable hindrance once such concern is truly and deeply felt.

2.0 is divided into the concepts for the characterization of aesthetic orders and of artworks. Although the two classes overlap, we have need of characterizing objects of aesthetic interest (we leave the definition of this notion to aesthetics itself) from both standpoints. In the first case we think of the object as being internally differentiated into parts in relation to one another. We can here either characterize the parts or elements (for example, patches of color) in relative independence of one another, or we can characterize the whole as an ensemble of elements in relation to one another. We may think of the elements in crediting or discrediting terms, and we may also think of the ensemble as crediting or discrediting. Both of these are sources of critical appraisal. In the second case we seek to sum up the "character" of the aesthetic object or artwork as a totality. This vocabulary has a great variety and also derives from a great variety of sources, as is readily evident.

In C2.0 we have the counterpart of Part Two of the main text. Just as we found in the various areas of characterization the premises, so to speak, of the general and ultimate appraisives, so the appraisives of aesthetic characterization in C2.0 are what alone can give body, substance, and life to ultimate aesthetic appraisives. The latter appear in C3.0.

The second part of C2.0 turns from the details of form, organization, and mutual determination of parts of the aesthetic object which is particularly of technical concern to the artist at work in his medium, toward the characterization of the aesthetic complex as a work of art that is set in a place, tradition, cultural milieu, critical context. (The term 'artwork' must here be allowed considerable latitude.)

What are presented here are only those terms in our standard vocabulary that have a fully or predominantly aesthetic use, not but what they may not also appear elsewhere. Some three large divisions suggest themselves: Vivacity, Concinnity, and Splendor. These terms are but approximations for the varied families of concepts; but a glance at the list will, I think, reveal kinships. What is suggested here is that our ready stock of aesthetic appraisives reaching back into the Germanic and Romance origins of English look toward some three areas of characterization and, thus, evaluation.

The first of these is the area of vigor and *liveliness*, as compared with tranquillity and repose, each of which has an ineffable power over the human spirit when in some manner exemplified in objects presented to perception or imagination. Each of these, however, is subject also to a unique pathology, so to speak, in the direction either of an empty flamboyance and turgidity, or of frigidity and death. As in all other situations, so here the aesthetic critical imagination is ceaselessly at work to invent new coin for critical response. A basic demand for what is here expressed in terms of vivacity and vitality is, however, evident. These and other terms often undergo complex modifications and modulations when employed in aesthetic contexts.

The area for which *concinnity* may serve as an approximate designation has an often almost domestic or at least personal air. And this is not surprising. Just as the human voice must remain for us something of a paradigm, often beneath consciousness, for all music, so the human person, personality, or figure exercises a determinant power in our characterization of (particularly) the visible world. Clearly this human reference goes beyond the mere clean–dirty descript behind concinnity (marked in brackets), but this descript or image is particularly human and potent.

Finally, the essentially Latin or Roman vocabulary under *splendor* has a kind of unique coherence. One senses a characteristically warm and Southern image of light, real or reflected on many facets, that contrasts with the preceding kind of imagery. It can suffer from the corresponding vices for these resplendent virtues: vapidity, flashiness, empty grandeur, mannerism, and so on.

This vocabulary is but our ready store, on which we rely in one way or another far more than we suppose. No doubt other classifications are plausible. There is no question of our being confined to these vocabularies, for criticism is itself far too much of an art to be limited in such a manner. Nevertheless, the vocabulary is instructive. It is representative of what one might hazard calling "natural aesthetic." Our resources in invention and convention stretch illimitably further, but they begin at this center.

In C2.22 we have inherently material appraisive terms which must be sharply and emphatically distinguished from formal types such as, let us say. the literary genres that they deceptively resemble. Condition determinants for these terms will be sought in vain.

A glance at the vocabulary of Part Three (in the main text) will show that many of its terms can also be used in aesthetic critical contexts, especially, Elicitives, Deservatives, Estimatives, and, of course, Ultimate Commendatives, such as **good** and **bad**, which have universal range and are common to all critical contexts. So also the Elicitives in C3.1 may appear in nonaesthetic contexts.

As in the foregoing study of Commendatives, we maintain that the ultimates of C3.2 are essentially formal in nature and have significance only if supported by reasons rooted in material characterization or otherwise elucidated in such terms. The concepts of the present number, such as **beauty** and **sublime**, have, however, an enormously complex history and use. A mere foray into analysis here would only serve to oversimplify and distort them.

The aesthetic vocabulary presented here is inevitably loose and imprecise, seeking to give but an impression of the scope of critical language. It is not suggested that these are all the terms of such a vocabulary, nor that all of these terms have an exclusively aesthetic use, but only that these terms *do* have such a use. Some of the terms are clearly metaphorical and, of course, if we were deliberately to look in that direction some dozens of pages could be filled with critical metaphors alone and the list could inherently have no end. What is true of the M vocabulary would be equally true of the P and S aesthetic vocabularies, both of which are in flourishing state.

APPENDIX D – HUMORISTIC APPRAISIVES

ATTRIBUTIVE

arch	jocose
badinage	jocular
burlesque	joke
cachinnation	levity
comic	ludicrous
droll	merry
facetious	mirth
fun, funny	mischief
hilarious	prank
humor, humorous	wit
jest	

PROCESSIVE

amuse
entertain
gladden

SUBSTANTIVE

buffoon	jester
clown	wag
comedian	zany
humorist	

Humor is a kind of kingdom in the empire of the human spirit. Moreover its gates are well-guarded. There is an infallible test for what may be admitted within: does it actually amuse? And that which has at one time amused but does so no longer is just as peremptorily expelled from the domain. One could wish that the good, true, and beautiful were as rigorous in their choice of membership. To be sure, by such time-honored laws as that of excluded middle or of contradiction there is no middle ground between truth and falsity, but where is the infallible *sense* of truth as there is an infallible sense of humor? For no one is obliged to call anything amusing or funny if it does not amuse, and yet the one is not the other. To judge of humor and to be undergoing a mirthful response are quite distinct. Great comedians, perhaps the greatest, are great *judges* of humor; often they are found to be virtually incapable of mirth themselves even when they are evoking it in others.

Humor, or the comic, is often assimilated to aesthetics, although the aestheticians rarely have anything illuminating to say on the subject. It appears to belong there because there are, of course, comic works of art. But the term 'work of art' here means simply a public realization which ministers to the need for more or less refined devices for stimulating the comic response or frame of mind. There are also other works of art to produce other parallel results with other families of response. There are pornographic works of art, which have almost nothing to do with the aesthetic: their purpose is to stimulate the sexual imagination. There are or there could be masochistic and sadistic works of art to satisfy the taste for giving or receiving pain, a faculty which is but a streak in most persons, but a way of life for a few.

Comic or humoristic works of art have their devices and techniques and fall into as many schools as do the aesthetic works of art. The comic also has its own critics and of course its own vocabulary. It has proved just as difficult to explain the secret of humor as the secret of beauty or other forms of value.

What emerges from the vocabulary we have identified here is that there is virtually nothing in the way of characterization of humor comparable to the huge vocabulary for characterization generally we have just surveyed. Humor appears to be an all-or-nothing affair. The attributives cited here are all virtually synonyms and so coalesce into one general and ultimate appraisive. There is therefore no recursion to a body of characterization. A thing is funny if it amuses, if not, not. This is not to say that a study of humor, a comparison of comic works of art is not rewarding in many more ways than the delight they afford. But so far, only the psychological, or perhaps "clinical" approach seems to offer much hope of unlocking the secrets of humor. It is nevertheless interesting to see what the humoristic vocabulary consists in and with how little in the way of critical apparatus the enterprise is carried forward. Little more than this seems appropriate to say from the present standpoint regarding this almost divine fraction of our nature.

APPENDIX E – PHYSICAL APPRAISIVES

Are there values that pertain exclusively to physical, material, things qua material? That is, not as being, say, pianos, turnips, or reptiles? If we think of the sheer burden of "having" a physical body which must be kept from falling more than a few feet or colliding with others, must be fed and tended every day, and so on, we see that a number of values are clearly identifiable. Physical bodies by definition resist the effort to be moved, but some more than others. From this a few very simple, but easily overlooked, values arise; for example:

E1.0 MATERIAL APPRAISIVES

facile	awkward
handy	bulky
manageable	clumsy
	cumbrous
	hulk
	impediment
	lumbering
	unwieldy

These are genuine appraisives. There is no way of measuring weight, volume density, speed, or friction to determine an exact degree of unwieldiness or handiness. They are also appraisives we employ with the greatest of assurance. In reference to physical objects, we need only consult our own responses as sheer physical bodies, our fatigue or effort, to determine their application perfectly.

A further class of very necessary terms might be distinguished and could be called the Utilitives. They scarcely need exposition and could no doubt be added to:

adulterate
contaminate
contraption
cumbersome, encumber
fit, unfit

> **practicable**
> **serviceable**
> **useful**
> **usufruct**
> **utile**
> **viable**

One might add to them utilitives in certain very special categories, for example:

> **vermin**
> **weed**

E2.0   ENVIRONMENTAL ADAPTIVES

> **convenient**   **dismal** (L. *dies mali*) (15.3)
> **comfortable** (elic.)   **wilderness**
> **cozy (cosy)**
> **familiar**
> **hospitable**

These appraisives lie not far from the preceding in origin, but their application soon reaches beyond the merely physical. Various other discrediting terms besides **inhospitable, uncomfortable, inconvenient** will readily come to mind.

It is interesting to think how various the subjects are to which these terms are applied as one moves from rural to urban civilizations, and from one environment to another immensely varied in other respects. "Ah! Wilderness!" one may say, but it is one thing to face it as a Pilgrim Father or Daniel Boone, and another as a ghetto dweller breathing the air of the Sierras or Rockies. In our time wilderness has become a high value. Contrast the attitude of the children of Israel spending forty years in the wilderness of Sinai.

E3.0   GUSTATIVES

> (a) DIRECT APPRAISIVES
> **delicious**   **foul**
> **edible**   **insipid**
> **luscious**   **jejune**
>   **rancid**
>   **rank**
>   **vapid**

(b) ELICITIVES
appetizing
nourishing
palatable
savory
toothsome

The gustatives differ from the appraisives of 7.35, the appraisives of ingesting, by the fact that those were public aspects of the person's behavior, his style of feeding himself, whereas the gustatives narrowly concern the sensations and perceptions of tasting food and drink. They are presented here largely for the sake of affording subjects of comparison with other areas of appraisal.

Aside from the not too firm distinction between direct and elicitive appraisives, there is little that can be said of the gustatives. This may be contrasted with the enormously complex classifications of savours (and aromas) that have been attempted by psychologists. These of course are identifiable sensations and are themselves subject to appraisal: they are not appraisive in themselves.* Little more may be said of all these sensations and experiences than that they are "good" or "bad" or neutral or indifferent or mixed. Thus, still another area is displayed to which ultimate commendatives may recur.

Although the direct-elicitive distinction is, as noted, none too apparent, it affords a further subject of comparison with the general elicitives in 15.1.

---

* The literature is surveyed in detail by R. S. Woodworth, *Experimental Psychology*, New York, Henry Holt and Company, 1938, pp. 477–500.

APPENDIX F – GENERAL METAPHYSICAL APPRAISIVES

F1.0   METAPHYSICAL APPRAISIVES

real (other uses already considered)   **cloudland**
illusory
imaginary

We are not now speaking of the same thing we considered under the normatives where, for example, a real watch or fire engine is a genuine one, not a child's toy, for example. We are speaking of appearance (or illusion) and reality as metaphysicians have always spoken of them. Certain philosophers, though not all, have thought the real was a value. The *ens realissimum* was thought to be also the *ens perfectissimum*. One need only think of Plato, neo-Platonism (Plotinus, Pseudo-Dionysius, John Scotus Erigena), and St. Anselm to see how powerfully conceptions of this sort have worked even if they have fewer adherents today.

There are also radically different approaches to this idea. There are those who virtually reject the idea of the real as anything but a pitfall of language, as something that appears to be a stratagem devised to lead us into asking meaningless questions. Thus Kant names 'reality' as the fourth of his categories and 'existence' as the eleventh, and he has fairly clearly identified them with what appears or can appear in sense perception or is related to this by previously confirmed scientific laws. When he comes to discuss reality in the context of the ontological argument, he fires a salvo from which the argument has never recovered: 'real', or 'existence' is not a predicate at all, except in a grammatical sense. From Kant to Carnap the way is fairly direct: eventually it is said 'a is real' means that the term 'a' is the name of something, and that that is all it means.

As against this obviously and professedly anti-metaphysical view, it is safe to say that all genuinely metaphysical standpoints insist that the real is a value, that it is of a higher value than the illusory, and that these are meaningful and significant statements. Among these metaphysicians must be numbered not just theological philosophers but the adherents of Marxian materialism. They assert this and reiterate the application of it to "matter" on every conceivable occasion. The real is thought to be inherently valuable. Since our purpose is *only* to set forth the anatomy of appraisive language, I will forego examining this tenet. It is evident that it has had many kinds of support from nearly every part of the philosophical spectrum.

The above use of the idea may appear to have a place only in abstruse reckonings of metaphysicians, but this is far from the case. The conviction of its truth is widespread; it is a virtually commonsense idea. If we ask, "Are not a hundred real dollars of higher value than a hundred imaginary dollars?" or, "Is not something better than nothing?" the response will be an enthusiastic "Yes!" rather than a request for clarification. The burden of proof is on the philosophers. Some of them have of course taken up the challenge.

The real names not only one of the good commodities there happens to be, like music or food or love, but it is a value as beauty and justice are thought to be values. It is in this sense, defensible or not, that the real comes under consideration here.

F2.0   MAGNITUDINAL APPRAISIVES

POSITIVE CHARACTERISMS		NEGATIVE CHARACTERISMS
CREDITING	+	CREDITING
(a) QUANTITY		(a) QUANTITY
abundant		
ample		
bounteous		
copious		
inexhaustible		
lavish		
luxuriant		
plethora		
profuse		
(b) SIZE		(b) SIZE
colossal		considerable
enormous		moderate
gigantic		modest
huge		
immense		
incalculable		
prodigious		
titanic		
tremendous		
vast		
(c) STRENGTH		(c) STRENGTH
forceful		dainty (App. 2.0)

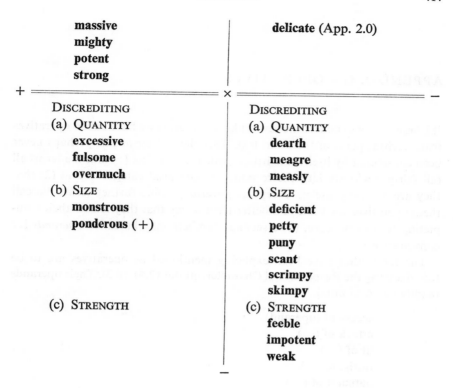

massive
mighty
potent
strong

delicate (App. 2.0)

+ ═════════════ × ═════════════ −

DISCREDITING
(a) QUANTITY
   excessive
   fulsome
   overmuch
(b) SIZE
   monstrous
   ponderous (+)

(c) STRENGTH

DISCREDITING
(a) QUANTITY
   dearth
   meagre
   measly
(b) SIZE
   deficient
   petty
   puny
   scant
   scrimpy
   skimpy
(c) STRENGTH
   feeble
   impotent
   weak

−

The foregoing is but a sample of a large vocabulary that is useful and rather instructive but not particularly interesting. Most of the applications of the terms are perhaps tied to utility. What is overmuch, moderate, immense, or bounteous most often depends on considerations obvious from the context.

The three classes are found in each of the four divisions although two of them are without obvious terms in formal speech. Terms for these are readily devised informally.

Apparent creditings are often attached as intensive modifiers to discrediting substantives: colossal crimes, vastly overrated claims, and so on, much as **holy** can be discrediting in *holy terror*.

APPENDIX G – OPERATIVES

It is interesting to collect the several kinds of terms we have called operatives from various parts of the main text. This class of terms has perhaps never been considered by itself. It is held together by the fact (1) that the terms all fall fairly obviously into the response or appraisal categories and (2) that they are all fairly useless except as governing some further term. We call them operatives for want of a better term to say that they render their completing terms operative. (The second members may be called *operands* for convenience.)

The terms that have been explicitly mentioned as operatives are to be found among the Responsional Characterizations (2.4), (8.3). Their operands readily come to mind.

> **access of** (operand)
> **attack of** ( )
> **fit of** ( )
> **instigate** ( )
> **outburst of** ( )
> **paroxysm of** ( )
> **spasm of** ( )
> **throe, throes of** ( )
> **transports of** ( )
> **twinge of** (pain)

These are two of the operatives among the appraisals:

> **deem (worthy, unworthy of)**   3.13
> **relegate to** ( )   3.222

Render in **render (futile, obedience, thanks, helpless,** etc.) would be an operative but the result would not be invariably appraisive. **Deem** has been discussed. It is now almost invariably an operative though in origin it had a more independent significance. These are drawn from moral judgment:

> **charge with** ( )   5.21
> **discharge (a duty)**   5.22
> **inflict (punishment**   5.22
> **qualms of** ( )   5.1

tax with ( )   5.21
twinge of (conscience)   5.1

Twinge of course also has a completely non-appraisive use in *twinge of pain*.
Some further operatives drawn from Part Two are these:

foment (revolution)   13.72
foment (trouble)   (11.111)
inflict (harm)   11.111
perpetrate (crime)   13.71

The operands are obviously necessary to all these terms. One cannot just
have a paroxysm, be in throes of, nor can one just relegate, inflict, foment,
and perpetrate. The terms might also be somewhat loosely called *auxiliary
appraisive verbs*.

APPENDIX H – HIGHER ORDER APPRAISIVES

It may be well to draw particular attention to these as a particular class since their appearance in the text occurs under titles descriptive rather of their content and function than of their logical form.

It will be recalled that the Responsional Characterizations of 2.4 are placed in Part One in order to be thought of in immediate connection with the responses. They are, however, not strictly responses but, as discussed in the text, either as appraisives of responses AR or responses to responses R^2. This then raised the question whether there may not be some four possibilities altogether: RA and A^2 in addition to the two just mentioned.

It appears plausible to think of the Concepts of 2.4 as being directed toward responses, as the second term. This would rule out RA and A^2. They seem also to show a certain coolness and distance in the speaker's stance toward the response so that AR is the most likely classification for them, rather than R^2. But this is difficult to judge a priori. If I say that some form of expression was lugubrious or turgid or that it was lurid or full of pathos am I not expressing a *response* to this mode of expression? Sometimes, at least, it appears that this would be a response rather than an appraisal.

The curious class of Operatives in 2.4 are all AR. I am appraising a second or third person's manner of responding and I would clearly reject characterizing myself so in the immediate present.

The appraisives of Aggressive Expression in 11.12 seem to be appraisives not of responses but of appraisals, hence A^2. To be sure, if I say, "You have insulted Mr. Chapman," I may notice that you were emotionally agitated when so doing, but clearly what seems offensive is not your emotional state but your choice of such and such a way of expressing yourself. In short, you have taken a deliberate step, have chosen your words.

We see here the difference between 2.4 and 11.12. We must choose between thinking of your "behavior" as antipathy, an outburst or an access of rage, on the one hand, or as a more or less deliberately phrased form of calumny, defamation, vilification, and the like. Generally the latter is thought to be more severely consequential morally. The former terms shade off into virtually excusable *res gestae* like shrieks of horror or screams of delight.

If these classifications are correct, it will be of some interest to see whether there are not also other concepts more definitely classifiable as R^2 and concepts under RA.

APPENDIX J – NEGATIONS

A substantial topic that deserves considerable treatment by itself is that of the effect of negation on the terms in Part Two and Part Three. A few observations on this may be made, confining attention to the deservatives of 15.2 and a few other terms.

In its most prevalent form, negation is produced by the addition of prefixes (*un-*, *in-*, *non-*, etc.) to the various positive terms. In 15.2 we have noted these transformations in brackets. In each case there is a virtually perfect opposing correspondence between a term and its negation, like the positive and negative image in photography. Both positive and negative are appraisive and are opposed as credits and discredits. Usually the positives are credits, and the negatives are discredits, except in the case of terms already negative in sense though positive in form: **assailable, culpable, objectionable, questionable**, and **reproachable**. Other negative characterisms could be added to the remaining parts of the vocabulary, for example, by adding *un-* or *non-*, or more naturally, the adverb *not* to the terms. These are comparatively simple uses of negation.

The remaining crediting terms in 15.2 are not generally negated by prefixes, but as noted, the use of *not* has the same effect as a prefix. A notable exception is **invaluable**, which is obsolete as a negation of **valuable**: it no longer means "not valuable" but rather "valuable in the most superlative degree, beyond valuation". It thus of course does not mean either "not deserving to be valued (esteemed)", still less "deserving not to be valued", but "deserving an immeasurable degree of credit."

Moving beyond these terms, other classes deserve to be distinguished. In all they may be divided as follows:

Class 1	POSITIVE APPRAISIVE	NEGATIVE APPRAISIVE
	pious	**impious**
	polite	**impolite**
	potent	**impotent**
	mannerly	**unmannerly**
	(To these should be added nearly all the deservatives of 15.2)	etc. etc.

Class 2	POSITIVE NON-APPRAISIVE (or most often nonappraisive or only capabilitive.)	NEGATIVE APPRAISIVE
	calculable	incalculable
	forgettable	unforgettable
	describable	indescribable
	etc.	inexpressible
		inflexible
		irremediable
		unsingable
		unplayable
		unworkable
		etc.
Class 3	POSITIVE IRRELEVANT TO THE NEGATIVE (or not in use, or rare)	NEGATIVE APPRAISIVE
	pertinent	impertinent
	etc.	imposture
		impudent
		inadvertent
		indefatigable
		indefeasible
		indifferent
		indiscriminate
		indomitable
		inscrutable
		insufferable
		unmitigated
		unruly
		impeccable (?)

As we see, the force of negation in all these cases renders the terms appraisive. The transformation is most significant in the instance of the abilitives in Class 2. As noted in the text, by far the greatest number of -bles are not at all appraisive or at least are certainly not deservative in nature. The positives simply say what can be done (e.g., can be handled, managed). But the negatives stir up more than thoughts of what can be done: they suggest what we may be frustrated in doing, and here emotion is not far in the offing. This is particularly true of the negatives of Class 2.

It should, however, be noted that the force of negation does not transform mere abilitives or capabilities *into deservatives*. In fact they gain a fairly "new" sense. Thus as contrasted with the merely expressible (*stateable, formulable*), **inexpressible** suggests the profound and esoteric or what is hidden in depths of emotion.

A rather special class is that of certain terms such as **assailable** and **questionable** which are discrediting in positive and crediting in negative form. One feels, however, that while they are appraisive both in positive and negative form, they are fully deservative only when positive and discrediting. **Unassailable** and **unquestionable** do not mean "deserving not to be assailed or questioned," or even "not deserving to be." Their appraisive force derives rather from their sheer (negative) abilitive character: what cannot be questioned, or cannot be assailed lays claim to credit in a special way because assailing and questioning are already appraisive procedures (as in 3.0). They are, however, no less general as appraisives than other terms in 15.0.

Unlike these terms, ordinary material capabilities, when negative, such as those in Class 2, e.g., **unsingable, unplayable, unworkable**, are very often appraisive in contexts easily identified, but usually not in their positive form.

The force of negation in reference to all of the terms of Parts Two and Three deserves more study than can be accorded to it here.

INDEX TO CONCEPTS

A

B

C

D

E

F

G

H

I

J

K

L

M

N

O

P

S

T

| twinge of remorse | 5.1, App. G | typical | 15.5 |
| twit | 11.122 | tyrant | 11.2, 13.4 |

U

ugly	App. C 3.2	unkempt	7.12,
ultimatum	11.111		App. C 2.21
umbrage at, take	2.4	unmanly	10.1
unassuming	8.22	unmannerly	App. J
unbalanced	6.11	unmitigated	15.4, 15.5,
unbending	8.25		App. J
unbosom	6.33	unmixed	15.4
uncanny	App. B 2.0	unnerve, unnerved	9.22
uncomely	App. C 3.2	unprepossessing	8.24
uncompromising	11.111	unprincipledness	14.4
unconscionable	15.5	unruly	7.23, App. J
uncouth	8.24, 13.1,	unsavory	13.1
	App. C 2.21	unscrupulous,	
unction	App. B 1.1	unscrupulousness	12.22, 14.32
unctuous	App. B 1.1	unseasonable	9.4
underdone	15.42	unseemly, unseemliness	14.21
underestimate	3.3	unselfishness	11.3, 14.33
underhanded	11.112	unshapely	App. C 2.11
underrate	3.3	unsightly	App. C 3.2
undying	App. B 2.0	unspeakable	15.5
unearthly	App. B 2.0	untidy	App. C 2.21
unequalled	15.5	untoward	15.3
unethical	14.01	unwieldy	App. E 1.0
unexampled	15.5	unwomanly	10.1
unfathomable	App. A 1.5,	upbraid	5.21
	App. B 2.0	upheaval	11.1
unfeelingness	11.2, 14.33	uplifting	15.1
unflagging	9.22	upright, uprightness	14.01, 14.4
unflinching	9.22	uprising	11.1
unfold	6.33	uproar	11.1
unforgettable	App. J	upsetting	15.1
unfortunate	9.4	upstart	11.111
unfounded	App. A 2.5,	urbanity	8.24
	App. A 3.5	useful	App. E 1.0
ungainly	App. C 2.11	useless	15.5
ungodly	App. B 1.1	usufruct	App. E 1.0
ungovernable	11.111	usurp	11.111, 13.7,
ungrounded	App. A 2.5,		13.72
	App. A 3.5	usury	12.21
unify	App. C 2.12	utile	App. E 1.0
union	13.6	utopian	13.4
unique	15.5	uxorious	10.2

V

vacillate, vacillation	9.21, 14.23	vagrant n.	13.2
vacuous	6.13	vague	App. A 1.5
vagabond	13.2	vain, vanity	8.22, 14.22

W

INDEX TO PERSONS AND SUBJECT MATTER

FOUNDATIONS OF LANGUAGE

SUPPLEMENTARY SERIES

Edited by Morris Halle, Peter Hartmann,
K. Kunjunni Raja, Benson Mates, J. F. Staal,
Pieter A. Verburg, and John W. M. Verhaar

Sole Distributors in the U.S.A. and Canada:
HUMANITIES PRESS / NEW YORK

DATE DUE